THE NEWS AT THE
ENDS *of* THE EARTH

The

NEWS

AT THE

ENDS

OF THE

EARTH

THE PRINT CULTURE *of* POLAR EXPLORATION

HESTER BLUM

DUKE UNIVERSITY PRESS *Durham & London* 2019

Printed in the United States of America on
acid-free paper ∞
Designed by Matthew Tauch
Typeset in Garamond Premier Pro
by Westchester Publishing Services

Library of Congress Cataloging-in-Publication Data
Names: Blum, Hester, [date] author.
Title: The news at the ends of the earth : the print culture of polar exploration /
    Hester Blum.
Description: Durham : Duke University Press, 2019. | Includes bibliographical
    references and index.
Identifiers: LCCN 2018040994 (print)
LCCN 2018047420 (ebook)
ISBN 9781478004486 (ebook)
ISBN 9781478003229 (hardcover : alk. paper)
ISBN 9781478003878 (pbk. : alk. paper)
Subjects: LCSH: Polar regions—Discovery and exploration—Sources. | Polar
    regions—History—Sources. | Explorers—Polar regions—Diaries. | Survival—
    Psychological aspects. | Climatic changes—Psychological aspects. | Human ecology—
    Psychological aspects.
Classification: LCC G580 (ebook) | LCC G580 .B58 2019 (print) | DDC 910.911—dc23
LC record available at https://lccn.loc.gov/2018040994

Cover art: The meteorologist, C. T. Madigan. Photograph by Frank Hurley. State Library of
New South Wales: [Home and Away - 36730].

This title is freely available in an open access edition (doi:10.18113/P8C085) thanks to the
TOME initiative and the generous support of The Pennsylvania State University. Learn more
at openmonographs.org.

CONTENTS

―――

ILLUSTRATIONS

CHRONOLOGY

Major Polar Expeditions by North Americans and Europeans, 1818–1922

Expeditions in shaded rows produced shipboard newspapers.

DATE	COMMANDER, SHIP	EXPEDITION	SHIPBOARD NEWSPAPER
1818	John Ross, *Isabella*	British, Northwest Passage	
1819–20	William Edward Parry, *Hecla* and *Griper*	British, Northwest Passage and Arctic exploration	*North Georgia Gazette, and Winter Chronicle*
1821–23	*Hecla* and *Fury*		
1824–25	*Hecla* and *Fury*		
1819–22	John Franklin	British, overland voyage to Coppermine River	
1829–33	John Ross, *Victory*	British, Arctic exploration	
1825–26	Frederick William Beechey, *Blossom*	British, Alaskan coast	
1836–37	George Back, *Terror*	British, Arctic exploration	
1838–42	Charles Wilkes, *Vincennes*, etc.	American, Antarctic and Pacific exploration	
1839–43	James Clark Ross, *Erebus* and *Terror*	British, Antarctic exploration	
1845	Franklin, *Erebus* and *Terror*	British, Northwest Passage	
1847–54	T. E. L. Moore, *Plover*	British, Franklin search supply ship	*Flight of the Plover, or the North Pole Charivari*

DATE	COMMANDER, SHIP	EXPEDITION	SHIPBOARD NEWSPAPER
1850–51	Horatio Austin, *Assistance*, *Resolute*, etc.	British, Franklin search	*Illustrated Arctic News*; *Aurora Borealis*; *The Gleaner*; *Minavilins*
1850–51	Edwin De Haven, *Advance*	American, Franklin search	
1850–54	Robert McClure, *Investigator*	British, Franklin search	
1850–55	Richard Collison, *Enterprise*	British, Franklin search	*Polar Almanac*
1852–54	Edward Belcher, *Assistance*	British, Franklin search	*Queen's Illuminated Magazine*
1852–54	Rochfort Maguire, *Plover*	British, Franklin search	*Weekly Guy*
1853–54	John Rae	British, overland Franklin search	
1853–55	Elisha Kent Kane, *Advance*	American, Franklin search	*Ice-Blink*
1857–59	Francis Leopold McClintock, *Fox*	British, Franklin search	
1860–61	Isaac Israel Hayes, *United States*	American, Franklin search, open polar sea search	*Port Foulke Weekly News*
1860–62	Charles Francis Hall (independent)	American, Franklin search	
1864–69	(independent)	Arctic exploration	
1871–73	*Polaris*	North Pole expedition	
1869–70	Carl Koldewey, *Germania* and *Hansa*	German, North Pole expedition	*Ostgrönländische zeitung* (East Greenland Gazette)
1875–76	George Nares, *Alert* and *Discovery*	British, Arctic exploration	*Discovery News*
1881–84	Adolphus Greely, *Proteus*	American, Arctic exploration	*Arctic Moon*

1879–81	George De Long, *Jeannette*	American, Arctic exploration	
1893–96	Fridtjof Nansen, *Fram*	Norwegian, Arctic exploration	*Framsjaa*
1897	S. A. Andrée, balloon	Swedish, North Pole expedition	
1897–99	Adrien de Gerlache, *Belgica*	Belgian, Antarctic expedition	
1901–2	Evelyn Briggs Baldwin, *America*	American, Arctic exploration	*Midnight Sun*
1901–4	Otto Nordenskjöld, *Antarctica*	Swedish, Antarctic exploration	
1901–3	Erich von Drygalski, *Gauss*	German, Antarctic exploration	*Antarktischen Intelligenzblättern* (Antarctic Intelligencer)
1901–4	Robert Falcon Scott, *Discovery*	British, Antarctic exploration	*South Polar Times; The Blizzard*
1910–13	*Terra Nova*		*Adélie Mail and Cape Adare Times; South Polar Times*
1903–5	Anthony Fiala, *America*	American, Arctic exploration	*Arctic Eagle; Polar Pirate; Vulture*
1903–6	Roald Amundsen, *Gjøa*	Norwegian, Northwest Passage	
1907–9	Ernest Shackleton, *Nimrod*	British, Antarctic exploration	*Antarctic Petrel; Aurora Australis* (book)
1914–17	*Endurance*		
1921–22	*Quest*		*Expedition Topics*
1907–9	Frederick Cook, *John R. Bradley*	American, North Pole expedition	
1908–9	Robert Peary, *Roosevelt*	American, North Pole expedition	

DATE	COMMANDER, SHIP	EXPEDITION	SHIPBOARD NEWSPAPER
1908–10	Jean-Baptiste Charcot, *Pourquoi-pas?*	French, Antarctic exploration	
1910–12	Amundsen, *Fram*	Norwegian, South Pole expedition	
1911–14	Douglas Mawson, *Aurora*	Australian, Antarctic exploration	*Adelie Blizzard*; *Glacier Tongue*
1912	Knud Rasmussen and Peter Freuchen	Greenlandic-Danish, Arctic exploration (first of six Thule expeditions)	
1913–16	Vilhjalmur Stefansson, *Karluk*	Canadian, Arctic exploration	

BOOKS ON ICE

Early in 2006 I visited the Grolier Club, a cloister for bibliophiles in New York City, in order to see the exhibition *Books on Ice: British and American Literature of Polar Exploration*. Curated by David H. Stam and Deirdre C. Stam, librarian-scholars and polar book collectors, the show recast Arctic and Antarctic exploration history as book history; on many expeditions, the Stams proposed, "books seem to have been as essential as pemmican, primus stoves, fuel, and furs."[1] The exhibition featured significant editions of voyage literature from both Arctic and Antarctic ventures over the centuries, as well as a range of other polariana. This miscellany included illustrations of the Arctic regions depicting (and, in at least one case, drawn by) Inuit translators and guides, such as an image by Inuk interpreter John Sacheuse (or John Sackhouse, Hans Zakaeus) of the "first communication with the natives" held by John Ross's British Northwest Passage expedition in 1818. Also on hand was a wooden case that had held a portable library, one of many provided by the American Seamen's Friend Society to naval and merchant ships. Robert Peary had carried the portable library on his North Pole expedition of 1905–6 and again in 1908–9. Virtually all polar ships had libraries, and the Grolier Club exhibition contained the catalogue of the books in the ship's library on the *Discovery*, Robert Falcon Scott's first Antarctic command. A sound recording made by Ernest Shackleton and released by *Edison Phonograph Monthly* under the title "My South Polar Expedition" was among the more notable ephemera. Perhaps the most pathetic item was the edition of Alfred Lord Tennyson's *In Memoriam: Maud, and Other Poems* carried to Antarctica by a member of Scott's final, fatal expedition, one volume of which was found near the frozen bodies of the polar party.[2]

I was riveted. At the time I was completing a book on the literary culture of early American sailors, and I brought to the Grolier Club both my scholarly interest in the history of maritime books and an omnidirectional avidity for narratives of polar exploration. In a display case halfway through the exhibition I saw an unfamiliar artifact that at once unified my interests and seemed to stand as their apotheosis: an 1852 facsimile of the *Illustrated Arctic News* (1850–51), a shipboard newspaper written and published in the North by the men of the HMS *Resolute*. As I would come to learn, the contents of the paper were largely comic and playful, featuring detailed medical reports on the worrisome decline of the sun as winter advanced; a story about an inflatable named Benjamin Balloon getting "high" on "Hydro-Gin"; notices of a companion newspaper (the *Aurora Borealis*) from the expedition's sister ship; and reviews of shipboard theatricals.[3] The newspaper combined manuscript hand with printed headers and other typography produced, remarkably, on one of the first Arctic expeditionary printing presses. Sailors adapted the press to their use in the Far North in multiple ways: a note in the paper, in one example, specifies that "the large type headings as well as the Arms and devices were cut on board by the Seamen."[4] The *Illustrated Arctic News* was created during the total darkness of polar winter by icebound sailors who were searching for the members of a vanished—and perpetually searched-for—British Northwest Passage expedition launched by Sir John Franklin in 1845 aboard the ships *Erebus* and *Terror*. To this day most of the bodies of the men have never been found, other than a handful of remains of individual sailors who died at various points earlier in the expedition. One of Franklin's missing ships, the *Erebus*, was finally located on the Arctic seafloor near King William Island in the summer of 2014, 167 years after the first searches, by a state-sponsored submersible mission led by Parks Canada. The second ship, *Terror*, was located in Terror Bay in the fall of 2016 by a private expedition. In the nineteenth century, however, only scattered relics of the expedition (and scattered graves) were discovered, including a copy of Oliver Goldsmith's *The Vicar of Wakefield* found on the ice.

In the Grolier Club, the sight of the *Illustrated Arctic News* activated not only my fervor but my archival instinct as well, and moved me to proclaim to my companion, "Here is my next book." When I made this assertion I knew nothing about the *Illustrated Arctic News* beyond the information contained on the exhibit display tag. From my reading in polar history I was familiar with the decades-long search for the Franklin expedition. As a nineteenth-century Americanist, I could not help but notice references to

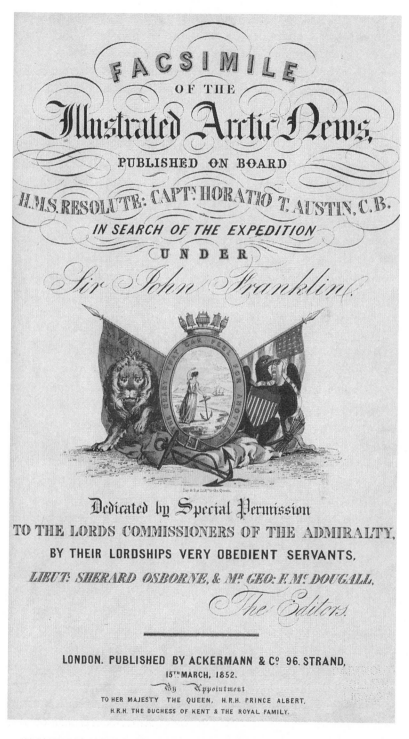

FIG PREFACE.I — Title page, *Facsimile of the Illustrated Arctic News, Published on Board* H.M.S. *Resolute,* Captn *Horatio T. Austin,* C.B. *in Search of the Expedition under Sir John Franklin* (London: Ackermann, 1852). COURTESY OF DARTMOUTH COLLEGE LIBRARY.

the hunt for the *Erebus* and *Terror* in the media of the period; Frankliniana was its own mania for a time in the Anglo-American midcentury, and its traces are visible in periodical, literary, and other historical accounts. The existence of literary cultural work by sailors was not news to me either, as mariners' engagement with and production of narrative writing has been the ongoing focus of my scholarship. What was unfamiliar—and what impressed me as so strikingly, declaratively different about the *Illustrated Arctic News* at that moment in the Grolier Club—was the revelation of the presence of an actual printing press, a far-from-standard piece of nautical equipment, aboard that icebound Arctic ship.

The press was used, surprisingly, in service of media circulation largely within the confines of the expedition's ships themselves. Of all the ways that a polar expedition might find to pass the tedium of a long, dark, immobilized winter, I wondered, why would crew members feel an imperative not just to write a newspaper but to print it as well? And not to print it upon their return home to London or another metropole but to print it somewhere around latitude 75° N, well north of the Arctic Circle in the Canadian archipelago, for an imagined community defined only by (and necessarily limited to) the members of the expedition, the actual community, themselves? I was arrested by their employment of the very form of the newspaper, an uncommon genre in sailor writing. Yet as I would discover, the *Illustrated Arctic News* represents only one of many coterie newspapers created by polar voyagers throughout the nineteenth and early twentieth century in what became a standard practice of such ventures, however little known today. Looking at the *Illustrated Arctic News* for the first time, I was curious to learn if the climatic and geophysical extremity of the polar regions, as well as their nonhuman scale—which was tracked in the scientific recordkeeping done by polar ventures as a matter of course—would also register within the quotidian pages of an expedition's gazette. The genesis for this book, in other words, was a question freighted with multiple implications, both then and now: *What is the news at the ends of the earth?*

That is how the book began, but books on ice, like ice itself, are not fixed in place. Nor do they maintain a consistent state of matter. When I began researching and writing *The News at the Ends of the Earth*, I was also closely reading contemporary news reports emerging from the Arctic and from Antarctica: news of climate change, of resource extraction and its attendant land and water claims. I followed the twenty-first-century media reports with one eye cast on the nineteenth-century research in which I was engaged. My questions about the news at the ends of the earth took on more detail and more urgency: How does polar news circulate? What is its temporality in a region without familiar patterns of diurnal time? What knowledge do the Arctic and Antarctica impart to the human and nonhuman world in Anthropocenic time, in deep or geological time? Do the forms of media chosen by expedition members—newspapers and other ephemera—have something to tell us about what kind of communicative media and narrative structures can help us represent our current age of climate change?

I came to realize that twenty-first-century news of polar resource circulation and climate observation, facilitated by textual and other media representation, was not just a contemporary analogue of the story I was telling about the nineteenth and early twentieth centuries: it was the same story.

ACKNOWLEDGMENTS

The idea for this book was first conceived in a club for book lovers, and it is a tremendous pleasure to thank the many libraries and archives that have made its realization possible. I am in debt to the librarians and staff of the following institutions and collections that I was fortunate to be able to visit while researching this project: the Stefansson Collection at Dartmouth College; the Scott Polar Research Institute at the University of Cambridge; the National Maritime Museum in Greenwich, London; the Library Company of Philadelphia; the American Philosophical Society; the American Antiquarian Society; the New-York Historical Society; the John Carter Brown Library; the Huntington Library; the Smithsonian National Museum of American History Archives; the Peary-MacMillan Arctic Museum; the Cincinnati Historical Society and Library; the Free Library of Philadelphia; the Historical Society of Pennsylvania; the G. W. Blunt White Library at Mystic Seaport; the British Library; the Royal Geographical Society; National Archives of the United Kingdom; the Biblotèque Nationale de France; the Libraries and Archives of Canada/Bibliotèque et Archives de Canada; the Polarmuseet in Tromsø, Norway; and special collections libraries at Duke University, University of Pennsylvania, Columbia University, Penn State University, Harvard University, University of Toronto, Bowdoin College, New York University, and the University of Michigan. Librarians at a number of repositories I was not able to visit in person have been liberal with their knowledge and their materials, and I thank the New Zealand Antarctic Heritage Trust, the Alexander Turnbull Library of New Zealand, the South Australian Museum, the Greenland National Museum and Archives, and the Alfred Wegener Institute for Polar and Marine Research in Germany. Institutions work when the people associated with them are thoughtful, discerning, helpful, and ethical. Jim Green, Michael Winship, David Stam and Deirdre Stam, Sandra Stelts, and Paul Erickson have guided, advised, and inspired my archival research over many years and have been models of friendship and professional collaboration.

The National Endowment for the Humanities has underwritten my work on this project for a number of years, and I gratefully acknowledge the NEH Long-Term Post-Doctoral Fellowship at the Library Company of Philadelphia that inaugurated my research in 2010; the NEH-sponsored 38th Voyage of the whaleship *Charles W. Morgan* that gave me more insight into shipboard life and labor; and the year-long NEH Fellowship in 2014–15 that allowed me uninterrupted writing time. My research at the archives and institutions listed above was also supported by research awards and grants from the following: the Bibliographic Society of America's McCorison Fellowship for the History and Bibliography of Printing in Canada and the United States, Andrew W. Mellon Foundation Fellowship at the Huntington Library, William Reese Company Fellowship at the John Carter Brown Library, and a Franklin Research Grant from the American Philosophical Society. Two Residential Scholar Awards from the Penn State Institute for the Arts and Humanities/Humanities Institute, as well as the support of the Penn State English Department, College of the Liberal Arts, and Center for American Literary Studies, have also been instrumental to my work, and I thank Mark Morrisson, Susan Welch, Michael Bérubé, Lauren Kooistra, Sue Reighard, John Christman, and Robin Schulze. I am grateful to Robert Levine, Dana Nelson, Donald Pease, and Priscilla Wald for their support of my work over the years. For sharing their knowledge and materials (both institutional and private) I also thank Connie King, Elaine Hoag, Naomi Boneham, Ted Widmer, John Pollack, Douglas Wamsley, Rachael Green, Paul O'Pecko, June Phillips, and Thomas Walker.

My scholarship has benefited enormously from conversations with colleagues at a number of colleges and universities at which I've had the privilege to present parts of this book in progress. For their kind attention and vital input, I thank audiences at Notre Dame University's Unauthorized States Symposium; Harvard University; The Futures of American Studies Institute at Dartmouth College; UC Santa Barbara Interdisciplinary Humanities Center; University of Maryland; University of Kentucky; New York Metro American Studies Association; Cornell University; Center for Cultural Analysis at Rutgers University; UCLA's Americanist Research Colloquium; Rumowicz Literature of the Sea Lecture/Seminar Series, University of Rhode Island; Freibert/Wittreich Symposium, University of Louisville; University of South Carolina; McNeil Center Biennial Graduate Student Conference; CSUS and F. Ross Johnson Distinguished Speaker Series, University of Toronto Centre for the Book and the Centre for the Study of the United States; University of Delaware; University of Massachusetts–Boston;

Princeton University; CUNY Graduate Center; Oakland University; UC Irvine; Pomona College; Rice University; University of Miami; University of Oxford; Early American Literature and Material Texts Workshop, McNeil Center for Early American Studies and Library Company of Philadelphia; University of Nottingham; University of Sussex; Ecole Normale Supérieure de Lyon; Université Sorbonne Nouvelle Paris 3; University of Pennsylvania; Bowdoin College; Baylor University; Perilous Passages Symposium at Bayreuth University; University of Michigan; Ice³ Symposium at Columbia University; CUNY Victorian Conference; Florida International University/ Bayerische Amerika-Akademie; Archipelagoes/Oceans/Americas Symposium at Brigham Young University; Movement and Mobility Symposium, Texas A&M University–Corpus Christi; Yale University; and Northwestern University. I am very grateful to my hosts, interlocutors, great friends, and longtime mentors at these talks, who include (roughly chronologically) Ivy Wilson, Elisa New, Donald Pease, Eric Lott, Elizabeth Dillon, Emily Zinn, Robert Levine, Jeff Clymer, Sarah Chinn, Shirley Samuels, Brigitte Fielder, Alex Black, Jonathan Senchyne, Meredith McGill, Chris Looby, Martha Elena Rojas, Aaron Jaffe, Tatjana Soldat, Gretchen Woertendyke, Jeannine DeLombard, Martin Brückner, Ed Larkin, Cathy Matson, Sari Edelstein, Holly Jackson, Rebecca Rosen, Sarah Rivett, Duncan Faherty, Jeff Insko, Rodrigo Lazo, Kyla Wazana Tompkins, Judith Roof, Tim Watson, Jason Bell, Lloyd Pratt, Marcy Dinius, Hannah Murray, Graham Thompson, Pam Thurschwell, François Specq, Hélène Quanquin, Cécile Roudeau, Jazmín Delgado, Evelyn Soto, Don James McLaughlin, Tess Chakkalakal, Susan Kaplan, Dan Walden, Tim Cassedy, Kelly Wisecup, Kelly Bezio, Jason Payton, Melissa Gniadek, Karin Hoepker, Susan Scott Parrish, Fritz Swanson, Maggie Cao, Rebecca Woods, Talia Shaeffer, Richard Kaye, Tanya Agathocleous, Caroline Reitz, Martha Schoolman, Heike Paul, Brian Russell Roberts, Mary Eyring, Sarah Salter, Dale Pattison, Sarah Weston, Hyoun Yang, Wai Chee Dimock, Corey Byrnes, and Harris Feinsod.

For searingly smart readings of draft chapters of this book, I am in debt to Martha Schoolman (with whom an unsurpassed friendship began with a conversation about Captains Littlepage and Shackleton twenty years ago), Stephanie Foote, Scotti Parrish, Sarah Mesle, Sarah Blackwood, Kyla Wazana Tompkins, and Dana Luciano. For conversations about the polar regions over many years, I thank P. J. Capelotti, El Glasberg, and Penn State Polar Center colleagues Pernille Sporon Bøving, Eric Post, Andrew Carleton, and Russ Graham. For their oceanic poetry, I thank Elizabeth Bradfield and Craig Santos Perez. Kenn Harper offered valuable insight into Inuit culture and the Inuktitut language. For C19 Americanist friendship that lifts me up and teaches me something new every day, I deeply thank everyone mentioned above, plus Monique Allewaert, Sari Altschuler, Nancy Bentley, Mary K. Bercaw-Edwards, Jennifer Brady, Carrie Tirado Bramen, Michelle Burnham, Rachel Buurma, Siobhan Carroll, Lara Cohen, Brian Connolly, Pete Coviello, Pat Crain, Colin Dickey, Betsy Duquette, John Durham Peters, Amy Elias, Elizabeth Freeman, Amy Greenberg, Ellen Gruber Garvey, Naomi Greyser, Melissa Homestead, Carrie Hyde, Leon Jackson, Virginia Jackson, Jamie Jones, Catherine Kelly, Wyn Kelly, Ari Kelman, Greta LaFleur, Caroline Levander, Gesa Mackenthun, Stacey Margolis, Tim Marr, Barbara McCaskill, Steve Mentz, Michele Navakas, Meredith Neuman, Eden Osucha, Sam Otter, Chris Parsons, John Pat Leary, Carla Peterson, James Peterson, Chris Phillips, Joe Rezek, Seth Rockman, Jason Rudy, Karen Sanchéz-Eppler, Sarah Scheutze, Kyla Schuller, Dana Seitler, Kirsten Silva Gruesz, Caleb Smith, Jacob Smith, Stephanie Sobelle, Gus Stadler, Jordan Stein, Laura Stevens, Claudia Stokes, Ed Sugden, Lisa Swanstrom, Elisa Tamarkin, Steve Thomas, Bob Wallace, Ken Ward, Lenora Warren, Eric Wertheimer, Ed Whitley, Edlie Wong, Nazera Wright, Xine Yao, and the extended community of the McNeil Center for Early American Studies.

It has been an honor and a joy to work with the wonderful Courtney Berger and Duke University Press on this book. I thank Courtney most warmly for her superlative editorial insights and support, and particularly for helping me think through this book's engagement with media studies. I also am grateful to Sandra Korn for her close care, Christopher Catanese for expertly shepherding the book through production, Judith Hoover for careful copyediting, and Chris Robinson for his great marketing assistance. Two anonymous readers provided remarkably incisive comments and suggestions, and I am hugely thankful to them for their intellectual generosity and their contributions to the final product.

Portions of this book have been revised from earlier work, and I acknowledge with gratitude the editors and publishers of these pieces. An earlier version of chapter 5 was published as "Charles Francis Hall's Arctic Researches," in *The Sea and Nineteenth-Century Anglophone Literary Culture*, edited by Steven Mentz and Martha Elena Rojas (New York: Routledge, 2017), and has been revised and expanded for this book. Several pages of chapter 2 and the conclusion have been reworked from "The News at the End of the Earth: Polar Periodicals," in *Unsettled States: Nineteenth-Century American Literary Studies*, edited by Dana Luciano and Ivy Wilson (New York: New York University Press, 2014), "Melville in the Arctic," *Leviathan* 20.1 (2018):

74–84, and "'Bitter with the Salt of Continents': Rachel Carson and Oceanic Returns," *Women's Studies Quarterly* 45.1–2 (2017): 287–91. My thinking on ice and Antarctic ponies has developed from short essays I wrote for *Avidly* and for the *Los Angeles Review of Books*, and I thank the superb editors of those pieces, Sarah Blackwood and Sarah Mesle.

At Penn State I am thrilled to have such dear friends and colleagues as Janet Lyon, Michael Bérubé, Jamie Bérubé, Robert Caserio, Kris Jacobson, Julia Kasdorf, Philip Ruth, Ben Schreier, Sarah Koenig, Susan Squier, Gowan Roper, Anne McCarthy, Courtney Morris, Dan Purdy, Debbie Hawhee, John Marsh, Sean Goudie, Tina Chen, Jessica O'Hara, Cynthia Young, Zachary Morgan, Elizabeth Kadetsky, Ebony Coletu, Scott Smith, Colin Hogan, Erica Stevens, Eric Vallee, Nate Windon, Ting Chang, Miriam Gonzales, Liana Glew, Eric Norton, Dustin Kennedy, and Tyler Roeger.

The academic lady feminism and dear friendship of Janet Lyon, Lisa Surwillo, Sarah Blackwood, Claire Jarvis, Sarah Mesle, and Kyla Wazana Tompkins inspire and teach me. Mary McClanahan keeps me sane. For good and especially for bad I thank Lisa Beskin, Katherine Biers, Fiona Brideoake, Pete Coviello, Karo Engstrom, Stephanie Foote, Elizabeth Freeman, Geoff Gilbert, Susan Gregson, Katherine Lieber, Cris Mayo, Britt Metevier, Michael Metevier, Frank Ridgway, Pam Thurschwell, Sarah Leamon Turula, and Joan Stroer White. I am lucky to have friends like Lisi Schoenbach, Ben Lee, Daryl Kovalich, John Mancuso, Amanda Mancino-Williams, Nigel Roth, Emily Zinn, Jim Kearney, Jeremy Braddock, Rayna Kalas, Mary Richardson Graham, Patrick Richardson Graham, Patrick North, Billie Jo North, Don Becker, and Toni Jensen; how I wish we all lived in the same town.

Martha Schoolman, Caitlin Wood, Orly Schoolman-Wood, Jamie Taylor, Andrés Villalta, Javi Taylor-Villalta, and Leo Taylor-Villalta have been the core of my people—our "friends who are family"—for twenty years; they buoy me every day.

I would match the strength and resilience of my parents, Carl Blum and Maureen Blum, against any polar explorer alive or dead. They always keep moving, no matter the challenge or the conditions, and I hope I can continue to keep up.

And to my radiant, electrifying, brilliant partner and child, Jonathan Eburne and Adelaide Blum Eburne, who always do a good show and have fun with it, who bring wit, artistry, adventurousness, fierceness, justness, curiosity, and topgallant delight to our every moment together: this book, like its author, is dedicated to you.

INTRODUCTION

POLAR ECOMEDIA

.... decrease in the number of blizzards, failure of the
Ross Sea to freeze, absence of very low temperatures on the Barrier ....
..... bitterly regretted their failure to keep Meteorological records ....
records of the British Antarctic expedition were unearthed from the highest
shelves of the lumber rooms of the libraries and were perused with avidity ...
..... the great question of the day was, Does climate change?
— GEORGE SIMPSON, "Fragment of a Manuscript Found by the People of
  Sirius 8 When They Visited the Earth during Their Exploration of the
  Solar System," *South Polar Times* (1911)

The ocean has a very poor respect for daily papers.
— WILLIAM HENRY GILMAN, *Letters Written Home* (1858)

Polar exploration produces writing. Whether from the Northwest
Passage–seeking Arctic voyages of the early nineteenth century or the
"heroic age" of Antarctic ventures in the early twentieth, the most consistent outcomes of historic polar missions were not expeditionary feats but
narrative accounts of the voyages. Expeditions were not particularly successful if judged by the standard of whether or not they fulfilled their voyage objectives; nearly all historical British and American polar missions can
be said to have failed if our evaluative criteria are whether parties navigated
the Northwest Passage, flagged the North or South Poles, or traversed Antarctica. As a geologist who participated in two Antarctic expeditions (and
who contributed articles to both expeditions' winter quarters publications,
Aurora Australis and the *Adélie Mail and Cape Adare Times*) characterized

it, the four phases of polar exploration history are "(a) The voyage south from civilisation. (b) Winter and summer at winter quarters. (c) Spring and summer sledging. (d) The catastrophic phase. (May or may not occur)."[1] Loss and death thinned many voyages, which were salvaged in the public imagination by tales of valor or endurance. Expeditionary writing told these stories. In 1880 an American naval officer and North Polar explorer, George De Long, entered in his journal, "I frequently think that instead of recording the idle words that express our progress from day to day I might better keep these pages unwritten, leaving a blank properly to represent the utter blank of this Arctic expedition."[2] Yet continue to write he did. And even after his ship *Jeannette* was annihilated by the ice and twenty of the thirty-three men aboard had perished—De Long himself among the dead—his journals remained in circulation. What do the narratives of polar exploration tell us? In large part, stories of extremity. In their meteorological, geographical, and political remove from the usual variances among nation-states or global precincts, the polar regions have been figured as impossibly remote. Today rapidly accelerating anthropogenic climate change (the evidence for which has been particularly stark in the Arctic, and increasingly in Antarctica as well) has rendered the atmospheric state of the planet itself extreme. As a result, human futurity too is in a state of extremity. Among proliferating challenges, our Anthropocenic moment has produced a crisis in how scholars think and write about humans, the nonhuman world, and the earth itself, in imagining both our present and across time.

Of all the responses to extreme environmental conditions that were attempted by polar expedition members of the long nineteenth century, perhaps the least known are a body of printed ephemera and other tenuous informational media created aboard icebound ships in the darkness of high-latitude winters. These ephemeral works include a rich, offbeat collection of Arctic and Antarctic ship newspapers, as well as notes in bottles, letters and cairn messages, rescue notices printed on silk and lofted by fire balloon, playbills, songs, menus, and maps constructed of organic materials, all of which polar sailors used to mark time and communicate information. *The News at the Ends of the Earth* studies transitory printing and textual circulation amid extreme climate processes, in moments when human life itself has seemed ephemeral, whether during a British Northwest Passage expedition in the 1820s, an American search for missing Arctic explorers in the 1850s, a Norwegian sprint to the South Pole in the 1910s, or in the face of the devastating effects of anthropogenic climate change on polar icecaps today. In the polar regions the production of works of textual ephemera is a testimonial to (and fuel for) resilience, perhaps counterintuitively. As a category of transient objects and evidentiary media, ephemera record temporary moments, instances in time; the material artifacts and texts themselves are neither crafted to last nor presumed to warrant preservation. The etymology of the term for the genre itself bears a special charge when invoked in the polar regions: "ephemera" comes from the Greek ἐφήμερος or *ephémeros*, lasting only one day. At latitudes approaching 90° N or S in the lands of the midnight sun and the polar night, the sun rises and sets only once per year, and thus the single day that ephemera are meant to last can have a duration as long as six months. In polar spaces outside of conventional diurnal measures of time, where human life is difficult to sustain and where resources are both scarce and endlessly sought, explorers consistently turned to fugitive modes of written expression. When safely back home, expeditions may have produced weighty volumes of their voyages in substantial print runs, yet while icebound during a winter darkness that lasted for several months, expeditions printed nonce works. Their reasons for doing so, and to what effect, are the focus of this book. Arctic and Antarctic sailors made a conscious genre decision in choosing to print newspapers and other forms of ephemera: in a polar environment, newspapers no longer regulate diurnal time but instead call attention to (and help relieve) its attenuation. The paradox of printed ephemera—which have the seeming permanence of print but are in their form designed to be dispersed and disposed of—registers the variable, atemporal challenges of life, humanistic thought, and global ecology in the Anthropocene.

The texts and other varieties of media that emerge from and describe Arctic and Antarctic conditions take many forms; the frozen zones have been generative of written and other communicative media by and for travelers, indigenous residents, imaginative writers, scientists, and artists, past and present. Indeed the resources, hydrography, geography, and climatology of the polar regions have been of persistent interest throughout modernity. Scores of expeditions have traveled to the Far North and South since the sixteenth century, in the name of discovery and science, primarily, although imperial and commercial missions (largely unsuccessful) underwrote their attempts. Martin Frobisher's voyages in the 1570s to the southern part of what is now called Baffin Island were sponsored by the Muscovy Company, for example; Henry Hudson's 1610 expedition to the bay he named was supported by the British East India Company and the Virginia Company; and William Baffin (1616) sailed up the coasts of Greenland and Baffin Island in the aspirational name of the Company of Merchants of London,

Discoverers of the North-West Passage. The force of polar attention among Europeans and Americans was felt most keenly in the nineteenth and early twentieth centuries, however. Polar expeditions in the long nineteenth century included those helmed by the Americans Charles Wilkes, Elisha Kent Kane, Isaac Israel Hayes, Charles Francis Hall, Adolphus Greely, Anthony Fiala, Matthew Henson, Robert Peary, Donald MacMillan, George De Long, and Frederick Cook; the Germans Carl Koldewey and Erich von Drygalski; the Britons William Edward Parry, John Ross, John Franklin, George Back, John Clark Ross, Edward Belcher, Horatio Austin, John Rae, Francis Leopold McClintock, George Nares, Robert Falcon Scott, and Ernest Shackleton; the Frenchman Jean-Baptiste Charcot; the Norwegians Fridtjof Nansen, Otto Sverdrup, and Roald Amundsen; and Douglas Mawson, an Australian. The majority of these ventures were sponsored by their national governments in a tradition associated with British and Norwegian exploration. Relatively elite compared to other nautical missions, polar crews ranged in size from a dozen to almost two hundred men; most took fewer than fifty men, and Hall initially traveled alone in his first expedition, before joining an Inuit community on Baffin Island. The launches and returns of these voyages were closely followed by the Western public, and polariana appeared in a variety of literary and visual cultural forms, from poetry and panoramas to magic lantern shows and the lecture circuit. The practice of the expeditions generally followed this protocol: after sailing as far north or south as possible during the brief polar summers, polar crews would plan to winter over in a harbor with relatively stable ice, their vessels encased by the frozen ocean. The men lived aboard ship or in huts during the total darkness of polar winter months and prepared for overland and ice sledging operations (either dog-, pony-, or man-hauled) in early spring, for the purposes of hydrography, meteorological research, scientific experimentation, or a sprint to "flag" the poles. The latter feat took nearly one hundred years of steady attempts.

While quartered in the land-, ice-, and seascapes of the polar regions, expedition members—mostly white Westerners not indigenous to the frozen zones—produced an enormous volume of writing (and, eventually, photography, videography, and many other forms of data and textual production) in order to document what they saw, felt, heard, missed, experienced, counted, observed, and lost. The chapters that follow attend to the written materials created and circulated by American and European polar expedition members between 1818 and 1914 that exclusively originate in and have a special circulation amid the polar regions. (These writings historically complemented the similarly huge output of scientific recordkeeping done by polar voyagers, including magnetic dip observations, hydrography, geological sampling, zoological collection, core sampling, and temperature readings—many of which serve as data records for present-day climate scientists. Such scientific literature constitutes a genre of evidence that has supplemented this book but does not play a central role in it.) I concentrate instead on the print production and forms of writing that were generated in the polar regions by Europeans and Americans with the express design for circulation within the polar regions alone, among exceptionally constrained publics composed largely of the members of the expeditionary ships themselves. Such texts are informed by Inuit, Yupik, Iñupiat, Sami, and other Arctic indigenous knowledge and histories, even when this body of knowledge is not always explicitly credited by white Westerners. Central to the polar texts under discussion in this book are the series of little-known and rarely (if ever) studied Arctic and Antarctic newspapers written by expedition members for distribution among each shipboard community's "private family circle," as one Arctic newspaper described it, or what another paper called "*our own little circle.*"[3] I study not just the content of the writings, but also the way they were made, used, collected, organized, printed, circulated, saved, or discarded. My interest is in the production and means of distribution of this media, whether in the form of the newspapers exchanged aboard isolated, icebound ships among members of a crew, or in the form of the notes and letters thrown to the commerce of the frozen North, such as messages left in cairns, cast adrift in bottles, or launched in hydrogen gas balloons. From the nineteenth century to today, as I argue more broadly, the planetary implications of these texts and print media paradoxically emerge from their very non-utile, motile, ephemeral, iceboundedness.

In our contemporary Anthropocenic moment of accelerating Arctic and Antarctic polar ice sheet collapse, human life on Earth can itself feel ephemeral, both because of and despite humans' irreversible impact on global climate and the geological record. The evanescent printed records generated in polar extremity, I argue in this book, offer conceptual and formal devices for describing, comprehending, and, most ambitiously, surviving climatic extremity. These texts, which constitute one form of what I call *polar ecomedia*, are examples of environmental writing by which, in turn, we might imagine—and with hope mediate—climate change and ecological extremity today. One broader critical question animating this study of Arctic and Antarctic printing and ephemera, in other words, is what genre of writing, what communication medium, emerges from and is demanded by the Anthropocene?[4] The story I tell in this book draws from but does not recapitulate historical expeditionary accounts of endurance and privation. I instead explore what literary and communicative forms the outlandishness of Arctic and Antarctic conditions inspire and, more important, what kinds of textual and media circulation they can sustain. Such media are "socially realized structures of communication," in Lisa Gitelman's terms; in this book, and in the Anthropocene epoch in which the news at the ends of the earth bears heavily on all life on the planet, media must be understood to be realized both socially and environmentally.[5] The ecomedia materials under discussion in this book occur in different narrative, textual, or circulatory forms than those typically associated, critically speaking, with the polar regions or other ecological spaces, and will likely be new to readers for these reasons. My focus is on projects such as Ernest Shackleton's editorship of the *South Polar Times*, a typescript newspaper published in Antarctica beginning in 1902 for Robert Falcon Scott's crew (among whom Shackleton was initially third officer), rather than on *South* (1919), his popular first-person narrative of the *Endurance* expedition. In the same vein, I study Charles Francis Hall's technological contrivances for writing in igloos in −40° temperatures, as detailed in the hundreds of ephemeral notebooks that survive his seven years of residence with the Inuit, rather than his published personal narrative, *Life with the Esquimaux* (1864), or the various accounts of his final, shattering voyage. I devote attention as well to other archives and forms of thought that organized themselves around the poles, whether messages left in cairns and other provisional caches fashioned from rock and ice, oceanic dead letters, "open polar sea" and hollow earth theories, or Inuit epistemology and indigenous lifeways.

What white Westerners thought of as communication had to adapt to the ecological realities of polar communication. Polar voyagers did not immediately or automatically become producers and consumers of ecomedia upon reaching the icefields, and their experiential transformation is part of the story of this book. For example, Anglo-American expeditions built cairns from local rocks, inside of which they stored messages and supplies. But for the Inuit, cairns, or Inuksuit, transmit messages in their very shape and construction; they are sufficient unto themselves as communicative media, and do not encompass written information. What Inuksuit communicate, however, was not legible to British expeditions engaged in Franklin searches, which often destroyed the rock forms in hopes of finding letters or a food cache. (In response to a lecture I gave on this material, media studies scholar John Durham Peters quipped, "Destroying cairns in search of a message is the *point* of media studies.") But if polar expeditions have functioned in Western history as impetuses for generating narratives, writing on ice and about ice in the Anthropocene may be scarcely more legible than writing on water.

In attending to today's breaking news from the polar regions while tracking down historical polar expeditionary newspapers across dispersed archives, I have kept in mind the motivation governing David H. Stam and Deirdre C. Stam in staging their *Books on Ice* exhibition over ten years ago: the notion that within expeditionary history, "books seem to have been as essential as pemmican, primus stoves, fuel, and furs."[6] The resources (fuel, dried meats, skins) invoked in the Stams' comparison are all demanded by and, in some ways, emerge from the polar regions. What I propose is that the media of production and distribution, survival and loss that constitute polar writing, in the form of newspapers, cairn messages, and other ephemeral inscriptions in icebound regions, are Arctic and Antarctic resources as well. In studying writing from the geophysical ends of the earth—at this moment of climate-focused news envisioning the anthropogenic ends of the earth—I argue for finding unexpected resources for futurity in forms of polar evanescence.

Ice Cycles

Ice bears its own temporality, in nonlinear cycles. European polar exploration began in early modernity as a search for faster routes to new commercial markets via a Northwest Passage; industrialization in the late eighteenth and nineteenth centuries drove both the colonialist imperatives and resource needs that have today led to fossil fuel scarcity. Human overconsumption of resources has been unequally distributed globally, as the developing world bears the brunt of anthropogenic climate change and has benefited the least from the industrializing forces that have caused it. Temperature increases register differently in the polar regions as well. The Paris Agreement of the United Nations Framework Convention on Climate Change (2015) seeks to limit temperature rise in the next century to 1.5–<2°C above pre-industrial levels. Yet the Arctic is a climate multiplier: a 2° global rise in temperature would actually result in an increase of 3.5–5°C in the Arctic.[7] The very global warming propelled by fossil fuel usage in the past few hundred years is now melting the Arctic regions and enabling oil- and gas-hungry nations to bring new extractive technologies to bear in the Far North. In other words, the global trade interests of early modernity, which launched the first Northwest Passage expeditions, in turn inaugurated industrialization's appetite for fossil fuels and increased human energy consumption. The oil and gas deposits now targeted for extraction would not be accessible had not the carbon usage that necessitates their mining produced the irreversible warming effects presently melting the polar ice sheets.

In a number of cases there is in fact a direct link between contemporary resource extraction and polar ephemera. In 1960, during a period of oil and gas company reconnaissance of the northernmost islands of the Canadian archipelago, expeditionary messages from a series of mid-nineteenth-century Arctic voyages were uncovered, extracted from cairns by scouts from Imperial Oil, the petroleum company J. C. Sproule, Round Valley Oil, and the well-drilling outfit Dominion Explorers Limited. "One of the by-products of the search for oil and gas in the Queen Elizabeth Islands has been the discovery of a number of records left by early Arctic expeditions. These records were normally left in stone cairns, or buried near them," Canada's Department of Northern Affairs and National Resources records reveal; in 1960 "no less than nine records are known to have been found in the Arctic Archipelago, seven from expeditions taking part in the search for Franklin."[8] These include a land possession claim to the region left in 1851 by the Briton Erasmus Ommanney of the *Assistance*; various locational notes and lists of provisions cached in 1853 by his countryman Edward Belcher's Franklin search; a declaration of "possessions of all the Arctic islands north of North America from 60 deg. West Longitude to 141 deg. West and as far North as 90 degrees North" made in 1909 by the Canadian Joseph-Elzéar Bernier; and a 1917 note from an American, Donald MacMillan, that his Crocker Land expedition had recovered messages from George Nares's 1875 British Arctic expedition.[9] (Crocker Land itself turned out not to exist.) There is no telling what future fossil fuel extraction in the Arctic will exhume, or what or whom it will bury.

The polar expeditions launched by Europeans and North Americans beginning in 1818 are usually historicized within the context of the broader exploration and colonization projects of the long nineteenth century. And yet the initial Arctic ventures of the period were inaugurated and enabled, in some ways, by short-term global climate change. As reported by members of the Anglo-American Arctic whaling fleet in 1816 and 1817, a couple of uncommonly warm winters off the west coast of Greenland produced greatly reduced sea ice in Far Northern waters. Likely a result of the varying global climate effects resulting from the massive eruption of Mount Tambora in Indonesia in 1815, this meteorological anomaly is more commonly identified in America and Europe for its cooling effects, which produced the notorious "Year without a Summer" in more temperate climes in 1816. (The very cold, rainy summer kept inside a summer pleasure party that included Mary Shelley, who then began composing *Frankenstein*, the frame narrative of which features an Arctic expedition to find a warm open polar sea.) The warmer than usual temperatures in the Far North that were produced by this temporary oceanographic anomaly buoyed nineteenth-century theories of an open polar sea beyond the northern ice and aided the transit, for example, of William Edward Parry's 1819–20 Northwest Passage expedition. Parry's advances, in turn, gave encouragement to future expeditions, which fared less well as Arctic ice coverage returned in subsequent decades. But if short-term global climate change launched Anglo-American polar exploration when the idea of an open polar sea was only a fantasy, today global warming has turned the dream of a warm Arctic into a reality. The Northwest Passage is increasingly ice-free in the summer, and several circumpolar nations are refurbishing Arctic bases that had been abandoned in the Cold War, ostensibly to protect future Arctic trade via the Northern Sea Route.

The medium of ice is itself only one incarnation of a substance that takes three seemingly incommensurate forms: liquid, gas, solid. As such, ice is both ephemeral and durable. Ice in the Arctic and Antarctica appears both silent and still and yet is spectacularly on the move, and not just in epochs of climate crisis: in its vibrancy ice carves valleys, levels mountains, and deposits moraines over hundreds of miles. "Here was a plastic, moving, semi-solid mass," Elisha Kent Kane wrote of a glacier in Greenland, "obliterating life, swallowing rocks and islands, and ploughing its way with irresistible march through the crust of an investing sea."[10] Beyond even a planetary scale, the melting of the polar ice sheets has in fact measurably changed the tilt of the earth. Elizabeth Leane and Graeme Miles find in this shift a profound reorientation of humans' relationship to the planet itself: "At a time when we are still confronting the impact of our actions on the biosphere, this realization of our ability to inadvertently change the orientation of our planet in space, even by a tiny amount, gives a new dimension to the Anthropocene: we live not so much *on*, now, but in uneasy partnership *with* a body spinning through space."[11] In the polar regions ice groans, cracks, screams, hisses, forms and liquefies in hours. For the Inuit of Kangiqsujuaq, ice even provides temporary caves beneath the surface of the ocean into which hunters can crawl to harvest mussels. Ice also tells stories that are hundreds of thousands of years old. Those who study paleo-oceanography (the history of the ocean) and paleoclimatology (the history of the earth's climate) can read in ice core samples narratives of past volcanic eruptions, forest fires, rising seas, and flowers. As this book details, the variable elements of the polar environment bring into stark relief how textual and other media forms communicate in extremity.

While it may be a given to recognize that the past bears lessons for the future, this book does not and cannot observe linear temporality on a human-centered scale, both in topic and in evidentiary material: thanks to the more or less simultaneity of all human activity within the scope of planetary time, plus the acceleration of melting ice, one measure of the temporal distinctions between the nineteenth century and the twenty-first has collapsed. By this I mean that when we frame our thinking within the terms of the recently designated epoch of the Anthropocene, defined as the period of measurable human geological impact on the earth, we are forced to reckon with other geological scales of time, those that go beyond the human. *Homo sapiens*, for example, evolved 250,000 to 400,000 years ago, and within that frame the distinction between 1818, 1914, and 2017 CE barely registers. Furthermore, in terms of planetary time—scientists now calculate the earth's age at 4.55 billion years—400,000 years is itself a relative blip. Perhaps this is why it is famously difficult to envision or otherwise represent the temporal scale of the earth outside of the compass of human action and thought. Often these visualizations are keyed to a human scale, such as in Stephen Jay Gould's well-known metaphor in *Time's Arrow, Time's Cycle*: "Consider the Earth's history as the old measure of the English yard, the distance from the King's nose to the tip of his outstretched hand. One stroke of a nail file on his middle finger erases human history."[12] Such images represent a characteristically Anthropocentric imagination of the inhuman scale of deep time.[13] Given this context, what we understand as artifacts of history necessarily register within different scales of pastness and require variable indices of temporal dynamism. The work of interpreting such artifacts is not just a matter of being mindful of the conditions that produced them and the forces that make them available to be read today; the very temporalities of that pastness must collapse.

The visual forms emerging from the polar regions today—a polar bear clinging to vanishing ice, a blighted industrial drilling site atop the permafrost—in some ways bear the metaphorical legacy of nineteenth-century racist stereotypes of the "vanishing" Native, made pathetic, distant, and inevitable in his twilight. As such, the only narrative they provide is one of inevitability. They are clichés in other ways, too; a *New York Times* staff photographer working to visualize climate change via drone imaging suggested, "A lot of the iconography that we've seen depicting climate change has been very similar. I think many people feel oversaturated with images of glaciers calving into the ocean and polar bears on a piece of ice floating in the sea."[14] The media perspectives usually granted of the polar regions in their moment of exhaustion, of vanishing, have not yet found a narrative frame sufficient to their oceanic and planetary contours. Climatic specificity matters here: as regions simultaneously fluid and terrestrial, inhabited and not, stateless and multiply contested, the Arctic and Antarctica (while emphatically not the same geophysically or demographically) provide different substructures than the rest of the terrestrial earth for knowledge repositories and circulation. Here is an example of these very qualities of the icebound world, as illustrated by the contemporary poet and naturalist Elizabeth Bradfield in her poem "Polar Explorer Robert Falcon Scott (1912)." Bradfield captures the motility of the body of the doomed explorer while in Antarctica. On their mission to reach the South Pole, Scott and his Southern Party companions trudged across the frozen continent, "manhauling" sledges in defiance of climate adaptation strategies before dying on the ice. Their bodies could not be recovered and were heaped with stones in lieu of burial by their reserve crew a year later. Denied a seaman's traditional sea burial, Scott rests atop frozen water. But Bradfield reminds us that his body is nevertheless on the move in death too:

> his body, still wrapped in its reindeer bag, still swaddled
> in his tent's frayed silk, flag still tattering, his body
> may have reached the Ross Sea
> through the slow torrent
>
> of the ice shelf. All the days he plodded,
> the land was sliding back beneath him, treadmill
> to the sea where he at last is given
>
> a sailor's burial,
> maybe today, sunk and drifting.[15]

Even in Antarctica, the polar region anchored by a land mass, there is no terrestrial fixity for burial; the dead can no more stay put than can an Antarctic ice sheet. If we think of Scott's body as a communicative medium, as Bradfield's poem imagines it, we can make connections to other stories: to nautical traditions of sea burial, to the deadly consequences (in both directions) of a colonial subject's maladaptation to local conditions, to nonlinear understandings of movement in time and space. Polar ecomedia, I argue, allow us to apprehend the archive of human toil and tragedy—and, significantly, the nonhuman processes of accumulated and diminishing ice—that constitute the news at the ends of the earth.

For a model of polar ecomedia and its arbitration by ice, consider George Murray Levick's photographic notebook. Levick was a zoologist, surgeon, and photographer on Robert Falcon Scott's British Antarctic expedition to the South Pole aboard the *Terra Nova* (1910–13), the venture on which Scott and four companions famously died on the ice on their disappointed return from the pole, having learned that Norwegian Roald Amundsen had reached 90° s thirty-four days before them. Levick stayed in reserve to study Adélie penguins and thus survived the expedition as part of the Northern Party. Along with the geologist Raymond E. Priestly, Levick produced a Northern Party newspaper, the *Adélie Mail and Cape Adare Times* (1911–12); his pen name was "Bluebell." The handful of Northern Party readers of the *Adélie Mail and Cape Adare Times* would have learned of ongoing penguin mischief at Cape Adare from the paper's "Police News," which was dominated by accounts of domestic violence, such as the following: "Tubby Flipper was charged with severely illtreating his wife, who, it appears, is a very industrious woman and much liked by her neighbors. . . . Judge C. no sooner heard the case read out than he sentenced the prisoner to 21 days hard labour, the judge remarking that he intended to put a stop to the disgraceful habit of wifebeating which had become the habit at Cape Adare. The prisoner was removed swearing horribly."[16] Upon his return from Antarctica Levick wrote a then-scandalous pamphlet—in Greek—titled "Sexual Habits of the Adélie Penguin," in which he accurately described autoeroticism, necrophilia, homosexuality, and nonprocreative sex among the penguins. The pamphlet was denied publication but circulated privately; it was excavated and published in 2012.[17]

But Levick's provocative penguin studies are not my ecomedia focus or archaeological practice here. Levick's less vivid writings included a journal listing the details of his photographic exposures. When the expedition left its base hut at Cape Evans, Levick left the notebook behind, by design or chance; its existence became lost to the historical record, for a time. Global warming has led to more extensive summer thaws in Antarctica, much as it has throughout the planet. In recent years the New Zealand–based Antarctic Heritage Trust has unexpectedly found photographic negatives from Shackleton's Ross Sea Party of 1914–16. (Media reports of their rediscovery were sent to me by friends who know of my research; nearly every week, still, they resurface to my attention via Facebook's "On this Day" feature, making the news seem ever-new.)[18] Also found were five crates of whisky and brandy from Shackleton's *Nimrod* expedition of 1907–9.[19] In the summer of 2013, exactly one hundred years after the *Terra Nova* expedition had ended in tragedy, the icemelt runoff around the hut at Cape Evans (also managed now by the Antarctic Heritage Trust) exposed a notebook, Levick's photographic notebook, still legible. It was restored, digitized, and then returned to the hut at Cape Evans—returned, that is, to the ice, just as the three bottles of Shackleton's whisky were returned to his Cape Royds hut after analysis and chemical reproduction.[20] The reinstatement of Levick's notebook in Antarctica was a source of surprise and consternation to some responders to news reports in October 2014 on the discovery of the notebook. While it is not my scholarly habit to cite internet commentary, I was struck by the observation of a commenter writing as "Sage-on-the-Hudson" in a sentiment echoed by others: "After being placed in a new binding, the notebook was sent back to Antarctica. Why? To be read by the penguins? Since there are no museums, libraries or permanent settlements on the continent, that would seem its own exercise in pointless futility."[21] While the commenter might not have made use of the archival resources I analyze in this book, he could have tarried a while at Cape Evans virtually: Scott's hut has been made available to digital travelers in extraordinary detail via Google Street View. In nonpolar spaces, the program's mapping function allows one to walk through a neighborhood, a route, or a streetscape, even if one cannot deviate from the road or sidewalk, cannot penetrate most buildings or go off road. In Antarctica, though, the only viewing option is interior (at least it was in 2014, when Sage-on-the-Hudson left his comment). The Street View of Scott's Antarctic hut to which one has access offers remarkable detail of the well-maintained stores in the hut, but the route beyond the hut is arrested at the lintel. Google Street View shows one limitation of nonpolar modes of thought: rather than giving us magisterial vistas of Antarctic icescapes, our view is bounded by terrestrial infrastructure.[22] Subzero temperatures are a great preservative, which is why Scott's supposedly temporary hut remains intact a century later, as does one at Cape Royds built by Shackleton a few years later. While the two explorers' huts may not be "permanent" in any human-scaled temporal sense, their preservation (both by Antarctic climate and by the Heritage Trust) ensures that the Cape Evans and Cape Royds huts are, in fact, "museums" and "settlements" in all the ways that count in the polar regions. And as *The News at the Ends of the Earth* will show, they are libraries as well, storehouses of ecomedia circulation.

Levick's notebook is an exemplar of polar ecomedia. A manuscript notebook of photographic data collection, it was buried in the ice in one

FIG INTRO.1 — George Murray Levick's photographic notebook before restoration.
© ANTARCTIC HERITAGE TRUST, NZAHT.ORG.

polar age and offered up by the ice a century later as a result of the climatic change induced by the very industrialization that now drives polar resource extraction and of which polar expeditions were a part. But the notebook is not a museum artifact, abstracted from its polar milieu and catalogued as ephemera, even as it is available digitally. It is back at the scene of its original circulation as expeditionary media, a record of data production tracking the habits and conditions of nonhuman populations in Antarctica. Unlike Western modernity's history of envisaged resource extraction in the polar regions, Levick's notebook is a polar resource that has been put *back* on the ice. Who—or what—will next take it up from the melting ice to read anew?

Polar Periodicals

Levick's notebook is continuous with other forms of polar recordkeeping, both in its creation and circulation and in its mediation by polar climate. The chapters that follow turn more specifically to texts that not only remained in (or, in the notebook's case, were returned to) the polar regions but were created and printed there. Beginning in 1848, the year of the first Franklin searches, many expeditions brought printing presses, which are not usually classed among nautical supplies. With such presses, polar-voyaging sailors wrote and printed newspapers, broadsides, cairn messages, and other reading matter beyond the Arctic and Antarctic Circles. The polar expeditions I discuss range from William Edward Parry's first Arctic voyage on the *Hecla* and *Griper*, which launched in 1819, to Douglas Mawson's Antarctic voyage on the *Aurora*, which concluded in 1914. There were at least twenty-seven newspapers published by expedition members during this period. In addition to the *Illustrated Arctic News* (HMS *Resolute*, commanded by Austin, 1850–51), the newspapers I read include the *North Georgia Gazette, and Winter Chronicle*, the first Arctic newspaper (HMS *Hecla* and *Griper*, Parry, 1819–20); the *Flight of the Plover, or the North Pole Charivari* (HMS *Plover*, Moore, 1848); the *Aurora Borealis* (HMS *Assistance*, Ommanney, 1850–51); the *Weekly Guy* (HMS *Plover*, Maguire, 1852–54); the *Queen's Illuminated Magazine* (HMS *Assistance*, Belcher, 1852–54); the *Polar Almanac* (HMS *Enterprise*, Collinson, 1853); the *Port Foulke Weekly News* (*United States*, Hayes, 1860–61); the *Discovery News* (HMS *Discovery*, Nares, 1875–76); the *Arctic Moon* (*Proteus*, Greely, 1881–84); the *Midnight Sun* (*America*, Baldwin, 1901–2); the *Arctic Eagle* (*America*, Fiala, 1903–5); the *South Polar Times*, a lavish, extensive newspaper published by Scott's National Antarctic expedition on the *Discovery*, as well as the expedition's offshoot, a more informal newspaper called *The Blizzard*, for pieces deemed unsuitable for *South Polar Times* inclusion (1902–3); the first book published in Antarctica, *Aurora Australis*, written and printed by members of Shackleton's 1907–9 British expedition aboard the *Nimrod*, who also created the newspaper *Antarctic Petrel* (1907–9); the *Adélie Mail and Cape Adare Times*, written by the Northern Party on Scott's second, fatal expedition on the *Terra Nova* (1910–13); and *Adelie Blizzard* (*Aurora*, Mawson, 1911–14). In several instances, newspapers were suppressed by commanders (such as the underground papers *Gleaner* and *Minavilins* (*Resolute*, Austin, 1850–51) or did not come to planned fruition (such as the *Polar Pirate* of Fiala's 1903–5 mission). Periodicals were not confined to Anglo-American ventures; the German Arctic expedition led by Carl Koldewey aboard the *Hansa* (1869–70) published the *Ostgrönländische Zeitung*, and the Norwegian Fridtjof Nansen's *Fram* expedition (1893–96) circulated the manuscript newspaper *Framsjaa*. Mawson's Australasian Antarctic Expedition was the first to establish a radio link to the outside world; the *Adelie Blizzard* is thus the first paper to include news of the outside world via cable reports, and the last paper, chronologically speaking, that I treat in this book.

The New Georgia Gazette
and
Winter Chronicle

Monday November 28th 1819

We owe an apology to the Public
for having delayed the insertion
of this letter until a long after
the performance to which it alb-
uded took however we that
so much of our second Number
had been occupied by the affairs
of the Theatre, that we had hardly
room in our last to mention the
managers expedience although
not having last our selves obliged
in justice to our correspondent
on this subject, to lay before
the letter which is we now
submit to our readers as
well as the songs which
were sung by Mess. Horner
and others, and which will
be found in the last page of the
present Number.

To the Lady of the Winter Chronicle

Sir

I received with expressing the
infinite delight I felt in witnessing
the entertaining performance of
Friday evening which few could
hesitate to pronounce the ablest of
anything of the kind that
has ever ___ succeeded it
in this country; and which it
might be justly stated will more
be surpassed by any future
Theatre towards this arid
& genial clime; where it would
be admitted the wind can never
____ they said some expense
inconvenience from empty letter
done than I should recommend
the old Gentleman in the blue
to damn Coverts transport
a little of his accumulated wealth
by supplying his time therefore
impairments with some further
the allowance

THE WEEKLY GUY.

No. v.]   Friday, Dec. 3, 1852.   [Gratis.

Having made the 'amende honorable' at
the conclusion of our paper, by apologising for
its late appearance last week, we little thought
any further allusion to the subject would be at
all necessary. In fact we consider the boasted
'freedom of the press' a dead letter, a hoax, if
we are not at liberty to come and go as pleases
best ourselves and our friends. Even to mention
it, is perhaps conferring undue importance to a
contemptible joke perpetrated against us on
Monday, in the shape of a report industriously
circulated to the effect, that our 'Guy' had come
to an untimely end, having been stolen, or stray-
ed, or otherwise made away with. Possibly in
this case as in many others, 'the wish was father
to the thought.' But it is the very reverse of any
feeling of annoyance that induces us now to al-
lude to the subject; on the contrary, we heartily
thank the perpetrators for the attempt, and
would feel great pleasure in bestowing on them
our meed of praise, if we could but discover a
single gleam of wit in the joke, either as to the
matter or the manner thereof. We must therefore content ourselves with the expression of

POLAR ALMANAC,

for the

YEAR OF OUR LORD 1854,

being the seventeenth year of the reign

of

HER MAJESTY QUEEN VICTORIA.

Printed on board

of

Her Majesty's Ship Enterprise,

in

Camden Bay

Latitude 70°08′North. Longitude 145°29′West.

by

Henry Hester Captains Coxswain,

Vivat Regina.

FIG INTRO.5 — *Weekly Guy* 5 (3 Dec. 1852). John Simpson Papers, 1825–1875. DAVID M.
RUBENSTEIN RARE BOOK AND MANUSCRIPT LIBRARY, DUKE UNIVERSITY.

FIG INTRO.6 — *Polar Almanac.* John Simpson Papers, 1825–1875. DAVID M. RUBENSTEIN
RARE BOOK AND MANUSCRIPT LIBRARY, DUKE UNIVERSITY.

These publications were produced in great part for a reading audience
of the mission's crew members. As Lara Langer Cohen has argued about
amateur newspapers in the 1870s and 1880s in the United States, such communities are "not just an *effect* of print"; "community is also the *cause* of
print."[23] The logic applies to polar newspapers as well. Concocted originally as a stratagem to combat the physically and mentally debilitating trials
of a sunless polar winter, the newspapers generated near the poles were generally comic or parodic. The *Port Foulke Weekly News* of Isaac Israel Hayes's
United States expedition, for example, facetiously adhered to periodical
expectations. As Hayes described it, "There is a regular corps of editors
and reporters, and office for 'general news,' and 'editorial department,' and
a 'telegraph station,' where information is supposed to be received from all
quarters of the world, and the relations existing between the sun, moon,

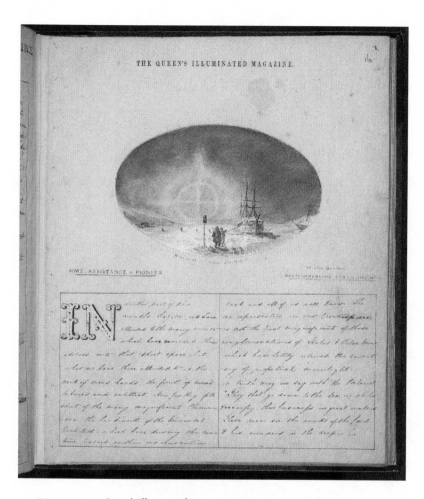

FIG INTRO.7 — *Queen's Illuminated Magazine*. Barrow Bequest vol. 6, Add s 35305.

and stars are duly reported by 'reliable correspondents,' and pictorial representations of extraordinary occurrences are also received from 'our artist
on the spot.'" (This expedition consisted of only fourteen men; it should
go without saying that there was no "telegraph station" at latitude 81° N in
1860.) The *Port Foulke Weekly News* was not alone in its "farcical" inhabitation of the expected beats for a newspaper, and Hayes's description of its
contents can stand for a general one: "There is a fair sprinkling of 'enigmas,' 'original jokes,' 'items of domestic and foreign intelligence,' 'personals,'
'advertisements,' &c., &c., among a larger allowance of more pretentious
effusions."[24] Hayes's quotation marks designate the different sections of the

FIG INTRO.8 — *Port Foulke Weekly News*. Manuscript newspaper aboard *United States*, Isaac Israel Hayes's Arctic expedition, 1860–61. NEW-YORK HISTORICAL SOCIETY.

THE
DISCOVERY NEWS.

SATURDAY. NOV, 27, 1875.

All readers of the "News" will learn with astonishment that so large a section of its readers as the whole of the Nor-Westerly Community have as yet found no subject upon which to dilate in its pages. Many causes may be assigned for this state of affairs, but doubtless it would be hard to find the real one, a multiplicity is no doubt at work, and the result is the rather melancholy one that our wit and humour column remains unfilled. Least said is however soonest mended, and it may be that the intellectual charms of that district are even now mustering themselves to storm the maiden fortress, we will therefore not give way to green-sickness but smilingly and blushingly await the onset, in full hopes that another week will have brought a conclusion to the preparatory measure hitherto at work.

It is a beautiful and instructive thing to observe the artificers at their labours under the masterly direction of our skilful architect. The theatre, at which their time is uow employed, is almost complete, and its appearance already goes far to verify the prediction as to its success uttered in this paper last week.

It is considered advisable by a correspondent that in future no one journey to any distance from the ship greater then a hundred yards unarmed; noises have been heard in the wardroom at night utterly unlike any a dog can make, and yet evidently issuing from a large and powerful animal; a sort of a medium between the sneezings of a drayhorse and the contemptuous grunts of a pig, these must have been vented by a Polar bear; those who will persist, after this warning in circumambulating the mile would do well to begin at the other end, and thereby elude the animal's observation, they would moreover find it a pleasing change in the monotony of that somewhat unromantic trudge.

The public will be glad to learn that Dr. Ninnis has kindly consented to furnish the Discovery News with a weekly weather notice; this, the only true and authentic account will considerably enhance the value of our paper.

We beg here to state that the thanks of all on board are due to the unflagging industry and zeal of their printer Benjamin Wyatt; without the unsparing attention to the work which he has evinced, it would have been impossible for this paper to have gained the popularity and success it has met with.

Thoughts on the Floe

I consider the aspects of nature here, are more impressive than in many other regions.

The snow-clad mountains in their shadowy darkness at even-tide, the brilliant moon surrounded by a clear and cloudless sky, and which alike illumes and shadows all, impart s to all around an appearance with which one finds it difficult to draw a comparison.

On this scene one gazes with awe and silent admiration, as conscious midst all this Giant Creation, of man's insignificance. What countless myriads of such as we, have been swept from this earth out of sight, and not a single natural law been disturbed, or a moments cessation been caused in the silent march of creation. Our civilization and familiarity, certainly has a tendency to make us pass with little thought or notice the wonderful works of nature on earth and air; but I think it is almost confined to the few who visit these regions, to observe the Majesty of the great Creator as exemplified on the third natural element.

As the majority of our ideas of grandeur and importance are formed from comparisions, so from a falling brook or rivulet we build up our imaginations, until we eventually form an idea even of the great Niagara; familiarity having made us conversant with the devious and uneven course of our brook or rivulet through all its vicissitudes; and thus we allow our mind to multiply and create the magnitude and phenomena of bodies of water - and often err but little. Furthermore we ought to bear in mind when viewing this scene, that the potent force of these immense masses of ice is equal to its grandeur and sublimity; the expansive force of water when freezing being known to rend asunder the stoutest rocks and strongest vessils in which it may be contained. The motive force imparted to it by wind and waves is directly in unison with its other characteristics, this force being such that no floating construction known or likely to be known can withstand it, its solidity and firmness of flotation (by virtue of its formation) being proof against any resistance on its part.

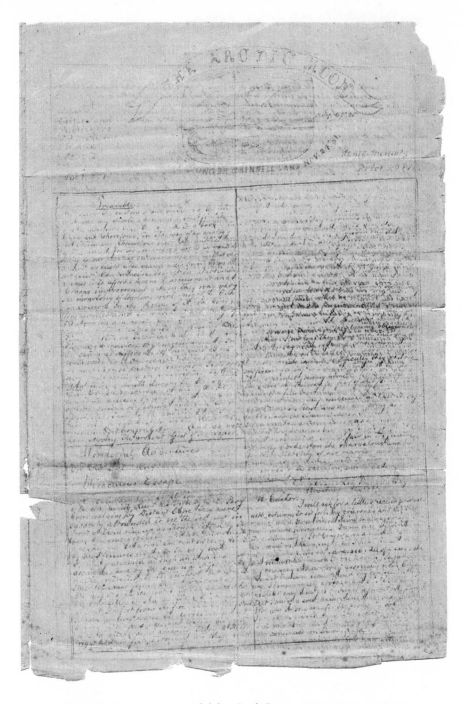

FIG INTRO.10 — *Arctic Moon*. Adolphus Greely Papers, 1876–1973. COURTESY OF
DARTMOUTH COLLEGE LIBRARY.

FIG INTRO.11 — *Midnight Sun*. Ernest deKoven Leffingwell Papers, 1900–1961. COURTESY OF DARTMOUTH COLLEGE LIBRARY.

FIG INTRO.12 — *Arctic Eagle*. Harrie H. Newcomb Papers, 1897–1958, MS 257. GEORGE J. MITCHELL DEPT. OF SPECIAL COLLECTIONS AND ARCHIVES, BOWDOIN COLLEGE LIBRARY.

FIG INTRO.13 — *South Polar Times.* COURTESY OF DARTMOUTH COLLEGE LIBRARY.

paper, of course, but they also serve as ironized scare quotes referring to the performance of quotidian habit in the Arctic.

In many ways we might see newspapers as the social media of polar expeditions. Contributions to polar newspapers, for instance, focused on interpersonal or canine affairs (intrigues among the sled dogs were a popular topic); the scientific and exploratory aims of the missions rarely made the pages of the gazettes. "The place for scientific results is not here," a note at

FIG INTRO.14 — *The Blizzard*. MS 856. SCOTT POLAR RESEARCH INSTITUTE, UNIVERSITY OF CAMBRIDGE.

the end of a contribution to *Aurora Australis* explains, "but rather in the contemplated meteorological, geological, and mineralogical memoirs of this expedition."[25] The poetry that appears in Arctic and Antarctic printing is droll and aspires to wit; it includes special-occasion menus in verse ("The Dessert's much as usual—you'll all know the reason/ 'Tis difficult here to get things out of season");[26] complaints about polar problems such as condensation ("And in the middle of the night/ In our sleeping bags there's a riot./ Someone turns and screws about,/ And gets in such a pet,/ Says he cannot sleep any more,/ 'Cause his sleeping bag is wet");[27] and parodies of well-known literature ("Once more unto the beach, dear friends, once more/ Or live for ever on the legs of crabs").[28] And yet this content amplified—even as it was designed to ease—the time and distance between the expeditions' location and resources and the usual journalistic and literary center of the metropole.

But if polar newspapers were a form of social media, a collective production of unbounded diffusion while in extremity, then they embody

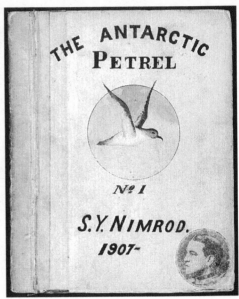

FIG INTRO.15 — Ernest H. Shackleton, ed., *Aurora Australis* (Antarctica: Printed at the Sign of "The Penguin" by Joyce and Wild, 1908). JOHN CARTER BROWN LIBRARY.

FIG INTRO.16 — *Antarctic Petrel*, no 1. British Antarctic Expedition, 1907–9. MS-0261. ALEXANDER TURNBULL LIBRARY, WELLINGTON, NEW ZEALAND.

boundedness at the same time, as their producers were literally confined to ships while wedged in ice. Produced in regions and at times of year hostile to demarcations of hour, day, and global positioning, Arctic and Antarctic newspapers did not regulate time so much as they marked its dilation. Polar publications model possibilities for oceanic inscription in geophysical spaces resistant to terrestrial commonplaces. They also constitute an important resource in themselves: they become an alternative medium by which expedition members worked through questions of time, space, and human duration in climatic extremity. The Arctic and Antarctic regions have long presented imaginative and strategic impediments to stable possession, given the geophysical challenges of sustaining human life. But when faced with the natural antagonism of the extremity of polar conditions, nineteenth-century expedition members did not draw blanks; they printed gazettes.

The very act of *printing* texts in the Arctic and Antarctica represents an attempt to make a mark in an icy, oceanic environment hostile to customary forms of inscription, whether locational, imperial, or infrastructural.

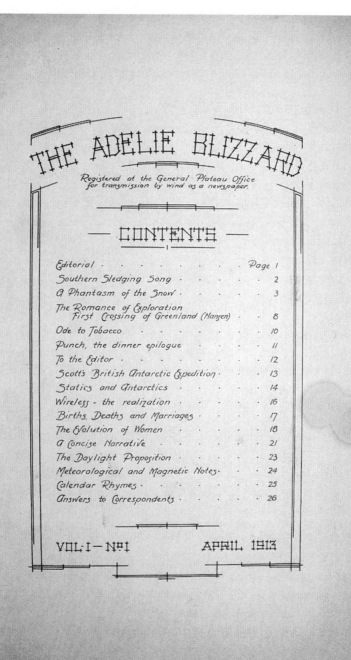

THE ADELIE BLIZZARD

Registered at the General Plateau Office
for transmission by wind as a newspaper.

— CONTENTS —

VOL. I — No 1   APRIL 1913

FIG INTRO.17 — *Adelie Blizzard.* SOUTH AUSTRALIAN MUSEUM, AUSTRALIAN POLAR COLLECTIONS.

(Analogously, a robotics project by scientists at the University of Southern California and NASA aimed at installing a large-scale 3D printer on the moon for building structures shows a similar drive to imagine production infrastructure in extreme environments; that 3D printer would be the polar press of the future.)[29] And yet the fact that all the printed materials are fugitive pieces demonstrates a recognition of the fleeting ephemerality of human life in climate extremity. This is the insight that polar ecomedia furnishes: it is ephemera designed to encode its motion and its ice-carved retreat in its very creation. If, in Stephanie LeMenager's observation, "climate change represents, among other things, an assault on the everyday," then the forms of everyday life will not only change under climate crisis but will reflect it in their content and creation. In her astute extension of the implications of climate news to the very form of *news* itself, LeMenager continues, "Climate change 'news' fails to be 'news' insofar as it implies an end to the everyday itself. . . . Extreme weather, including superstorms and severe drought, and all of these conditions that are taking hold *as conditions* rather than as events shift the ground of habit and call attention to the profoundly ecological, interdependent state of humanity."[30] LeMenager introduces the genre of the news to conversations about Anthropocene writing by invoking Henry David Thoreau's lofty rejection of periodical information:

> I am sure that I never read any memorable news in a newspaper. If we read of one man robbed, or murdered, or killed by accident, or one house burned, or one vessel wrecked, or one steamboat blown up, or one cow run over on the Western Railroad, or one mad dog killed, or one lot of grasshoppers in the winter—we never need read of another. One is enough. If you are acquainted with the principle, what do you care for a myriad instances and applications?[31]

LeMenager's gloss on this passage is that Thoreau hated the concept of the news "because it implied that 'the world' is a disposable externality, a serial fiction with an iterative and forgettable plot."[32] Yet to my reading Thoreau (who was well up on the polar expeditions of his time) is noting the collapse of temporal distinctions, read ecologically, as well as calling for serial—if asynchronic—forms of information to emerge from the natural world itself.[33] In other words, he calls for those in "the world" to be attentive not just to the natural world, but to the natural world-as-media. In the polar regions, the genre of the news and the medium of the newspaper are self-conscious registers of the ephemerality of life in climate extremity. Rather than the banal, quotidian repetition that riles Thoreau, the evanescent nature of *news* is the subject of polar papers. If climate change disrupts the notion of the everyday, then we might see in the extremities of polar climate a disruption of diurnal timescales, as well.

Ecomedia at the Ends of the Earth

By naming icebound newspapers, cairn messages, and other expeditionary ephemera *polar ecomedia* I do not intend to argue simply that these polar exploratory communication materials are the bits and pieces that constitute a different class of ecomedia. More broadly, I am interested in how we might understand the ephemera of historical polar expeditionary communities within ongoing scientific and humanistic conversations about how the environment and forms of communicative media are mutually constituted—and mutually in flux and degeneration. The continuity of these questions across historical time is one of the primary arguments of *The News at the Ends of the Earth*. The term "ecomedia" denotes, for one, the technological media used to register complex systems of ecological and environmental change. It indicates as well an approach to thinking about the imbrication of media forms (whether art, film, data visualization, etc.) within systems and environments. My use of the term understands these two definitions as fundamentally intertwined within the polar landscape.[34]

The coinage "ecomedia" has been used in recent years by some scholars in media studies (in conversation with work in media archaeology, dead media, and ecocriticism) in analyzing forms of nonprint media, such as film and photography, that offer ecocritical perspectives on the relationship between humans and the natural world.[35] Media archaeology unearths communicative technologies that have been superseded, discarded, or rendered obsolete, on the logic that narratives of supplanted media can inform our understanding and deployment of communicative media today. They *inform* both in the sense of providing information and in giving form, revealing the processes by which historical media are constituted and subsequently dismantled or preserved. In Jussi Parikka's account, media archaeology understands "media cultures as sedimented and layered, a fold of time and materiality where the past might be suddenly discovered anew, and the new technologies grow obsolete increasingly fast."[36] The practice of media archaeology seeks to disrupt narratives of smooth technological advancement told by conventional progressive histories. "If *history* is a term that means both what happened in the past and the varied practices of representing that past," Lisa Gitelman writes of media and history, "then media are historical at several different levels." Media are artifactually of the past, for one, but they also produce a sense of pastness—and thus a temporal collapse—as "using media also involves implicit encounters with the past that produced the representations in question."[37] What distinguishes polar expeditionary media from other forms is that their very creation and reproduction occur under conditions of transience and displacement. Not confined to the standard ephemeral genres they inhabit (the newspaper, the blank form), polar ecomedia are produced—and subject to modification and obsolescence alike—in extremity, ecologically and geophysically. Their inevitable desuetude occurs within an environment in which human life and nonhuman geological and aqueous processes alike are precarious. Yet for all this precarity, polar ecomedia such as periodicals and blank forms presume a futurity, readers and writers to come. Within such extreme environments, polar ecomedia are not just responding to climate conditions but encoding their effects within the very evolution of the media themselves.

In *The News at the Ends of the Earth* my extraction of works of polar ecomedia from expeditionary history is in part an attempt to imagine sustainable communication cultures, ones whose revelatory power emerges in concert with the ecologies in which they are produced. In his work on "ecosonic media," Jacob Smith argues for a "green-media archaeology," in which the exhumation of abandoned technologies likewise functions "as part of a search for more sustainable media cultures of the future." Smith cautions scholars of media archaeology, though, not to relegate the communication devices of the past to some "quirky" cabinet of curiosity; they persist.[38] Polar ecomedia are situated in the time of the Anthropocene, and as such are continuous both with an arc of modernity predicated on resource extraction and global commerce and a futurity that must reckon with their planetary effects. I join media archaeologists in affirming the weird temporalities of polar communicative texts. Telling stories like these, Parikka writes, requires beginning "in the middle—from the entanglement of past and present, and accept[ing] the complexity this decision brings with it to any analysis of modern media culture."[39] If, as Siegfried Zielinski writes, "media worlds are phenomena of the relational," then the ecomedia produced *within* conditions and locations of climate extremity communicate *about* climate extremity, both in form and content.[40] In his striking work on elemental media environments, John Durham Peters characterizes media as "vessels and environments, containers of possibility that anchor our existence." In arguing that environments can be seen as media (just as media are themselves environments), Peters proposes that media "not only send messages about human doings and our relations with our ecological and economic systems; they are also . . . constitutive parts of those systems."[41] It is in this sense that polar ecomedia differentiate themselves from contemporary works of ecomedia, which strive to represent or communicate ecological conditions to its viewers, auditors, or readers. Polar ecomedia surpass representation to exemplify in their very ephemerality the processes of drift, erasure, acceleration, and change endemic to Anthropocene life.

Writing about and in the Anthropocene is a "question of *mediation*," or how "media operate conceptually in geological time," as Tobias Boes and Kate Marshall stipulate, and the work of media archaeology in this sense is, in part, to excavate the layers of accumulation even while recognizing that such conceptual work only contributes to the accretion.[42] Mediation in this case is not arbitration or resolution but rather a condition that forms (or calls into awareness) a connection.[43] The term "polar ecomedia" likewise does not necessarily refer to the mediating element itself but rather to the aggregate product of the intercession between the nonhuman environment and the human agents existing within and shaping it. In this book I am working from and speaking to the fields of the environmental humanities, material textual studies and the history of print, oceanic studies, and the literature and history of polar exploration; my reworking of ecomedia in a polar context reflects this critical genealogy throughout the book.[44]

Questions of linguistic or conceptual insufficiency have been occupying environmental humanities scholars and others attentive to climate change in recent years. On the one hand, as Dipesh Chakrabarty has argued in a foundational essay, the crisis calls for academics to set aside disciplinary distinctions—"to rise above their disciplinary prejudices"—as all human history, from the vantage point of the Anthropocene, is contemporary.[45] On the other hand, as Rob Nixon writes, the Anthropocene presents a broader representational challenge: "how to devise arresting stories, images, and symbols adequate to the pervasive but elusive violence of [the] delayed effects" of "slowing unfolding environmental catastrophes."[46] One appeal of Anthropocene-framed thinking to humanities scholars is its necessary disruption of modes of inquiry organized around disciplinary boundaries, as Tobias Menely and Jesse Oak Taylor observe. By understanding "the Anthropocene as a narrative," they propose, we recognize the "inherently fictional and yet epistemologically productive quality of any periodizing marker."[47] Academic distinctions are not the only categories reshaped by Anthropocenic thinking; the nature of knowledge itself is at issue. "What does it mean to generate knowledge in the age of climate change?" ask Ian Baucom and Matthew Omelsky, observing that "climate change discourses have reshaped the contemporary architecture of knowledge itself, reconstituting intellectual disciplines and artistic practices, redrawing and dissolving boundaries, but also reframing how knowledge is represented and disseminated."[48] In her work on climate fiction and the Anthropocene, LeMenager sees in climate change a "struggle for genre," or "the struggle to find new patterns of expectation and new means of living with an unprecedented set of limiting conditions." The concept of the "everyday," in turn, "frays in this unique moment of global ecology," an observation that has implications for understanding polar newspapers, as I discuss further below.[49]

Scholars working in the environmental humanities have been bringing humanities methodologies and critical thinking to information generated, in part, by the sciences and other disciplines. One of the benefits of this approach, as Nixon says, is that "creative people are using objects to try to release stories about the Anthropocene that have the capacity to inform and surprise."[50] For LeMenager and Stephanie Foote, a key to this "capacity to inform and surprise" is the humanist's skill with storytelling, a narrative and argumentative strategy that "provides adaptable points of view, ways of seeing the world that can be picked up, pieced apart, borrowed and bricolaged into modes of resistance and response."[51] Genre fiction and other modes of art and expression have been responsive to climate change for several decades, even if Amitav Ghosh questions why "serious fiction" has not made climate change a topic worthy of the imagination.[52] As Foote suggests, one question might be whether aesthetic production is even the way to approach slow-moving climate change; Timothy Morton proposes that climate change is too enormous a concept or reality for the human mind to grasp fully.[53] What these various interventions share is an interest in the play of narrative form, a commitment to disciplinary heterogeneity, and a conviction of the inadequacy of previous timescales, whether academic or geological.

Polar media require different critical modes. Although their production and circulation is exceptionally constrained in practice, the sphere of their influence is oceanic in its implications. In examining ecomedia and other polar circuits of knowledge, I am alert to literary and textual production and circulation in oceanic terms, on a scale beyond the human and outside of linear time and space. In considering what epistemic forms and practices are sustainable in the Arctic or Antarctica, I explore what forms of oceanic exchange (both imaginative and material) are continuous with polar ecomedia—that is, exchange not defined by relations between nation-states or by linear trajectories.[54] Oceans cover 71 percent of the earth, but human visualizations of the globe insistently privilege a terrestrial perspective; most students are trained to recognize the shapes of continents, but not the bodies of water that give them form. As the seas are rising as a result of the melting of polar ice caps, the contours of the land that interrupts the aqueous globe are themselves transformed, whether low-lying islands or coastal cities. Oceanic studies is invested in recognizing the artificiality and intellectual limitations of certain kinds of boundaries—national, political, linguistic, physiological, temporal—in studying forms of literary and cultural influence and circulation.[55] The sea must be "a space of circulation because it is constituted through its very geophysical mobility," in Philip E. Steinberg's formulation.[56] A fundamental premise of oceanic studies is that familiar patterns of relationality (capital, national, planar, human) dissolve in the space and time of the sea. If, in other words, many scholars now view history from the bottom up, or nations in terms of their transnational or hemispheric relations, or the colonizer as seen by the colonized—to gesture to just a few reorientations of critical perception in recent decades—then what would happen if such scholars took the oceans' nonhuman scale and depth as a first critical position and principle? While transnational forms of exchange (whether cultural, political, or economic) have historically taken place via the medium of the sea, only recently have humanities scholars paid attention to that medium itself: its properties, its conditions, its shaping or eroding forces. The sea is "continually being reconstituted by a variety of elements: the non-human and the human, the biological and the geophysical, the historic and the contemporary," as Steinberg characterizes it, and in turn modes of oceanic thought are themselves predicated on relations whose unfixed, ungraspable contours are ever in multidimensional flux.[57] Still, much as the polar regions are oceanic spaces that frustrate imperial or national ambitions, they are governed by geophysical forces and biological habits different from the fluid, unfrozen nautical world. In this sense, the question governing this book is not just *what* is the news at the ends of the earth, but *when* and *where* is the news at the ends of the earth.

Oceanic spaces are not friction-free, as the examples in this book demonstrate, and nor are the other environmental channels that support communications infrastructure, as recent critics have noted. The need for study of the very materiality of the infrastructure supporting networked communications—a materiality too often de-emphasized or hidden—is perhaps most evident in the rhetorical erasure of the hardware that enables the cloud to exist in wireless communications. Media and communication studies, as Nicole Starosielski writes, have "focused on the content, messages, and reception of digital media and paid less attention to the infrastructures that support its distribution."[58] An example of a counterpoint to such neglect is Michael Warner's recent work on the power grid (and on what it means to go offgrid). He highlights the pervasive abstraction of the idea of the grid, an abstraction that does not make visible what form of primary energy—oil, gas, coal, solar, wind, or geothermal—fuels the secondary electricity in use when flipping a light switch, say.[59] In her work on undersea cables, Starosielski too observes that when "communication infrastructures are represented, they are most often wireless . . . directing our attention above rather than below and reinforcing a long-standing imagination of communication that moves us beyond our worldly limitations."[60] In bringing into relief the apparatuses that undergird resource and media networks, both Warner and Starosielski note that these circuits are imagined as frictionless. Or, as John Durham Peters puts it, "Infrastructuralism shares a classic concern of media theory: the call to make environments visible."[61] In Starosielski's formulation, the result is "a cultural imagination of dematerialization: immaterial information flows appear to make the environments they extend through fluid and matter less." In arguing against the notion that a "fluid" environment is smooth or turbulence-free, Starosielski is not using fluidity as a metaphor: she is analyzing the actual oceanic environments through which digital cables pass. But these are not stable or untroubled environments, as she argues in her description of the "turbulent ecologies" of digital media: "Turbulence is a chaotic form of motion that is produced when the speed of a fluid exceeds a threshold relative to the environment it is moving though. . . . Turbulence is rarely a direct and purposeful opposition to flow. Rather, it describes the way that social or natural forces inadvertently create interference in transmission simply because they occupy the same environment, in the end contributing to the network's precariousness."[62] In conceiving of the undersea world as part of the network of contemporary digital communications itself, Starosielski provides a schematic for thinking of Arctic and Antarctic spaces too. The polar regions are both fluid and ice-stalled; while geophysically removed from modern trade routes, the Arctic in particular has nevertheless been a speculative global passage for many centuries, a fantasy of planetary access that global warming is increasingly making a reality.

The ephemera and other forms of polar ecomedia created by polar expedition members provide a provocative model for understanding the oceanic contours of literary exchange. What forms and practices of thought are sustainable in the Arctic or in other regions beyond the political world, in the actual Ultima Thule? What do these knowledge practices tell us about human acts of inscription in and on a natural world under increasing threat? Polar exchange in the form of newspapers is, on one hand, the most quotidian in the world; the distance between the *Illustrated London News* and the *Illustrated Arctic News* is not that great. On the other hand it can be seen as the most eccentric, in the sense that the supposed blankness and barrenness of the polar regions both exceed the kinds of traffic we think of as part of global or intranational exchange and also stand as its limit.

Ultima Thule

The polar regions are ever in the headlines. Interest in the Arctic and Antarctica is at a new pitch in our present moment of anthropogenic climate change and resource depletion. The late eighteenth-century advent of industrialization marks the beginning of the Anthropocene, in some accounts, and the measurements for such study are geometrically proliferating in our present moment.[63] For one, Arctic ice is melting at potentially catastrophic rates as a result of climate change, turning the warm open polar sea of nineteenth-century fancy into an oceanic reality in parts of the Arctic North in recent summers. Circumpolar oil and gas reserves are increasingly targeted for mining in response to human fossil fuel overconsumption. Five nations (Canada, Denmark, Norway, Russia, and the United States) have coastal claims to the North Pole, and thus by extension to any mineral rights in its radius. Russia even planted a titanium version of its national flag on the seafloor at the North Pole to secure its assertion. The Canadian discovery of one of John Franklin's ships on the seafloor in the summer of 2014 prompted that nation's prime minister Stephen J. Harper to avow that finding the British ship, lost for 169 years, "strengthened Canadian sovereignty in the North," which had been one of the Harper administration's broader aims.[64] (Indeed in 2017 the U.K. Ministry of Defense transferred ownership of the two ships to Canada.) In May, 2015 U.S. President Barack Obama authorized the oil giant Shell to resume drilling in the Chukchi Sea off the Alaskan coast, although Shell ultimately pulled out after accruing over $4 billion in exploratory costs. Obama did conclude his presidency with sweeping environmental protection orders for the Arctic and other U.S.-claimed oceanic spaces under the power of the Outer Continental Shelf Lands Act (a law that came into being in the mid-twentieth century to secure U.S. oil and gas drilling rights, ironically); Donald Trump granted new Chukchi Sea well permits to an Italian oil company in July 2017, however, and in early 2018 moved to open to drilling all U.S. claims to Outer Continental Shelf lands. Russia and other Northern powers have been re-opening circumpolar naval bases and commissioning new icebreakers for their northern fleets. At the same time, in unanticipated news, a substantial portion of the immense West Antarctic ice sheet was determined in 2014 to be on the verge of unstoppable disintegration, which will lead to a precipitous rise in global sea levels; in 2017 it was reported that "miles of ice [are] collapsing into the sea."[65] Satellite footage of the Yamal peninsula in Siberia has shown giant new holes in the earth, and while the initial images looked as if they could have been created by hoaxical hollow earth websites, the craters seem to have been caused by methane gas explosions triggered by the thawing permafrost and rising air temperatures caused by climate change.[66] As the methane holes in Siberia warn us, holes in the earth are not only the cause of climate change (via drilling and other modes of resource extraction) but also the product of it, as methane gas is released from the softening permafrost. Long-dormant diseases are rising from the thawing permafrost as well. However remote and inhospitable Antarctica and the Arctic might remain for the lived experience of most humans, the global significance of the regions registers across space and time—well beyond our present moment, even as the Arctic, in particular, has been in many ways an Anthropocenic bellwether.

Recent literary and theoretical explorations of the environmental humanities, oceanic studies, deep time, environmental justice, and planetarity all reflect a growing interest in the long-reaching global effects of recent human actions, for human agency in the Anthropocene, as Boes and Marshall have argued, must be "radically open to nonhuman influences."[67] At the same time Dana Luciano cautions us to be mindful that "the 'Anthropocene' was not brought about by all members of the species it names"; the human toll in the Anthropocene is more commonly visited upon indigenous people and those in the developing world, populations not always included in notions of a "humanism" figured as universal but shored up by racial and imperial violence.[68] Stacy Alaimo has similarly maintained that "questions of social justice, global capitalist rapacity, and unequal relations between the global North and the global South are invaluable for developing models of sustainability that do more than try to maintain the current, brutally unjust status quo."[69] These and other critical interventions recognize the finitude of human technical and mechanical control over and around the globe. For historical polar explorers, these mechanical limits existed to be tested. Today the insatiable demands by industrialized and developing nations for fossil fuels have refigured the Arctic and Antarctica again as bountiful—at least for capitalism. The early nineteenth-century mania for Arctic exploration, the early twentieth-century obsession with Antarctic missions, and our present turn to both polar regions in an attempt to maintain human resource-consuming habits all coalesce around resources, whether natural or intellectual, and include a recognition of their limits. The news reported from the ends of the earth has consequences not just for the North and South Polar regions themselves but for the planet.

The polar regions might be said to speak in the sense that their ecological motility discloses information about our planet's past and threatened future. The Arctic and Antarctica are, in turn, given expression by humans in various forms of writing and other media. These have included voyage accounts and expeditionary diaries, such as Parry's *Journal of a Voyage for the Discovery of a North-West Passage from the Atlantic to the Pacific* (1821), Elisha Kent Kane's *Arctic Explorations: The Second Grinnell Expedition in Search of Sir John Franklin* (1856), and Apsley Cherry-Garrard's *The Worst Journey in the World* (1922); poetry, fiction, and film on ice as sublimity or terror, such as Samuel Taylor Coleridge's "Rime of the Ancient Mariner," John Carpenter's *The Thing* (1982), and Elizabeth Bradfield's *Approaching Ice* (2010); Arctic indigenous communications, trade routes, and travel networks, such as the Inuit navigational landmark cairns known as Inuksuit; data and accounts from climatologists, ecologists, glaciologists, biologists, and other scientists, such as the information used to track anthropogenic climate change; and visual and plastic artistic creation, such as the paintings of William Bradford and Peder Balke, the films of Guido van der Werve, the photography of An-My Lê, the installations of Olafur Eliasson, and the printmaking of Pitseolak Ashoona.

In nineteenth-century fiction and poetry, the realms of ice were imaginatively encountered beyond the reach of geophysical or temporal regulations. Readers could travel to the milky, boiling South Polar seas of Edgar Allan Poe's *Narrative of Arthur Gordon Pym* and the warm open Arctic sea that was Captain Walton's objective in *Frankenstein*; stand poised on the verge of the hollow earths of "Adam Seaborn's" *Symzonia* and James De Mille's *Strange Manuscript Found in a Copper Cylinder*; or step out of nation-time in Harriet Prescott Spofford's "The Moonstone Mass" and in Captain Littlepage's Arctic reveries in Sarah Orne Jewett's *Country of the Pointed Firs*. Polar sublimity in works of fancy drew from the published journals and voyage narratives of Arctic and Antarctic explorers in the period. While the extremities of the actual worlds described in expeditionary accounts of the frozen zones may not have reached the fanciful pitch of their fictional interpreters, the voyage narratives, too, brought news of a region outside of easily classifiable Western notions of geoplanetary space or diurnal time. The poets and novelists of the nineteenth century turned to the language of the Burkean sublime to frame their imaginary encounters with the Arctic, drawing from polar expeditions' extensive coverage in print. They emphasized the North's frigid stillness, and in an ideological move analogous to that of early Europeans in the Americas, inaccurately described the Arctic as an uninhabited wasteland.

Actual expeditionary venturers, on the other hand, met the unutterable or annihilating aspects of polar experience not with the awestruck silence of the sublime but with a density of textual production, in a variety of genres. The *Illustrated Arctic News* and the nearly thirty other shipboard newspapers and other polar ecomedia that I have researched across dispersed archives constitute one form of text through which sojourners to the Arctic and Antarctica mediated their experience. While researchers in media studies have been in rich critical conversation with ecocritics, scholars of book history or the history of the material text have had relatively few sustained engagements with the environmental humanities. This book aims to kindle more such dialogue by attempting to reconcile the structural estrangement of print culture from ecocriticism. In its isolation from industrial centers, Arctic coterie publishing and other forms of ephemeral inscription are positioned to provide fresh perspectives on the polar regions and print spheres alike. Arctic and Antarctic printing also gives us new ways to think about literary publics. If, in Michael Warner's provision, a public "comes into being only in relation to texts and their circulation," then what kind of public is constituted by a newspaper created by and for thirty-odd men on a single frozen-in ship, a thousand miles from the nearest English reader?[70] If for Benedict Anderson a newspaper produces imagined communities, what happens when those communities are not anonymous or broadly dispersed but constitute the entire "nation" in a single intimate body?[71]

The Arctic and Antarctica have functioned as teloses for conceits of global influence from early modern mapmaking to our resource-hungry present. The extent and implications of this reach—from polar vortices to rising seas—is only increasing, and oceanic forms of ecomedia demand that we reconceive of the relationship between message and audience, at a geographical as well as temporal remove. The geophysical distance of the

Arctic and Antarctica from standard or expected print and communication spheres is one condition of this reorientation. The modes and organs of transmission of texts within polar and oceanic environments are often incommensurate with our usual understanding of print circulation. Polar news emerges from and records other temporalities, whether in the form of lost expeditions, the geologic history discernible in polar ice, or the future global destruction scried in melting ice. In these ways we might think of polar news as always belated, or ever frustrating linearity.

Questions of resource identification and management, Arctic and Antarctic preservation and exploitation, and climatic variation have ever been the lede for stories about the polar regions. How did the first largely white, Western voyagers beyond the Arctic and Antarctic Circles understand the scale of their own news as it circulated within the geophysical space of the poles? *The News from the Ends of the Earth* takes that question literally, exploring the difference in resources—both material and intellectual—presented by polar spaces. By *resources* I refer both to the ecological substance of the polar regions, in their remove from predictable routes and terms of exchange, and to the imaginative and ecomedia output of polar exploration, which is often ephemeral and itself does not follow recognizable circuits. *The News at the Ends of the Earth* is attuned to the tension between the oceanic or global ambitions of polar voyages and the remarkably tenuous and circumscribed conditions of their practice.

I open this book with three chapters on the newspapers and other printed materials created in the Arctic and Antarctica and discuss how expedition members used the generic form of the periodical to work through questions about their time, place, and impermanence in the polar regions. The final two chapters turn to forms of ecomedia such as Arctic dead letters and Inuit knowledge circulation, both of which have broader critical and theoretical implications for the study of the environmental humanities and literary history alike. The chapters do not strictly observe chronological order, for polar history is not a narrative of linear progression, as I have been suggesting. Accounting for polar ecomedia, from the nineteenth-century expeditionary age to the present, demonstrates instead the asynchronous nature of oceanic forms of exchange. Both the evidentiary basis and intellectual ambitions of this project argue for the revelatory force of ephemera.

The first Arctic newspaper, the *North Georgia Gazette, and Winter Chronicle* of Parry's first Arctic expedition (1819–20), was a novelty and provoked some unexpected questions about how expedition members contributed (or else acted as NCs or noncontributors) to the shipboard community. Yet as I discuss in chapter 1, "Extreme Printing," the availability of printing presses aboard Arctic-voyaging ships beginning in 1848 transformed the practice of newspaper production among polar sailors. The output from Arctic presses was conditioned by and responding to specific polar environmental conditions, I argue. The genre of the newspaper—an ephemeral form associated with diurnal time—was put to use by Arctic- and Antarctic-voyaging sailors in their meditations on polar temporality, community, and circulation. Once tabletop printing presses found their way aboard ship, expedition members adapted them to their literary and theatrical ends. Chapter 2, "Arctic News," examines the rich variety of post-1848 Arctic newspapers, including the *Weekly Guy*, the *Discovery News,* the *Port Foulke Weekly News,* the *Arctic Eagle*, the *Illustrated Arctic News*, and the *Aurora Borealis*, newspapers by ships engaged in the search for Franklin in the early 1850s, as well as other forms of printing related to shipboard theatricals and entertainments. The forms of exchange that took place within the pages of these newspapers in the second half of the nineteenth century had a more expansive sense of contribution and collective exchange, both within the expeditions themselves and within the polar regions more generally.

Expeditions to Antarctica in the early twentieth century—the so-called heroic age of exploration—produced the most lavish of all polar publications. Shackleton was central to two of the most elaborate ventures: the *South Polar Times*, which he edited while an officer on Scott's British *Discovery* expedition of 1901–4, and *Aurora Australis*, the first book printed in Antarctica, which was published by members of Shackleton's own *Nimrod* expedition of 1907–9. The book, published in about one hundred copies, of which eighty-plus are extant, consists of 120 pages of mixed-genre material, bound with the materials that were at hand, from orange crates to horse halters to boxes that once contained stewed kidneys. The heightened professionalization of the book arts practiced by Antarctic voyagers is just one distinction between publications of the North and the South: the subject matter of Antarctic periodicals turns more explicitly to climate change and environmental science, and chapter 3, "Antarctic Imprints," examines the increased expertise of the onetime amateur polar publishers within the context of an increase in narrative accounting for the planet's climatic variability.

Newspapers were not the only media to circulate among polar expedition members, as the second part of *The News from the Ends of the Earth* details. Chapter 4, "Dead Letter Reckoning," ranges widely over a form of ecomedia that I call "Arctic dead letters." These consist of the cairn messages, notes in bottles, cached documents, mail, and other periodic circuits of delivery or connection in geophysical spaces that would seem otherwise to frustrate human exchange networks. Polar expeditions were required to leave messages in cairns or other outposts at regular intervals, in multiple copies, often on preprinted forms in six languages. Other official documents were printed aboard ship. Even though thousands of bits of paper were distributed throughout the Arctic in the nineteenth century, it was exceptionally rare for one of these messages to be found or received; most remained in circulation for an open-ended period of time and may yet emerge today, as ice melts and permafrost thaws. In their risk of annihilating dispersion and their potential for ceaseless drift, Arctic dead letters exemplify the unboundedness of polar ecomedia in its attenuated temporality, randomness, and motility.

The career of the unconventional American Charles Francis Hall is a somewhat different example of an exchange of knowledge whose circuits are both routine and extravagant within and without the Arctic regions in the long nineteenth century. The fifth chapter, "Inuit Knowledge and Charles Francis Hall," focuses on Hall's accounts of the circulation of subsistence and intellectual knowledge as well as historiography between himself and Inuit residents of the Arctic regions. Hall was unusual among most nineteenth-century Anglo-American explorers in choosing to adapt to indigenous lifeways; his relationship to nautical epistemology as practiced by white sailors was more complicated (and violent). His exceptional path to and within the Arctic, accompanied along the way by the Inuit couple Ipiirviq and Taqulittuq (or Ebierbing and Tookoolito, as they were known to the American public), helps to delineate how Arctic indigeneity has been figured within oceanic models of intellectual circulation.

I close *The News at the Ends of the Earth* with a brief coda on a thwarted Arctic expedition and on matters of life and death. Subsistence and mutual cooperation have become especially urgent issues in the Anthropocene. But although the temporalities of life and death are usually conceived in human terms, this book joins other humanities work on the Anthropocene in shifting our scales of relation from the human to the nonhuman, from the global to the planetary, and, in my argument in particular, from the terrestrial to the oceanic.

The course of my work on this project in some ways mirrors the trajectory of the British and American explorers I study. Initially I brought to my polar archival findings a scholarly approach practiced in my earlier work in oceanic studies, maritime narratives, and material text studies. The topography of this research, however, has demanded additional methodologies for my critical navigation, drawn from the environmental humanities, Anthropocene studies, and media studies. The archives of ice ring with a special ethical urgency today. I thought my preoccupation in recent years with the news coming out of the Arctic and Antarctica was a consequence of being an ecologically concerned citizen in the Anthropocene, a by-product of my historicist impulses; it turns out, though, that the archive of news from the polar regions in the past several hundred years (and across geological time) was speaking to me as well. It is my hope in this book to amplify what that deep and motile repository of polar ecomedia can tell us.

=================

ONE

EXTREME PRINTING

Captain Parry! Captain Parry!
Thy vocation stops not here:
Thou must dine with Mr. Murray
And a quarto must appear.
— SAMUEL TAYLOR COLERIDGE, "Captain Parry" (1825)

. . . North Cornwall has not had as yet its Caxton.
— advertisement for *Queen's Illuminated Magazine* (1852)

Polar newspapers were created and printed in conditions of extremity in multiple senses. The expeditions for which newspapers formed the shipboard social media, for one, were journeying toward latitudinal extremes approaching 90° S or N. Polar expeditions had infrequent contact with an Anglophone public after a point, and thus the potential for circulation of the media they produced was necessarily exceptionally limited. While their isolation was not complete—in the Arctic, Anglo-American explorers had frequent contact with Inuit and other indigenous peoples and routinely employed Inuit guides—Western expedition members, in their cultural chauvinism, imagined themselves at a supreme distance from others. The meteorological conditions and attendant environmental hardships of life in the polar regions are also notoriously extreme; the mechanical acts of writing and operating printing equipment become challenging in turn.

This chapter describes how sailors came to print at the polar ends of the earth, concentrating on the outfitting, mechanics, and production of presses and printed materials in the polar regions. (The second and third chapters turn to analysis of the literary and informational content of the papers.) The material and intellectual strategies they brought to bear in mediating the particular challenges of creating printed texts in extreme conditions gave shape to the forms of communicative texts I am calling *polar ecomedia*. Printing presses were first stocked on Arctic ships in service of the search for Sir John Franklin's missing Northwest Passage expedition aboard the ships *Erebus* and *Terror*, which had left Britain in 1845. The presses were almost immediately requisitioned, however, by crew members for their entertainment during the sunless months of the polar winters. The materials that polar expedition members printed using the presses may reasonably be seen as the curious or charming incidentals of the leisure hours of a collective formed by circumstance. But polar periodicals tell us more than the news (or a mocking facsimile of the news) from the cramped cabins of icebound crews. The ephemeral form of the newspaper is crucial to this story: *news* conveys information that interrupts a moment in time, even as *newspapers* are characterized by their periodicity, their marking of time. In Walter Benjamin's formulation in "The Storyteller," newspapers provide information but not stories; the storyteller, who offers the benefit and the intimacy of experience, recedes in an age of impersonal information distributed via newspapers. Sailors, those notable travelers and yarn spinners, are storytellers in Benjamin's account—and the conditions for storytelling, stillness and boredom, are certainly in place in the polar regions. Yet the form of the newspaper, considered in Benjaminian terms, does in fact have utility for sailor storytellers. Arctic and Antarctic voyaging sailors turn to the genre of the periodical not to convey news in the form of information—the content of the papers is parodic, light, and farcical—but to structure their meditations on polar temporality, community, and circulation.

Expeditionary newspapers produced in the Arctic and Antarctica are forms of media that are both shaped by and consciously responding to polar environmental conditions. Newspapers are understood to be periodic, marking daily time. Polar winter, however, is relentlessly nocturnal, out of time. While polar winter rhythms would be disruptive to any unused to their temporal irregularities, they were especially so to sailors accustomed to watch-oriented discipline, in both senses of "watch." An Antarctic winter, for example, unsettled Otto G. Nordenskjöld's work with the Swedish Antarctic Expedition in both its labor and literary dimensions; while in polar darkness, he wrote, "A thing that I missed above all things was regular, ordered work. All the preceding pages must have shown the difficulty there was in arranging such labour, whether indoor work or outdoor."[1] In crafting gazettes, newspapers, and periodicals, expedition members explicitly mark the weirdness of their time and place. They are simultaneously imposing diurnal order on a region without sun and rather seriously calculating what goes awry when temperate forms of periodical writing are imposed on an intemperate world. This is how quotidian newspapers become polar eco-media: produced by and within the outlandishness of the Arctic and Antarctic environments, they theorize ephemeral ways of reading and writing in and about the polar regions in their very pages.

We see this most clearly in one of the few extant photographs of the actual act of polar printing.[2] The photo, *Printing the "Arctic Eagle"* was taken during the Fiala-Ziegler Expedition (1903–5), a U.S. attempt to reach the North Pole on the ship *America*. In the image we see a series of bunks, the crowded sleeping quarters of the seamen; this is not an officer's private cabin. Three men are abed, wrapped in wool blankets, in positions of repose and observation.[3] In the foreground are a pair of fur boots. The focus is on the printer, Spencer Stewart, who served as the expedition's assistant commissary: he is clad in a wool sweater, with a pencil tucked behind his ear. Seated on the edge of the bunk of one of the reclining men, Stewart straddles a hand-operated tabletop press, which appears to be a Boston-produced Golding Official Press. (The name "Golding" is just perceptible on the curved side of the press.) Judging from the machine's size relative to the printer—and from the size of the press's production, the newspaper *Arctic Eagle*—this was probably the Official model no. 6, with a chase size of 8¼ in. × 12½ in.[4] A thick stack of folded paper, presumably copies of the *Arctic Eagle*, is visible on the left. Just above the printer's right hand the type case is discernable, and the blurred man in motion working with it would be Seaman Allen Montrose, who, according to Commander Anthony Fiala, "had been a wandering newspaper typo before he took to following the sea."[5] The photographer must be squeezed within the frame of the door. Since Commander Fiala himself had previously been the art director and photographer for the Arctic paper's namesake, the *Brooklyn Daily Eagle*, we might guess that he operates the camera here.

This remarkable image makes visible the situational intimacy of the mechanics of the production and circulation of shipboard newspapers. Our idiomatic sense of a paper emerging "hot off the press" has a different tactility when the press (its ink, in particular) would have to be thawed for use. The heat and breath of the cluster of bodies in bed around Stewart and Montrose is conjured by this glimpse of printing the *Arctic Eagle*, the very

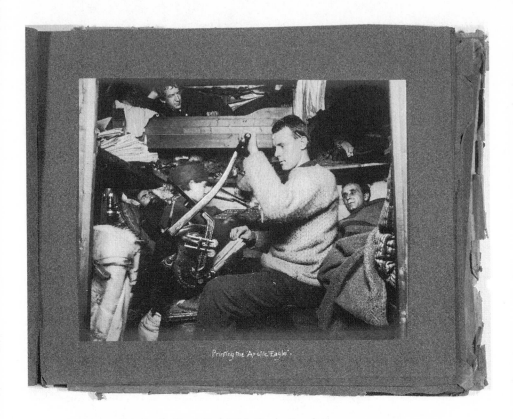

FIG 1.1 — *Printing the "Arctic Eagle,"* Fiala-Ziegler Expedition. PRIVATE COLLECTION.
USED WITH PERMISSION.

body heat and breath that is likely providing much of the room's meager warmth. Unlike the abstracted, invisible, imagined communities of Benedict Anderson's classic formulation regarding newspapers, polar periodicals are produced quite literally in the laps of their readership. Notions of print circulation and the political and social bodies of the ship's community take on new meanings in this context. Half of the men within the space framed by the photograph are in bed; does this imply that the *Arctic Eagle* is a morning paper? or a very late evening edition? The usual temporalities of newspaper publication, as we will see, do not matter—or they signify differently—in an environment in which the sun might not rise for as many as 120+ days and in which the crew has no easily observable means of marking time.

We cannot tell what time it is in the photograph, nor can polar newspapers mark diurnal or other serial time in the customary manner of the genre. Nautical time is a factor in this ecology as well; sailors' schedules are typically divided into four-hour blocks of time known as "watches," although the standard four-hour watches at sea become attenuated during the relative calm of polar nautical labor. While these are responsive to a twenty-four-hour calendar, a rotating watch system does not establish a natural division between morning and night for nautical laborers. (The American explorer Donald MacMillan was among those who addressed this problem by wearing a twenty-four-hour watch.) The photo *Printing the "Arctic Eagle"* captures in one frame several of the topics that this chapter on polar printing illuminates: the extremity of the circumstances in which polar periodicals were produced and circulated, and the attendant difficulties this produced; the intimacy and social forms of this particular media; and the collectivity of the papers' creation. Polar ecologies shaped the media forms with which voyagers marked time and established community, however ephemerally.

Neptune's Newsrooms

Printing presses were originally brought to the Arctic to assist in the broad dispersal of messages in the decades-long search for the sizable missing British Northwest Passage expedition commanded by Sir John Franklin, which launched in 1845 with 129 men on two ships, *Erebus* and *Terror*. (I treat this search in greater detail in chapter 4.) Once tabletop printing presses were aboard ship, and after winter storms made fire balloon messaging and the other official uses of the devices impractical, expedition members sought to pass the dark winter hours by adapting the technology to literary and theatrical ends. The presses produced broadsides and playbills for shipboard theatricals, copies of songs and occasional poems composed by mission members, and the community newspapers that I discuss in the next several chapters. Sailors even carved their own large-font type and emblems from the ship's store of spare lumber stocked for repairs, although wood is at a premium in regions north of the timberline. A number of Arctic expeditionary newspapers were published in the second half of the nineteenth century, including the following Anglophone papers: the *Flight of the Plover, or the North Pole Charivari* (1848); the *Illustrated Arctic News* (1850–51) and the *Aurora Borealis* (1850–51), companion papers by sister ships engaged in the search for Franklin; the *Gleaner* and *Minavilins* (1850–51), underground papers suppressed by ship commanders; the *Weekly Guy* (1852–53); the *Queen's Illuminated Magazine* (1852–54); the *Polar Almanac* (1854); the *Ice-Blink* (1853–55); the *Port Foulke Weekly News* (1860–61); the *Discovery*

ROYAL ARCTIC THEATRE.

Ich Dien

H.M.S. ASSISTANCE.

Manager: Captⁿ Ommanney

Patronised by Captⁿ Horatio Austin C.B.

GRAND ATTRACTION FOR THE NEW YEAR.

On Thursday the 9th of January 1851, the Favorite Actors of the Ships Companies present will perform the truly laughable

FARCE OF THE

TURNED HEAD.

To be followed by the Grand Farcical Tragical Melo-dramatical Serio Comic

PLAY OF

BOMBASTES FURIOSO!!!

which will be produced by the Officers of the Squadron. The only Lady in this piece, has been engaged at an Enormous Sacrifice, it being her first appearance on any Stage!!!

The whole to conclude with the entirely

NEW PANTOMIME OF

ZERO!

OR HARLEQUIN LIGHT!!

Written expressly for the occasion by a talented member of this expedition. In which the celebrated Clowns will introduce some of their favorite airs.

Doors open at 6 oClock __ Commence at 6_30.

ROYAL INTREPID SALOON

GRAND ATTRACTION!!!

On Friday, January the 17th 1851, the Performance will commence w^t the celebrated Gallantie Show of

MOVING FIGURES!!

And conclude with the

LIFE OF A SAILOR!!

in Six Steps.

Several Comic Songs will be sung between the performances.

The following Talented Company will appear.

Miss^{rs} Lewis, Urquhart, and T & H Morg

Doors open at 6 oClock. __ Commence at 6_30.

N. B. Children in arms not admitted

N.B. The large type headings as well as the Arms and devices were cut on board by the Seamen.

FIG I.2 — *Facsimile of the Illustrated Arctic News 3 (31 Dec. 1850), 31.* In the bottom right of the image a note indicates that the "large type headings as well as the Arms and devices were cut on board by the Seamen."

News (1875–76); the *Arctic Moon* (1882–83); the *Midnight Sun* (1901); and the *Arctic Eagle* (1903–4). Including papers by non-Anglophone crews on other European expeditions, such as the German *Ostgrönländische Zeitung* (1869–70) and the Norwegian *Framsjaa* (1893–96), there were at least seventeen Arctic newspapers between 1848 and 1904, and several others that were conceived of and not carried through (such as the *Polar Pirate*, 1904).[6] More than half of the British and American commanders of Arctic expeditions in the nineteenth century were involved at some point with a shipboard newspaper.

The existence of literary culture aboard ships and among sailors is not in and of itself unusual over the course of the nineteenth century. Many long-voyaging ships were provided with libraries; sailors read histories, novels, and periodicals, intensively reading (and sharing among themselves) the stock of reading material at hand. And polar voyages, which could plan on enforced periods of relative inactivity during the winter, had larger libraries than many ships. Franklin's *Erebus* and *Terror*, for example, had three thousand volumes between them. The catalogue for the *Assistance* (engaged in a Franklin search), which was printed aboard ship in 1853, lists novels by Jane Austen, James Fenimore Cooper, Herman Melville, and Walter Scott (plus Scott's *Letters on Demonology and Witchcraft*) among scores of volumes of polar history, voyages, and navigational science.[7] Some sailors kept personal journals, while officers contributed to shipboard textual production in the form of logbooks, ship accounts, progress diaries, and—on more official, grander expeditions—narratives of their voyages and discoveries, which often became strong sellers.[8] This was enabled in part by the unusual rates of literacy among seamen, estimated at 75 to 90 percent by the mid-nineteenth century; on polar expeditions, which were more high profile and often more selective, the figures were likely higher.[9] As a laboring class their literacy was encouraged by onboard schools on naval ships (focused on mathematics and navigation as well as letters, all necessary for nautical advancement) and a maritime culture in which leisure time was often spent in storytelling or in theatricals, a particular mainstay of British naval practice adopted at times aboard U.S. ships. The second number of the *Illustrated Arctic News* was pleased to report on the newly created seaman's school in "Summary of the Month's Proceedings": "Well done!—Education, & improvement are twins. Encourage & foster the one, the other must follow. The Schoolmaster is indeed afloat."[10] During the American Lady Franklin Bay Expedition of 1881–84, Commander Adolphus Greely established a "triweekly" school at which "arithmetic, grammar, geography, and meteorology were taught. . . . For a time Dr. Pavy instructed two men in French. The educational qualifications of the men were very good, and there was but one of the party on its original formation who was unable to write, and he acquired that attainment during our stay."[11] These proportions were typical of polar expeditions. When not engaged in reading or navigational exercises, the leisure hours of polar expeditionary crews were also occupied with dancing (for exercise, by design) and theatrical productions, all of which were long-standing traditions of naval recreation and diversion.[12]

Only on polar expeditions did publishing shipboard newspapers become a frequent activity, even an expectation; newspapers are otherwise rare among seamen's leisure customs. The first North American Arctic newspaper was not printed but circulated in manuscript, and was in several ways anomalous: it was an experiment not repeated on polar missions for decades, for one. What is more, the paper produced conflict instead of cooperative vision. In the manuscript *North Georgia Gazette, and Winter Chronicle* (1819–20) of William Edward Parry's first Arctic expedition, the question of community was quite explicitly debated within the paper itself, as contributors arranged themselves rhetorically against the NCs or "Non-Contributors" to the paper.[13] Aboard the *Hecla* and the *Griper*, Parry's ships, this literary economy was defined by the officer corps, by and for whom the paper was created. The *North Georgia Gazette, and Winter Chronicle* was later printed in London a year after the expedition's return, in response to "the interest which the Public took in all that had passed during the voyage."[14] But the details of the Arctic context in which the expedition's officers (who constituted the paper's stringers) understood their impish attacks on journalistic noncontribution had no resonance when replayed back within national borders. Articles that suggested the mission's collectivity was fragile or threatened, even if humorous, were in fact suppressed upon the voyage's return to Britain. The economies of literary circulation—of the barely public sphere of the polar mission—were in flux in this first Arctic paper (discussed in chapter 2); their terms would continue to change in subsequent expeditionary newspapers.

Decades after this first manuscript experiment, polar newspapers were resurgent. They shared a number of qualities in common. Their content was light and farcical, in large part, and offered satiric commentary on polar environmental conditions. Arctic and Antarctic newspapers were produced during the several months of polar darkness in which expeditions wintered over, their ships bound by ice and their crews relatively stilled—and, as David H. Stam and Deirdre C. Stam have argued, looking for ways to mark the time.[15] The process of marking time by expedition members was, in turn, stamped by polar conditions. In the Arctic and Antarctica, extreme printing became more than a novelty or a curiosity: expedition members used the ephemeral periodical form of the newspaper as a counterpoint to (and a satiric commentary on) the temporal and ecological distortions and extremities of the polar regions. The nearly simultaneous and necessarily limited production and consumption of these texts by polar voyagers represents an unusual print circuit—intensified but not exceptional—that emerges from the intersection of the ecological, geographic, scientific, and nationalist aims of expeditions; the manual labor performed by polar voyagers; and developing technologies of print and literary culture.

Understood as passenger entertainment and edification, shipboard newspapers in and of themselves are not unheard of when created by nonlaboring travelers, as Jason R. Rudy has demonstrated compellingly in the context of nineteenth-century British long-voyaging passenger ships to Australia and other settler colonies. Emigrants to the British colonies had high literacy rates and commonly produced newspapers during their lengthy passages, originally in manuscript form, and later on printing presses; passengers could subscribe to the paper in order to ensure a souvenir copy at the end of the voyage.[16] During an 1891 voyage undertaken by the British passenger liner *City of Paris*, for example, a gazette was "printed on board" by the travelers; its object was to provide "interesting reading during spare moments." The headnote to the "Miniature Newspaper" concludes that if the publication "serves as a souvenir of the voyage to friends at home it will accomplish the object for which it is intended."[17] A substantial portion of the content of such papers was poetry, Rudy has found, in the forms of both parodic rewriting of popular contemporary poetry and original verse, often nostalgic in tone. My research in a range of maritime collections finds that passenger papers were somewhat less of a tradition in the North American context. The Kemble Maritime Ephemera Collection at the Huntington Library, for instance, holds records for over 925 shipping companies, mostly passenger cruise ships operating between 1855 and 1990. Only thirty-six shipboard newspapers appear in the twenty-four thousand records in the collection. Of these thirty-six, the majority consist of wire telegraphy news, supplemented by ship-specific menus and social calendars. In North American ship papers there are relatively fewer poems written by passengers in the manner described by Rudy, in which British emigrants used the national poetic form to reimagine themselves as colonial subjects. We are given a glimpse of this process (in a return to the imperial homeland) in the

Austral Chronicle, a biweekly journal published aboard a large passenger ship traveling from Sydney to London in 1886. The paper's prospectus observes, "No town in any English-speaking community, inhabited by like numbers to those now afloat in the 'Austral,' would or could exist and hold together without its newspaper. Then why should the population of the 'Austral' not have its newspaper?"[18] The editors of the *Austral Chronicle* seem to be classic Andersonian subjects, imagining national communities afloat. Yet passenger liner newspapers (as well as polar periodicals, as we will see) were imagined communities with a crucial difference: their addressed constituency was not imaginary but fully and wholly present. The *Cunard Cruise News*, for example, described itself as "the only newspaper issued the world over that has a circulation of one hundred per cent in its community."[19] The function that papers serve in establishing community is oriented less to an abstract notion of the nation and more toward a motile, ephemeral, and yet entirely at hand collectivity.

What kind of public did the editors of and contributors to polar newspapers have in mind? There exists a mutually constitutive relationship between an association and its newspaper, as Tocqueville describes it in *Democracy in America*: "A newspaper . . . always represents an association, the members of which are its regular readers. That association can be more or less well-defined, more or less restricted, and more or less numerous, but the seed of it, at least, must exist in people's minds, as evidenced by nothing more than the fact that the newspaper does not die."[20] These communities took many forms throughout the eighteenth and nineteenth centuries. Tocqueville's claims are derived from the smaller, voluntary associations he observed in the United States in the 1830s, what Anthony Ashley Cooper, third Earl of Shaftesbury, identified in the previous century as forms of "private society," an oxymoron whose axes of meaning have subsequently converged.[21] The elements Anderson stipulates as essential to the literary genre of the national newspaper are also found in smaller collectives on a local or private scale, such as the assembly of seemingly unrelated parts into a fictive whole conjoined only by their "calendrical coincidence," their temporal or spatial proximity.[22] For Anderson the newspaper and the book are necessarily "mass-produced industrial commodit[ies]" that can reach a large and dispersed population seemingly simultaneously; he finds "community in anonymity."[23] Shaftesbury's coteries, on the other hand, along with Tocqueville's voluntary associations, are characterized by their intimacy and their ephemerality rather than by their vast scale or their facelessness.[24] To what extent, then, can the national and the anonymous attributes of the newspaper themselves be imagined, even when the circulation of the newspaper is restricted? I am interested, in other words, in how the genre of the newspaper is itself imagined by communities: how the idea of a public becomes "constitutive of a social imaginary," in Michael Warner's formulation.[25] That is, if for Anderson newspapers allowed a broadly dispersed population a sense of belonging to the imagined community of the nation, then the polar newspapers, in an alternative move, enable a close-knit local community—one flung far from the geophysical place of the nation—to establish an imagined community apart from it. Not the "silent privacy" of newspaper reading "in the lair of the skull" that Anderson describes, polar newspapers were read aloud and in common to the collective.[26] The polar community both constitutes and is constituted by the newspaper's production. Polar newspapers emerge from a place of paradox within these discourses of newspaper, print culture, community, and nation, as they are tiny bodies of shared interest that in and of themselves constitute the mass totality of a culture. Unlike the associations mentioned by Tocqueville, or the coffeehouse coteries described by David Shields, which were contained within a broader world of sociability and print, the polar literary communities were completely isolated from any possibility of communication with other polities or individuals—even if their missions represented a nation's interest.[27] The newspapers that Arctic expeditions produced, then, are at once mass-market-produced commodities and privately circulated bits of ephemera.

We see something closer to this model on North American ships whose passengers, in contrast to those on British liners, were perhaps more likely to be traveling for leisure or employment than emigration. Among the handful of poems by passengers appearing in the Kemble Maritime Ephemera Collection's newspapers we find a lofty ode to the voyage; a comic bit of doggerel about alcohol use ("Pure water is the best of drinks, / That man to man can bring, / But who am *I* that *I* should have / The best of anything"); and a poem titled "Creeds" by a Mrs. E. Alsheimer of Phoenicia, New York, who declares that she "takes no heed of [her] neighbor's birth," yet in her racist sense of magnanimity will grant anyone "a white man's place on earth" as long as he is "clean."[28] Several East Coast ships traveling to the California gold fields in 1849 had manuscript newspapers written by fortune seekers. Boasting—inaccurately—that theirs was the "only paper published on the Pacific Ocean," the editors of *Bound Home or The Gold-Hunters' Manual* of 1852 felt an expansive sense of their periodical's reach: "Our facilities are greatly increasing in every direction for opening and extending our different agencies in every part and portion of the habitual globe, having lately formed extensive arrangements in China, Pekin, Nankin, the Feejee Islands, the North Pole, the Red Sea, the Spacific Isles, and the Solar Peas."[29] The final two malapropistic markets cheerfully admit the folly of the ambitions of the *Bound Home*. The *Emigrant*, the organ of the *Alhambra*, bound for San Francisco from New Orleans, featured navigational updates as well as poetry written by the ship's captain. The captain's final contribution to the *Emigrant* offered the following benediction to his Gold Rush passengers:

> Your saddle bags shall yet be filled
> With Sacramento's glittering ore.
> Your doubts and fears shall all be still'd
> And troubles come not near you more.[30]

The voyages on which these newspapers were produced, it is important to note, were experienced by the papers' contributors as one-way trips: emigrants and Gold Rush fortune-seekers would generally not be making a return passage on the vessel. The time they had to pass aboard ship was a time in transit from one mode of life to another, for unlike sailors, the sea was neither the space of their work nor the time of their permanent leisure.

Sailor newspapers, written entirely by the laboring crew of a vessel rather than by passengers at relative leisure, are far more rare. Why are they singular? Seamen are at work and cannot leave their job site at the end of a day to return home; even when off duty they remain on call. While mariners made time for literary and other forms of imaginative exchange when they could, the forms of collective work such as the creation of newspapers would be difficult when a ship was under way. To give some rough perspective: the National Maritime Museum in Greenwich, England, preserves records for thousands of ships; of just *six* manuscript newspapers from long-voyaging ships of the nineteenth century identified in their holdings, only three papers are written by seamen (the other three are passenger newspapers). While this is obviously not the total number of seamen's newspapers in the period—and very likely not the total among the holdings in the National Maritime Museum—it is proportionally similar to what I have seen in twenty years of archival research on sailors. (This relational rarity also provides some context for my surprise when first encountering the *Facsimile of the Illustrated Arctic News*, as described in this book's preface.) The extremity of polar environmental conditions accounts for the difference between the relative anomaly of sailor-produced newspapers on long-voyaging ships and their prevalence on Arctic and Antarctic expeditions. Polar ships, unlike other oceangoing vessels, were immobilized by ice for a substantial part of the year, and their crews—smaller in number than those on naval vessels, in general—had more time and space for communal efforts. The broader literary culture of sailors is robust, as my earlier work documents; within that culture, though, the genre of printed shipboard newspapers composed entirely by polar expedition members is unique.[31]

The very presence of printing presses at sea in the nineteenth century is likewise unusual in the time before ship-to-shore wireless telegraphy became practicable in the late nineteenth century. In the infrequent occasions when presses were employed on ship, they were generally in the service of colonial activity or warfare.[32] The terms of surrender for a temporary defeat of Simón Bolívar by Royalist forces in Venezuela in 1815, for example, were circulated via a broadsheet printed aboard a Spanish naval ship, under the imprint "Frigata Diana Imprenta del Exèrcito Expedicionario" (The Expeditionary Army Press of the Frigate *Diana*).[33] There were other forms of extreme printing in the period, as well. U.S. soldiers printed battlefield newspapers during the Civil War and Spanish-American War on portable presses, as James Berkey's work has explored.[34] Elizabeth Harris notes of the Civil War, "Command posts in the field needed to turn out notices and orders, soldiers of some units produced weekly or 'occasional' newspapers, and traveling printing offices were very desirable."[35] Presses were hauled onto the ice during various "Frost Fairs" on the Thames River in London, on those occasions when the river froze solid and deep enough to sustain a city fair. In 1683, for instance, the printer Croom sold commemorative postcards from the frozen river. In 1814, when as many as ten presses were in operation at the Frost Fair, a 124-page book, *Frostiana; Or a History of the River Thames in a Frozen State*, was printed on the ice.

Extreme printing provides an enduring record of a temporary event. A card, newspaper, or playbill printed in an exceptional space or circumstance is an instantiation of something more permanent (or at least, something occurring in a different temporality), designed to commemorate an event fleeting, tenuous, never intended to last. In the case of a Thames River Frost Fair, a printed postcard can be seen as a textual monument to the rarity of the river's total solidity—the printedness itself becomes momentous. Yet periodical print is itself a category of ephemera, designed to be used and discarded in turn. Like Frost Fair printing, polar newspapers commemorate a temporary community formed by climatic extremity. The particular properties of Arctic ice add a special element to the extremity of this form of printing too. While the period of a frozen-over Thames may be of far shorter duration than a wintry Arctic, its shallow river ice is relatively stable. In the Arctic, sea ice is ever in motion, and ships wintering over in the North are at risk of being squeezed, pitched sideways, crushed. A sunless winter aboard an ice-locked ship would seem to provide stasis and a longer interval for the exercise of printing newspapers than other extreme forms of printing enjoy, and the winter's relative stability would be more suited to a newspaper's seriality. Yet the paper's ephemerality—both generically and materially—is kept forcefully in play by the challenges posed by the climate to the physical and mental integrity of the newspaper's community.

Unlike other transitory instantiations of pressrooms, Arctic publishing is significant for the very genre of its periodical production, the content and organ of the newspaper itself. A newspaper—unlike a postcard or a book—suggests an ongoing duration: it is an ephemeral, cyclical issuance with a presumption of continuity and futurity. In a region without diurnal time during the winter months, newspapers are conditioned by and responding to different temporal and ecological conditions. Polar periodicals are works of ecomedia: means of communication whose form, content, production, and circulation provide opportunities for their creators—and for Anthropocene observers today—to reframe their, and now our, understandings of ecological spaces and of human endurance in tenuous conditions.

From Grub Street to Trap Lane

Ephemera nevertheless requires hardware. Polar voyage narratives, newspapers, and admiralty records are frustratingly short on specifics about the outfitting of the presses that traveled to the ends of the earth, and are also reticent on the details of the make and model of the equipment. Printing presses did not become easily portable until the second half of the nineteenth century; in 1848, the year a press was first put to use on an Arctic expedition, industry design standards likely meant that this first Arctic press was larger than a tabletop model. Later presses, however, appear to have been smaller manufactures such as the Golding Official letterpress used on the Fiala-Ziegler Expedition discussed earlier (as seen in figure 1.1). Elaine Hoag's superb bibliographic scholarship on the printing aboard the Franklin search ships makes the case that between 1850 and 1854 the various expeditions had with them secondhand Albion or Columbian half-sheet demy presses (such as on Edward Belcher's *Assistance* mission) or folio-foolscap-size Stafford or Cowper bellows presses (such as on Rochfort Maguire's *Plover*). The *Plover's* bellows press was purchased by the Admiralty, according to an invoice in its records: "Izod, Messrs.: To be paid £5 bill for supply of a bellows press &c for the Plover."[36] Another press had recently landed from a returning expedition needed to be repaired.[37] Others could have been spare machines from the Admiralty's own printing shops.[38] It is somewhat surprising that complete lists of press materials—tabletop press model descriptions, paper type, ink volume—do not make it onto the provision lists for Arctic voyages, which customarily engaged in exhaustive provisioning accounting practices, denoting every box of nails, roll of twine, tin of potted meat, and pair of woolens. (Hoag argues that cuts in Admiralty funding at the time might explain the "haphazard outfitting" that landed older presses on Franklin search ships and, in turn, produced the uncharacteristically scant historical record regarding the provisioning of such presses.) The circumstances of their presence aboard ship is otherwise mentioned in passing if at all, for the most part: "A printing-press was given to the expedition by the Admiralty for printing balloon-papers," which were brief messages printed on brightly-colored silk or oiled paper and distributed in bundles attached to the lit string of a hydrogen balloon (see chapter 4). "There were no printers in the squadron, but some of the officers soon learned the art; and besides balloon-papers, play-bills, and announcements of fancy dress balls, were regularly sent to press," reports the preface to *Arctic Miscellanies* (a collection of the articles in the shipboard paper *Aurora Borealis* that was later published in London in 1852).[39] Maguire, who served on the Franklin search ship *Plover* at Point Barrow, Alaska (1852–54), reported in his journal, "A small printing press formed a part of the liberal supply granted to us by their Lordships on leaving London."[40] Among the miscellaneous collected papers of that particular expedition's surgeon is a newspaper clipping advertising Waterlow's Autographic Press, which was a lithographic copying mechanism rather than a typesetting press. (If that device were on ship, it could have been used for the duplication of shipboard letters, memoranda, or cache records, or for the reproduction of illustrations, as in at least one case an expedition brought with it a set of images from London to supply an anticipated shipboard paper.[41]

There was a press aboard the *Assistance* to print silk and paper balloon messages for the Franklin search; it was not used to print the ship's manuscript newspaper *Aurora Borealis* but instead was put into service producing a shipboard library catalogue, playbills, poems, and advertisements for amusements. An article in the *Aurora Borealis* cheekily entitled "The Rise and Progress of Printing in the Arctic Searching Expeditions"—in just the first year of Arctic printing—documents how the *Assistance* crew moved quickly to bring their own "industry and artistic merit" to transform the materials on hand. "The press, and materials belonging to it, were only sufficient for the purpose of printing the papers attached to the balloon," we learn; "hence a limit was placed to the ambition" of the expedition members. (This indicates that it likely was a small tabletop press designed for printing social calling cards at home, which are about the size of the balloon messages.) Refusing to accept such limitations, the *Aurora* reports, the crew—in a demonstration of the kind of mental and mechanical "improvements arising from leisure and emulation"—carved new large-type capital fonts, including "the shaded letter, the double-lined letter, and the white letter in black relief." For their final printed program of the Royal Arctic Theatre's season, the crew continued to improvise, amplifying the ambition of the artistry of their carved emblems and devices; on the playbill, "the coat of arms, the Prince of Wales's plume, the delicately-carved rose, shamrock, and thistle, the border of oak leaves, acorns, and laurel, spoke well for the industry and artistic merit of all concerned."[42] A mania for printing was created among the crew, "The Rise and Progress of Printing" attests:

> The eagerness with which all the productions were sought after, requires to be seen to be understood. The applicants for copies were not content with impressions on paper, but every variety of material went to press in a most ludicrous manner; silk pocket-handkerchiefs, shirts, calico, satin, and even a blanket. Here we fancied the *furor* would have ceased, but, to our surprise, one person brought a monkey-jacket, and another a chamois-leather.
>
> This indeed must have been gratifying to the printers; and, to their credit be it spoken, during the greater part of three days there was a rapid despatch of business. May they, in their future attempts, succeed as well. Should the art of printing at this establishment continue to improve at the same rate as heretofore, we will back our Arctic press against the world.
>
> In years to come, every little *souvenir* of our sojourn here will be prized for the recollections it will give rise to—of the comfort and amity that existed among the members of the "Austin happy family."[43]

In these early moments of Arctic printing, the novelty of the presence and performance of the press itself was paramount, judging from the baroque range of media on which sailors printed. They were proud too of their ingenuity in creating new type blocks for the press; an article in the *Queen's Illuminated Magazine*, which had printed headers but was otherwise mostly handwritten, reports, "The Headings and Large Capital letters too are a proof of the taste of Lieut. May, and the skill of Bery and Young."[44] (Walter May was an expedition artist, Benjamin Young the ice quartermaster.) To think of these fabrications as "souvenirs" thus makes them consistent with the mementos printed during Thames Frost Fairs— their outlandishness of production, not their content, was the point. As newspapers became more habitual with polar exploration, the genre itself became the focus of the energies (and the creative expression of the assemblage) of the "happy family" constituted by a ship's crew.

Edward Belcher included his expedition's press among a list of the literary materials comprising the ship's extensive library, which featured religious volumes, travel narratives, histories, popular novels (including Melville's *Typee* and *Omoo*), and titles such as *Bathing and Personal Cleanliness*.[45] While the library's holdings were supplemented by personal contributions, Belcher indicates that the press was provided by the Admiralty: "The libraries furnished to each vessel contained all that was asked, which, aided by private collections, left nothing to be wished for in that department. A very excellent printing press, with full type, was supplied to the leading commands, and was found useful."[46] In the Admiralty accounts for 1852, a line item on April 5 authorizes Belcher "to procure a Printing Press for use of the Expedition Est. £15."[47] The diary of the assistant surgeon and quartermaster for the Fiala-Ziegler Expedition, Charles Seitz, mentions that the ship was provided with "a fine library and a printing press and papers from the *Brooklyn Eagle*," the paper for which Fiala had written before turning Arctic explorer.[48] As my discussion of a photograph from this expedition at the opening of this chapter conjectures, this was a Golding Official tabletop press. A full-page feature in the *Brooklyn Daily Eagle* on its Arctic sister publication affords one of the only detailed breakdowns of an Arctic press outfit, specifying the various forms of type aboard the *America* (but not the press model). Noting that the press and type had been saved for a time by the crew—at no small effort—after the ship had been crushed by the ice, the *Brooklyn Eagle* reports that production on the paper helped pass the eighteen months the expedition spent hoping for rescue. But during the crew's final thirty-mile trek to a relief ship, the press and type had to be abandoned, and Fiala details to his old Brooklyn colleagues precisely which type he has been unable to return:

One font 9 point old style, in one Rooker job case.

One package type and spaces, 9 point.

One font of 18 point head letter in one case.

23 Articles and items, set in minion, in 17 packages (2 sets of proofs of this matter furnished).

Two casts of heading "The Arctic Eagle" with parallel rule cast under, also one brass parallel rule to match.

One brass column rule for first page.

One brass column rule for second page.

Dashes—3 styles.

Borders, column width—4 patterns.

One double column composing rule.

One single column composing rule.[49]

In its level of specificity the *Brooklyn Daily Eagle* feature devotes an attention to the materiality of the Arctic press outfitting that reflects a journalist's interests and expertise—rather than that, say, of a career naval officer. Fiala's printing experience did not necessarily translate to nautical expertise, it should be noted; he was an object of contempt in the eyes of some of his crewmen, one of whom, George Shorkley, kept a notebook of his most absurd statements, which he called "Fialisms." Just one example, with Shorkley's parenthetical commentary: "(While his face and hands were blue and his teeth chattering)—'I feel that I was born for the Arctic. While strong men shiver in heavy furs, I am uncomfortably warm in ordinary attire.'"[50]

It is conceivable that there was a printing press aboard the *United States*, Isaac Israel Hayes's 1860 expeditionary ship, even though his men produced the *Port Foulke Weekly News* as a manuscript paper. Hayes's voyage narrative does not specify a press, although the opening prospectus of the *Port Foulke Weekly News* offers the following (possibly satirical) explanation for its scribal rather than print publication: "We hurried our paper through the press, without using our new font of type," an urgency that was compelled by the desire "to please" the paper's "borrowers and non-subscribers" alike— who must then not "criticize, or make remarks concerning typographical appearances." The newspaper is imagined here as an organ that can unify a potentially fractious crew and create the conditions for a "happy family," as the *Aurora Borealis* did aboard the *Assistance*. Since the *Port Foulke Weekly News* came out well, the prospectus continues, "we will probably reserve

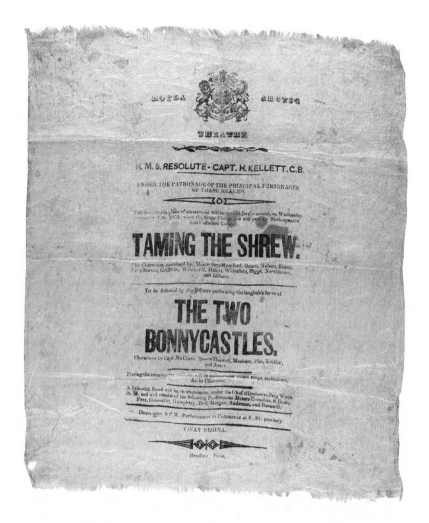

the type to make either balls of, for the purposes of sending dispatches to, and dispatching any troublesome neighbors."[51] (These "troublesome neighbors" requiring dispatches by way of lead ball ammunition would include polar bears, which are very dangerous to humans in the polar North, despite the light tone taken here.) An expedition's crew could stop using a press it had previously employed in newspaper publication too. For example, the first three numbers of the *Arctic Eagle* were printed, while the fourth was in manuscript hand, but the men of the *America* had a fair excuse not to take

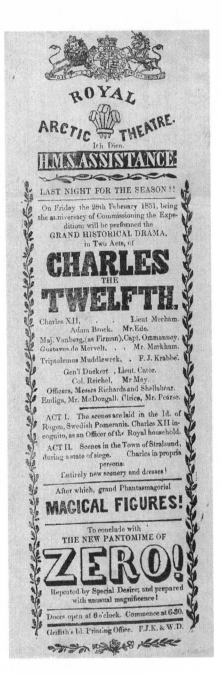

FIG I.4 — Royal Arctic Theatre playbill, printed on pink paper. General Reference Collection c.45.i.11. © THE BRITISH LIBRARY BOARD.

FIG I.5 — Royal Arctic Theatre playbill, printed on blue paper, possibly a proof sheet. General Reference Collection c.45.i.11. © THE BRITISH LIBRARY BOARD.

FIG I.6 — Playbill advertising a performance during the Franklin search, 1850–51. It is printed in black on linen with a seam down the left hand side and a line of stitching at the bottom. TXT0089. © NATIONAL MARITIME MUSEUM, GREENWICH, LONDON.

the trouble to set type: in the interim, their ship had been demolished by ice. The prospectus for the *Queen's Illuminated Magazine* was printed, and the newspaper had printed headers, but the paper was generally handwritten and hand-illustrated; the same is true for the *Illustrated Arctic News*, which had elaborate and extensive printed headers and printed theatrical announcements but was otherwise in manuscript hand. The first fully printed Arctic paper was the *Weekly Guy* (1852).

FIG I.7 — Playbill produced on board HMS *Intrepid* during the Franklin search led by Sir Edward Belcher. Printed in black and red on cream silk. TXT0090. © NATIONAL MARITIME MUSEUM, GREENWICH, LONDON.

In at least one other instance, a proffered press never made it on ship, as Carl Koldewey reports of the German Arctic expedition of 1869–70 aboard the *Hansa*. "We thought that . . . we ought to follow the example of our predecessors," Koldewey writes of the origin of the manuscript newspaper *Ostgrönländische Zeitung* (East Greenland Gazette), which, like a number of other Arctic newspapers, was edited by the ship's surgeon. "Unfortunately, a small printing press, given by the printing-house at Bremerhaven, had not followed us on board. In order, therefore, to have two copies, one for the cabin and one for the forecastle, we had to take the trouble to write it."[52] The distinction drawn here between the cabin (occupied by the officers) and the forecastle (occupied by the common seamen) was common to general shipboard hierarchies and was certainly a factor in the fractiousness displayed by and in the manuscript newspaper of Parry's first expedition's newspaper, the *North Georgia Gazette, and Winter Chronicle*. But by this point in this history of nineteenth-century Arctic expeditions most polar newspapers had more explicitly leveled such nautical class structures, at least in their rhetorical insistence on the equal value of the contributions (and printing skill) of the "men" or common seamen. Other than possible differences in national naval traditions, the need for two copies of the newspaper aboard Koldewey's *Hansa* may reflect instead the practical obstacles to general dissemination of the periodical when produced by manuscript hand rather than on a printing press. On Hayes's *United States* expedition, which had a manuscript paper, there were only fifteen men, making it among the smallest of polar ventures in the period; the need for multiple copies was likely not as urgent. The *Illustrated Arctic News* too counted "the men" both among its contributors and its printers; as the preface to *Arctic Miscellanies* (a collection of *Aurora Borealis* articles) testifies, "Several of the men, too, became adepts in the art of printing, and set up in type, songs and other trifles, chiefly of their own composition."[53]

Albert Hastings Markham's memoir provides the fullest description of the outfitting and layout of an Arctic printing establishment. He notes that each ship in the expedition "had been provided, before leaving England, with a printing-press, and an officer and seaman [Lieutenant George Giffard and Able Seaman Robert Symons] had been instructed in its use." The printers issued a prospectus for their printing "firm," as Markham calls it, which promised that they would "carry on the Noble Art of Printing in a Style & with a Rapidity hitherto quite unattainable.[54] It was difficult for Giffard and Symons to carve out space for their venture on the ship, however, as Markham's memoir testifies:

> The "cost" and "trouble" . . . that were expended in obtaining a convenient place in which to carry out the "noble art of printing," were caused by the fact that our photographers were equally anxious, with our printers, to possess themselves of the small cabin lately occupied by my cousin [Clement Markham], and which is so grandiloquently alluded to as "extensive premises." In fact, for some little time it was a very sore and vexed question between those two celebrated and energetic firms. Trap Lane was so called in consequence of the after-hold being immediately outside the door of the cabin; and it occasionally served as a very disagreeable kind of man-trap when, through inadvertence, the hatch had not been replaced. As this part of the ship was, during the early part of her com-

mission, in total darkness, owing to the pile of stores that were stowed in every available corner, it is no wonder that unsuspecting individuals should occasionally have fallen into the trap!

Our printing-press was, it is almost needless to say, of great use to us during the winter; for, although it never printed very much for the public service, it was constantly called into requisition for the purpose of striking off programmes for our dramatic and other entertainments; and on such important events as birthdays and Christmas-day we indulged in the extravagance of printed bills of fare. On the whole the printing establishment on board the "Alert" tended very materially to beguile the tedium of our long nights, and must therefore be regarded as a decided success.[55]

We see here, first of all, the exceptionally constrained physical spaces in which the crew members were operating in general aboard ship, however amusingly conjured in the idea of the icebound ship constituting a "city." The "extensive premises" of the printing office, according to the prospectus, are located "within half a minute's walk of the foremost Quarter Deck Ladder, and easily accessible to all parts of the city."[56] Markham observes that ironic remarks about the grand quarters—and their attendant hazards—disguise some actual tensions among the printers and the photographers: to claim any corner for creative work could be a battle, as the photographers would be engaged in expeditionary work, not art for the sake of art alone.

More provocatively, Markham here makes a distinction between the "public service" in support of which the printing press could be put to use, and its counterpart—which would presumably constitute the "private." The public service would likely be linked to the expedition's mission to attempt the North Pole (Markham is describing George Nares's 1875–76 large British Arctic Expedition), although he notes that the press is not employed to this end. The expedition members take it up instead for their private use, which, crucially, does not mean *individual* use. The private function performed by the press attends to the ship's body as a whole in printing "programmes for our dramatic and other entertainments," Markham writes, as well as "printed bills of fare" for communal holiday meals and birthday celebrations. We might generally associate newspapers with a public function, but polar newspapers violate one of the definitions of a public in the sense that all of its members is intimately known to one another.[57] It is against this particular concept of publicness that Markham defines the Arctic Press's function throughout the ship as "private."

The language of "privacy" and "private use" to indicate ship-wide community recurs in Arctic newspapers. The *Port Foulke Weekly News* begins

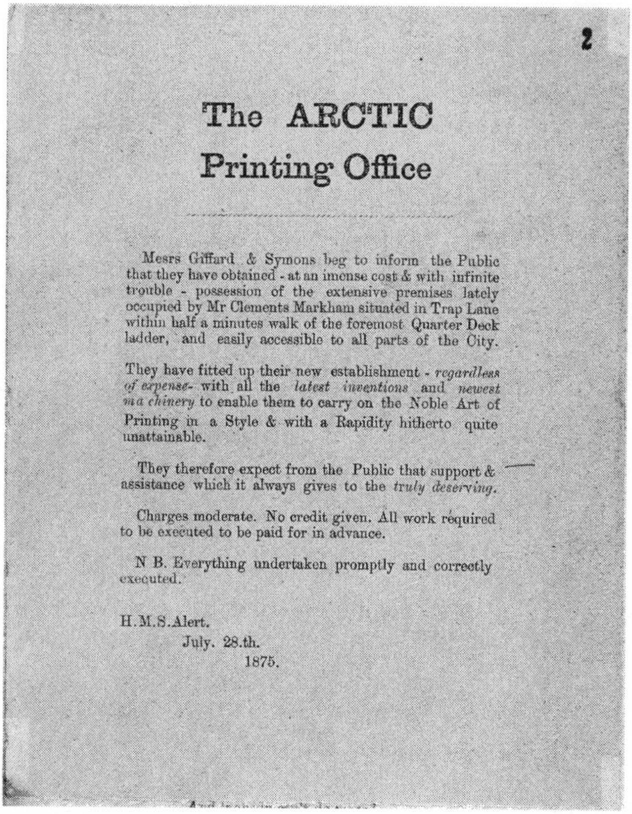

The ARCTIC Printing Office

Messrs Giffard & Symons beg to inform the Public that they have obtained - at an imense cost & with infinite trouble - possession of the extensive premises lately occupied by Mr Clements Markham situated in Trap Lane within half a minutes walk of the foremost Quarter Deck ladder, and easily accessible to all parts of the City.

They have fitted up their new establishment - *regardless of expense*- with all the *latest inventions* and *newest machinery* to enable them to carry on the Noble Art of Printing in a Style & with a Rapidity hitherto quite unattainable.

They therefore expect from the Public that support & assistance which it always gives to the *truly deserving*.

Charges moderate. No credit given. All work required to be executed to be paid for in advance.

N B. Everything undertaken promptly and correctly executed.

H.M.S.Alert.
July. 28.th.
1875.

FIG I.8 — The Arctic Printing Office advertisement. May/13/2.
© NATIONAL MARITIME MUSEUM, GREENWICH, LONDON.

with an invocation of the "private family circle" that comprises the entirety of the paper's readership and the crew, in a representative example.[58] Within the pages of the newspapers, gazettes, and weeklies, editors and contributors alike demonstrate an awareness of the relative privacy of the circumstances of their periodicals' distribution, given the absence of a reading community beyond that of their shipmates. Yet at the same time they recognize that polar newspapers are calling into being an Arctic public defined not just by proximity or happenstance but by specific ecological conditions. Within the space of the newspapers we can see expedition members working out ideas of how communities can be both public and private, how transient assemblages can form worlds elsewhere, even in the face of geophysical and ecological extremity.

Amateur Communities

Shipboard-printed newspapers increasingly became standard to the leisure and community-building practices of Arctic expeditions, and eventually Antarctic ones; they remain so to this day.[59] The forms of exchange that take place within their pages reflect a learned, experiential sense of the relationship between the polar environment and what we might call a polar imprint: the mark that expeditions sought to make on what the poetic imagination of the day held to be the Arctic's sublime blankness. Polar newspapers also demonstrate an expansive sense of contribution and collective exchange, both within the expeditions themselves, and within the polar regions more broadly. Expeditionary interest in the genre of the newspaper is a reflection of the broader cultures of print in the nineteenth century, in both Britain and the United States, in which newspapers played significant roles as organs of nationalism and examples of amateur literary production. At the same time, newspaper production is consistent with polar expeditionary culture itself, in its imperative to produce volumes of writing as a hedge against polar blankness. As polar gazettes became conventional to expeditionary practice, certain periodical and aesthetic conceits became literary conventions among expedition members as they explored the genre of the newspaper as a way to meditate on—and mediate—questions of Artic temporality and isolation.

In all cases, Arctic literary imprints, ephemera by the definitions of literary genre, have been treated in turn as ephemeral to the histories of polar exploration, which tend to mention Arctic newspapers alongside theatricals and shipboard libraries in a brief paragraph or two describing winter pastimes.[60] The exception is the excellent bibliographic work on polar publishing done by Elaine Hoag and by David H. Stam and Deirdre C. Stam, as well as Elizabeth Leane's analysis of Antarctic newspapers.[61] Arctic imprints constitute a small and dispersed archive found in the miscellaneous folders, generally, of those expedition members whose papers have been collected in archives, and—among this already small class—within the smaller subset of those who kept samples of polar printing as souvenirs. (Hoag estimates the total number of imprints produced in the Arctic in a five-year stretch at midcentury, the height of the Franklin searches, at around one hundred; she doesn't work with Antarctic material.)[62] A collection of printed theatrical playbills from the Nares British Arctic Expedition (1875–76) held at the Scott Polar Research Institute, for instance, had been preserved by an able seaman on the mission named William Maskell; his daughter donated them to the archive in 1942. John Simpson, a surgeon on several Arctic expeditions, tucked theatrical programs into his journal of one voyage. In another example, a librarian at the Virginia Historical Society came across what she characterized as a "curious scrap of paper" in the society's holdings while researching a website feature on a different polar mission. The tattered paper, partly printed and partly inscribed in ink, is an 1850 balloon dispatch from the HMS *Resolute* engaged in a search for Franklin. In a 2013 blog post written on the balloon message, the librarian Katherine Wilkins wonders, "How could a scrap of paper be retrieved from the Arctic circle and placed in the collections of the Virginia Historical Society in Richmond, Virginia?" The repository does not know the provenance of the item, she continues, which suggests "that it has been in our collections for a long time. We may never learn how we acquired this unique item."[63] In my own research for this book, I have traveled to thirty-odd archives in five countries, the majority of which hold only a single periodical or a handful of examples of Arctic or Antarctic imprints. The archival presence of the balance of these imprints, in turn, is not readily apparent from library finding aids, which have historically privileged the printed voyage accounts and correspondence associated with polar exploration.[64] In my research for this project, I have seen multiple versions of the same couple of playbills printed from this press on different media: paper (of various colors), linen, silk, and chamois (see figures 1.3–1.7). Some of the newspaper and theatrical advertisements that survive are printed on yellow or blue paper and may be proof sheets, which could explain their presence in the archive as reserve copies.[65] In the playbills one can also observe examples of the emblems as well as the hand-cut large-type font made by the sailors in the titles "TURNED HEAD!" and "MAGICAL FIGURES" and "BOMBASTES FURIOSO!!!"[66] This heterogeneity of material reflects, in part, the novelty of the practice of Arctic printing and the attendant desire to preserve souvenirs on fancier fabric. The National Maritime Museum, for instance, holds several playbills printed on brightly colored silk that had been elaborately framed for display by their mid-nineteenth-century preservationists. The relative volume of such commemorative souvenir production is a primary reason such playbills remain in the "Uncatalogued" or "Miscellaneous" folders of prominent expedition members.

The elusiveness of this material reflects, for one, the ephemerality of a moment in time, a season, an expedition carried out in the absence of diurnal measurements of days, abstracted from contact with the state sponsors of most ventures other than via the singular national time kept by sea clocks

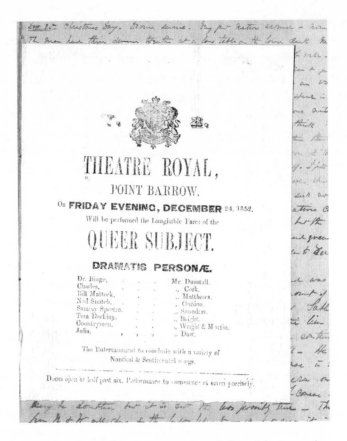

FIG 1.9 — *Queer Subject* theater program tucked into John Simpson's "Account of Voyages." Box 1, Folder: Account of Voyages, John Simpson Papers, 1825–1875. DAVID M. RUBENSTEIN RARE BOOK AND MANUSCRIPT LIBRARY, DUKE UNIVERSITY.

keyed to the Greenwich meridian. Rather than a mechanism for passing time, newspapers, as well as letters and logbooks, become a measurement and codification of it. In addition, the elusiveness of polar periodicals within archives is consistent with the imperfect preservation histories of periodicals more generally, especially for amateur publications or those created by nonelites.[67] These media were never designed to stay, to stick, to make it to the shelf; they were as transitory as the ship or the ice, always on the move.

In their newspaper incarnations, polar ecomedia bear affinities in some ways with the amateur periodicals of the latter half of the nineteenth century. Both were enabled by the wide availability of desktop printing presses, which gave nonprofessionals access to parlor (or cabin) publication. Small presses were initially manufactured for use by tradesmen look-ing to economize on job printing costs, but as Elizabeth Harris describes, "almost as an afterthought, manufacturers advertised the same apparatus [do-it-yourself printing presses] to children and amateur printers." Hobby presses were a hit; between 1860 and 1880 the "number of press-making companies tripled."[68] Tabletop presses in the home were used primarily to print calling cards or other social documents, but younger people—mostly white, middle-class boys—used the presses to create their own newspapers. We see an example of this dual function in the *Boys and Girls Favorite*, an amateur paper out of Grand Rapids, Michigan. One "prize" for a reader who could furnish twenty-five additional subscribers to the paper was a "beautiful printing press for boys and girls, worked by hand, Cards, Hand-bills, Circulars, in fact, all kinds of printing can be done with neatness and dispatch. Just the thing all boys and girls want. Given for twenty-five new names."[69] The process of generating new subscribers to the paper was also a process of generating new outlets for print, both periodical and social.

We see some of the differences between amateur periodicals of the tem-perate and polar zones on display in the career of Isaac Israel Hayes, who had experience with recreational papers both as an Arctic explorer and as a surgeon in Pennsylvania. He had first traveled to the Far North with his fellow Philadelphian doctor-turned-polar-explorer Elisha Kent Kane on the 1853 Second Grinnell Expedition in search of Franklin's lost ships, and when Hayes returned from his own command of an 1860–61 Arctic expe-dition, he found that the United States was engaged in the Civil War. He became the surgeon in charge of Satterlee Hospital in West Philadelphia, the large Union medical center known for treating thousands of casualties from the battle of Gettysburg. There Hayes established a library as well as a hospital newspaper—written and printed by convalescing soldiers—for the sake of their mental health and amusement. According to an article in its first number entitled "Our Printers," the *West Philadelphia Hospi-tal Register* "is printed and published, within the walls of the Hospital.— The type is set up, and the press-work performed by Soldiers, whose names are given below.—convalescent patients, partially disabled by service in the field."[70] The *West Philadelphia Hospital Register* describes a lecture course (a general midcentury amusement also popular aboard polar ventures), and the first topic was a familiar one: "The Surgeon in Charge [Hayes] will in-augurate the course by a Lecture on the Arctic Regions." (Subsequent lec-ture topics similarly trended heavily toward Arctic themes.)[71] There was at least one crucial distinction between the *West Philadelphia Hospital*

Register, however, and the two Arctic newspapers with which Hayes had been associated (the *Ice-Blink* of Kane's Second Grinnell Expedition and the *Port Foulke Weekly News* of Hayes's own command of the *United States*). A fundamental aspect of U.S. amateur newspaper publishing in the second half of the nineteenth century was exchange, the process by which publishers of small-circulation sheets sent copies of their papers to other amateurs in expectation of returns in kind. This custom was facilitated, in part, by very low postage rates for newspapers. The second issue of the *West Philadelphia Hospital Register* reported, "We have the pleasure of welcoming, already, a number of newspaper exchanges, which are placed immediately into the hands of eager readers. We tender to our brethren of the quill (scalpel) our affectionate *greetings*."[72] Other medical institutions had papers as well, as Benjamin Reiss's work on asylums in the period reveals; the *Opal* of the New York State Lunatic Asylum in Utica (which began publication in 1851) exchanged with 330 other periodicals.[73] Exchanges were not practicable, of course, for Arctic papers, or for shipboard papers more generally. In this way the ship circulates differently than other supposedly heterotopic spaces, such as the prison.[74]

In the 1870s and 1880s in the United States the amateur journalism trade was remarkably robust. There are fifty-five thousand amateur newspapers in the American Antiquarian Society's holdings alone, the great majority produced by teenage boys—comprising the first teenage print subculture, Lara Langer Cohen has argued. Cohen's work with this particular archive has revealed that much of the content of the late nineteenth-century American amateur newspapers was tedious, repetitive, and largely beside the point. "Instead of creating an outlet for one's own thoughts," she writes, "it appears that one started an amateur newspaper to join a community of other amateurs. This community is not just an *effect* of print, as has often been argued of other print cultures. Community is also the *cause* of print." Cohen's latter point equally applies to polar print cultures. The audience for amateur newspapers, she continues, "largely seems to have consisted of other amateurs."[75] Amateur papers achieved an audience of their fellows by participating in cultures of exchange; many hobby papers printed within their own pages the titles of the papers with whom they were in an exchange relationship.[76] An amateur paper published in the port town of New Bedford, Massachusetts, took the obligations of exchange particularly seriously; an editorial statement in the first number of *Shells and Seaweed* promised, "We will exchange with ALL amateur publications. No sample copy fiends need apply, unless their request be accompanied by a stamp."[77]

A concern about the "fiends" who request sample copies without sharing in kind pops up again and again in its pages; what seems monstrous about such fiends is their nonparticipation in a print culture based on reciprocity.

Concerns about nonreciprocity were central to the first Arctic newspaper, the *North Georgia Gazette, and Winter Chronicle* (1819–20). But it preceded *Shells and Seaweed* (1884)—and indeed the amateur journalism movement—by over a half century. While polar newspapers share many generic and technological affinities with the amateur boys' newspapers of the late nineteenth century, they were not directly inspired by them, nor by the papers of the English public schools, which also postdate the first Arctic papers. Indeed a great number of naval officers left school early to go to sea. One officer on Parry's first expedition wrote in a private letter about the ship's manuscript newspaper, the *North Georgia Gazette, and Winter Chronicle*, "When it is considered at what an early period the officers of the navy are sent to sea generally at eleven or twelve years of age and that the education which they receive on board can scarcely be supposed to be on the best or most enlarged plan it will we think be admitted that many of the papers in the North Georgia Gazette are far superior to what might reasonably be expected and such as would not discredit the more regular scholar and practised writer."[78] Newspapers were part of a culture of periodical publication that flourished in Britain and the United States over the course of the nineteenth century. In Adriana Craciun's account, polar exploration more broadly benefited from an expansion of print in the period. Beginning in the early nineteenth century, British Arctic expeditions produced published narratives as part of a formalized relationship with the London publisher John Murray; in turn, "the voyage account authored by the ship's captain [became] increasingly important to the business of exploration."[79] As the scholars Craciun, Janice Cavell, and Russell Potter have documented, Arctic expeditions in the second half of the nineteenth century generated enormous media attention, particularly in response to the search for Franklin's missing expedition.[80] Thus while the newspapers printed by polar expedition members aboard ship during sunless, ice-stalled winters were not direct analogues to the broadsheets of the temperate metropoles, they were enabled in some ways by similar impulses.

In publishing their news in polar periodicals, as I have been arguing, Arctic explorers were, in part, seeking to re-create the forms of temporal regularity and imagined community that newspapers have historically been understood to serve in the period—only in this instance doing so in extravagantly outlandish conditions. The process of *printing* their news and engaging in the satiric imagination of its broader periodical circulation offered expedition members a particular manner of inhabiting and reflecting upon the genre of their literary production, one that emphasized their ecologically extreme perspective and acknowledged their ephemerality within that space and time.

Polar Imprints

Putting thoughts to words and words to print reverberates in other ways, as well. The dedications and apologia in the opening numbers of polar papers make strong claims for what one paper called an "intellectual revolution" among seamen. (They also make claims for the mental health benefits provided by the amusements of periodical play, as chapter 2 discusses in more detail.) According to the *Aurora Borealis*, "the general public appear to have no conception" of sailors' nonmanual skills. "The popular opinion seems to be, that the literary attainments of British sailors seldom exceed the acquisition of some boisterous song, and that only the very erudite amongst them can succeed in scrawling a letter to their friends at home." To the contrary, the paper of the *Assistance* continues:

> [Here] we find articles written by veteran tars, whose home since boyhood has been upon the sea, that would not disgrace the pages of some of our magazines. These men with frames of iron, with a courage and a stern endurance that nothing can subdue, show themselves possessed of a delicacy of imagination and a power of perception that one has great difficulty in reconciling with the honest roughness of their appearance. . . . The men from before the mast, who contributed to the "Aurora Borealis," are amongst the most exemplary in Her Majesty's service.[81]

The men "before the mast" are the common seamen aboard ship, the nonofficers and the "veteran tars," whose literacy rates were notably high for a laboring class.[82] To be sure, it is in an expedition's self-interest to promote a view of common sailors as powerful in mind as well as body, even in a document for internal circulation. But the evidence bears out the periodical's claims. The Nares expedition of 1875–76, for example, consisted of two ships of sixty men each. During the Arctic winter the ships established a school for sailors, which included instruction in navigation and history. "Only two men out of the entire ship's company were unable to read and write," recalls Markham, "and these two men were placed in a class with two others, who were unable to read and write English." (The nonreaders in English were from Denmark and Gibraltar.) The literacy class "was presided over by the doctor, who kindly volunteered to devote himself to the instruction of the 'cripples,' as they were facetiously called."[83] Such facetiousness indicates that their illiteracy was relatively unusual. The elite Markham found himself impressed by the knowledge and intellectual curiosity he found among the common seamen with whom he fraternized during his Arctic voyaging. "I was much surprised at the extensive Arctic knowledge which they possessed," he wrote, "showing that they had read largely on this subject, and were anxious to learn yet more."[84] There was also a makeshift academy and a Reading Room on the *Assistance* during the immobilized inactivity and darkness of polar winter. In addition to working on the paper *Aurora Borealis*, the men of the "lower deck" (that is, the seamen) organized themselves into "schools on the Lancasterian system," in which the stronger students taught the less able; subjects included navigation, steam, seamanship, arithmetic, and even modern languages and music.[85] Sherard Osborn, who commanded a support tender for the *Resolute* and *Assistance* Franklin search ships in 1850–51, merrily recollected the sight of "tough old marines curving 'pothooks and hangers' [practicing their letters], as if their very lives depended on their performances, with an occasional burst of petulance, such as, 'D—the pen, it won't write! I beg pardon, sir; this 'ere pen will splutter!' which set the scholars in a roar."[86] The biological discipline at work here is regulatory but directed more immediately toward personal community than state imperatives.

In the *Aurora Borealis* "articles were contributed by the commanders, officers and men, of the expedition. Some of the papers are from the pen of the venerable Admiral Sir John Ross, and others, and not the least interesting, are from rough and weather-beaten tars before the mast."[87] George Murray, a quartermaster or petty supply agent, was judged the "best writer" among those contributing to the *Aurora Borealis*.[88] This nautical class-leveling was common in post-1848 Arctic papers. The prolific printer aboard the Belcher expedition, for example, was a seaman named H. Briant, rated "musician"; he contributed poems to the *Queen's Illuminated Magazine* in addition to his printing work. We see the literal mark of his labor in an inky fingerprint left at the bottom of a proof sheet from one of the expedition's official dispatches, a blank cairn record, preserved in the British Admiralty Records.[89]

One of the great archival pleasures of the text of this project has been just such encounters with the mark of the hand of labor upon the material of mechanized production, however limited in its industrial scope. Briant's

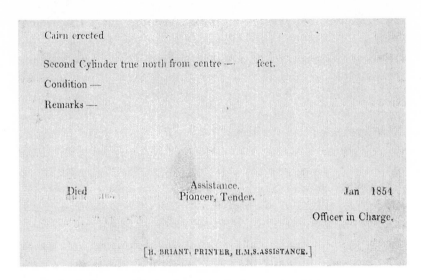

Cairn erected

Second Cylinder true north from centre —   feet.

Condition —

Remarks —

Died   Assistance,   Jan 1854
                    Pioneer, Tender.
                                                    Officer in Charge,

[H. BRIANT, PRINTER, H.M.S.ASSISTANCE.]

FIG I.IO — H. Briant, Printer. Documents Relating to Arctic Expeditions, ADM 7/195. NATIONAL ARCHIVES, LONDON.

fingertip, a hand-stitched folded hem on a pink silk-printed Arctic song composed on ship, a broken tooth enclosed with a commemorative printed menu: these flaws or remnants constitute less errata or variant than aide-mémoire of the exceptional intimacy within which the extremity of these printed texts were produced. As the labor of letterpress printing itself was generally trade work, it is not surprising that seamen would be involved in typesetting and working the shipboard presses. Key within an Arctic context, though, is how frequently officers and men were working the presses side by side, creating different forms of naval and textual community. Able Seaman Symons of the *Alert* on the Nares expedition also acted as a printer and contributor, standing shoulder to shoulder with a lieutenant, Giffard. The sister ship of the *Alert* likewise had a press, and on the *Discovery* Able Seaman Benjamin Wyatt was the printer. The Scott Polar Research Institute holds a printed "Education Sheet" from the *Discovery* expedition, presumably designed to give the printers some practice in setting type. In it we see how the men are using the medium of print to work through the terms of their maritime experience. The sheet runs through the alphabet, assigning a word to each letter according to custom—but several of the nonstandard word choices reveal something about the tastes and backgrounds of the printers: "And.Bee.Cat.Dog.Ear.Fig.Gin.Hop.Inn.Jug.Kit.Loo.Man.Noon .Oil.Pence.Quay.Rot.Sin.Tin.Urn.Vex.Win.Yes.Zinc."[90] While the first five or six words might be examples used by any schoolchild in practicing alphabet words, contributions such as "gin," "loo," "quay," "rot," and "sin" show a kind of louche devolution better associated with working seamen. The nautical class known as the "men" printed on many other expeditions as well. Kane's *Ice-Blink* (1853–54; Second Grinnell Expedition, a Franklin search) was composed by "authors of every nautical grade: some of the best from the forecastle."[91] Rochfort Maguire notes in his diary of his time on the *Plover*, "In the Printing department a man named Daw a Seaman, is making himself very useful [in helping to produce the *Weekly Guy*]."[92] On the Fiala-Ziegler Expedition of 1903–5, the *Arctic Eagle* was printed by the "assistant commissary steward, the youngest man in the field department; the compositor [was] Seaman Montrose, who had been a wandering newspaper typo before he took to following the sea." A woodcut formed a special cover for the *Arctic Eagle* to commemorate Christmas in 1903; it shows the ice-beset ship in the background and two expedition members raising brimming goblets in the foreground, sled dogs at their feet. The engraving was created with a "chisel and pocketknife by [the ship's] assistant scientist porter."[93]

When Arctic newspapers were not offering testimony in support of the cultural bona fides of their crewmen in earnest, edifying tones, they were doing so in the very spirit of fun and frolic with which the periodicals were launched. The publishing schedule of the *Arctic Eagle* was "whenever convenient"; the "maiden effort" of the paper was designed as a "flyer; feeler, as it were, to test the market for such a paper among the reading public of Franz Josef Land." The public for the unpopulated Far Northern Russian archipelago was, of course, constituted solely by the crew of the ship, as the *Eagle* acknowledges: "We can confidently assert . . . that it is the only paper in six hundred miles."[94] Such was the case with all Arctic periodicals, even as they might jestingly have an eye on other markets. "We fear not the frowns of the Temperate Zone," the prefatory matter to the *Illustrated Arctic News* states, for these Far North newsmen, "being of a peaceable disposition, would deprecate wrath, or jealousy on the part of the Titans of the Southern Press, who may fear our entering the field as competitors in these Regions." While London printers are certainly "Titans," especially compared to amateurs on the *Resolute*, the southerliness of their northern European location is globally relative. The *Illustrated Arctic News* continues its sport by assuring the printers of the metropole that "unless Old England be overtaken by a night of three months duration, it is not our intention to appear again in the Editorial line."[95] This self-deprecation makes claims for the legitimacy of the seamen's publications in positioning the *Illustrated Arctic News* as an object for jealousy or competition, however impudently.

One basis for this comparison, or this sense of competition with London or other metropolitan papers, may be the fact that shipboard clocks are synchronized with Greenwich Mean Time for longitudinal location purposes. Moored in Arctic ice for months or years, expeditions were navigationally tethered to the prime meridian, even as their daily lives were synchronized to polar temporalities, displaced by many meridians. The editors of polar newspapers recognize that one expectation of contemporary media, however, is to erase such temporal distinctions in the name of broader and swifter communication. As the preface to a collection of articles from the *Aurora Borealis* explains, "A great paper like the [London] 'Times' no longer addresses itself to one empire or to a single people. The telegraph and the railroad have destroyed space, and a truth now uttered in London in a few minutes later vibrates through the heart of France, or is heard on the shores of the Adriatic."[96] Yet even as the *Aurora Borealis* served as the "public organ of the little world" constituted by "Captain Austin's squadron in the Arctic Seas," that little world itself was not networked with U.S. or European spheres of communication; the "truths" published in this Arctic organ resonate only among the members of Austin's ships. "We fear that the time is far distant," the preface concludes, "before 'the peoples' of Europe will feel any of the brotherly spirit which animated 'the Austin Happy Family.'"[97] Dispersed European "peoples" cannot share the intimacy of the expeditionary "family" unit, for one. But the sentiment also underscores a different point: as an example of ecomedia, the *Aurora Borealis* is networked with the polar region, not with the temperate world. Note, too, that the preface to the *Aurora Borealis* selections stresses that "the time is far distant" when such networks might be joined: the Arctic is figured as both temporally and spatially extreme.

Yet even in their acknowledgment of the distance of the Arctic papers from the printing centers of the "Temperate Zone," both in their geographic location and in their fabrication, polar periodicals hew to literary formal expectations. In their dedications, preambles, and preludes, for example, Arctic newspapers offer the kind of conventional apologia familiar to readers of first-person narratives, even as they recognize how unusual their periodicals were, relatively speaking. "We follow the custom of our brethren of the quill," the preamble to the *Arctic Moon* (of Adolphus Greely's American Lady Franklin Bay Expedition, 1881–84) observes, "who generally devote a column of their first issue of a newspaper—like the preface to a book—in whys and wherefores, in the way of an apology for introducing themselves upon the public." Published semimonthly (at a waggish list price of 25¢ per issue) from Fort Conger in Grinnell Land (lat 81°44′, long 64°45′), the *Arctic Moon* invited "articles in poetry or prose, short or long, serious or facetious." As the musical ability of the expedition members is relatively poor, the author of the preamble admits, "we have more than ordinary justifications in prescribing, the *Arctic Moon* twice a month during the days of darkness," since the expedition's "predecessors in the realm of the ice king have long ago established the precedent" of a shipboard newspaper.[98] The apologia that prefaced the earlier *Illustrated Arctic News* (1850), the precedent-setters mentioned in the *Arctic Moon*, had recognized that paradox in claiming novelty in the production of an all-too-familiar periodical form. Using the conventions of publishing to argue for its lack of convention, in other words, the *Illustrated Arctic News* had made this part of the paper's raison d'être: "Where merit cannot be pleaded, novelty, as in Bloomerism, may avail."[99] A periodical in the Arctic was as dislocatingly out of place as Bloomers or pants were on a woman; both became Anglo-American fads in the 1850s nevertheless. The *Weekly Guy* in 1852 had been billed as a curiosity: "ANOTHER NOVELTY!!!"[100] The expedition's initial novelty had been an Inuit dance, also advertised via printed playbill—albeit only as a "GREAT NOVELTY!!," with two exclamation points rather than three. (A journal kept by a crew member observes, "The Notice headed 'Great Novelty' was turned out of hand by the Compositors in a very creditable form, but they regret that they have not four times the number of types.")[101] It did not take long for exceptional novelties to become expectations, commonplaces aboard Arctic ships. But this is a function of nautical practice: when a method or technique is effective or an improvement upon former custom, it becomes regularized in common. We have seen already how one ship responded to a dearth of fonts—they carved their own. "Whatever is wanting, we must endeavour to supply," the advertisement for the *Queen's Illuminated Magazine* states. These needs include "A Morning Paper and its *Latest intelligence*! . . . Periodicals Papers &c, where will they come from if not created by our selves? . . . The Printing Press has been we fear, but little appreciated, by the sagacious if not intelligent inhabitants of these realms, and North Cornwall, has not had as yet its Caxton." (William Caxton was the fifteenth-century merchant, writer, and printer who introduced the first printing press to England in 1476.)[102]

The printedness of words had its own ecological value to expedition members, both as a mark of the degree and quality of Arctic light and as

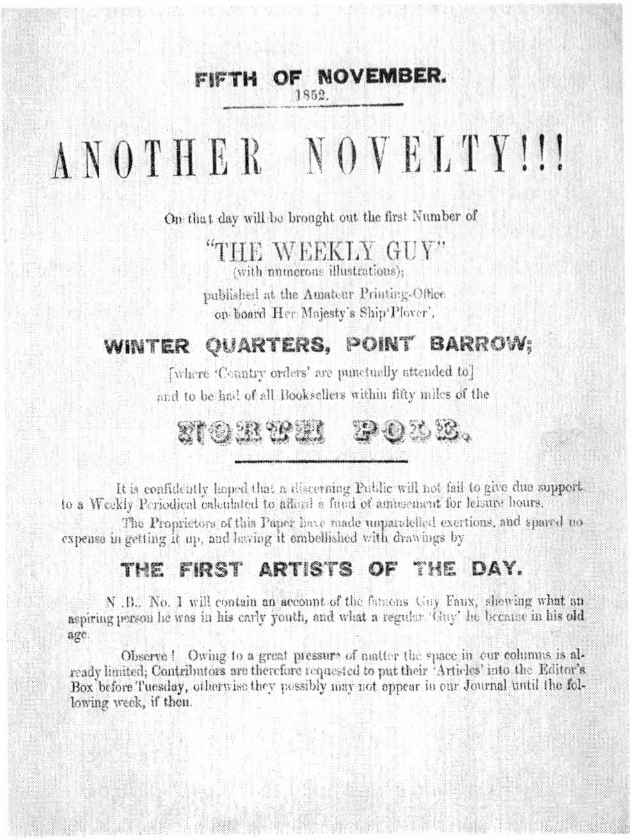

FIFTH OF NOVEMBER.
1852.

ANOTHER NOVELTY!!!

On that day will be brought out the first Number of

"THE WEEKLY GUY"
(with numerous illustrations);

published at the Amateur Printing-Office
on board Her Majesty's Ship 'Plover',

WINTER QUARTERS, POINT BARROW;

[where 'Country orders' are punctually attended to]

and to be had of all Booksellers within fifty miles of the

NORTH POLE.

It is confidently hoped that a discerning Public will not fail to give due support
to a Weekly Periodical calculated to afford a fund of amusement for leisure hours.

The Proprietors of this Paper have made unparalleled exertions, and spared no
expense in getting it up, and having it embellished with drawings by

THE FIRST ARTISTS OF THE DAY.

N.B.. No. 1 will contain an account of the famous Guy Faux, shewing what an
aspiring person he was in his early youth, and what a regular 'Guy' he became in his old
age.

Observe! Owing to a great pressure of matter the space in our columns is already limited; Contributors are therefore requested to put their 'Articles' into the Editor's
Box before Tuesday, otherwise they possibly may not appear in our Journal until the following week, if then.

FIG I.II — Advertisement for the *Weekly Guy*. Box 4, Miscellaneous
Printed Material 1844 Nov.–1875 Jan. 20, undated, John Simpson Papers,
1825–1875. DAVID M. RUBENSTEIN RARE BOOK AND MANUSCRIPT
LIBRARY, DUKE UNIVERSITY.

a gauge of their distance from comparative comfort. It was common on expeditions to judge the degree of winter darkness by whether or not it was possible to read a copy of a newspaper at noon. During the Second Grinnell Expedition, Kane wrote in his journal on 14 January 1855 that it was "growing lighter," a relief, as it "has now been fifty-two days since we could read [newspaper] type, even after climbing the dreary hills."[103] With the disappearance of the sun in 1875 during the Nares expedition, the commander recalled, the "noon twilight was insufficient to enable us to make out the words in a 'Times' leading article, when the paper was held up facing the south." Nares then calculated with some grimness, "We have yet eighty-seven days of more intense darkness to pass through."[104] Late January "raised the spirits" of those on the expedition, as each day brought "an increased arch of twilight.... At noon of the 28th we were able to read on the floe a few lines from the leading article of the 'Times.'"[105] Edward Moss's account of this expedition adds texture to Nares's account: "The words 'Epps's Cocoa,' in type nearly half-an-inch long, were easily read, but the 'breakfast' in small type between them was utterly illegible. It was just possible to spell out 'Oetzmann' in clear Roman type five-sixteenths of an inch long; and after much staring at the page, held close before the eyes, we managed to make out 'great novelty' in type one-fourth of an inch long." Moss also gives an example in large font, bold type of what is "LEGIBLE AT MID-DAY."[106] The Norwegian Fridtjof Nansen also used the newspaper-sunlight gauge on his *Fram* expedition; on 27 January his crew could "just see to read *Verdens Gang* [The Course of the World, a Norwegian newspaper] about midday."[107]

Why did the form of the newspaper serve as the standard for gauging polar solar radiance? The small type of newsprint may have been variable across the nineteenth century, but it provided a familiar measure across ships and over time; more light is required to read tiny type, naturally. The leading article of the *Times* of London, used by the Nares expedition in 1876, appeared in what today we would measure as six-point font. Newspapers were cheap, widely available, disposable, and carried on virtually all ships, making them an accessible basis for comparison. More evocatively, papers are tied directly to the sun's rise and fall. In temperate latitudes, periodicals are generally daily, diurnal; whether in morning or evening editions, their temporality is irrevocably linked with the sun's periodicity. In employing a newsprint light meter for polar practice, expedition members acknowledge both the expectations of printedness and its daily practices, and their estrangement from it. Printed text, and its scarcity, becomes a marker for the distance between temperate latitudinal regularity and polar latitudinal extremity: If a daily paper has no daily sun by which to be read, are days still a measure of time?—of information?

Printedness represents different things at different times in the polar regions, however. George E. Tyson's diary of his survival of the *Polaris* expedition achingly records the loss of the ship's store of books after he and eighteen others are separated from the leaking ship:

No Bible, no Prayer-book, no magazines or newspapers—not even a *Harper's Weekly*—was saved by any one, though there are almost always more or less of these to be found in a ship's company where there are any reading men. Newspapers I have learned to do without to a great extent, having been at sea so much of my life, where it is impossible to get them; but some sort of reading I always had before. *It is now one hundred and seven days since I have seen printed words!* What a treat a bundle of old papers would be! All the world over, I suppose some people are wasting and destroying what would make others feel rich indeed.[108]

Tyson is counting the days since he has seen printed words. What does this longing for print represent when expressed by someone actually adrift in the Arctic, untethered from ship or shelter? His lament is all the more striking in the face of the extremity of his condition: he wrote these words while on a diminishing ice floe upon which the nineteen *Polaris* survivors— refugees after the murder of their ship's captain, Charles Francis Hall, and the loss of their ship—traveled eighteen hundred miles over six months before their rescue. They survived on seal that their Inuit companions were able to hunt from the floe, and on the few stores they managed to salvage from the ship. No one, apparently, salvaged the *Harper's Weekly*. And yet what Tyson highlights is the very ephemerality of print in temperate latitudes, which people who do not happen to be on a loose floe in the Arctic are "wasting and destroying." In this instance print is a stabilizing, regulatory entity, its neat ruled lines in fixed contrast to the errancy of the movement of the *Polaris* survivors.

Print is likewise a "comfort" to Fridtjof Nansen and his crew, and not just when it is visible by the light of the returning sun. When Nansen and his men leave their ship and are camped in their winter quarters for the dark season, they pine for printed matter: "How we longed for a book! . . . The little readable matter which was to be found in our navigation-table and almanack I had read so many times already that I knew it almost by heart. . . . Yet it was always a comfort to see these books; the sight of the printed letters gave one a feeling that there was after all a little bit of the civilized man left."[109] There is no human Other invoked in this passage to provide a supposed "savage" counterpart to the "civilized man" Nansen imagines; the erosion of civilization in the Arctic is instead conflated with a loss of access to readable print. What is important to note in both Tyson's and Nansen's situations is that neither has access to a printing press and thus cannot readily produce new forms of printed ecomedia. Tyson is in desperate survival mode on an ice floe that is breaking up; Nansen's physical location is less tenuous, but his expedition does not have a press, although it does produce the manuscript newspaper *Framsjaa*. Their distress is thus especially keen.

For those expeditions that did have access to presses, though, the polar regions still presented many challenges. The following section describes how polar ice, often evoked in imaginative conjurations of polar spaces or Arctic sublimes in this period, was often a deterrent to textual creation in polar spaces themselves. The printed and other textual media that expedition members ultimately produce are polar ecomedia in the sense that they account for—reflect or incorporate in some way—the very icy conditions in which they were produced, despite manifest hardships.

Ice! Ice!! Ice!!! Is the Handwriting on the Wall

Arctic printing had its mechanical privations, some of which might be readily imagined. Resupplying the press was not an option in the Far North. On the Franklin search ships *Assistance* and *Resolute* printing became "so great a passion" that "at length their stock of paper was run out."[110] The variable range and quality of the materials on which playbills and other ephemera were printed—linen, cloth, silk, oiled paper, chamois—also suggests the limited range of supplies aboard ship, although those substrates were likely also used to create commemorative copies. The extreme cold was an issue as well. Frozen ink had to be melted for each printing session. (An ingenious solution to this problem was invented by the American Charles Francis Hall in maintaining his journals in −40°; it is described in chapter 5.) A note appended to a theatrical playbill by the printer Briant during Belcher's expedition alerted the crew to this contingency: "N.B.—The business of the Printing Office is considerably retarded, in consequence of the ink freezing on the rollers.—Printer's Devil."[111] So widely recognized a consequence of Arctic printing was frozen ink and other writing materials that the circumstance could be invoked for comic effect, as it was in one article, "Departure of the Travelling Parties," a mock diary detailing the brutal conditions experienced by sledging teams while establishing forward depots of provisions: "The M.S.S. here ceases in consequence of the Ink having become solid, an evil which might have been remedied, had not the pencils been already used for fuel." The same article sardonically reports that on 3 October the party "awoke, horribly hot—Ther. −17°."[112] The punchline is that −17° is far warmer than conditions had been for the men, working usually in temperatures below −50°. (Temperatures are given in Fahrenheit unless otherwise indicated.) Extreme temperatures in Antarctica had an effect on the very color of the ink used to illustrate the caricatures in *The Blizzard*, the lighter sister publication to the *South Polar Times* on Scott's 1901–4 *Discovery* expedition: "The severe weather . . . has even affected the ink used in printing, changing it from blue to green, and from green to purple; so if [caricature subjects] do not see the delicate contour, the regular features, and the noble expression that their looking glasses would lead them to expect . . . they must blame the low temperatures which have of late affected the office machinery."[113] Ink was not the only artistic pigment in demand; in fashioning sets for the Arctic theatricals aboard *Assistance*, for example—a ship on which there was "a scarcity of paint"—the resident artist had to improvise paint combinations: "He was reduced to mixtures of 'Day and Martin,' black ink, black-lead, whitening, washing blue, glue, and other unusual ingredients, consisting of chimney-soot and lamp-black, to complete his picture."[114] There may not have been a rich palette of paint colors aboard this particular Arctic mission, but the officers at least had shined shoes, as the reference to the shoe polish brand Day & Martin indicates.

These were not conditions conducive to writing. "I daily applied myself to mental work," wrote Adolphus Greely, yet "the ink froze nightly at my head."[115] A reader of the *Weekly Guy* (the paper for the *Plover*, 1852) wrote to the paper's editor, "I would fain be a contributor to the pages of your periodical," but the sunless winter of their icebound world was an obstacle to inspiration rather than its source: "The hoar winter here conceals from sight / All pleasing objects which to verse invite."[116] There was nothing particularly inspirational about such extreme conditions for Hayes. "Our readers no doubt think it very funny to write an Editorial; thermometer below zero, ink frozen, imagination congealed, memory gone with the summer; thoughts in the sunny south, and feet wrapped up in furs. But there's no fun about it," he complained in the *Port Foulke Weekly News*. "The editor has a very uneasy chair. His bed is not a bed of roses, but a bed of ice. He eats ice, he drinks ice and he even smells ice. . . . Ice! Ice!! Ice!!! is the handwriting on the wall:—The 'MENE, MENE, TEKEL UPHARSIN' of the Arctic Editorial Belshazzar."[117] There will be no futurity in human underestimation of the dominion of ice, Hayes's biblical analogy makes clear.

Ice was destructive to literary cultures in more secular ways, too. Shipboard condensation was an ongoing problem throughout nineteenth-century polar exploration history. Because the interior of the ship was warmer than the exterior, human breath would freeze and the walls would sweat, forming clouds of icy vapor or thin sheets of ice that had to be chipped away. In a scrapbook photo kept by Anton Vedoe of the Fiala-Ziegler Expedition, ice crystals appear thickly clustered on the beams above and alongside the men; the ice looks like badly fraying contemporary asbestos fibers or fiberglass insulation.[118] "Every week or ten days throughout the winter we had to remove from our cabins the ice caused by the condensation of the moist air where it came in contact with the cool outer walls," recalls Robert Peary. "Behind every article of furniture near the outer wall the ice would form, and we used to chop it out from under our bunks by the pailful."[119] Such was the trade-off for having temperatures above freezing in the cabins of the ship; condensation produced the great "annoyance" of "the incessant drip in our cabins and elsewhere on board." The "disagreeable drip" was destructive to books and paper, naturally, and they had be removed from shelves and any position in which they might come into contact with the ship's sides or beams. Markham found it "decidedly unpleasant, whilst writing, to have a continual stream of water pouring down upon your head and upon your paper." One of his messmates, however, "had brought an umbrella with him, and this being spread over his chair protected him from the wet, and thus enabled him to read or write in comparative comfort."[120] A sound plan, indeed, even as one questions why an umbrella would be a necessary item to bring to a High Arctic expedition. When paired with the shoe polish, these trappings of gentlemanly custom show one aspect of maladaptation of British expeditionary preparation to local conditions. A more utilitarian nautical supply might have been a locker for the ship's library. As David H. Stam has shown, on two of his expeditions Peary brought loan libraries in wooden cases that had been provided by the American Seamen's Friend Society.[121] But as Peary's narrative suggests, even lockers did not prevent damage to books caused by condensation: "Books were always placed far forward on the shelves, because if a book were pushed back it would freeze solid to the wall. Then, if a warmer day came, or a fire was built in the cabin, the ice would melt, the water would run down and the leaves of the book would mold."[122]

In such non–climate controlled conditions, other book arts were necessarily practiced as well. The doctor on Fridtjof Nansen's expedition sets up a bookbindery, "greatly patronized by the *Fram*'s library"; this becomes a necessity both on account of condensation and because "several books that are in constant circulation, such as *Gjest Baardsens Liv og Levnet*, etc., etc., are in a very bad state." (Gjest Baardsen was a notorious early nineteenth-century Norwegian thief and escape artist, and this volume, his autobiography, was very popular.) The most extensive trade in the book arts aboard ship, however, is the "manufacture of diaries," Nansen writes, of which every sailor is a producer.[123]

In addition to diary writing and the requisite shipboard recordkeeping and journaling, expedition members supplemented their store of theatrical texts by composing their own.[124] A partial list of plays performed in the Arctic follows, organized in rough chronological order and divided into two generic categories. I have culled this list from playbills, polar periodicals, and voyage narratives; those designated with an asterisk were composed by expedition members aboard ship:

FARCE/COMEDY

* *The North West Passage: or, the Voyage Finished* (*Hecla* and *Griper*)[125]

Miss in Her Teens (*Hecla* and *Griper*)

The Liar (*Hecla* and *Griper*)

The Citizen (*Hecla* and *Griper*)

A Bold Stroke for a Wife (*Hecla* and *Griper*)

The Mayor of Garratt (*Hecla* and *Griper*)

Bon Ton; or, High Life above Stairs (*Hecla* and *Griper*)

Heir-at-Law (*Hecla* and *Griper*)

Queer Subject (*Plover*)

The Original (*Plover*)

* *Fun, Foolery, Frolic, and Mirth* (*Amphitrite*)

Box and Cox (*Amphitrite* and *London*)

King Glumpus (*Investigator*)

Raising the Wind (*Investigator*)

Slasher and Crasher (*Assistance* and *London*)

* *Arctic Pantomime of Zero, or Harlequin Light* (*Resolute* and *Assistance*)[126]

Who Speaks First? (*Resolute*)

The Scapegrace (*Assistance*)

The Irish Tutor (*Assistance*)

The Silent Woman (*Assistance*)

Turned Head (*Assistance*)

Bombastes Furioso (Assistance)

Married Life (Assistance)

The Lottery Ticket (Assistance)

Legerdemain (Intrepid)

Taming [of] the Shrew (Resolute)

The Two Bonnycastles (Resolute)

* *The Countryman (Advance)*

The Blue Devils (Advance)

* *Little Vulgar Boy, or Weeping Bill (Alert)*[127]

* *The Arctic Twin (Alert)*

* *The Ice-Bound Regions (Alert)*[128]

The Chops of the Channel (Alert)

Catch a Weasel (Alert)

Aladdin, or The Wonderful Scamp (Alert)

Vilikins and His Dinah (Alert)

Area Belle (Alert)

Money Makes the Mare Go (Jeannette)

The Siamese Twins (Jeannette)

The Irish Schoolmaster (Jeannette)

HISTORY/TRAGEDY/DRAMA

Hamlet (Assistance)

Charles the Twelfth [A Night with Charles XII. of Sweden, or, A Soldier's Wife's Fidelity] (Resolute and *Assistance)*

Nearly all theatrical performances aboard expedition ships were of one-act farces of the nineteenth century. Many were comedies of manners, and their situational humor may have come, in part, from the opportunity they afforded sailors to cross-dress and engage in various acts of class, gender, and ethnic transgression. They were hugely popular with the crew members, despite open-air performance temperatures that could range in the teens.[129] Arctic plays written in situ were themselves farces, reflecting this distinct generic preference. They include *Arctic Pantomime of Zero, or Harlequin Light*, a farce featuring evil sprites named Frost-Bite, Scorbutus, and

Hunger. "Turning all the dangers and inconveniences to which we are exposed in these inhospitable climates into evil spirits that are leagued against us," the farce stages those malign spirits as "continually watching every opportunity to surprise an unfortunate travelling party, till at length their power is destroyed by the appearance of the more puissant good spirits, Sun and Daylight."[130] It proved a hit; the Royal Arctic Theatre performed the *Pantomime of Zero* on a number of occasions, according to extant playbills. The "original pathetico-comico-burlesque operetta" *Little Vulgar Boy*, written by Chaplain William Pullen ("poet-laureate" of the Nares expedition), was a dramatic adaptation of a poem in *The Ingolsby Legends*, a popular midcentury collection of folk tales and ghost stories. And on Parry's first expedition, when the ship's scanty stock of plays had been run through, Parry wrote a five-act musical entitled *The North West Passage: or, the Voyage Finished*. Its plot described the expedition's hoped-for progress through the Bering Straits (which would have meant achieving the Northwest Passage, which the expedition did not in fact accomplish) and a return home to the Prince of Wales pub to regale their sweethearts with stories of their exertions. The very few dramas or histories performed by polar voyagers seem to reflect either those works' exceptional popularity or familiarity, in the case of *Hamlet*, or a theme of spousal fidelity that would resonate with men on a long voyage.

A talent for dramatic composition and interest in the genre more generally is in line with the observations recorded in the "Literature and Art" column of the *Port Foulke Weekly News*, produced by Hayes's *United States North Pole* expedition. On that venture too "there is an evident preference for dramatic entertainments." Second Mate Henry Dodge, the literature columnist and coeditor of the paper, continues the "Literature and Art" report by noting that the general "taste in literary matters is not inclined to the religious or to the fictitious;—A large invoice of both this class of books having been packed away on Friday morning, as unmarketable."[131] Dodge's own tastes, according to Commander Hayes, esteemed periodicals over religious works, fiction, or plays; by earlier November 1860 the editor had "already consumed several boxes of 'Littell's Living Age' and the 'Westminster Review.'"[132] Dodge's periodic excess registered not just in literature: he was a notorious drunk, according to private diaries kept by several expedition members, even if this behavior is not documented in Hayes's *Open Polar Sea*.[133] (This discrepancy between expeditionary accounts demonstrates that official voyage narratives rarely, if ever, give the full story of personnel matters.) His alcohol abuse did not interfere with his work for the expedition newspaper, though; Dodge was a frequent and talented contributor.

In a provocative and bitingly funny "Literature" column in the *Port Foulke Weekly News* with which I will close this chapter, Dodge writes, "We are such an enlightened set of mortals that Books are unnecessary either for our amusement, or knowledge." In fact, Dodge writes blithely, "we know enough." Demonstrating their collective knowledge, he boasts:

> We all know who wrote Shakespeare; we all know that John Bunyon wrote Paradise Lost; we all know that Napoleon Bonaparte was the greatest general of his age, until he was defeated by Caesar the Great, who in his turn was defeated by General Walker, who is now the greatest man alive. We all know that in 1942 a man by the name of Columbus discovered the New World, in a small vessel called the "Great Eastern," and that he opposed the landing of the Pilgrims, in which engagement he was killed. . . .
>
> What, then, is the use of books? It is a great deal better to employ our time in learning the art of spinning yarns, and in acquiring a knowledge of the valuable sciences of "cribbage," "faro," "vingt et un," "Kimi, &c." . . .
>
> Then who cares for books; is it not better to be able to amuse "my mess" with yarns, which are of old standing, may be a hundred years old (in which of course "I" am the principle actor) than to be able to answer our "learned Astronomer" why we have so many successive months of darkness and light here? Of course it is! Then overboard with the books! who cares for "general information"? Not I! I would rather read one copy of the "N. Y. Ledger" or "Clipper," than the whole ships company's collection of books.[134]

Within the pages of a ship's newspaper, Dodge elevates the value of newspapers over books. He cites as proof of the exhaustion of books' value the sufficiency of knowledge gained by the crew of the *United States*. But their knowledge is, of course, inaccurate, comically so. Instead sailors trust their own yarn spinning, storytelling practices. Dodge is wittily playing with the idea of sailor knowledge—what I have called maritime epistemology or the "sea eye" and what Margaret Cohen has called sailors' "know how"—as more properly the province of experience and oral history than abstract book knowledge.[135] Yet Dodge's humor is also at the expense of the kind of information that newspapers provide, and in this sense he anticipates Walter Benjamin's well-traveled sailor-storyteller, long on experience and ill-served by "general information." Yet for Dodge (unlike Benjamin), the impoverished media form providing unwelcome information is books rather than the newspapers that Dodge embraces.

Dodge's "Literature" column stresses the communal vividness of sailor forms of narrative media and the collective experience represented therein. In the case of the *Port Foulke Weekly News* of Hayes's *United States* expedition, and the papers of polar expeditions more broadly, the challenge of collective experience is building and representing community in geophysical and climatic extremity. The printing press became a tool in facing that challenge.

TWO

ARCTIC NEWS

And indeed, what they wanted to talk about all along, was the Ocean. Somehow they could not get to the Topick. Neither Clock really knows what it is,—beyond an undeniably rhythmick Being of some sort,—tho' they've spent most of their lives in Range of it, sometimes no more than a Barrel-Stave and a Hull-Plank away. Its Wave-beats have ever been with them, yet can neither quite say, where upon it they may lie. What they feel is an Attraction, more or less resistible, to beat in Synchrony with it, regardless of their Pendulum-lengths, or even the divisions of the Day. The closest they come to talking of it is when the Shelton Clock confides, "I really don't like Ships much."
— THOMAS PYNCHON, *Mason and Dixon* (2004)

I would rather read one copy of the "N.Y. Ledger" or "Clipper," than the whole ships company's collection of books.
— HENRY DODGE, "Literature," *Port Foulke Weekly News* (1860)

Thomas Pynchon's novel *Mason and Dixon* features two sentient, chatty sea clocks who are curious about the relationship of linear, terrestrial time to the weird temporalities of the sea. Stashed together briefly on the remote South Atlantic island of St. Helena in the mid-eighteenth century, the clocks discover that the cadence of the sea allows their sensitive pendulums to speak to one another, as the first epigraph details. The clocks understand that the ocean is "an undeniably rhythmick Being of some sort" and feel an "Attraction" to those rhythms. Yet both the Ellicott Clock and the Shelton Clock (made by eighteenth-century clockmasters so named) find it "more or less resistible, to beat in Synchrony with it, regardless of their Pendulum-lengths, or even the divisions of the Day." The irregularity of the swells both compels the clocks and repels them; to join in oceanic Synchrony would be a rejection of the imperial time they are designed to keep. As entities whose function is to ensure that sailors are tied to the metropole (to Greenwich Mean Time) for the sake of navigational accuracy, the clocks must, to their vague regret, stand in permanent obliquity to the time of the sea. This is why the Shelton and Ellicott clocks "somehow . . . could not get to the Topick" of the Ocean, even though it is "what they wanted to talk about all along."

Arctic sailors too are looking for ways to stage conversations about oceanic registers of time. They too find that remaining in touch with Greenwich time puts them at odds with the ecological rhythms that structure their polar life. Shipboard newspapers, as this chapter describes, became the mechanism for their conversations about polar temporalities. Arctic newspapers began as a novel way for expedition members to amuse and distract themselves during the darkness and relative inactivity of a polar winter, in the same spirit in which crew members mounted theatricals and participated in other entertainments such as dancing, magic lantern shows, lectures, and singing. Dramatic performances and dances might concede some limitations in staging and orchestration aboard an icebound ship thousands of miles from London or Philadelphia, yet the structural expectations for the participants and audience of a play or a waltz do not materially differ in the Arctic. This is not, however, the case for newspapers. If newspapers are generally defined by their seriality, topicality, accessibility, diversity of coverage, and compass of address, then Arctic newspapers were in violation of these terms nearly across the board. In a region without diurnal time measurements, papers did not appear regularly. The majority of ships had no interaction with the rest of the Anglophone world (and thus no possibility for broader news reports or circulation) for at least six months of the year. Contributors to Arctic papers signaled their awareness of a lack of material with which to populate the sections of a conventional paper by creating parodies of them: mock classified ads or comical real estate sections. Shipboard papers might have been available to the vessel's crew, but they rarely circulated or were much acknowledged publicly upon an expedition's return home. The members of the community constituted by polar papers were always within one hundred feet of each other, even though they might be flung far from the reach of other Anglophone readers.[1]

A crowded, competitive British journalistic field helped drive interest in Arctic exploration early in the nineteenth century, as scholars have detailed;

the various London and other British metropolitan papers sought to scoop not just each others' gazettes but also the voyage narratives that publishers (particularly John Murray) would publish with the Admiralty's imprimatur shortly after expeditions returned home.[2] The journalism produced by actual polar expedition members has not been the focus of scholarship to date, and when Arctic newspapers are briefly mentioned they are seen by such critics as amusing provincial analogues to their more established cousins. Yet Arctic papers are not simply displaced, parodic versions of the familiar periodical metropolitan or national titles. As I argue in this chapter, in their creation of Arctic newspapers polar sailors are attempting to work through an appropriate textual response, in both temporal and literary terms, to the nonnormative time and nonnormative forms of community and everyday life in which they find themselves in the ice of polar winter. A theater may operate without formal alteration in the Arctic, in other words, but when mounted in polar spaces a daily or weekly newspaper becomes generically eccentric. In exploring what kind of media is sufficient to polar spaces, British and American expeditions in the North explore their own relationships to the regulatory functions of literary genres associated with nationalism, to the space of shipboard community, and to Arctic time. In the loose, comic form of the newspapers produced by expedition members, we see their acknowledgment of the futility—the incongruity—of impressing serial, diurnal, and national temporal narratives upon Arctic spaces.

This chapter focuses on polar newspapers aboard British and American expeditionary ships in the Far North, with attention to their putative objectives, the literary content and generic range of contributions to the papers, and the climatic and material conditions that structured the continuation or cessation of the periodicals' circulation. The responsibilities of literary citizenship within such an Arctic periodical community became the preoccupation, in fact, of the first polar paper (the *North Georgia Gazette, and Winter Chronicle*), which predated others in the genre by nearly thirty years but did not succeed on the terms established by its expedition leaders, as the opening section of this chapter describes. After the *North Georgia Gazette*, the sphere of circulation of newspapers in the North changes from one restricted to the officers, to a broader practice of marking time that incorporated the entire expeditionary crew. Subsequent Arctic papers likewise demonstrate a reconception of the relationship between expeditionary crews and polar environmental spaces in both place and time. The newspaper genre of polar ecomedia comes into being as a result of the habits and practices that are designed to ensure survival and endurance while overwintering. What Arctic papers achieve, ultimately, is the formulation of a generically sophisticated theory of polar writing.

The Winter Chronicle of Their Discontent

The first polar newspaper, the *North Georgia Gazette, and Winter Chronicle* (1819–20), was not printed but rather circulated in manuscript.[3] The *Winter Chronicle*, as it was called within its own pages, was written in the Arctic by the officers of William Edward Parry's British Northwest Passage Expedition, which consisted of nearly one hundred men, about twenty of whom were officers. Parry pioneered the tactic of deliberately spending the winter on the ice; whereas previous Arctic missions had foundered if unable to return to open water before the cold season set in, Parry prepared for and embraced the prospect of a long, frozen sojourn above the Arctic Circle. Winter recreation included plays and dancing, and "In order still further to promote good-humour among ourselves, as well as to furnish amusing occupation, during the hours of constant darkness," Parry wrote, the ship would "set on foot a weekly newspaper." He named Captain Edward Sabine (who helmed the expedition's sister ship) as editor and hoped the gazette would serve the purpose of "diverting the mind from the gloomy prospect which would sometimes obtrude itself on the stoutest heart."[4]

The newspaper's charge to bring recreation and pleasure to its intimate sphere of circulation, however, found a more electric transference than Parry had anticipated. Over the course of its issues, the newspaper's sense of fun and play began to curdle over a staged feud between the contributors and the noncontributors, or NCs, to the paper—all of whom were officers. But when the expedition's success and popularity resulted in republication in London of the *North Georgia Gazette, and Winter Chronicle*, Parry suppressed many of the most barbed articles on the NCs. The wit that had circulated among their coterie was disallowed from circulation in the literary sphere outside of the ship's own economy. The expedition officers' presumptions of private, intimate, collaborative mutuality were compromised in and altered by publication, in other words, and the effect was to call into question the very premises of joint endeavor and mutuality undergirding the expedition itself. The broader result was that neither Parry nor any other Arctic commanders would attempt another shipboard newspaper for nearly thirty years. While the content of the *Winter Chronicle* was similar to the contributions that would characterize later nineteenth-century Arctic papers, its mode of community and spatial address differed. For Parry and the other officers who wrote for the paper, the tether of "home" (whether understood as Britain, the Admiralty, or naval hierarchy) was strong. The *Winter Chronicle* does not evince the epistemological commitment to writing from and about polar spaces that later papers would have; the form of the periodical had not yet adapted itself to the ecologically specific conditions consistent with later polar ecomedia. The example of Parry's paper is key to understanding the rich body of Arctic newspapers that would ensue later in the century.

The initial number of the *Winter Chronicle* proposed to circulate the paper "amongst the Officers of the Expedition," who acted as content providers; editor Edward Sabine claimed that he was "wholly dependent on the Gentleman of the Expedition" for the success of the paper.[5] The contributions were delivered anonymously and published pseudonymously.[6] As in later papers, the tone of the contributions to the *Chronicle* reflect its recreational aims: articles include reviews of shipboard theatricals in addition to the lyrics of expedition-themed songs written and performed at the ship's winter quarters. Other genres featured in the paper are riddles and enigmas, mock-advertisements and notices, and analyses of the social habits of the expedition's dogs. One "Nauticus" tried to submit a mathematical problem, but it was rejected for its simplicity; it failed to "exercise the ingenuity" of the crew (1:15).[7] Even though the paper's editor, Captain Sabine, later wrote that "at the time [the issues] were composed, not the remotest idea was entertained of their fulfilling any other purpose than that of relieving the tedium of an Arctic Winter, and perhaps of afterwards affording amusement to a few private friends at home," the *Chronicle* was in fact printed in London a year after the expedition's return, in response to "the interest which the Public took in all that had passed during the voyage." In the prefatory note to the printed edition of the paper, Sabine trusts that the contributors "may be allowed to claim from the general reader the same indulgence, which they would have received, had the perusal of the Chronicle been confined to the partial circle to which they originally intended it should have been limited" (v).[8] The implied reader of the *Winter Chronicle* remains Arctic-bound, even as Sabine's language evokes the conventions of first-person narrative writing: an apology for deficiencies of circumstance, which we are told have been uncorrected upon publication.

Yet despite Sabine's promise that "no alteration has been attempted in the respective papers, in preparing them for the press," the printed edition nevertheless excised a good number of articles and letters from the manuscript version. The decision about which pieces to cut seems to have been made by Parry himself.[9] One might expect that the expurgations made for the sake of public circulation of the gazette would be of material that was racy, crude, or nonsensical. This is not, however, the case; Parry's censorship focuses largely on articles that concern a supposed feud among the officers on the question of who is adequately contributing to the expedition's mission. The majority of the excised pieces consist of an ongoing series of editorials, letters, and fictional stories proposing outlandishly violent reprisals against the NCs. The NCs are singled out for not contributing specifically to the paper, I will stress; there is no indication that their contributions to the broader polar mission are deficient. This is not to say that concerns about the noncontributors did not make it into the print version; in fact the contents of the late issues in volume 21 of the *Chronicle* were increasingly dominated by articles on the NCs. At their most mild, the articles wonder whether the noncontributors lack the wit to contribute; at their most heated, the contributors threaten to multiply behead the "many-headed monster, the *Encea Borealis*, vulgarly called N.C.," or to brand their counterparts "with a red-hotte ironne, fashioned after the letters N.C." The latter, in fact, is drawn from the one piece Parry identified for omission that for an unknown reason made its way into the paper: an example of the genre of fiction in which a narrator finds a superannuated manuscript account, which he in turn presents to the reader. In this short fiction, the found manuscript describes an expedition to the Arctic in which certain members refuse to participate in "merrie-making"; the captain withholds their rations in punishment, for "those which do not benefitte the Communitie, the Communitie is not bounded to benefittee *them*" (MS *Chronicle* No. 9). These tensions, while real, were largely rhetorical. No sailors were branded or beheaded on the expedition. Parry's identification of the pseudonymous contributors shows that the fight was pitched between and among the top-ranking officers writing variously as NCs and as contributors.

But even though the tone of both the printed and the excised articles is satirical, the rhetorical playfulness of the attacks on the noncontributors cannot disguise a very serious concern: that not all expedition members were fairly sharing in the mission's labors and in its rewards. The suppressed pieces, in particular, reveal an escalating distress and mock anger over the differences between the contributing and noncontributing members of the expedition. Sabine's notion of a "partial circle" of readers is key to this tension. And as a reflexive gesture to the severely limited circulation of the paper, it is also disingenuous, like all such gestures in genres of coterie writing.

The articles in the *North Georgia Gazette, and Winter Chronicle*—and indeed those of later polar newspapers as well—are finely tuned to their intimate sphere of circulation, given all the inside jokes and event- and place-specific references. In the *Winter Chronicle* this attention is most keenly felt in terms of the paper's role in fostering and reflecting collaborative labor. The paper's existence was wholly reliant on full participation in its production, the editorial statements said repeatedly. In just the second issue of the paper, Sabine was sounding the alarm to those who had not yet contributed: "I would also remind those who are yet silent, that *now* is the time when support is most needed; when, if every person will put his shoulder to the wheel in earnest, (and each individual may command his own exertions,) there can be no doubt that your Paper will go on with spirit" (2:15). Sabine's metaphor of self-directed manual labor aside, this call for writerly work was issued to a coterie within a coterie: the twenty-odd officers sharing exceptionally tight quarters with nearly eighty "men," the seamen not holding officer status.

We see this worry about the failure of collectivity in a poem directed to the NCs by one of the expedition's lieutenants, writing as "Timothy Tickle'em." In the poem—which was one of the ones Parry struck from appearance in print—we learn of the contributors' plan "to tear their characters to bits" upon the expedition's return home:

> The Churls, I vow, who *cannot* write
> Aught to be hang'd, or shot outright,
> As useless Vermin who destroy
> The food we should alone enjoy
> But wherefore spend our words in vain,
> When all our hints inflict no pain?
> We'll roar it out to all the world,
> When once again our sails are furl'd:
> . . . .
> Thus, my dear friends, we'll serve each knave,
> Who does not chuse to send his stave,
> And if we can't excite their shame,
> At home, at last, we'll brand their name. (MS *Chronicle* No. 14)

This poem excited "considerable foment" among the NCs, we learn from a suppressed letter to the editor, written by Parry himself. The vow, when back in England to "shame" or "brand" the name of those who did not contribute, is seen in other contributions, such as the punishment mentioned above of branding the letters NC on an offender's cheeks. What is notable is that these threats to expose the noncontributors to the broader social and professional world—however humorously intended in the manuscript or coterie newspaper—are nevertheless censored from the public record of the printed newspaper. They wished to keep the rhetorical exercise of noncontribution within the world of the expedition only.

Even though threats of beating or hanging noncontributors are not meant to be taken literally, one presumes, a response from a supposed NC-sympathizer (identified as Lieutenant Henry Parkyns Hoppner, a very frequent contributor to the *Chronicle*) in the form of a letter to the editor (likewise censored from the print version) seems to take the larger social and professional threat more seriously. The poem by Timothy Tickle'em, the correspondent writes, "seemed to express a degree of malice that I imagined never would have been permitted to creep into [the *Chronicle*'s] columns, which I always fancied, were originally intended to afford amusement to *our own little circle*." The writer's stress here on the "*little circle*" of this coterie newspaper's audience is significant; the frequency of the attacks on those not writing for the paper means the noncontributors had legitimate reasons to fear losing face in the social and professional spheres back home. What is more, the NCs' concerns seem to have been ongoing, as the letter continues: "The spiteful pleasure which your Correspondent anticipates in pointing out the Non-Contributors to those who have no concern in the affair will, I fear, give just grounds for strengthening the apprehensions that many entertained before, of similar intentions" (MS *Chronicle* No. 15). The fear on behalf of the NCs of the possibility of a "stain on their characters" seems to hit a nerve; the letter from the defender of the noncontributors concludes, "Although the N.C.'s may be wrong, still they do not deserve . . . that stain upon their Characters which this, and some other Articles are likely to impress on the minds of readers who are unacquainted with circumstances" (MS *Chronicle* No. 15). This remark, made by a pseudonymous contributor, shows a presumption of an audience outside the orbit of their polar sphere. The social tension staged is palpable here, and the paper's editor, Captain Sabine, appended a judicious note to the letter of protest, which said that Sabine would have questioned the letter-writer had he known who he was. The "lines in question did not strike us as written with any such ill-design," Sabine explains, but allows that although "we may . . . have been mistaken, but we really do not perceive what occasion any individual amongst us can have for a 'malicious feeling' toward the persons who have not written for the Winter Chronicle" (MS *Chronicle*

No. 15). This measured justification stands in contrast to the bombastic affectation of the newspaper's previously published threats against the bodies and reputations of the noncontributors.

A follow-up letter from the author of the threatening poem, Timothy Tickle'em (again, one omitted from the London publication of the paper), asks facetiously what the NC fear—that the "Admiralty will seek out the names of those two or three individuals out of 20, who have never written for the Winter Chronicle?" No, the contributor argues; "the N.C.'s must know, that the knowledge even of the *existence* of a paper among us must necessarily be confined to a very limited circle; & that whatever stigma is brought upon them on this account, is one of their own seeking." The presumption of intimacy, of a private society outside of state relations, is key to this contributor's position, as he continues: "If the contributions to the Winter Chronicle were to be regulated by law, like the Income-tax, according to each man's *ability* to contribute, it is evident how woefully the N.C.'s would be in arrears!" (MS *Chronicle* No. 16). This letter relocates the social threat of noncontribution to the immediate officer coterie of the expedition itself rather than the broader English professional world. It also suggests what may be lost in translation when polar ecomedia is removed from polar spaces.

As it turns out, Parry's manuscript edition of the *Chronicle* reveals that the proportion of contributors was far less than that claimed in the letter quoted above (that is, that only "two or three individuals out of 20" were NCs). Parry's copy identifies virtually all the authors of the pseudonymous contributions, and we find there were a total of ten contributors. Three of the ten, however, contributed just one or two pieces to the paper. The seven frequent contributors were Parry, Captain Sabine, several other lieutenants, and the ship's clerk and purser. The three who made only a few contributions, however, were all midshipmen, the lowest class of officers. And among these midshipmen is one John Bushnan, whom Parry identifies as the author of the letter from "N.C."—his only contribution to the *Chronicle*. Midshipmen, who had just begun their professional naval careers, would have the most to fear from threats to their reputation. This would be especially true in the case of the *Chronicle*, in which the spats and disputes are all staged among high-ranking officers writing pseudonymously.

But officers, of course, were not the only members of the expedition. None of the "men" aboard ship—the able seamen, boatswain's and carpenter's mates, eighty-odd all told—seems to have contributed to the paper. Nor is it clear that they necessarily read it, although the men serving at the officers' mess would have the occasion to overhear the reading aloud of the *Chronicle* over a meal and to spread its contents among the common seamen.[10] Perhaps a seaman might have been given one of the manuscript copies of the paper, but it would likely have been something acquired under the table. This sense is reinforced by another unprinted letter to the editor. This short note is signed by "Timothy Hint" and expresses pointedly the stresses of keeping labor expectations in balance. Here is the note, in full: "It is a well-known fact in the Natural History of Bees, that a certain part of the year, the working Bees confederate to turn the *Drones* out of the Hive; perhaps some one of your Correspondents may know at what part of the year this circumstance usually takes place, and whether it differs in different climates" (MS *Chronicle* No. 14). Worker bees do virtually all of the labor in the beehive, including catering to the drones, whose only function is to be available to impregnate the queen bee—at which point the drone dies. Also relevant, given the Arctic setting, is the fact that the turning out of the drones from the hive usually happens in early winter, when the *Winter Chronicle* was launched. The letter, written by second-in-command (and *Chronicle* editor) Sabine, could indicate a coded fear, however wry, that the workers (that is, the common seamen of the voyage) might feel collectively mutinous against the drones (the officers). The potential for insurrection would be no laughing matter at sea, of course, where mutinous sailors potentially faced death. Less than two months before the *North Georgia Gazette, and Winter Chronicle* shut down production, a letter from a correspondent named "Peter Plainway"—Parry himself—asserted a resurgence of collective work and goodwill. Notably, this letter appears in the fourteenth volume of the London version, where it was printed in place of the provocative Timothy Tickle'em poem, which had opened that particular issue in the manuscript version of the *Chronicle*. Parry claims that it "is evident, that the number of [the paper's] Correspondents is weekly increasing. . . . The N.C.s!—but alas the very name is now almost extinct" (14: 53). "Extinct" in the printed *North Georgia Gazette*, perhaps, but alive and kicking in the manuscript version, and therefore among the officers during the expedition.

Parry had intended for the newspaper to "emplo[y] the mind" and "divert the leisure hours"; he had anticipated no "unpleasant consequences" of giving his men a literary outlet for their opinions.[11] Yet the expedition's surgeon, Alexander Fisher, reveals in his own narrative of the voyage that there was, in fact, reason to worry about the consequences of giving the men license to free expression. Fisher's narrative is taken from the journal he kept during the voyage; the following concerns about the *Winter Chronicle* were presumably recorded before its first numbers appeared:

> I have no doubt but it will answer its end, that is, of diverting the men; but . . . I am not quite so certain of its answering its purpose so well, for I have seen one or two instances, and have heard of many more, where newspapers on board of ship, instead of affording general amusement, and promoting friendship and a good understanding amongst officers, tended in a short time to destroy both . . . until at length the paper, instead of being the source of amusement and instruction, becomes the vehicle of sarcasms and bitter reflections.[12]

Fisher was himself a noncontributor. A contemporary review of the *Chronicle* (one not familiar with the unexpurgated version of the gazette) pointed out that injunctions against wounding the feelings of members of the group serve only to weaken the junto's literary output; forbidding hurt feelings is "a law as destructive to mirth and quizzery, as that of political libel would be to free opinion. . . . It seems absolutely to have assisted the climate to freeze up the spirit of *fun* altogether."[13] During Parry's first expedition, the newspaper did not serve the function of plays on British ships, which were understood to be safe, contained spaces for playacting resentments and disrupting hierarchies. In fact, in one striking example sailors on a prison ship staged a play about the Haitian Revolution.[14] Parry would go on to command two more successful Arctic expeditions, with increasingly elaborate costumes and props for theatricals. Yet he never again permitted a newspaper.

Joking about noncontribution by high-ranking officers was all very well when it was an internal matter, a private manuscript newspaper. But as the more incendiary pieces in the *Chronicle*—all written by major officers— were withheld from the version printed for the public, the actual attribution of the suppressed articles says a good deal about how Parry's men imagined the intelligibility of their experience to the broader world, how they imagined their literary collectivity as something apart from their professional collectivity. This bifurcation would not continue, as future Arctic expeditionary papers did not confine their contributor list to the officer corps and ceased to consider the metropoles of the temperate zones as at all part of their orbit of circulation.

British and American polar expeditions launched less frequently in the 1830s; the British Admiralty was conserving its resources, and the United States devoted its oceanic expeditionary energies to the Exploring Expedition led by Charles Wilkes (1838–42). When Sir John Franklin's Northwest Passage expedition sailed in 1845, it was the first British mission in nearly a decade. (George Back had led the single Royal Navy mission of the 1830s.) Newspapers also returned to the Arctic in the late 1840s, after nearly three decades in which expeditions chose other winter pastimes. Their reemergence was an effect, in part, of technological innovations in portable tabletop printing presses; the presses were initially designated for use in the Arctic to print thousands of rescue ship location notifications to aid in the search for the lost Franklin expedition. The searches that began in 1848 for Franklin and his men inaugurated a new boom in Arctic exploration, which in turn gave rise to the shipboard newspaper production and printing that would become a new convention in polar expeditionary practice. An important factor among the reasons polar papers caught on with expeditions in the second half of the nineteenth century (and were of less interest in the 1820s and 1830s after Parry's initial experiment) was the availability of tabletop printing press technology, as I discussed in chapter 1. The form of the newspaper in turn gave polar venturers an intellectual space in which to experiment with notions of both time in the absence of diurnal regulation and the "new" in the face of monotony.

Franklin's ships *Erebus* and *Terror* and their combined crew of 129 men had sailed in 1845, and by 1847 there were concerns in Britain that there had been no word of the expedition in two years. The *Plover* was one of the first Franklin searches, engaged as of 1848 in that "important mission to relieve our fellow countrymen in distress."[15] The *Plover* was provided with a small press by the British Admiralty—Elaine Hoag suggests that this press might have been folio-foolscap size—which on the *Plover*'s subsequent voyage of 1852–54 would be employed in printing relief messages designed for distribution with the Yupik and Inuit of the western Arctic.[16] The *Plover*'s surgeon, John Simpson, established a newspaper in 1848 entitled *Flight of the Plover, or the North Pole Charivari*.[17] Its objectives, Simpson wrote in its inaugural number with a medical-professional interest, were "to employ the hours of idleness on our passage in mental exercises, that may, we hope be conducive to the general amusement and hilarity of our small society."[18] The *Flight of the Plover* was to be published monthly, the first issue proclaimed on March 1, 1848. The early spring date is notable, as this season of production would not continue to be observed for later Arctic periodicals, which were written during the winter months in which ships were stilled by ice and polar night.[19] Subsequent periodicals began in October or November and generally lasted (if they carried on that long) until January or February, when the returning light and increased work of the spring sledging season turned the crew's attention to different forms of exercise, mental or otherwise. Simpson stresses the need to cultivate "amusement and hilarity" among the crew in order to maintain morale during a long, uncomfortable, and potentially fruitless cruise. Unlike the earlier *North Georgia Gazette, and Winter Chronicle*, whose circulation was limited to the mission's officers, the *Flight of the Plover* and all subsequent Arctic papers extended the "amusement" of the paper to the entire crew.

The form of hilarity taken by the *Flight of the Plover, or North Pole Charivari* was not the crudity by which sailors were stereotyped in the nineteenth century (although it should be acknowledged that polar missions staffed a somewhat more elite class of seamen). The newspaper was born of literary jokes and puns, as a poem by Lieutenant William Hulme Hooper insists. As he details in its origin story, an untitled poem that forms part of the first issue's opening article, Hooper and four shipmates were clustered intimately in his cabin, "at least *three* in, *one* half without," playing the literary dozens:

In converse pleasant, yarns now spinning
On books or morals sage debating
One on our ears had puns a drumming
The rest him for them soundly rating
"What a rum cove must that queer prophet
He of Khorassan veiled, I mean,"
Says one: "of whom Tom Moore made profit
In Lalla Rookh, as if he'd been
A most enchanting sort of creature—
Fancy his phiz now all who can
What'ere you think I'll bet I'll beat your
Most horrid pictures of this man—
He must have been a Knowing Codger
To cheat his victims with a veil,
What an infernal artful dodger!
To make so slight a screen avail."

. . . .

"A serpent's mouth and forked tongue his is
T'enchant the maidens while they're kissing."
At this we laughed & talking went
Of other Books to take a [blank]
Until one evening well nigh spent
"I vote" says one, "we copy *Punch*"![20]

The idea is greeted rapturously by Hooper's companions, who fall to naming suggestions, after which Hooper determines that "if none else will chaper / I'll edit, sure, myself the Paper." The verse displays an awareness of the contemporary literary scene, as well as a capacity for playful critique of various of its elements. The proposal to copy *Punch*, the widely popular British satirical weekly, sets an editorial tone that would be followed in most Arctic newspapers: the contents of the papers were generally comic and farcical. The subtitle of *Punch* was *London Charivari*, which is given a nod by the *North Pole Charivari* subtitle of *Flight of the Plover*. A charivari is a noisy, discordant, mock serenade or din, often made crudely with pots and pans; thus the papers' titles and subtitles conjoin lofty ambition with humorous self-deprecation about the instruments employed in the contributors' literary soundings. The poem also demonstrates the familiarity of the crew with literary taste and convention: for one, they joke about the seeming superiority of conversations about "books and morals" to the making of bad puns (their frequent practice, in fact); they then engage in speculation about Thomas Moore's *Lalla Rookh* (1817), a popular Orientalist romance featuring a veiled prophet from Khorassan, or Persia. The *Plover* crew members' interest is in the "phiz," or face, beneath the veil: What must the prophet have been concealing?

Their fascination with the disguised oracular figure might reflect the attraction of anonymity to men confined to a small ship with little privacy; it could at the same time be a nod to the practice of anonymous article submission that was routine with polar periodicals, as well as to many magazines back in the metropole. The crew members' discussion invokes Dickens's "artful dodger" from *Oliver Twist* and shows sufficient ease and facility with the contemporary literary scene to mock it. (Other popular novels in circulation on Arctic expeditions included *Pickwick Papers*, *Two on a Tower*, *The Old Curiosity Shop*, *Tom Jones*, *Gulliver's Travels*, *The Lady of the Lake*, *Pride and Prejudice*, *Typee*, and *Omoo*.)[21] An omitted word at one point in the poem—at least, a word omitted in the copy of the *Flight of the Plover* that Simpson brought home; the original edition may have included it—seems to be a vulgarity that raises the rhetorical stakes of this mockery. Imagining what is beneath the veil of the prophet of Khorassan, Hooper speculates: "'A serpent's mouth and forked tongue his is / T'enchant the maidens while they're kissing.' / At this we laughed & talking went / Of other Books to take a [blank]." In order for the final line to scan, and to rhyme, the empty space left in the page should signify a trochee that rhymes with "kissing." It seems likely that the missing words are "piss on" or "piss in."[22] One of the functions of polar periodicals is to stand as social media, as in-house scandal sheets; there are inside jokes to which nonexpedition members will not have access. Thus while this may be a metaliterary joke, the men of the *Plover* may also be lampooning someone in particular. The comfort of the contributors with dispersing irreverence among the crew as a whole marks another difference from the *North Georgia Gazette*'s more narrow and more anxious mode of address. This inaugural poem fulfills the objective that Simpson claimed for the *Flight of the Plover*, that "fun and frolic" would mix with "more sober narration" to the "good and laudable" end of fostering community and providing mental exercise.[23] This aim was shared with other Arctic papers.

The *Illustrated Arctic News* of the *Resolute* (commanded by Horatio Austin during a Franklin search in 1850–51), another Franklin search expedition, was likewise founded on "amusement," designed "to relieve the monotony of sunless days—to show to all, that fun & good fellowship, may exist" in constant night.[24] Provocatively the *Illustrated Arctic News* differentiates the "strange, & ever changing phenomena of Nature" in the "desolation of Land & Ice" into which the mission has ventured, from the "the ruins of an old World" which also invite the crew's contemplation. Within the context of exploratory expeditions more generally, the language of old and new worlds is inescapably imperialist or colonialist, primarily associated with the Columbian encounter with the Americas. Such suggestions are in part inevitable, given the northern Canadian location of the Northwest Passage ventures and related Franklin searches. Yet Arctic expeditions did not long retain a vision of any practical colonialist future in the Far North, despite the presence of Inuit, Iñupiat, Sami, Yupik, and other indigenous communities; attention quickly shifted more fully to the other telos for Arctic exploration: resource extraction and commercial transportation via the Northwest Passage. (We can see an echo of this interest in global exchange in the Oriental imagery of the *Lalla Rookh* invocation in the *Flight of the Plover*.) The articulations of Old and New World imaginaries within polar periodicals, then, refer less to imperial

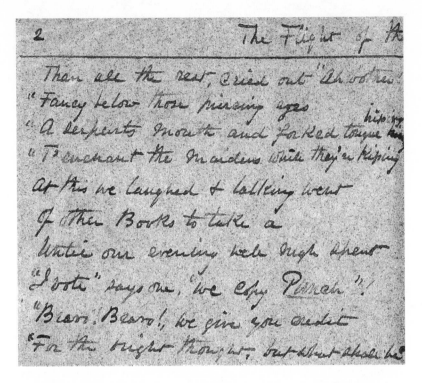

FIG 2.1 — Detail from *Flight of the Plover, or the North Pole Charivari* 1 (1 Mar. 1848):
2 (Editor's Folio), Box 1, Folder: Accounts of Voyages, John Simpson Papers, 1825–1875.
DAVID M. RUBENSTEIN RARE BOOK AND MANUSCRIPT LIBRARY, DUKE UNIVERSITY.

fantasies than to the sense of total removal and abstraction from their known world felt by expedition members, immobilized in regions without familiar communication or transportation networks, without light. In this sense Anglo-American expeditions were ever in error, as Inuit communication networks were robust; the refusal of many white Westerners to engage with or credit indigenous knowledge has been costly in multiple ways for hundreds of years.[25] Even if the atemporal remoteness of the Old World rendered it unavailable to their Arctic lives—which could not be characterized as day-to-day lives, in the absence of the diurnal regulatory orb—polar crews could nonetheless create worlds anew from the "strange, & ever changing phenomena" of their frozen world within the compass of their own imaginative purview.

A sense of world-encompassing "ruin" might be underwriting the legitimate concern expeditions had for the psychological equilibrium of their crews, given their long-term isolation in sunless Arctic winters. For this reason, in part, shipboard newspapers were conceived of as a tonic to "enliven the dull solitude of our winter, and under its benign influence dispel dark despondency from our minds," as a review of the *Aurora Borealis*, a newspaper published by the *Assistance*, the sister ship of the *Resolute*, explained in the *Illustrated Arctic News*. To the "dark rigours of an Arctic Winter" and the "dreary waste of these inhospitable regions," the review continues, the "brilliant coruscations of wit" on display in Arctic newspapers would bring "lustrous rays of light."[26] Twenty-five years later the mental health benefits of shipboard newspapers had been well established. Indeed a stipulation that crew members contribute to the general society on ship was part of Arctic recruiting; as Albert Hastings Markham, second in command of the British Arctic expedition of 1875–76, recalled, "'Can you sing or dance? or what can you do for the amusement of others?' were questions invariably addressed to candidates for Arctic service by the board of officers appointed to select from the numerous applicants who presented themselves."[27] By the time of George Nares's 1875–76 expedition, a newspaper was an Arctic expectation. "Every effort was made to preserve the health of the crew," the expedition's surgeon recorded in the mission's official proceedings, "and to alleviate as much as possible the monotony of the dreary winter. A newspaper was printed periodically."[28] To the Admiralty and to commanders, a primary objective of the publication of Artic newspapers was mental health (as "it is, in fact, very necessary to exercise both the physical and mental powers of the men during the dark months"), although this might not be our primary association with the function of periodicals more generally— unless we think of this form of health in terms of the enlightenment ideal of an educated public as a common good.[29] But this sense of community was no abstraction; shipboard communities constituted the entirety of the world imagined by Arctic publications, and the healthy operation of such communities could be a matter of life or death.

In emphasizing the health benefits afforded by the newspaper, periodicals noted that the editorial function was frequently taken up by the ship's doctor, whose medical services, ideally, would then be little required thanks to the crew's salubrious labors. The Norwegian explorer Fridtjof Nansen appointed his ship's doctor as the "irresponsible editor" of the manuscript paper written during the *Fram* expedition (1893–96; the gazette was called *Framsjaa*, or "news of, or outlook from, the *Fram*"). A poem entitled "Winter in the Ice" in the opening number explains:

The doctor here on board has nought to do, boys;
Not a man to test his skill among the crew, boys;
Well may he look blue,
There's nought for him to do,
When every man is strong and hearty too, boys.
"Now on the *Fram*," boys,
He says "I am," boys,
"Chief editor of newspaper for you!" boys.[30]

The newspapers aboard the *Fram* and elsewhere not only serve as the means of producing health among the community; they become the evidence for the health of the shipboard society in a mutually constitutive relationship. And in the case of Arctic exploration, health is also measured in terms of boredom—here, the doctor's own.

In safeguarding the mental health of polar expeditionary crews, Arctic newspaper production was not at odds with Arctic expeditions' broader missions, including the grave work of Franklin expedition rescue and recovery. To amuse is to divert the attention, and in providing amusement polar papers created beguiling regulatory mechanisms for exercising and passing time. The opening number of the *Queen's Illuminated Magazine* (published during Edward Belcher's command of the *Assistance* in its 1852–54 cruise) was quick to argue:

> Has Amusement aught to do with the sacred duty of the Search for the Squadron of Franklin? We answer—Yes!—isolated as we are from the rest of the world, buried as it were for awhile from intercourse with our fellowmen, and on the eve of a long night in which days, weeks, aye! months, will pass uncheered by the Sun's glorious beams, we shall have much to tax our patience and spirits.—Next to healthy exercise for the body, nay, we opine before it, is cheerful exercise for the mind—Reading, is no doubt, beneficial to some, but all cannot sit down for hours poring over books; for such, the Magazine offers a field in Writing and Composition—and furthermore we believe it will be found, that the publication of this Gazette will form a topic of communication, & we trust, *kind* criticism, which will serve to break the dull monotony of our daily torture.[31]

There is a special urgency in relieving the "torture" visited upon Arctic expedition members, not simply isolated but "buried" in their abstraction from intercourse with the Old World that had been invoked in the *Illustrated*

Arctic News. Reading is insufficient to counteract the torture of monotony; the act of creation, the practices of literary and textual production, are essential for stimulation. Markham saw this drive to imaginative production as a psychological concern as well, observing that once a ship was icebound, "the seaman has little to do but reflect on, and possibly brood over, his situation. It is, therefore, absolutely essential that some means should be devised to drive from him all unpleasant thoughts, and to make him feel that it is in his power to relieve the tedium of what would otherwise be a long and monotonous winter."[32] A fear of "brooding" seamen is a concern about individual nonproductivity, a fear that depressive interiority renders the sailor powerless. And the sense of agency awakened in the men by the creation of a newspaper—having something "to do," in Markham's terms— is necessarily *collective*: health itself, within the context of a confined crew, is not individual but shared in common.

The very collectivity of the intellectual work in producing an expeditionary newspaper is key to the enterprise. When ships are in motion, nautical labor is itself communal: sailors are organized into watches and can achieve most principal maritime tasks (hoisting or furling sail, bracing against the wind, making repairs) only by working jointly. Expeditionary newspapers in polar winters remind sailors—relatively fixed in place and relieved of the constant sheet adjustments and rigging labor done while aloft and actively under sail—that their community, their labor, is held in common. Both poetic imaginaries and popular histories tend to stress the solitude of polar exploration, and it is certainly the case that after a certain point polar-venturing ships move beyond the scope of contact with most other humans (or, in the case of Inuit, Iñupiat, Sami, Yupik, or other indigenous encounters, beyond the range of engagement with what Eurocentrism would consider "civilization"). If exploration is conceived as solitary by those who do not engage in it, then newspapers are emphatic in confirming to expedition members that they are part of a collective—a lesson learned in the Arctic after the fractiousness that compromised Parry's early nineteenth-century attempt in the *North Georgia Gazette, and Winter Chronicle*.[33]

These lessons could extend beyond shipboard life. While the need to *mark* time may be exceptional to polar exploration given climatic and geophysical conditions, the need to *pass* time with a community was not. By the time of the *Midnight Sun* of 1901 (and throughout the Antarctic missions of the early twentieth century, as chapter 3 details), publishers of polar periodicals were able to "rest in the feeling that no apology is needed for the existence of the paper. That the publication fills a want in the community, there need be no question." Polar papers had become naturalized, and so too had their editorial staffs: emerging from the Arctic icescape to serve as editors of the *Midnight Sun*, for example, were "Mr. P. O. Larbear, and Mr. S. Eal."[34] And yet the nature in which these publications are produced is an uncanny one for Anglo-American expedition members. Accustomed to the periodicity of morning, afternoon, and evening editions, British and American crews titled their papers with an ironic eye to the extremely prolonged temporality of the usual markers of newspaper frequency. Thus a daily paper in London or New York might be the *Sun*, published every twenty-four hours, while its Arctic counterpart would be a paper called the *Midnight Sun* or the *Arctic Moon*, whose periodicity would be attenuated. American North Pole explorer Anthony Fiala treated this contingency as comic in an interview with the newspaper for which he used to work, the *Brooklyn Daily Eagle*: "We had two day editions and one late at night. You see, up there we have only one full day and one night a year, so that it gave us plenty of time for fresh news between editions."[35] For the explorers, there might be humor or pathos or resignation in the recognition that a daily edition of the *Midnight Sun* would appear once in three months. If in London or Philadelphia the mechanics of the production of the daily news had been previously invisible—the morning paper in the lower latitudes simply *appeared*, the agents of its production invisible—then the circumscription and ephemeral location of expedition members require them to take up the means of production.

Hyperborean Curiosities of Literature

Like nineteenth-century Anglo-American newspapers more generally, Arctic periodicals featured a selection of light verse and other poetry.[36] In many instances, the poems take as their subjects the expeditions' aims or activities, matter that seldom is treated in other contributions to Arctic newspapers. So much of the narrative prose that seamen produce in their other, more formal expeditionary writing is devoted to the scientific and navigational aims of the missions; perhaps only poetry, in its periodical forms, is a distinct enough form of expression to distinguish newspaper writing about the expedition from official prose. In the first number of the *Illustrated Arctic News* the "Traveller's Evening Song" encourages the present expedition members while remaining mindful of the lost Franklin crew: "With hope renewed, then on we go, / England must not blush for us! / And with fresh vigour cross the floe, / In search of those before us."[37] The missing expedition was never far from the thoughts of the men of the *Assistance*, as the poetic "Epilogue" to the final theatrical performance of the Arctic winter season stresses: "One sole regret we had, until to night, / That those so near, could not with us unite; / And in this mimic world the hours beguile."[38] The invocation of a "mimic world" is arresting: the theatrical stage is the primary simulacrum, but so too is the expedition itself, creating the trappings not just of home society but of home *time*, beguiling the hours with evening performances staged in ceaseless darkness. Many poems were composed to commemorate occasions, whether theatrical or calendrical. Upon the reopening of the Arctic Theatre in November 1875 during the Nares expedition, a playbill distributed to the audience announced, "To-day we welcome you, and not To-night, / For all is noon with us—all summer bright."[39] The playbill marks the absence of diurnal celestial divisions, but mordantly inverts the actual light conditions that obtain in mid-November in latitude 82° N, when all would be not noon but midnight. A narrative poem about the expedition, written several months later, in March 1876, faced this circumstance more squarely: "The sun never shone / Their gallant crews upon / For an hundred and forty-two days; / But no darkness and no hummocks / Their merry hearts could flummox: / So they set to work and acted Plays."[40]

Whether their aims were Franklin rescue or recovery or "discovery" of the Northwest Passage or North Pole, expeditions were necessarily limited in the work they could do in winter by the darkness and cold. In an illustrative case, although the "daily sea routine" while under sail on one expedition required that morning watches begin at 4:00 a.m., the "winter routine" pushed morning watches back to 6:45, a significant sleep-in by comparison.[41] Winter labors consisted of planning for spring sledging trips (voyages by sled, pulled by dogs or men), recordkeeping, climate and magnetic observation, and maintenance of iced-in ships. The men hunted for Arctic game, in part for scientific observation, in part for sustenance, whether musk-ox, fox, bear, or seal, although these proteins were not always pleasing to the palate of Anglo-Americans, to their detriment in combating scurvy. They especially avoided the exemplary antiscorbutic raw seal, a staple of Inuit diets. The difficulty the hunters of the *Resolute* had in landing Arctic fowl inspired the poem "Stray Shots" in the *Illustrated Arctic News*. In the absence of eider duck trophies for consumption or specimen preservation, the poet finds material for comic verse and addresses a song of experience to the hunters:

Thus like your lead, you'll scatter round,
Knowledge by long experience found—
Your Artists then at any rate,
The "Arctic News" will illustrate
And as sage Punch can not here roam,
Supply his place 'till we reach home.[42]

Expertise is absent in both their wit and their huntsmanship, this poem admits with self-deprecating humor, and the men of the Arctic are scattershot in their various literary and hyperborean aims, grazing and missing their targets indiscriminately. This strategy is analogous to the forms of cairn messaging circulation described in chapter 4 and to the voluminous production of texts in the Arctic regions more generally by Anglo-American expeditions: the more material that is generated, the more they multiply their chances of making contact.

Like the passengers on British settler colonial voyages whose shipboard poetic parodies Jason Rudy has described, some Arctic sailors produced burlesques of well-known poems.[43] The continued popularity of Poe's "The Raven" nearly six decades after its original publication is evident in a reincarnation of the poem as "The Ravings" by a contributor to the *Arctic Eagle* in 1903. "The Ravings" refers to a fateful moment when the crew of the Fiala-Ziegler Expedition realizes that the encroaching ice will compel them to abandon their trapped ship, *America*, which had been seriously threatened by ice once before and which was eventually broken up by the pack. (Fiala's crew of thirty-eight men were rescued eighteen months later.)

Once, in Arctic night most dreary
While the ship's crew rested—weary
Of the task of building sledges
        That had been built once before,
With the sound of moorings slacking,
Suddenly there came a cracking
As of pack-ice closer packing—
        Crowding in toward the shore—
        All of this and then some more.

Fiala, roused by this commotion
In the lonely Arctic Ocean,
Instantly, with optic psychic,
        Saw the ghost he saw before.

Quoth he "Man or devil, hark'ee—
Speak to me from out thy parkee—
Tell me—(if though knowest, mark'ee)—
    Tell me this now I implore—
    Only this, I ask no more:

Can she twice withstand the crushing
Of the pack upon her rushing—
Lying here at outer ice-edge,
    Far from the protecting shore?"
Spake the ghost, with grin ungainly—
"Listen—I will tell thee plainly
That thou strives to save her, vainly
    Her bones share with mine this shore,
    Here they'll rest forever more."

. . . .

Thus, dismantled, crushed and dying,—
But with colors bravely flying—
Our good ship lies on the ice pack,
    Doomed to sleep on Teplitz shore.
On the bridge, the parkee spirit
Shouts his order 'till we hear it
All about the ship or near it.
    Sometimes we can hear his roar.
    From our cabin on the shore—
    Sometimes his—and sometimes more.[44]

This "parkee spirit"—a nautical ghost or flying Dutchman or ancient mariner—remains on the doomed ship in the familiar tradition of maritime spirits. Here, though, his ghostly voice issues from the oracular hole of the hood of a winter parka, his face invisible, much like the veiled face of the prophet of Khorassan invoked in the *Flight of the Plover*. "Parka," like "anorak" (or "annuraaq" in Inuktitut), is a word imported into English usage from northern indigenous languages (*parka* is an Aleutian term related to the native Nenet languages of Russia), and thus the parkee spirit is tethered to the Arctic both rhetorically and culturally. Like Poe's raven, the occult figure of the parkee spirit signals a threat of madness. The poem also provides a sense of polar repetition: the men of the expedition have been through loss and rebuilding challenges before. In the poem's repetitions

The Ravings.

(With apologies to Edgar Allen.)

Once, in Arctic night most dreary,
While the ship's crew rested—weary
Of the task of building sledges
    That had been built once before,
With the sound of moorings slacking,
Suddenly there came a cracking
As of pack-ice closer packing—
    Crowding in toward the shore—
    All of this and then some more.

Fiala, roused by this commotion
In the lonely Arctic Ocean,
Instantly, with optic psychic,
Saw that ghost he saw before.
Quoth he "Man or devil, hark'ee—
Speak to me from out thy parkee—
Tell me—(if thou knowest, mark'ee)—
    Tell me this now, I implore—
    Only this, I ask no more:

Can she twice withstand the crushing
Of the pack upon her rushing—
Lying here at outer ice-edge,
    Far from the protecting shore?"
Spake the ghost, with grin ungainly—
"Lister— will tell thee plainly
That thou strivest to save her, vainly,
    Her bones share with mine this shore,
    Here they'll rest foreve mo e."

Anthony, with eyeballs starting,
Thro, his pale lips slightly parting
Breathed a prayer—then jumped himself
    As he had never humped before.
While the "Chief" cursed timbers crashing,
The "Old Man", with bull's eye flashing,
Down the narrow gang-plank dashing
    Dragged "chronometer" ashore.
    Only this?—well, perhaps more.

Later, Hartt with tears surprising,
Muttered that the water, rising,
Made the ship unsafe to stay on—
    Something he'd ne'er said before.
To Fiala—"You show sand, sir;
But I'm now in full command, sir;
And I order you to land, sir,
    Be so good to climb ashore,
    I am last—." And then some more.

Those at home may have a notion
That the mystic Arctic Ocean
Offers deeds of valor only,
    To our manhood's precious store;
But all those who— joyed or grieving—
Saw our little party leaving,
Realize that I'm not weaving
    Fiction in with History's lore—
    This there is— and then some more.

Thus, dismantled, crushed and dying,—
But with colors bravely flying—
Our good ship lies on the ice-pack,
    Doomed to sleep on Teplitz shore.
On the bridge, the parkee spirit
Shouts his order 'till we hear it
All about the ship or near it.
Sometimes we can hear his roar
    From our cabin on the shore—
    Sometimes his— and sometimes more.

TO OUR BUGLE AND DRUM.

"The awful silence of an arctic night." Who said it? Liar! Liar!! Come to Teplitz Bay. Ha! Ha! Ha! Listen! Did you notice any peculiar note in my voice? Are my eyes glassy and wild? My God! Am I going mad? Only this morning while I was sleeping safely, as I supposed in my bunk, suddenly without any warning there burst in upon me the greatest, the most fiendish roars of discord that Arctic explorer was ever damned to listen to. In an instant the atmosphere assumed a hellish sulphurescent hue and I was knocked into a trance out of which I awakened near noon together with several others suffering from a frontal headache and a peculiarly nervous, irritable condition. Oh! for the clear, cool, silver tinkle of the mess bell ringing out the death knell of this aborted monstrosity of a once fair militar!

Arise! some St. George and slay this hollow headed, bass voiced demon and his long winded, ear splitting second. Charge! you faint hearted, and stamp out this scourge. Must I continue to listen through the long winter to this Arctic parasite in his constantly increasing inopportune outbursts? May I have a haven to which I may flee— the dog tent, where amongst their howls and growls I can again pick up the harmonizing vibrations which make life worth living.

"Activity is necessary to success— rest by change of activity."

The above was submitted by our genial Commissary as his slogan. We shall have to see the Steward about this.

The Commanding Officer hinted the other day that he picks up anything he sees laying around loose. Hang onto your caps and mittens!

FIG 2.2 — "The Ravings," *Arctic Eagle* 1.3 (1903): 4, Harrie H. Newcomb Papers. GEORGE J. MITCHELL DEPARTMENT OF SPECIAL COLLECTIONS AND ARCHIVES, BOWDOIN COLLEGE LIBRARY.

and rote rhymes we get a sense of the commonplaces and familiar rhythms of Arctic life.

At several moments proxy versions of what is supposed to be Inuit or Yupik literature appear in Arctic newspapers. The examples of indigenous prose and verse follow closely the forms and rhythms of Anglo-American genres, which suggests either that the seeming translators hewed closely to available models or, far more likely, that the examples are inventions of or very loose adaptations by the white crew members. Here are two instances; the first comes from the *Plover*, engaged in Franklin searches in the far Western Arctic. An article entitled "Hyperborean Curiosities of Literature" appearing in the *Weekly Guy* in 1852 promises a translation of an "unpublished volume of Esquimaux poems" under the title "Esquimaux Anthology." The poem "O-Ki'-O-Me (Winter Season)" is a song of subsistence hunting:

1

In the winter, oh! how nice,
    Yang-a, yang-a, ya-ang-ah!*
With sledge and dogs upon the ice,
    Yang-a, yang-a, ya-ang-ah!*
Clothe'd well from top to toe',
Fur without and fur below,
With loose coat to keep out snow,
    Yang-a, yang-a, ya-ang-ah!*

2

When the sky is calm and bright,
    yang-a &c.
We in snow can sleep all night,
    yang-a &c.
Then in cheerful happy mood,
Fetch we home the whale flesh good,
To our huts for winter food,
    yang-a &c. . . . .

*This is the burden of every Esquimaux air with which we are acquainted, and is the same now as when the people were first visited. The origin of the time-honored word "Yang-a" is lost in the most remote antiquity.[45]

Sealing and sledging songs would certainly be in use by Inuit and Yupik hunters, and as most Anglo-American expeditions employed indigenous guides and provisioners they would have had exposure to Inuktitut and Yupik airs (the *Plover* was located in Point Barrow, Alaska, and the local "Esquimaux" would likely be Iñupiat, or Alaskan Inuit peoples). Topically "O-Ki'-O-Me" is reasonably consistent with Inuit practices. And yet the song's emphasis on the pleasure and happiness the cheerful hunters take in their ample fur outfits in the face of winter exposure might reflect more the white Westerners' relative boredom, immobilization, and ill preparation in cotton and wool than anything else. The song's chorus—"Yang-a, yang-a, ya-ang-ah!"—is the only untranslated part of the poem, which suggests that it functions as a nonsense refrain, an element common to Western poetry as well. The poetic refrain is described by Edward Hirsch as a "universal device of archaic and tribal poetries," an accompaniment to "communal labor, dance, and song." Like polar periodicals themselves, refrains are ways of marking time.[46] And like nautical labor, refrains are collective. At the same time, though, "Hyperborean Curiosities of Literature" figures the Iñupiat as a people out of time, ancient: the "origin of the time-honored word 'Yang-a' is lost in the most remote antiquity." In characterizing the Esquimaux in such terms, this piece in the *Weekly Guy* summons clichés of prehistoric indigenous primitiveness, while still establishing a "time-honored" traditional history for them, one that uses Western poetic forms to express the simple pleasures of subsistence practices—the very practices to which Anglo-Americans were largely slow to adopt.

A second instance in which indigenous writing purports to appear in Arctic newspapers comes from the *Aurora Borealis*, in a call-and-response sequence of articles that is more evidently massaged by white writers. The Anglophone historical record provides some background on the subject of the articles, Qalasirssuaq, one of a number of indigenous Greenlanders who ended up in service to British and American whaling voyages or polar expeditions in the eighteenth and nineteenth centuries. The young Inuk guide served on the *Assistance* after being engaged by the expedition at Cape York, Greenland. Qalasirssuaq (the modern Inuktitut spelling of Kallihirua) was renamed Erasmus York by the officers of the *Assistance*, in nods to Commander Erasmus Ommanney and the location where he was taken aboard.[47] The crew nevertheless called him Kalli and taught him English. Qalasirssuaq eventually traveled to Britain, where he had some measure of fame and where he attended St. Augustine's College, a missionary school for the Church of England. He died young, in 1855, the terrible, all-too-common fate of indigenous peoples brought to the imperial metropole. After his death a clergyman published *Kalli, the Christian Esquimaux*

(1856), which went through several editions in London and New York. *Kalli* includes a poem adapted from lines spoken by one of the men aboard the *Assistance*; it paints a somewhat different picture of the teenage Qalasirssuaq's ostensibly willing decision to join the British expedition. The poem describes "little" Qalasirssuaq as weeping and straining his eyes "to try if he could see again / His mother and his home." But ice is forming in the inlet, and the captain prefers to press on rather than return the "sad" boy to a maternal embrace. Kalli "learn'd to make the best of it" in the end.[48]

The *Aurora Borealis* features another side of Qalasirssuaq. In his supposed reply to an article claiming that "Arctic Highlanders" (Esquimaux) are dull and incapable—part of a broader piece on the inferiority of northern indigenous peoples—"Calahierna, alias Erasmus York," first wonders why, if white men are so smart, they would leave relatively temperate England for the frozen regions of the North.[49] The initial droll tone of this response does not last, however, and Qalasirssuaq shifts to a series of paeans to the imagined magical powers of the whites, who "must be an extraordinary people": they launch explosives that "multiply the many stars that pave the heavens"; send aloft "extraordinary round skins" to which are attached "long slips of pretty coloured paper" as part of the balloon messages designed to aid the Franklin search; and they read by "looking for hours into a series of leaves bound up together," through which "good and bad Augerkoks [shamans] talk." In this particular Inuit iteration of the trope of the talking book the white sailors stay true to Jack Tar type, rejecting wholesome literature in favor of salacious reading and "prefer[ring] the tongue of the bad Augerkoks to that of the good." Qalasirssuaq also guesses that "two different genii preside" over the expedition's four ships, much "as birds are propelled by wings."[50] All the racialized clichés of native awe in the face of imperial mastery are in play here: the spirit ships propelled by unseen forces, the wonder book, the whites' command over the firmament and the natural world. It is easier for the white men of the *Assistance* to invoke Kalli the awestruck primitive, in other words, than to be alive to the plight of Qalasirssuaq the denaturalized boy sobbing for his mother. This distance is reinforced by the general unwillingness (with some exceptions) of British and American sailors to learn Inuktitut or other indigenous languages, relying instead on native translators. The *Queen's Illuminated Magazine* made a joke of the British crew's language limitations in a postscript to an advertisement for a new "Sub Editor": "No one need apply without he can read & write Esquimaux—Danish—Russian & Double Dutch."[51] If there are limits to indigenous knowledge, in the racist understanding of white sailors, it is consistent with their own fatigue with the forms of knowledge available to them, however they try to ease such rhetorical performances with humor.

Nuts for the Arctic Public

Polar periodicals were largely light and diverting, as I have said, and this tone is expressed in a variety of ways. Arctic newspapers by and large did not replicate the official voyage logs and accounts of daily mission progress, so the "news" in the newspaper rarely was topical or sober; since the entire crew was engaged in expeditionary work, a periodical's function was less to inform than to amuse. Exceptions came when contributors found either drollery in expeditionary conditions or foibles, or poetic pathos in the futility of Franklin rescue or recovery. One such instance is the "FATAL ACCIDENT" suffered by "Benjamin Balloon," one of the eight-foot hydrogen inflatables used aboard the *Resolute* for the purposes of Franklin search message distribution. Tragic Benjamin "literally inflated himself" by getting into the "cask containing Hydro-Gin"; his overindulgence in this gaseous form of gin rendered him so "light-headed" that he floated away, lost. His recovery was actively sought by the crew, however, as he had on his person "papers to a great amount . . . Drafts at sight, on the firm of Messrs Cash and Case."[52] The witticism about drunk Benjamin Balloon imagines him absconding with papers or currency, which in this context consists of the printed location messages designed for potential receipt by the missing Franklin men (discussed in chapter 4). There is an additional punning jest in the name of the financial firm: Artic expeditions would use the device of the cache (pronounced "cash") to leave messages and supplies and would enclose the written and printed notices themselves in cases.

When it came to more explicit forms of humor, a variety of styles were in practice. Jokes, enigmas, puns, and conundrums were popular—some groaners, some knee slappers. One indication that the *Aurora Borealis* was indeed functioning to amuse its public is a letter to the editor from "Ennui," who had brilliant expectations of power in the winter months; instead, however, Ennui finds that he is "miserable and wretched," as "Mirth, Cheerfulness, Laughter, and Fun" have rendered his place aboard ship superfluous.[53] Contributors made use of italics and other emphatic devices to ensure that no reader missed their punning meanings, such as in a letter to the editor of the *Aurora Borealis* from a polar bear: "I offer you my

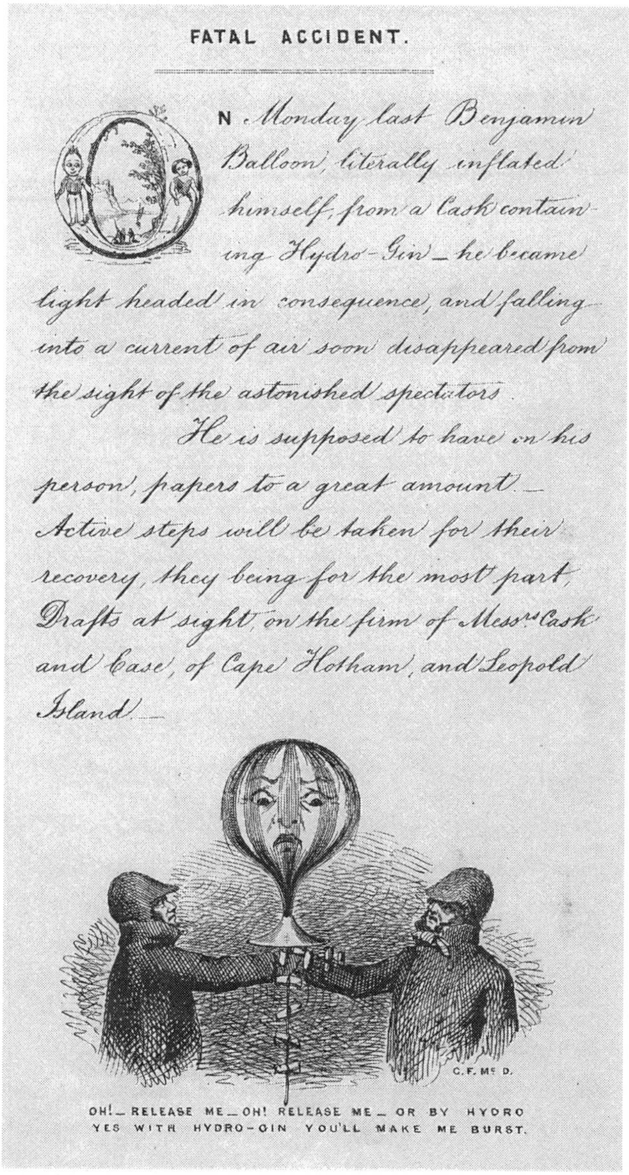

FATAL ACCIDENT.

O N Monday last Benjamin Balloon, literally inflated himself, from a Cask containing Hydro-Gin — he became light headed in consequence, and falling into a current of air soon disappeared from the sight of the astonished spectators.

He is supposed to have on his person, papers to a great amount — Active steps will be taken for their recovery, they being for the most part, Drafts at sight, on the firm of Messrs Cash and Case, of Cape Hotham, and Leopold Island.—

C. F. McD.

OH! — RELEASE ME — OH! RELEASE ME — OR BY HYDRO
YES WITH HYDRO-GIN YOU'LL MAKE ME BURST.

FIG 2.3 — "FATAL ACCIDENT," *Facsimile of the Illustrated Arctic News*, 8. Note the bundles of messages tied to the balloon's string.
COURTESY OF DARTMOUTH COLLEGE LIBRARY.

(bear) bare thoughts to make known amongst my race. You are aware my deeds are too frequently *seal*-ed with blood wherever my *ice*-olated track is found. I prefer the *bear*-ded walrus to a *tender* turkey. The awful *paw*-city of our race had better be believed than felt."[54] A one-liner in the *Illustrated Arctic News* managed to incorporate the names of all four ships in the squadron, here capitalized: "A good Pioneer must be a Resolute man. Few men however Intrepid, but have felt the want of Assistance."[55] The *Midnight Sun* of the Baldwin-Ziegler Expedition never published a second number, which might not be surprising given the quality of the opening joke of the only issue: "The ice pilot stated to Capt. Jo. Hanson this morning that he had observed open water on ahead. [Whose head?] Ed."[56] Some jokes made wordplay with Arctic terms and conditions:

CONUNDRUMS

Q. Why should we in our present position be considered very knowing?

A. Because there's nothing green about us.—

Q. Why are Parhelia like Indian Hunting Boots?

A. Because they are mock-suns. (moccasins.) [57]

While many of these witticisms are legible to readers today (whether or not they produce laughter out loud, and whether or not the joke is explained in the paper, as "mock-suns" is), a number of them make reference to what are clearly inside jokes among crew members. As the social media of polar expeditions, newspapers need not always explain their jokes; indeed many are the inside references that I am unable to decode. But these private jokes serve a strategic genre function as well, stressing the Arctic site-specificity of their transparency.

The comfort that crews felt with the conventions of newspapers and newspaper publishing is evident in other forms taken by periodical humor. These include parodies of news articles, satirical letters to the editor, farcical reports on the state of the weather, stock market tickers, and classified advertisements. An article titled "State of the Country" in the *Port Foulke Weekly News* covers domestic and foreign affairs in the language of seizure, war, and the "right of conquest"—only the territory ("dominion") claimed is found to be barren and unoccupied, with the point emphatically made in the discovery of two dead "inhabit[ants]," doubly nonthreatening for being a boy and an old woman. They are nonetheless "secured."[58] In mocking the language of imperial conquest, this writer is also acknowledging that the polar regions had proved not to be fit for the usual practices of Anglo-American colonialism.

The author of a letter to the editor saluting the "laudable enterprise" of the production of the *Arctic Moon* is gladdened to know that those expedition members who have been "confined to their homes for so many months, by cold and darkness," will now have relief from being "doomed to total ignorance of the most important things in the world," that is, "their neighbors' doings." For this wit, the primary purpose of a newspaper is to provide social gossip, "the doings of all personages living in high circles (I do not refer to the Arctic Circle)."[59] One object of social reporting is Mr. Sol, the "brightest luminary of the Arctic world," whose health is in a "low state" of decline as the fall advances.[60] A gentleman less predictable than Old Sol makes an appearance in the *Queen's Illuminated Magazine*, in a speculative etymological essay about the role of the paper's editor:

> The term Editor I affirm & maintain was originally derived from *Boxers*—Head hitters, one who was capable of giving the hardest raps—Johnson defines it as one who reviews or prepares any literary work for publication but before the great and dirty (vide Boswell) lexicographer had his being, words were commonly spelt as pronounced and amongst the Cockneys was spelt—Ed—iter (Head Hitter) as they pronounced it.... Therefore I propose that Johnson be corrected and in lieu it should be put as follows.—
>
> Editor—One who is capable of giving hard raps and also reviews any literary work for publication.[61]

The irony of this definition is that much of the time editors write about the need for more submissions, which can be slow to come, especially as the polar winter drags on.

Arctic classifieds are arguably the most consistently funny segments of polar papers (at least, to a reader today). This may be because the source of their humor is located less in private expedition or personnel-specific jokes than in the vagaries of supply deficiencies or in the absurdity of juxtaposing classified ad conventions with polar conditions. Take the real estate notices, for example. In the *Arctic Eagle* we find the following attractive parcels: "CHOICE BUILDING LOTS FOR SALE. Desirable location with unrestricted privileges. Swept by an ocean breeze."[62] Mindful that the "ocean breeze" might bring seventy knot winds and −70 degree temperatures, a notice in the *Queen's Illuminated Magazine* proposes "an exchange of abode with any gentleman, seeking solitude and a bracing climate"; in return, what is "*wanted* for immediate possession" is "a large House in the neighbourhood of London—the advertiser tired of a secluded life, is desirous of an abode close to a public thoroughfare whilst a cheerful prospect embracing at least a dozen trees, some grass, and one *cow*, are absolutely indispensible."[63] Rather than lamenting the scarcities attendant to Arctic life in terms that might depress community spirits, contributors use the conventions of newspaper section offerings to turn insufficiency into comedy.

Expeditions were short not just on grass, cows, and trees but on supplies of alcohol and other diversionary materials. This was generally a strategic provisioning choice, given the potential for abuse in close quarters. Drinking jokes are frequent in polar periodicals and highlight both unslaked thirsts and occasional overindulgences. An ad for the Arctic Tailor Shop promoting "spring styles" in fur clothing (sailors were historically proficient with sewing needles) stipulated expectantly that goods "taken in trade must be marked 'XXX' on the head and supplied with spigot."[64] (The risks of such unfettered access to spirits can be seen in their effects on Henry Dodge, the second mate of the *United States*, who was continually drunk and belligerent, according to a shipmate.)[65] The device of the want ad was also used in the *Aurora Borealis* to tease the dramatic members of the ship's company for the vaporous bombast in the theatrical playbills: "WANTED IMMEDIATELY.—A supply of gas for the Royal Arctic Theatre: the large quantity in the playbills, being found to be insufficient."[66] The "For Sale" section in the same paper promises the future production of a slim new volume, *Nuts for the Arctic Public*, "a very amusing and laughable little work, containing the original *bon mots*, puns, enigmas, charades, riddles, facetiae, and racy jokes of the well-known and amusing punster of the Expedition. A chapter will also be given on the most approved method of pulling a leg."[67] This particular ship, the *Assistance*, had several underground papers in addition to the *Aurora Borealis*. (According to my research, copies do not survive or are held privately.)

Polar instantiations of the conventions of comedy and of nineteenth-century textual forms could be ugly instead of benign. The British expedition led by Nares staged a series of minstrel shows as part of the "Thursday Pops" program, performed by the "Pale-O Christy Minstrels."[68] (The troupe's name gestures both to the longstanding U.S. blackface troupe Christy's Minstrels and to the term "paleocrystic," which is used to describe ice that is many years old, as would be the case in Arctic regions.) Costumes at the "Grand Bal Masqué" aboard the *Resolute* included "Highlanders," "Japanese," and "Niggers."[69] In the interlude between a performance of *Hamlet* and the farce *The Scapegrace* the audience aboard the Belcher expedition (1852–54) was presented with "Negro" songs and "a highly pathetic Story of NEGRO LOVE by Mr. J. REID, in full Negro Costume." (Reid was the expedition's ice master, or ice navigator.)[70] The *Jeannette* expedition under George De Long (1879–81) also staged minstrel shows, and on the program for one evening's event a crew member drew racist caricatures. The men on Adolphus Greely's Lady Franklin Bay Expedition (1881–84) performed "Plantation Melodies" and held an Indian "War Dance" in which they gave themselves "Indian" names, which they translated as "Yellow Hammer," "Bottom Dollar," "Freeze to Death," "Codfish Hater," and "Cheese Eater."[71] At the other pole, the crew of Robert Falcon Scott's first Antarctic expedition staged a minstrel show as the "Dishcover Minstrel Troupe" in 1902.[72] Other cruel performances took the form of taunts about the first African American polar explorer, Matthew Henson, who accompanied Robert Peary on several Arctic expeditions. In a newspaper reference to northern menu limitations, the *Arctic Eagle* printed the following racist joke: "Barring the possibility of Peary's aide Mr Henson—we are a thousand miles from the nearest coon, and yet there is a rumor that some one has got the Duke's spring chickens."[73] These were common forms of "humor" in the period, but it is not clear if such language acted only to accentuate the reach of the rhetoric of hate, or if it had a different resonance in the Arctic.

"Pretty Men"

Other texts are opaque—to expeditionary readers and to us today—not because of Arctic conditions but because of censorship. As I describe more fully in chapter 4, the British Admiralty required all written materials, "public and private," to be conveyed immediately and in full to naval officials upon an expedition's return. As a standard directive from the Admiralty agent put it, "You are hereby required and directed to deliver to me, the moment the ship anchors on England, all the charts, logs, journals, and memoranda, both of a public and private nature, which you may have kept during the time you have been on board the ship."[74] One aim of this stipulation was to ensure that accounts of the voyage would first appear under official Admiralty imprint, as Craciun argues. Furthermore, such regulatory practices help explain why the content of Arctic papers is relatively tame in their references to sexual desire and practices. The manuscript version of the *North Georgia Gazette, and Winter Chronicle* contained a transcription of a mysterious love letter supposedly tucked into a sewing kit, for example, as well as a letter concerning a romance between a sled dog and a she-wolf. (A "Spanish nobleman," the sled dog Carlo, had been sneaking off for assignations with "a lady of exalted rank, merit, & beauty, belonging to the Court of New Georgia," the Arctic region in which the expedition was located; the romantic pair were awaiting the arrival of the "Arch-bishop of the Frozen Regions to join their hands.")[75] These were among the articles omitted from the paper when it was reprinted in London upon the expedition's return.

When salacious material does appear in polar periodicals there is usually some measure of displacement between expedition personnel and the object of desire, as in the romance of the sled dog Carlo. Accounts of heterosexual relations with indigenous women appear in private journals but not official records; Harvey Scott Heywood, for instance, records numerous instances of boatloads of Esquimaux women visiting the *United States* when it is anchored off the Greenland coast in 1861. The men also attend native dances on shore, at which Heywood finds the women "kept going without mercy."[76] Longer-term relationships between British commanders and indigenous women were common but do not customarily appear in the heroic narratives of polar leadership; expeditionary histories have relatively little to say, for example, about Parry's close relationship with the Inuk mapmaker Iligliuk or about the children Peary and Henson fathered with the Inuit women Allakasingwah and Akatingwah, respectively.[77] Yet awareness of the Parry-Iligliuk connection was widespread enough for Coleridge to invoke it in a newspaper poem, "Captain Parry," after his third, less successful voyage to the Arctic: "Captain Parry! Captain Parry! / Thou hast had the devil's luck / Spite the gifted Secretary / And the charms of Eligluck."[78]

Also relatively rare are explicit acknowledgments of the queer sexual relations that would have taken place on most expeditions, however situational some may have been. The American polar hero and noted playboy Elisha Kent Kane—who had a sensationalized affair with Margaret Fox, one of the spirit-rapping Fox sisters—devoted a few pages of his Private Letterbook to a series of sketches of what he labeled "Pretty Men."[79] The *Queen's Illuminated Magazine* reveals a bit of homosexual panic in a fashion report on nautical dandies; illustrated by a sketch of heavily bundled men captioned "Fashions for October," the article "congratulate[s] our Arctic Readers, that no part of the clever definitions of a Dandy"—presumably, queer ones—"can be in any wise applicable to them." The word "dandy" has

FIG 2.4 — "Pretty Men," in the Arctic exploration letter book (private) of Elisha Kent Kane, 1820–1857, ca. 1850–51, Elisha Kent Kane Papers, Series IV, Bound Volumes Mss.b.k132, Volume 10. AMERICAN PHILOSOPHICAL SOCIETY, PHILADELPHIA.

a nautical definition, the article continues, not without accuracy: "It is a cutter reduced of her Main-boom because she has not men to manage it. . . . a ninny, a silly fellow[.] In modern usage a male of the human species who dresses himself? like a doll & who carries his character on his back [*sic*]."[80] In its anxious emphasis on gendered and nongendered pronouns, and in its insistence that true "character" is internal, the article reveals an uneasiness about masculine performances of seamanship and nautical costuming.

Clements Markham, a British explorer and later president of the Royal Geographical Society, kept accounts of hundreds of young naval officers in his *Arctic Navy List*; in his exacting attention to the details of their service,

Markham lists every part each man played in shipboard theatricals. Beyond strength, experience, or hardihood, he finds that the "most valuable qualifications for Arctic service are aptitude for taking part in those winter amusements which give life to the expedition during the months of forced inaction."[81] Of the veteran Arctic explorer Frederick William Beechey, for example, Markham writes:

In winter quarters at Melville Island he was Manager of the "Royal Arctic Theatre." The plays acted were:—

"*The Mayor of Garratt*;"

"*The Citizen*;"

"*A bold stroke for a Wife*;"

"*The Liar*;"

"*Miss in her Teens*;"

and "*The N.W. Passage, or the Voyage Finished*," an original musical entertainment.

Beechey acted Miss Biddy in "*Miss in her Teens*;" Philpot in "*The Citizen*;" Jerry Sneak in "*The Mayor of Garratt*;" Lady Minnikin in "*Bon Ton*;" and Simon Pure in "*A bold stroke for a Wife*."[82]

Only after this theatrical résumé does Markham record which ships Beechey commanded and the books he authored. A handful of historians who have referred to Markham's homosexuality, however, have received blowback from the polar enthusiast community.[83] A notable example of frank reference to queer sexual relations comes in a letter from Henry P. Hartt, the engineer on the Fiala-Ziegler Expedition, writing to the mission's surgeon, George Shorkley, from their winter camp. Hartt had been asked to occupy a room that had been shared by two shipmates, Charles Rilliet and John Trudens. "I objected," Hartt writes to Shorkley, "telling him that the room in question went by the name of the C—k suckers room. It seemed to surprise him very much, said he had never heard of it before, so of course I had to go and now I supposed I am classed as a sucker, but God. knows I am far from it." Later in that same letter, Hartt refers to a shipmate as "Oscar Wilde."[84] We see here the acknowledgment by most of the crew members (despite their leader's unawareness) of the homosexual activities in which Rilliets and Trudens engaged, even if the language used to describe them is not supportive.

In a striking and erotically charged letter to the Australian Antarctic explorer Douglas Mawson, a young woman writes to offer herself to the explorer—or rather to offer himself to him:

Dear Sir,

Will you take me as your cabin boy, a servant, on your antarctic expedition. I am a girl in the twenties, strong, healthy and fearless, & could make up as a boy perfectly. You will find the nimbleness of youth combined with the knowledge of woman, a very useful factor.

Yours truly

MARJORY COLLIER
Alias Jack Sëall[85]

Collier presents themself as Mawson's sea-all, his seal or his selkie, light and slippery and seeing all. The "nimbleness of youth" and the "knowledge of woman" made up in the body of a boy Jack Tar seems not to have caught Mawson's interest enough to accept the invitation, although he did keep the letter.

Polar newspapers gesture to queer desire and practice infrequently but playfully. Shipboard condensation problems were not confined to the crisis they presented to books and writing, as detailed earlier. Crew members' bedding would also freeze and then become saturated by the men's body heat; it often could not dry in the time afforded to its airing out. A sly poem called "The Arctic Twins" performed at the Arctic Theatre during the Nares expedition calls attention to this condensation problem with some homoerotic frisson:

And in the middle of the night.
In our sleeping bags there's a riot.
Someone turns and screws about,
And gets in such a pet,
Says he cannot sleep any more,
'Cause his sleeping bag is wet.[86]

Sharing furs was a common practice among the Inuit and other indigenous peoples; it preserved body heat and space within shelters and was adopted by Norwegian explorers such as Nansen, whose men slept three to a bag. British and American expeditions were less likely than Scandinavians to adapt to indigenous practices and materials for Arctic survival. Let us linger for a minute with the wet sleeping bag in this poem, which produces sleeplessness for the man "in a pet." The contemporary poet and polar naturalist Elizabeth Bradfield's poem "Against Solitude," from her collection on polar exploration, *Approaching Ice*, takes up this very issue:

> Leave your reindeer bag, damp and moldering,
> and slide into mine. Two of us, I'm sure, could
> warm it, could warm. Let me help you from your traces,
> let me rub what's sore. Don't speak. Your hair has grown long
> in our march, soft as my wife's. Keep your beard turned
> toward the tent's silk, your fusty breath—I know none of us
> can help it, I know, and truthfully I'm glad for any scent in this
>
> don't speak. How long has it been since my mouth
> has held anything other than ice and pemmican? Your skin,
> though wan and sour, is firm, delicious. Yes, your shoulder,
> your hip. I'd not thought how soft a man's hip would be,
> how curved the flesh above the backs of his thighs—listen
> do you hear the wind moaning, the ice groaning
> beneath us as it strains?[87]

The poem invokes the often communal or "public" nature of Arctic sex within furs in Inuit communities, as reported by surprised white guests in igloos in nineteenth-century travel narratives; the outsiders did not expect that shared bedding would be a site for sexual relations. In such circumstances, privacy takes on different meanings. A poem called "The Sleeping Bag" in the *South Polar Times* (written by the expedition photographer Herbert Ponting) toys with this concept by questioning whether outside and inside are discernible in animal skin bags: "If you turn the skinside outside, thinking you will side with that side; / Then the soft side, furside's inside, which some argue is the wrong side."[88] In Bradfield's poem, the convenient excuse of a "moldering" solo sleeping bag inaugurates an erotic moment. The situational nature of this particular homosexual encounter is indicated in part by the speaker's request that his partner not speak, that he keep his beard turned away so that the speaker might focus on his "soft" hip and his long hair, "soft as my wife's." The sounds of their lovemaking become the sounds of the wind and ice, both harmonized with and isolated to the polar regions.[89] In the "Arctic Twins" poem, by contrast, the fuss in the sleeping bag produces not sounds naturalized within the environment but a "riot"—perhaps here an indication of coercion or resistance.

Sexually suggestive language appears to have been present in some of the Arctic newspapers that were censored, seized, or otherwise suppressed, and evidence remains of the various forms taken by these acts of repression. The limited-edition London reprint of the *Illustrated Arctic News* (1850–51) was advertised as a facsimile edition, giving the impression that nothing had been altered. Yet the preface to the *Facsimile of the Illustrated Arctic News* reveals that "a few articles have been omitted for fear the bad taste of a long-shore Public, might lead them to object, on the score of raciness, for this we apologize to our gallant contributors."[90] The taste level of the "long-shore Public," or landspeople in coastal communities, is here suspect, rather than the taste of the sailors, which is the usual presumption. Mindful, maybe, of the judicious editing that had happened with the "facsimile" publication of the *Illustrated Arctic News*, Sherard Osborn, a British naval officer who contributed both to the 1850–51 paper and to the *Queen's Illuminated Magazine* of the subsequent Belcher expedition (1852–54), appended a note to the manuscript of the *Queen's Illuminated* in 1856: "This paper, must not be published or circulated publicly without the full consent of the contributors."[91] "Racy" was the default description of off-color materials in polar periodicals, judging from the frequency of its usage. In exercising "the right of rejecting what we considered unfit or injudicious to publish," the editors of the *Queen's Illuminated Magazine* explain, "What little we have not published has been solely on the score of—what shall we call it? extreme raciness!"[92] The proposed supplement to the *Aurora Borealis, Nuts for the Arctic Public*, had promised "racy jokes" in addition to puns, riddles, and bon mots.[93] One Mr. Trotter, a fictitious contributor of a letter to the editor of the *Weekly Guy*, guessed that many of the articles in the paper were written by the editors (in the absence of a diversity of submissions) and offered to be "a stand-by to supply you with good racy articles."[94] The late eighteenth- and nineteenth-century definition of "raciness" with reference to writing or speech, according to the *Oxford English Dictionary*, is "vigour, liveliness, robustness; lack of inhibition; suggestive or slightly indecent content or quality." Nansen flirts with raciness in *Farthest North* in his partial transcription of a poem in the *Framsjaa* entitled "Dog Rape on board the *Fram*," in which he describes a cold night aboard ship in which a harpooner and a kennelman are keeping watch. Just as a polar bear enters the poem—predator for the sled dogs—Nansen concludes his transcription "and so on."[95] It is not clear whether the "dog rape" refers to the poaching of sled dogs by a polar bear or encoded sexual violence.

Selective editing was one way that newspaper content was controlled, and in response, some writing went underground. Anton Vedoe's papers from the Fiala-Ziegler Expedition include a subversive pamphlet titled the *Vulture*, which has not been previously described in polar expeditionary history. It includes a suggestive photograph of a woman dressed as a mermaid; caustic rhymes about a shipmate whose body odor earned him the nickname Windy ("The roses red / The violets blue / Codfish stinks / And so do you"); profane jokes ("why is a baby like a seagull[?] Answer[:] One flits along the shore, the other shits along the floor"); and an incomplete limerick that begins "There was a man from Lynn / Whose pecker was spongy and thin."[96] In at least several cases (and possibly others, unrecorded in the archives to which I have had access) entire newspapers were commandeered by superior officers. A tantalizing trace is visible in the biography that Albert Hastings Markham wrote of his older cousin Clements Markham. Clements had contributed both to the *Aurora Borealis* (of the *Assistance*, on which he served as a young midshipman) and the *Illustrated Arctic News* (of the *Resolute*, its sister ship in the search for Franklin); his articles for the *Aurora Borealis* included a piece on trilobites. According to the biography—but mentioned in neither shipboard paper nor in expeditionary journals or narratives—two *additional* publications appeared subsequently on the *Resolute* and *Assistance*:

> In January yet another periodical made its appearance on board the *Resolute*. It was entitled *The Gleaner*, and had a humorous tendency. The editors were incognito, but their personality was suspected. Thereupon Markham, determined that the *Assistance* should not be behindhand in these matters, began the issue of another paper on board his ship. Under its title *Minavilins** he announced that "one of the editorial duties would be to keep a sharp watch on the *Gleaner*." Now, it happened that the second number of the *Gleaner* contained a scurrilous and quite unwarrantable attack on one of the officers of the expedition. This was Markham's chance. It was promptly answered by an article in *Minavilins* which not only withered up the *Gleaner* with scathing satire, but also emphasised his remarks by means of several humorous illustrations. But there was something worse than Russian censorship on that wintry icepack. This particular number was promptly confiscated by order of the senior officer, and at the same time both the *Gleaner* and *Minavilins* were suppressed altogether.

*"Minavilins" was a term well known and frequently used in the Navy to designate "odds and ends" that are lying about on the deck. It is now seldom used.[97]

A fifth newspaper was produced by the four-ship squadron, in fact, as Hoag reveals; a manuscript newspaper entitled *Artic Charivari* on the *Intrepid* (a supply tender) is mentioned in the journal of that ship's lieutenant, but no copies are extant.[98] Markham was so indignant at the suppression of the *Gleaner* and *Minavilins* that he came to the *Resolute*'s Grand Bal Masqué dressed as "Allegory," which his cousin wrote was "designed to illustrate the indignation which he felt at what he considered the unjust treatment he had received by the unwarrantable suppression of *Minavilins!*"[99] No one, however, seems to have understood the allegory.

Petering Out

The biggest threat to the longevity of Arctic papers was not censorship but the prolonged winters; the polar night distorted, ultimately, the efficacy of newspapers as temporal regulatory devices. The advent of spring brought increased work aboard ship to prepare for the season's sledge travel, which was one factor in the decreasing frequency and increasing slenderness of issues; still, the months-long darkness wore on sailor contributors, and they were not always able to generate material or sustain a publication schedule toward the end of the polar night. In early winter, when papers first launched, contributors had plenty of content to provide, as the editor of the *Aurora Borealis* describes: "When one of the French writers of the day was told the story of St. Denis having walked after decapitation, with his head under his arm, she wittily exclaimed: 'Ce n'est que le premier pas qui coûte.' So it has proved with the contributions to the 'Aurora.' The first steps taken, the rest were comparatively easy; articles at first came in tardily, but their followers have poured in measuredly and constantly, and an abundant harvest has been supplied to feed the flame of thought."[100] In its comparison to the French saint's posthumous mobility, this account of the paper's genesis casts its existence as miraculous, its stringers situational martyrs journeying to glory.

Toward the end of January, however, contributions slowed. Captain Carl Koldewey reported of *Ostgrönländische Zeitung* (East Greenland Gazette) of the German Arctic expedition (1869–70), "A new number of the paper appeared on Sunday, which, by its diminutive size, showed the decrease of material."[101] Sighed the editor of the *Illustrated Arctic News*, "Our Box—intended originally for literary purposes, produces only pipe-lights, and half-smoked Cigars."[102] Writing of "our old friend the Guy"—the *Weekly Guy* of a Franklin search expedition aboard the *Plover*—Rochfort Maguire lamented, "I feel sorry that the means at the disposal of the Editor, are not in any way, either mechanically or literary [sic], adequate to ensure Keeping up the publication with spirit—however we are promised an occasional number, when anything of unusual importance takes place."[103] The editor of the *Arctic Moon* of the Lady Franklin Bay Expedition, James Booth Lockwood, lamented the slowdown more sarcastically: "Contributors who are disappointed at not finding their articles in this issue are advised that it is on account of their non-receipt." Perhaps the problem lies in Arctic distribution limitations, the editor's note continues: "Owing to limited postal facilities, articles must be mailed on an early date to ensure their prompt appearance."[104] Polar weather also caused delays, as the *Weekly Guy* noted with acerbic surprise: "Who could have imagined that the icy barrier which encircled our good ship could have been so easily rent asunder and driven to seaward by the force of any gale? Or, who could have expected such a gale to produce its effects at midwinter? Who could have dreamed that any storm could have prevented the appearance of the 'Weekly Guy' on its accustomed day of publication? Surely not we. Nevertheless, the storm has been the cause of our delay."[105] Three weeks later, when the paper was delayed again, a "friend" (in scare quotes) submits a "riddle" to the paper: "Q. Why does the Weekly Guy resemble a good musician? A. Because it is never 'out in time.'"[106] As newspapers faded out of circulation with the coming of the sun, polar ecomedia struggled to be attentive to the temporalities of polar night.

The *Discovery News* of the Nares expedition found that by only late November there were particular voids in the paper's "wit and humour column," even as solicitations for material recognized the "unflagging industry and zeal of [ship] printer Benjamin Wyatt," an able seaman.[107] The *Discovery News* had been conceived of as a weekly, but "the supply of labour in the Printing office" was not sufficient to meet the demand upon it, and the paper's editor contemplated a move to a fortnightly schedule. In this instance, though, the attenuation was based not on a diminution of articles but other demands on the press itself: "the extra work consequent upon the commencement of the Theatrical season and the necessary use of type and time (which wait for no man) in setting up playbills &c."[108] Indeed Arctic sailors were "a litter-ary set," as Dodge of the *United States* expedition put it, jesting about the intellectual detritus produced by his shipmates.[109] In a "literary community like ours," a drop-off in contributions must convey a "sense of [contributors'] native modesty, and forbearance, feeling assured that they withhold from us the brilliant scintillations and magnificent coruscations of their taste and genius only for the purpose of giving a free field for displaying the talents of some younger aspirants."[110] Yet there is a risk to the editor in such modesty—however joshingly put—among contributors, Dodge finds in the penultimate issue of the *Port Foulke Weekly News*: "In the dim and shadowy, but not far off future, there indistinctly looms up the figure of our satanic looking imp, crying out for more copy while we in deep despondency are forced to give him as an answer, the raven cry—Nevermore. Let our friends rally around to spare us the infliction of this sooty scene of horror."[111] The invocation of Poe's "The Raven" in the *Port Foulke Weekly News* serves a similar function to its parodic rewriting in "The Ravings" in the *Arctic Eagle*: after a long night of labor—whether twelve hours or three months, intellectual or nautical—the toiler risks madness, disordered thinking.

An illustration of a "satanic looking imp" at the North Pole happens to play a curious role in the polar imaginary of the *Port Foulke Weekly News*, the manuscript organ of the *United States*, and I close the chapter on this point. The image appears in the December 1, 1860, edition of the paper and seems unrelated to other articles in it. (It is preceded by an article on volcanos by the expedition's commander, Isaac Israel Hayes, and followed by Dodge's "Grumbler" literary column.) The full-page illustration shows a flagpole planted at the center of a ring of concentric circles atop an arc of a sphere, but it does not fly a flag. Instead the pole is mounted by a mythical hybrid akin to a gryphon, with elements of a chimera present as well: the figure has the body, wings, and right arm or talon of an eagle; the right hind leg of a lion; the left hind leg and possibly the left forearm of a goat; a serpentine tail ending in a barb that resembles a harpoon or a compass arrow; and goat ears that resemble horns. The face of the figure is a perfect caricature of Commander Hayes, with his broad mustache and deep-set eyes. The gryphon-Hayes straddles the flagpole and holds a large, curious, v-shaped implement, which seem to be a dowsing rod composed either of antler or wood. The joint of the dowsing rod is serving as a shuttle for a bundled canine figure, which appears to be sniffing at the pole bushing or mounting

FIG 2.5 — Illustration by Harvey Heywood, *Port Foulke Weekly News* 1.4 (1860).
NEW-YORK HISTORICAL SOCIETY.

FIG 2.6 — [Isaac Israel Hayes] by Matthew Brady. BRADY-HANDY PHOTO-GRAPH COLLECTION, LIBRARY OF CONGRESS PRINTS AND PHOTOGRAPHS DIVISION, LC-BH83-1093.

bracket for the flagpole. A smaller mythical figure with what looks like a monkey's head stands on gryphon-Hayes's back, thumbing its nose at a winged, tailed creature also holding a dowsing rod of a different design.

What does this cartoon tell us about the North Pole–flagging ambitions of the *United States* expedition? As gryphons are seekers and protectors of treasure in mythological lore, Hayes's association with the hybrid beast aligns the objectives of the *United States* expedition within a history of imperial land-grabs in the name of resource extraction. Yet the other elements of the illustration suggest that finding the Pole will be a supernatural effort, one requiring the conjuration of mythical forces to achieve. Dowsing or diving—the practice of using a V- or Y-shaped rod to search for water or other organic resources beneath the earth—is considered a pseudoscience, and the figure of gryphon-Hayes intimates an occult route to the Pole. Hayes had planned to purchase sled dogs from Inuit communities in Greenland, but when his crew attempted to trade they found themselves with old, subpar dogs instead of the fresh teams Hayes had envisioned; eventually Hayes hired three native hunters. Thus the presence of the Inuit or "Esquimaux" dogs in the illustration might serve as another sign that the North Pole will not be obtained by the conventional means available to white Christians. What is more, Hayes was invested in discovering the supposed "open polar sea," the warm, ice-free zone beyond the Arctic ice caps, and the cartoon may imply that this aim is as fanciful as attaining the North Pole.

As it turns out, the story of the establishment of the shipboard newspaper has its own arresting take on a North Polar orientation, one that found the *Port Foulke Weekly News* providing a reorientation of the expedition's perspective on the world.[112] We see this in the following excerpt from the speech made by the paper's editor, George Knorr, upon its inauguration:

> Have we not left that vague border of the national domain far behind us? Yes, fellow-citizens! and it now devolves upon us to bring the vexed question of national boundaries, which has been opened by our enterprise, to a point—to a point, sir! We must carry it to the very Pole itself!—and there, sir, we will nail the Stars and Stripes, and our flagstaff will become the spindle of the world, and the Universal Yankee Nation will go whirling round it like a top. Fellow-citizens and friends:—In conclusion, allow me to propose a sentiment befitting the occasion,—A Free Press and the Universal Yankee Nation: May the former continue in times to come, as in times gone by, the handmaiden of Liberty and the emblem of Progress; and may the latter absorb all Creation and become the grand Celestial Whirligig.[113]

Knorr's reference to the "vexed question" of the "vague border" of the nation functions in several ways. Most immediately, he gestures to midcentury expansionist policies as well as to the sectional conflicts in the United States that would erupt into Civil War while the ship *United States* was far above the Arctic Circle, surprising the crew upon its return. Furthermore, the invocation of nationalist terms in which to cast "Liberty" and the "Free Press" was common to the period, when many newspapers (especially in Britain and Europe) were still subject to stamp taxes and governmental censorship. But Knorr's lack of clarity about the limits of the "national domain" also serves to raise the question of what relationship polar missions had to colonialist voyages. The language of sectional or national chauvinism was not absent from polar newspapers, although statist pride finds far less expression in the papers than it does in other, more public writing about national Arctic expeditions, such as official voyage narratives. Expeditions to the Arctic regions were not principally designed for territorial claiming (other than the imperialist imposition of place names), yet this passage records a cheeky awareness that behind the interests of science and hydrographic discovery lies a grander imperial ambition. This is especially seen in the use of the phrase "Universal Yankee Nation," which originated in the 1820s as a counterpoint to the South's "Virginia race." By midcentury, though, the Universal Yankee Nation was used more sardonically to describe a certain kind of New England ingenuity and proprietary expansiveness. Knorr's toast, then, becomes an acknowledgment of the forces of acquisitional control operating behind polar expeditions, while claiming a space for parodic world-making within the "vague" territory of the newspaper.

I see more than the tired metaphors of colonialism here, however playfully or parodically offered. Knorr invites us to reorient our critical perception, taking a proprioceptive stance—by which I mean one mindful of the place and conditions from which it originates—that looks to polar spaces not from a position rooted in an already established national space but from a new *point*, a new perspectival pole, a reorientation of our map of the world. And this world, polar periodicals tell us, is one out of step with the time, place, and practices of the temperate world. The centrality of an external, diurnal press to both the regulatory and the intellectual lives of the men is appreciated only in its absence; in flagging that pole more fancifully, Arctic travelers reorient themselves both at center and at periphery. Polar newspapers are also aware of the nationalizing and generalizing aspects of the genre of the newspaper; the *Port Foulke Weekly News* recognizes such moves as part of the demands of a newspaper. This point, like the "grand celestial whirligig" imagined by Knorr, sets us a-spin and allows us to imagine polar ecomedia at the ends of the earth.

THREE

ANTARCTIC IMPRINTS

How doth the gay explorer improve the rhyming minute
By editing a newspaper, and printing drivel in it
— [EDWARD FREDERICK BAGE], "To the Editor,"
Adelie Blizzard (1913)

Newspapers were a mechanism for sojourners in Arctic winters to comment upon and conceptually orient themselves within the unexpected vicissitudes of polar environmental spaces. By the advent of sustained Antarctic exploration in the late nineteenth century, when American and European polar interest shifted to the South, winter expeditionary newspapers had been institutionalized as a matter of course. This did not mean that Antarctic voyagers took for granted the technologies that enabled polar printing; in fact crew members amplified their textual production. In the most extreme example, several members of Ernest Shackleton's *Nimrod* crew (1907–9) were directed to a three-week course on operating a press at the London printing firm Sir Joseph Causton and Sons, Ltd.; the crew was *not* trained, however, in cross-country skiing or handling sled dog teams. Antarctic printing of newspapers and, in the case of the *Nimrod*, a 120-page bound book, complete with lithographs, was performed with an eye to the expeditions' patrons back home. The publications are monumental, artifactual; they feature elaborate illustrations, layout, and composition, as well as high-end photography and attention to the literariness or polish of their contents. In one case, submissions deemed too trifling or comic for the *South Polar Times* (which was published in four volumes over the course of two British Antarctic expeditions led by Robert Falcon Scott,

1901–4 and 1910–13) were shuttled to a companion paper, the lighter, slap-dash *Blizzard*.

A century of polar expeditions had habituated the Anglo-American public to stories of polar voyaging; as such, "the official narratives of all the expeditions might be supposed to leave almost nothing untold about life in the Polar Regions," James Murray and George Marston (two of Shackleton's men) write in *Antarctic Days*. Yet the books that were published for the general public, Murray and Marston point out, omit the "homely detail" that "alone can give a vivid impression" of polar life. By this they mean "the humours, the pathos, the commonplace of life on an expedition. The fact is that the funniest things about an expedition can never be told."[1] This assertion is made in a volume whose subtitle is, in part, *Sketches of the Homely Side of Polar Life*; it was published in a limited run of 280 copies. The circumscription of that edition was in fact common to media reflecting the "homely side" of Antarctic life. The first two volumes of the *South Polar Times* were republished in 1907 in a limited facsimile edition of 250, and the third volume in an edition of 350 in 1914; in 2002 the Folio Society produced a centennial edition of 1,000 copies. *Aurora Australis*, the first book printed, etched and lithographed, and bound in Antarctica (at latitude 77°32′ s), was produced in a run of less than 100 copies, eighty-plus of which are presently accounted for, either in university special collections, national archives, or private collections.[2] Antarctic imprints tended to circulate outside of the polar regions more reliably than Arctic ones, yet the sphere of that circulation was limited to an only slightly expanded coterie of expedition patrons, friends, and relations. To the extent that the circulation of Antarctic papers was responsive to the economic imperatives of mounting a South Polar expedition—which often required private patronage from philanthropists or commercial backers—the limited range of that circulation can be seen as a strategic form of accountability.

But even as these striking, boutique publications were mindful of their expeditionary sponsors, they were especially alert to local Antarctic conditions. The North and South Poles are not ecologically or geophysically identical, of course. While the Arctic regions consist of a vast area of ocean (in the nineteenth century, usually frozen) fringed by land, Antarctica is a glacier-covered land mass surrounded by the sea. The ice at both Poles is ever on the move. The large southern continent has a longer polar winter and historically colder, drier conditions than the Arctic. Unlike the Far North, which is rich in terrestrial megafauna such as musk oxen and polar bears, Antarctica has a relatively small population of land animals, as its megafauna are sea creatures such as seals. Ice at the North Pole is generally only several feet above sea level; the South Pole, by contrast, is at an elevation of 9,300 feet, crowning roughly 9,000 feet of ice sheet. The Arctic has been populated by indigenous groups for thousands of years, and the North American Arctic has been subjected to sovereignty and resource claims by nation-states for over half a millennium. Antarctica, by contrast, has no native human population and no permanent residents. Not until 1820 was Antarctica sighted by humans, and the first overwintering on the continent did not happen until 1898. At the turn of the twentieth century Antarctica was still relatively unexplored and little known compared to the Arctic. The Antarctic Treaty of 1959 established the southern continent as the province of science, where sovereignty claims are off-limits.[3]

Climate—and notably climate *change*—was a central concern to the newspapers of the polar South, although a topic not made explicit in Arctic papers. Why the difference?—in part because Antarctic missions were targeted at scientific inquiry more than were their northern counterparts, which were more nationalist or economic-driven in their focus on Northwest Passage trade routes. The Antarctic climate, furthermore, was still somewhat of a mystery to Northern Hemisphere residents. An article in the first number of the *South Polar Times* titled "Polar Plant Life" (1902), for example, remarks that even educated English people think of the South as marked by "warmth, tropical heat, beautiful climates, luxuriant vegetation and life." A dramatic contribution to the paper's second volume stages a conversation between returning Antarctic explorers and fashionable young ladies (in the company of "Mr. Nincompoop Poodlefaker"), one of whom presumes the South is warm and asks in ignorance, "And the natives and polar bears, were they very fierce?"[4] The perception of a temperate or tropical South Pole, teeming with life, was encouraged by fictional representations of the Far South, such as Edgar Allan Poe's *The Narrative of Arthur Gordon Pym* (1837) and James De Mille's *Strange Manuscript Found in a Copper Cylinder* (1888). The comparatively more hostile climate of the South Polar regions comes as a surprise to the educated English auditors invoked in "Polar Plant Life": the "North Polar regions are, as everyone is aware, far better known than the South, about which last, information has been far less obtainable. This is because expeditions to the North have been many and comparatively frequent, also whalers visit it every year; but there have been few expeditions to the South, and whalers rarely go there."[5]

Papers of the South deal more explicitly and more speculatively with climate change—not necessarily as we define the phrase today (as anthropogenic in origin) but as expedition members understood climatic changes through their habitual meteorological observation and recordkeeping. Whether in fiction, scientific articles, or jokes about constant talk of the weather (which proves to be a fascinating topic in Antarctica, much as it would bore society at home, they note), polar explorers tried to make narratives out of weather patterns, to bind up the environmental evidence of the southern continent. In the same fashion, their expeditionary publications were themselves collating partial glimpses of the inner world of the expedition for broader understanding and consumption. Expeditionary practices in Antarctica and the Arctic took different forms as well. Geophysical differences between the two polar regions help to account for some of the variety in the material texts of their various papers: the southern land mass permits the construction of huts and other semipermanent structures, providing both more space and more support for printing projects. Several of the expeditionary huts erected by Scott and Shackleton—intended to be temporary—still stand in good condition a century later, packed with supplies, including an almost edible hundred-year-old fruitcake uncovered in 2017, a testament to the preservation powers of the extreme cold and aridity.[6] By the early twentieth century, technological advances enabled expeditions to bring a range of camera types and, in the case of Frank Hurley of Shackleton's *Endurance* expedition, a "cinematograph machine," or early movie camera. Shackleton and Scott even experimented with motorcars, which proved to be another in a series of Anglo-American maladaptations to polar conditions. Mechanical developments were not necessarily responsive to Antarctic climate: Hurley had no more easy a time developing film at temperatures of −55° than printers at both poles had in maintaining the liquidity of ink for presses.

As was the case in the Arctic during the nineteenth century, roughly half of the Anglophone expeditions to Antarctica from 1897 to 1917—called the heroic age of exploration—published newspapers or other printed matter. The newspapers produced in Antarctica during this period include the *South Polar Times*, the *Blizzard*, and the *Adélie Mail and Cape Adare Times* (all of which were created by the men of Scott's *Discovery* [1901–4] and *Terra Nova* [1910–13] expeditions; the *Antarktischen Intelligenzblättern* (Antarctic Intelligencer) of Erich von Drygalski's German expedition aboard the *Gauss* (1901–3); the *Adelie Blizzard* and *Glacier Tongue* of Douglas Mawson's Australasian Antarctic Expedition (1911–14); the *Antarctic Petrel* of Shackleton's *Nimrod* expedition (1907–9), which also published a bound book, *Aurora Australis*; and *Expedition Topics*, the ship paper of the *Quest* (1921–22), Shackleton's final voyage, upon which he died.

All but *Aurora Australis* were typewritten; some notes on their production follow. The third and fourth volumes of the *South Polar Times* were produced on an Underwood typewriter by the editor, Apsley Cherry-Garrard, and the *Adelie Blizzard* was typed on a Smith Premier model, with stationery donated by John Sands and Partridge & Cooper.[7] Shackleton's *Endurance* expedition carried a Yost typewriter, as two photographs by the expedition photographer, Frank Hurley, reveal; one shows the machine in Shackleton's cabin, while the other finds it tumbled among the books, chocolates, and other detritus of a winter quarters cubicle shared by Hurley and the surgeon Alexander Macklin. The book *Aurora Australis*, "the first book ever written, printed, illustrated, and bound in the Antarctic," as Shackleton described it, was printed on an Albion press with a 10″ × 7″ platen; it was about 30″ high.[8] (The expedition also had a Remington typewriter, on which the *Antarctic Petrel* was produced.) In his sketch of the floor plan of their winter quarters hut, Shackleton gives primacy of place to the printing press and "printing machine," or etching press, positioning them centrally, flanking the dining table. The printers were ever mindful of coal dust and seal blubber oil detritus while pressing pages; once, the inking roller melted from too strenuous an application of the ink-thawing candle to the plate. The roller had to be recast, as Murray and Marston detail, as it was the "only one on the Continent."[9]

Shackleton's official narrative of the *Nimrod* expedition provides the fullest description of the operation of a polar press (save, perhaps, that of the former newspaperman Anthony Fiala cited in chapter 2), and I quote it at length in its instructive comprehensiveness:

> Through the generosity of Messrs. Joseph Causton and Sons, Limited, we had been provided with a complete printing outfit and the necessary paper for the book, and Joyce and Wild had been given instruction in the art of type-setting and printing, Marston being taught etching and lithography. They had hardly become skilled craftsmen, but they had gained a good working knowledge of the branches of the business. When we had settled down in the winter quarters, Joyce and Wild set up the little hand-press and sorted out the type. . . . The early days of the printing department were not exactly happy, for the two amateur type setters found themselves making many mistakes, and when they had at last "set up" a page, made all the necessary corrections, and printed off the required number of copies, they had to undertake the laborious work of "dissing," that is, of distributing the type again. They plodded ahead

FIG 3.1 — Herbert Ponting, "Mr Cherry-Garrard working on the South Polar Times," 1911, Cape Evans, *Terra Nova*. Ponting Collection, P2005/5/475. SCOTT POLAR RESEARCH INSTITUTE, UNIVERSITY OF CAMBRIDGE.

FIG 3.2 — Frank Hurley, "Frank Hurley and Alexander Macklin at home on the *Endurance*." ROYAL GEOGRAPHICAL SOCIETY (WITH IBG).

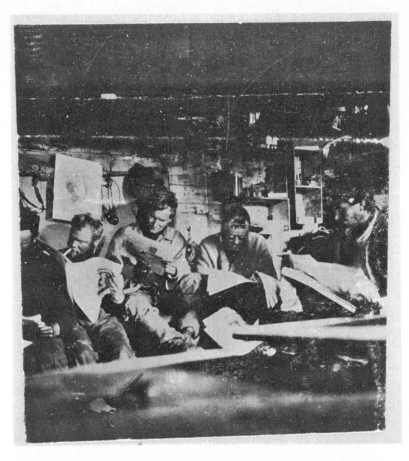

FIG 3.3 — Five men sitting in a hut or on board ship, reading newspapers. From left to right: Mac, Marston, Priestley, Murray, and Joyce. P59/61/97. SCOTT POLAR RESEARCH INSTITUTE, UNIVERSITY OF CAMBRIDGE.

steadily, however, and soon became more skillful, until at the end of a fortnight or three weeks they could print two pages in a day. A lamp had to be placed under the type-rack to keep it warm, and a lighted candle was put under the inking-plate, so that the ink would keep reasonably thin in consistency. The great trouble experienced by the printers at first was in securing the right pressure on the printing-plate and even inking of the page, but experience showed them where they had been at fault. Day meanwhile prepared the binding by cleaning, planing, and polishing wood taken from the Venesta cases in which our provisions were packed. Marston reproduced the illustrations by algraphy, or printing

FIG 3.4 — Ernest Joyce and printing press in his cubicle in the hut. P68/73/55.
SCOTT POLAR RESEARCH INSTITUTE, UNIVERSITY OF CAMBRIDGE.

from aluminium plates. He had not got a proper lithographing press, so had to use an ordinary etching press, and he was handicapped by the fact that all our water had a trace of salt in it. This mineral acted on the sensitive plates, but Marston managed to produce what we all regarded as creditable pictures.[10]

The resultant book bears the mark of the specialized printing firm that assisted the men of the *Nimrod*. It also showcases the resilience of materials in the polar regions. We see that resilience here in the form of the inventiveness of Bernard Day, ship's mechanic, whose bindings of the volumes of *Aurora Australis* repurposed the expedition's waste. Venesta was an early form of plywood, and the boards with which Day bound several score copies of the book reflect the variety of foodstuffs the expedition brought with it. Indeed those boxes of provisions, and the traces of their identifying stencils, now are used to help distinguish different editions of *Aurora Australis* from each other. In my own archival travels I have examined copies of *Aurora Australis* bound in boards bearing the stencils (sometimes in fragments) of the words "butter," "oatmeal," "pates," "fruit," and "stewed kidneys." Robert B.

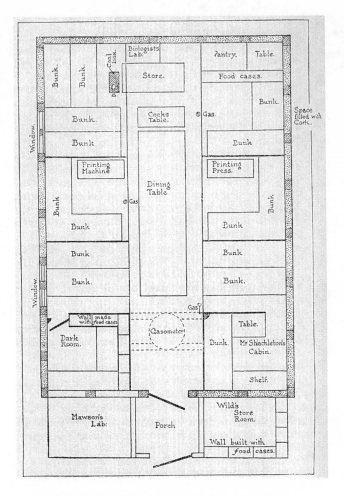

FIG 3.5 — Plan of the hut at winter quarters. From Shackleton, *The Heart of the Antarctic*, 91.

Stephenson's bibliography of extant copies of the book reveals the broader range of materials the Venesta boards had once contained, which include "tea," "jam," "pork pies," "kidney soup," "bottled fruit," "petit pois," "sugar," "Irish stew," "cutlets," "tinned fruit," "beans," "veal," "turtle soup," "syrup," "biscuits," "honey," and "chicken."[11] The domestic, quotidian details of the labels stamped onto the reclaimed Venesta bindings are in contrast to the images of privation, extremity, and alienation associated with Antarctic exploration.

The late nineteenth century through the end of the Great War is considered the heroic age of Antarctic exploration. It preceded what some have

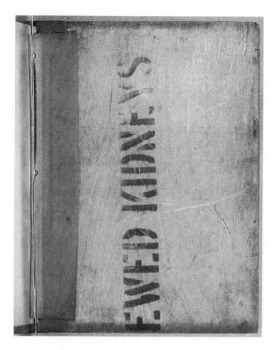

FIG 3.6 — Inside front cover of "Stewed Kidney" edition of Shackleton, ed., *Aurora Australis*. JOHN CARTER BROWN LIBRARY.

called the mid- to late twentieth century mechanical age, during which expedition members had access to improved communication, technology, outfitting—and airplanes. What made the heroic age heroic, then, was in great part the exceptional suffering endured by the first parties to winter over on the Antarctic continent, when their gear, resources, fuel, and clothing all proved to be inadequate. The two best-known Antarctic expeditions, led by Scott and Shackleton, were catastrophic losses. (Unjustly less familiar, and in some ways no less deadly, is Mawson's extraordinary march of 315 miles in 1912 after the death of two sledging companions and the loss of nearly all their food.) Scott and the four members of his party with whom he was attempting to be the first to reach the South Pole died on their return from the Pole, which they discovered had been flagged thirty-four days earlier by the Norwegian explorer Roald Amundsen. Shackleton and all the humans with him survived the *Endurance* expedition (1914–17) but lost the ship and suffered great privations. In both cases, however, expeditionary writing, photography, and other forms of polar media were salvaged by the survivors. Even on a march for their lives, when crew members of the *Endurance* were allowed to retain only two pounds of personal possessions, they still hauled heavy photographic glass plates taken by Hurley.

Before the *Endurance* was crushed by the ice, Hurley dove into the flooded ship to rescue his photographic output; he and Shackleton then selected 120 images, shattering the remaining four hundred plates so that the lensman would not be tempted to return to recover them.

The photographic plate selection process underscores the importance (as well as the changing meaning) of ecomedia circulation in polar missions while in Antarctica. On the one hand, Hurley's negatives are an instantiation of the increased technological professionalism brought to bear on Antarctic newspaper and media production. On the other hand, the destruction of nearly four-fifths of the negatives in the face of the loss of the *Endurance* testifies to the vicissitudes of Antarctic curation: Hurley's collection process is compelled under the threat of high-pressure environmental disaster rather than being driven by leisurely aesthetic selection. The rescue of the photographic plates likewise marks some distinctions between Arctic and Antarctic forms of media preservation: whereas the copy of the *Vicar of Wakefield* retained by Franklin's desperate men on their march from their abandoned ships might have brought them comfort or slight recreation, Hurley and Shackleton's photographic plates had no immediate office for the crew of the crushed *Endurance*. Instead the plates were curated and preserved for the benefit of a public situated a world away from Antarctica. In turn, the theoretical public imagined by Hurley and Shackleton in their dives into the fractured, ice-flooded ship has ever been mindful of the duress under which these photographic media were created.

The increased polar-specific professionalization of the onetime amateur, coterie publication reflects increased global attention to the climate and resources of the polar regions, as well as a growing narrative acknowledgment of the processes of climate change. The three most elaborate printed works of the Antarctic heroic age of exploration—the *South Polar Times*, *Aurora Australis*, and the *Adelie Blizzard*—are the objects of most of my attention in what follows; all were conceived of as monumental projects, and their production values and other aspects of their material texts bear out this ambition. All three typed or printed productions share an interest, for one, in notions of a polar verge or inner world, whether theoretically considered or fictionally created. In addition, all feature fictional sketches and nimble poetic parodies in which contributors comment upon climate change, weather, and other environmental conditions. These papers retain many of the comic elements of their Arctic counterparts—acrostics, caricatures, facetious stories about real estate and weather. A "To

Let" advertisement in the *Adélie Mail and Cape Adare Times*, for example, showcases a hut in an "airy and bracing situation. Surrounded by a large area of well-manured soil. . . . Beautiful weather. We are positively willing to guarantee that no wind of hurricane force shall blow for more than ten days running."[12] The discovery of "immense deposits of the mineral *ICE*" inspire an ad for mining investments, in another instance.[13] The winds in Antarctica are exceptionally punishing, which the *Adelie Blizzard* quipped would aid its distribution: the paper is "registered at the General Plateau Office for transmission by wind as a newspaper."[14] Yet Antarctic papers are also more self-consciously literary and more attuned to the meteorological and scientific aims of the expeditions. Still, as the title of Murray and Marston's volume of miscellany demonstrates, armchair polar travelers back in the metropole can expect only "sketches" of the "homely" aspects of polar life. (Murray and Marston use "homely" in the sense of ordinary, everyday, or simple.) The *South Polar Times*, *Aurora Australis*, and *Adelie Blizzard* are designed to be monumental, yet they can only ever provide *partial* views of Antarctic life, both in their formal limitations and in their status as works of ecomedia conditioned by climatic extremity. Even with only partial views, however, Antarctic publications are packaged to suggest more coherent narrative accounting, whether in the increasing number of texts meditating on the changing climate or in the bound material texts themselves. We might think of the production of these printed works as part of a sponsor-stewardship loop, designed as a form of payback. Newspapers and the first Antarctic book broadcast to their coterie producers that their polar mission endures, that the expedition survives with something to show for it. They bind up (both conceptually and in the sense of the material text of the bound volumes) the work that Antarctic explorers are doing to understand and represent the climate of the polar regions and how it is changing.

The partialness inherent in representations of Antarctic life and environment speaks to the challenges in using conventional textual or other media forms to convey climatic extremity. The elaborate productions of the Antarctic presses of the turn of the twentieth century are one formal experiment among many, as I discuss below. I begin, though, by lingering for a moment on a form of polar ecomedia that has been enabled by the social media technologies of our present: tweets from Antarctica. When presenting versions of the research in this book, I have routinely received comments such as "The papers sound like they served the same function as Facebook and Twitter do for us now." This is astute. In Arctic and Antarctic newspapers, contributors share witticisms, make observations on daily life, and relay inside jokes. They too circulate "fake news" (albeit for puckish effect). Like polar ecomedia, tweets and other social media posts are ephemeral. Like Antarctic missions, they have both private and public audiences; the glimpse they provide of the inner lives of their producers circulates only so long and so far.

Out of Time, Out of Place

The news out of Antarctica in the spring of '14 was terrible. Those attentive to the details of global climate change might assume that I refer to reports that first appeared in May of the looming, irreversible collapse of the West Antarctic ice sheet (the size of Mexico), the disintegration of which will produce a rise in sea levels of over ten feet in the next hundred years.[15] The fate of the West Antarctic ice sheet is so dire, however, that it no longer qualifies as news; it is a cataclysm, a visitation from a cinematic death contrivance born of human industrial activity. No, I refer instead to Shackleton's proposal to bring to Antarctica a string of unlikely, climate-tender work animals to pull the expedition's supply sledges: ponies.

Shackleton may be dead in nearly all media—in history books, most immediately—but in the spring of 2014 on Twitter, where he persisted a century later under the handle @EShackleton, he was preparing for the *Endurance* expedition (1914–17), his famous Antarctic voyage of material and animal loss and human perseverance and preservation. Between 2014 and 2016 the social media account in his name tweeted 140-character updates drawn from his journals, correspondence, and media coverage, issuing the posts one hundred years to the day, when possible, after the events. The account was curated by the new media artist Peggy Nelson, who "works with fragmented narratives, locative art, and media, both new and old."[16] While many tweets quote directly from expedition members' writing (as indicated by quotation marks), most are from Nelson's narrative paraphrase of the mission's activities. The expedition for which Shackleton was preparing on Twitter in the spring of '14 marked his third expedition in Antarctica, during a period of heavy interest in the region and a flurry of international expeditionary activity. He had been a lieutenant on Scott's first Antarctic command on the *Discovery*, an unsuccessful British-sponsored South Pole attempt (1901–4; not repeated on twenty-first-century social media). Shackleton next led a relatively less famous mission, also aiming for the South Pole, aboard the *Nimrod* (1907–9). The "race to the pole" in which

Scott (@CaptainRFScott on Twitter) subsequently found himself engaged with the Norwegian polar exploration legend Roald Amundsen (1911–12) was revisited on social media during the centenary of the two ventures; Scott, tragically (and, in the Anglo-American imagination, heroically) died in history as well as on Twitter on March 29, '12 (1912 and 2012). Since his social media death, Scott's Twitter account has been dormant, another internet ghost site. Like Shackleton, Scott was a pony enthusiast and brought nineteen Manchurian horses to Antarctica. The men gave them names such as Nobby, Jehu, Snatcher, Bones, Chinaman, Snippets, Blossom, and Jimmy Pigg. The animals that did not expire in transit died in Antarctica, as Scott himself did.

Ponies are not polar megafauna. And yet in two prominent early twentieth-century Antarctic expeditions, led by Scott and by Shackleton, Britons had brought the short, squat cousins of horses to the coldest, driest, and most inhospitable climate in the world. Why ponies? Unlike Siberian huskies and other dogs specifically bred for hauling sledges in the various northern Arctic regions, ponies are not known for their cold-weather hardiness. The Inuit, Sami, Chukchi, Yupik, and other indigenous peoples of the North do not use ponies, nor do Norwegians and other Scandinavians, whose adaptability to polar conditions consistently led to their Antarctic expeditionary success. (Neither the Inuit nor Scandinavians used motorcars, either, as both Scott and Shackleton attempted in Antarctica in the early twentieth century.) Equine labor was culturally familiar to the men who organized expeditions designed to reach the South Pole or to traverse the southern continent; they were less comfortable in thinking of dogs as beasts of burden, as northern peoples did. Dogs were domestic companions to Scott and Shackleton, while horses and ponies were working animals.[17] The ponies may have been an experiment, as hydrogen balloons bearing silk rescue messages were in the North, but the consequence of failure for the living animals is loss on a different scale of matter.

In reviewing his first command, on which ponies had proved equally ill-adapted to Antarctic conditions, Shackleton himself admitted, as he made it plain on Twitter in the spring of '14, "In hindsight, the ponies were a mistake." The ponies suffered from terrible seasickness on the ocean voyage. Their circulatory systems could not handle temperatures of −40°. Their narrow, tender hooves broke through the ice or fractured from the chill despite the small pony snowshoes crafted for them. They drowned, they died from cold, they were shot, they were eaten by the men—a posthumous service that had been planned from the start. "During my Nimrod Expe-

FIG 3.7 — Pony snowshoe from Cape Evans, Antarctica. British Antarctic Expedition, E 1910–13, Antarctica, N: 24a. SCOTT POLAR RESEARCH INSTITUTE, UNIVERSITY OF CAMBRIDGE.

dition, the ponies kept freezing," Shackleton acknowledged. "When they move about, they sweat. In extreme cold this means the ponies are constantly crystallizing. Dogs don't crystallize. They pant." Amundsen, flush from his international triumph of flagging the South Pole, took the time to drop by Shackleton's London office to offer him some advice—to "talk me out of ponies and into dogs and skis," Shackleton tweeted in paraphrased distillations of his journals, letters, and other narrative accounts. "Yes, I was considering using ponies again," he confessed; even more embarrassing, he wrote, "I had still not learned to ski." This was a British reluctance to adapt to polar conditions, joining the earlier Arctic expeditionary distaste at eating raw seal (a noted antiscorbutic recommended by indigenous peoples of the North), as well as the stubborn Anglo-American preference for wool clothing over the far superior skins worn by the Inuit and Sami and Scandinavians). "Amundsen was right. I knew he was right."[18] Would Shackleton bring ponies on the *Endurance* expedition, I wondered as I followed the social media stream in the spring of 2014? I hung on his Twitter feed as it unscrolled.

That I know the answer, know every outcome of every decision made on the now legendary *Endurance* expedition and its consequences for the less-fabled ponies, historically speaking, does not argue against the utility of the Shackleton Twitter feed as a genre of polar ecomedia through which to think through the place and time of literary and textual ventures. Both ponies in Antarctica and the textual form of the tweet are out of place. Twitter feeds are jumbled, nonsequential, heterogeneous streams of information. The microblogging platform is a medium premised on a form of immediacy, but in the case of the Shackleton expedition it is an anachronism—literally documenting events out of time. In their abstraction from the time and place of their original scene of writing or publishing, the tweets enact the asynchronicity of polar literary circulation in their limited, fragmented form. At the same time, Shackleton's tweets offer a narrative frame for encompassing the place and time of polar spaces within both the history of nations and within planetary time. Deep or geologic time keys its timescale to the age of the planet, estimated at 4.55 billion years; in this timescale the 100-year distance between Shackleton's expedition and "his" tweets might as well be a simultaneity. In a similar sense, my arguments throughout *The News at the Ends of the Earth* about the importance of nineteenth-century polar expeditions to understanding the twenty-first-century climate crisis are likewise mindful of planetary timescales.

In their brevity and motility, tweets re-create the sketch or glimpse form of the travel narrative genre of their period. They also, in this way, underscore that views of nature and human and animal adaptability are only ever partial. Tweets from Antarctica are akin to the nineteenth-century literary form of the sketch, the view, the peep, or the glimpse. Such short-form writing promises readers—or, in the case of Antarctic publications, expeditionary patrons—an access that is framed as glancing, partial, fragmentary. In her work on the form of the sketch Kristie Hamilton has called this pose a kind of "mass-market intimacy," a move from a centralized observer to a more ephemeral diffusion.[19] This generic withholding is in part an affectation, certainly, a gesture of rhetorical modesty that becomes conventional in the period. But we can see this also as a recognition of the futility of encompassing perspectives, a pushback against the taxonomic drives that likewise characterize the rise of professionalizing scientific discourse in the nineteenth century. The forms of the sketch, the glimpse, the peep, the view, and, we should add, the tweet are themselves elements of social media that provide a peep of the inner life of expedition members, one not covered by official voyage narratives. Indeed the newspapers are more properly miscellanies than newspapers—they are loose and comic and above all partial, generically and epistemologically at counterpoint to the exhaustively taxonomic records and journals kept officially by the expedition members at all other points of their time in the polar regions, however simultaneous that time may be.

The brevity and relative sociability of these forms does not mean that they are limited in their weight, however. The present-day polar explorer Felicity Aston, the first person to ski solo across Antarctica under muscle power alone, describes her own use of Twitter as a way to endure the isolation of her grand solo attempt. Aston had with her a satellite phone, but no matter how painfully, violently alone she felt many nights, never called her mother or a friend. Instead she sent SMS messages to her Twitter account, enough to leave a skeleton record of the voyage and satisfy a need to reach beyond the ice. (Aston did not carry a full-size journal because it would add too much weight for her to haul.) These tweets were not the only patchwork narratives of Aston's time in Antarctica. She had an mp3 player with her, loaded with music as well as audiobooks, including a lengthy history of England and an Agatha Christie mystery. But as the audiobooks were divided into chapters, and those chapters listed alphabetically, they did not play in narrative order; thus the murderer was revealed before there was a body, and the reigns of the Jameses and the Henrys and the Charleses disassembled and reassembled in Aston's mind along the long nightless kilometers.[20] Antarctica thwarts linear temporality and full accounting; seemingly accidental, erroneous, or coincidental patterns of correspondence register as causal properties of Antarctica itself rather than the vicissitudes of exploration or technological performance.

This was the case for Shackleton as well, most eerily embodied by the unaccountable phantom fourth man on the final push he and his fellow survivors made toward rescue on South Georgia at the end of his *Endurance* expedition. As he describes it:

> I know that during that long and racking march of thirty-six hours over the unnamed mountains and glaciers of South Georgia it seemed to me often that we were four, not three. I said nothing to my companions on the point, but afterwards Worsley said to me, "Boss, I had a curious feeling on the march that there was another person with us." Crean confessed to the same idea. One feels "the dearth of human words, the roughness of mortal speech" in trying to describe things intangible, but a record of our journeys would be incomplete without a reference to a subject very near to our hearts.[21]

Perhaps in this sense too the Antarctic ponies continue to haunt. Their thicker, shaggier coats might have made them hardier than Arabians but no less vulnerable to Antarctic winds. Compelled on Scott's expedition to jump from ice floe to floe, one pony fell into the frigid water and was rescued, whisky forced down its throat; a second pony could not be hauled out of the water and was killed by ice axe to keep it from being torn apart by circling orcas. "These incidents were too terrible," Scott wrote in his journal.[22]

Are ponies any more timely, any less absurd than humans when translocated to Antarctic spaces? Both humans and ponies are maladapted to continental conditions, suffering from inadequate shoes, poor nourishment, insufficient coats. Lawrence "Titus" Oates, for example, tended devotedly to the ailing, chilly ponies in Antarctica as a member of Scott's fatal expedition; he was tapped for the Southern Party that accompanied Scott on his dash for the Pole. On their return from 90° s latitude, devastated to have discovered that Amundsen's Norwegian team had preceded them to the achievement by five weeks, the British party was severely debilitated. Oates particularly struggled, plagued by terrible frostbite and gangrenous feet. His pleas to his companions to leave him behind were rejected. Lamed liked the ponies to which he had ministered (and which were later shot for food), Oates engineered his own mercy killing. In a blizzard, with temperatures at −40°, he performed a now-legendary act characterized as an exemplar of British heroic sacrifice: knowing he could march no farther, Oates said to his companions, "I am just going outside and may be some time" and stepped unshod out of the shared tent and into the storm, never to be seen again.[23]

The history of exploration is a history of death. There is the vast colonial violence of the usual practices of imperial ventures. There are the accidental deaths attendant upon what Kristin Jacobson has called "adrenaline narratives," stories of ascending Everest or free-soloing El Capitán.[24] It is easy to say that humans do not belong in places like Antarctica, but some choose to travel there for reasons that have their own centrifugal imaginative and scientific force. The heroic frame through which historic polar exploration is often presented hangs awkwardly when ponies enter the picture. Polar ponies stand with heads hung low from their doubled burden, hooves fractured from and fracturing the frozen terrain on which they stand. These are not chargers or stallions or steeds for conquerors; they are plodding, dumpy, matted beasts whose very name-ending encodes their diminution, their contingency within the story of polar exploration. Humans might feel

FIG 3.8 — "Breaking Camp, Southern Journey," Shackleton's *Nimrod* expedition. P62/3/4.
SCOTT POLAR RESEARCH INSTITUTE, UNIVERSITY OF CAMBRIDGE.

for these ponies—feel *as* these ponies—as the Arctic melts and the West Antarctic ice sheet collapses under our feet.

The Inner Life of the *South Polar Times*

Shackleton's first encounter with polar ecomedia came not in 2014 but in 1902, when he was serving as the third officer of the *Discovery* expedition, helmed by Scott in the latter's first, less fatal Antarctic command. (Shackleton was compelled to leave the expedition one year early because of ill health.) The young lieutenant edited the first volume of the *South Polar Times*, the expedition's typewritten newspaper, which was sumptuously illustrated by its shipboard artist, Edward Wilson. Published over the course of two expeditions across eleven years, it would ultimately run to four volumes, the fourth of which would be left incomplete after Scott's death during the *Terra Nova* expedition, over a decade after the *Discovery* voyage. In describing his plans for winter pastimes, Scott observes that "it was a very usual thing in the old Northern expeditions to hold classes for school amongst the men" (chapter 1 details this common practice), "but in those days many could not read or write." By contrast, the men of the southern expeditions (which began in earnest eighty years after the first Arctic expeditions) have the "accomplishments" of literacy, Scott boasts, and "are able to amuse themselves."[25] One element remained consistent between Arctic and Antarctic polar voyaging, as an editorial in the third volume written by Apsley Cherry-Garrard, by then the editor, pointed out: "Both in the North and South papers have been written during the famous Winter Night."[26] Nevertheless the southern explorers felt they had the intellectual and artistic edge; despite following "the example of the great national expeditions of past generations to the other end of the Earth," Scott's party felt that it was "no exaggeration to say that 'The South Polar Times,' in literary quality, in variety, and especially in its artistic features, has never been equaled in similar conditions."[27] The last statement is arguably true—or at least it was true until the bound book *Aurora Australis* was printed by Shackleton's *Nimrod* men five years later. This claim was made in a prospectus circulated to potential subscribers for a facsimile edition of the first two volumes of the *South Polar Times* to be printed in London after the *Discovery*'s return, and thus assertions of supremacy would make for good marketing. (The prospectus sought one thousand subscribers; the first two volumes were ultimately printed in a run of 250 copies.) The flyer summarizes the content of the first two volumes of the paper as comprising "something like 400 quarto pages, scarcely one of which is without its illustration, coloured or uncoloured, in the text or as a separate plate, illustrating life on board, portraits, caricatures, interiors, scenery, animal life, plant life, instruments, flags, coats of arms, sledging, sport, and many other things."[28]

Before polar winter set in, the "scheme" for the *South Polar Times* had been arranged. Both officers and men contributed to the monthly periodical, for which Shackleton served as inaugural editor as well as "printer, manager, typesetter, and office boy."[29] As Scott wrote in his journal, it had been decided collectively that each issue should feature "a summary of the events and meteorological conditions of the past month, certain scientifically instructive articles dealing with our work and our surroundings, and certain others written in a lighter vein." This "lighter vein" included

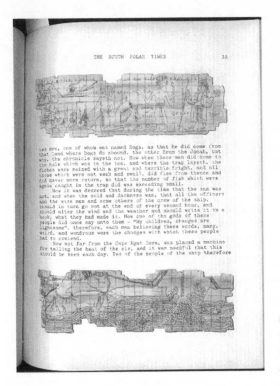

FIG 3.9 — Edmund Wilson illustration for "Leaves from an Ancient Papyrus," *South Polar Times* 2.2 (1903): 33.

"full-page caricatures, acrostics, and puzzles," which "the men contribute as well as the officers." In fact, Scott notes, in an echo of Clements Markham's observation about Arctic newspaper contributions, "some of the best and quite the most amusing articles are written by the occupants of the mess-deck, of whom one or two show extraordinary ability with the pen."[30] Its "super-excellence" reflects the crew's familiarity with a wide range of periodicals, as Albert Armitage, a *Discovery* expedition member, explained; the *South Polar Times* "was to combine all the best qualities of all the penny and halfpenny London dailies, together with those of the superior comic papers, as well as of the fourpenny-halfpenny and halfcrown monthly magazines."[31] In its regular features on expeditionary scientific activities and weather reports—reported straight, without irony or parody—the *South Polar Times* would differ from its Arctic predecessors, which rarely if ever gave sincere narrative accounts on such matters. They reserved the relation of such matters for their voyage narratives. The *S.P.T.* (to which the paper was referred in expeditionary writing and in its own pages) was designed to "give instruction as well as amusement," Scott testified; "we looked to our scientific experts to write luminously on their special subjects, and to

FIG 3.10 — Carved mahogany contribution box for the *South Polar Times*. From the British National Antarctic Expedition 1901–4 (*Discovery*), Y: 2002/2/2. SCOTT POLAR RESEARCH INSTITUTE, UNIVERSITY OF CAMBRIDGE.

record the scientific events of general interest, while for lighter matter we agreed that the cloak of anonymity should encourage the indulgence of any shy vein of sentiment or humour that might exist among us."[32] To ensure anonymous submissions, contributors deposited their materials, often written with disguised handwriting, in a customized wooden dropbox with an engraving of a rising, bleary-eyed sun on its face.

From its inaugural editorial, the *S.P.T.* had an eye to the differences between conventional newspapers and polar periodicals. "A pioneer of the Antarctic Press must necessarily differ in many respects from the papers of our Homeland, and the world in general," Shackleton pointed out. At home, or in "the world" that lies outside the frozen zones,

> I might stand at the door, and look in vain for the row of boys, each with his red-rimmed bicycle, ready to fly to the street corner with his bundle, the moment the paper leaves the printer's hands, and there unload to the grimy leather-lunged urchins of the pavement. In vain I might look for

the flaunting flag, and plastered sides, of that terror to nervous ladies, and mild old gentlemen, the high cart with its six foot wheels, which in half an hour spreads the news of the world from one end of the city to the other. I know we have not here as in England, the early train, which draws up at the many stations of Surburia, to deposit with the milk, bundles of still damp sheets, rolled off by the press in hours when all the rest of the world was asleep; sheets that in due time will be read propped up against the coffee pot or loaf. . . .

No; the surroundings are far different where this small paper starts its career. I look out of the door, and see a wide white world of snow and ice, with black volcanic peaks rising above the drift, and far in the snowy distance I see a great column of smoke from a chimney of no man's building, but from the great volcano Erebus, at whose foot our little colony dwells.[33]

The rich, evocative detail that Shackleton provides for this scene of home-land newspaper circulation shows wistfulness and nostalgia for the color-ful, riotous streets of the metropole. The "still damp sheets" of the outer-world newspaper arrive as predictably as the delivery of staples, even in "Suburbia"; this vision of domestic life accounts for various degrees of pe-riodical circulation, from the urban street corners to the quiet home. In-deed Shackleton emphasizes the multiple entities that handle or encoun-ter newspapers: boys, urchins, ladies and gentlemen, train conductors. The effect is to underscore the *s.p.t.* editor's own multiplicity of roles (Shack-leton as "printer, manager, typesetter, and office boy") while in the remote "wild white world of snow and ice," the fires of home and the pollution of industry replaced by a volcano, Erebus, named after a god of darkness and shadow.[34]

An earlier draft of Shackleton's editorial reveals details that he edited out for the version published in the inaugural *s.p.t.* Notably these details all have to do with diurnal time and the regularity of newspaper deliv-ery. Whereas the published editorial imagines suburban readers receiving "sheets that in due time will be read propped up against the coffee pot or loaf," a manuscript draft finds Shackleton envisioning "sheets that in due time ~~either at eight or nine A M~~ will be read propped up against the coffee pot or loaf."[35] The manuscript draft assigns diurnal and temporal specificity to the scene of a leisurely morning perusal of the paper, an hourly register that is reflective of the steady periodicity of the papers of the temperate zone. In another change, Shackleton cut from the printed version the following wish: "In writing this paper we think of those at home and hope that when ~~our~~ we return they may read it, and see how we amused ourselves ~~through the days of darkness, when the Sun played truant to us~~."[36] Why might he elide "eight or nine A M" from the version of the editorial statement that ended up in the Antarctic-printed *S.P.T.*? Why not retain the characterization of the sun's truancy during the polar winter? Shackleton could be looking to reduce references to temporal specificity within an Antarctic environment that, like the Arctic, is out of step—out of time and place—with the diurnal world of the homeland. In hoping that "those at home" might read the paper upon the expedition's return, the contributors might also wish to heighten the contrast between the bustle, textures, and colors of London (with its red bikes, grimy urchins, and postered wagons) and the white-and-black world of the southern continent. This is consistent with Arctic registers of polar temporality.

Southern papers, however, register their out-of-placeness in another dimension too. For within the paper itself the outer world was at times figured not as the homeland of Britain but as the world outside the confines of the "depths of the hold" where Shackleton and his *S.P.T.* volume 2 editorial successor, the physicist Louis Bernacchi, established their office. "Except for furtive interviews in the cabins of the various artists," Scott writes, "we of the *outer world* knew little of the progress of the venture until that fateful day the 23rd of April, when the sun disappeared for the first time below our horizon and the first number of the Journal was laid on the ward-room table by its smiling editor."[37] In aligning the newspaper's audience with the "outer world," Scott associates the publishers of the *S.P.T.* with the "inner world," which more generally was presented as the expedition itself. Any place that is *not* Antarctica is presented as the outer world within both the *South Polar Times* and the other writings of the polar crew members. Here are some examples. A poem in the *S.P.T.* written by the ship's lead stoker reimagines the "new world" as Antarctica to Britain's "Old":

By beaten roads the old world goes,
With noise of work and pleasure;
But those who must, mid snow and gust
Take out a new world's measure.
We know just why the order comes
"The Old World Wants to Know,"
So we bend our backs till the harness cracks
And go onward o'er the snow.[38]

In offering thoughts to the German expedition then stationed on the other side of the continent, Shackleton writes, "We and they are cut off in the same way from all connection with the outer world."[39] Otto Nordenskjöld's sojourn with a Swedish Antarctic expedition found him confessing that "one thinks so little of what can be taking place in the outer world"; although the expedition had brought stacks of newspapers from home, "these chronicles were something outside and foreign to us."[40] In the *Adelie Blizzard*, Mawson's expeditionary paper, anything outside of Antarctica is referred to as the "outer world."[41] By imagining their domestic home as external, Antarctic explorers reorient the polar regions as "internal."

To this day, in fact, scientists and others working in Antarctica use the phrase "the world" (from which Antarctica is, by implication, excluded) or "the external world" to distinguish the inner domain of the southern continent from the rest of the planet. A guide to the present-day culture of overwintering in Antarctica explains how ecological conditions during polar darkness contribute to this sense of internality. In the winter months, Antarctic veterans explain, "the visual field diminishes, so that even under a full moon you may not be able to see the mountains lying across McMurdo Sound that so dominate the summer landscape. . . . The world quite literally closes in. In this environment, people slowly divest themselves of concern about the external world."[42] In addition to the psychic and visual components of this foreshortening, there is a circumscription of mobility inherent to Antarctic winters. Today, the last flights to Amundsen-Scott South Pole Station from McMurdo Station occur in February or March of each year, when the sun is beginning its winter decline. Flights cannot resume until August at the earliest; anyone overwintering at the South Pole is immobilized there for about six months, with no possibility of travel back to the coastal base. This is because jet fuel freezes at −50°, and winter temperatures are lower than that point. The opening editorial for the *Adelie Blizzard* acknowledges that the polar desert could make explorers feel akin to Robinson Crusoe or his nonfictional analogue, Alexander Selkirk; yet "the fact remains that so far from being marooned, in the old sense," the men of the Australasian Antarctic Expedition experienced what the editor called—in quotes—"society."[43] By distancing the expedition members from a conventional notion of "society," the *Adelie Blizzard* opens up the possibility of new forms of community organization and social interiority, the rarefied club of those abstracted from "the world." These forms include the otherworldly.

The Inner World of Antarctica

Antarctica's extremity of weather and exceptional distance from the Northern Hemisphere contribute to a particular form of polar internalization. The supposed internality of the polar regions is not meant only as an ironic reversal of the usual sense of the North and South Poles as the ends of the earth. The language of "inner" and "outer" worlds had been common, in fact, in invocations of the polar regions throughout the previous century, most notably in the speculative fiction category of "hollow earth" writing. Several fictional pieces in Antarctic newspapers also contribute to the genre, as I discuss below. Hollow earth fiction traces its genealogy to the early modern period, if not earlier, if we include the underworlds of classical epics. Its zenith, however, coincided with the polar expeditions launched in the long nineteenth century. Holes in the earth, of course, must necessarily invoke the mining and extraction interests that have for centuries propelled "discovery" voyages. The large craters that have been appearing in Siberia in recent years both remind and warn us that holes in the earth are not only the cause of climate change (via extractive resource drilling) but also the product of it, as the Siberian holes are caused by methane gas explosions released by the rapidly warming permafrost.

Strikingly, nearly all hollow earth fictions set the Poles—usually the South Pole—as the entry point for the inner world. Often the region near the Poles, again particularly at the South, is fancied to be a tropical garden. The earth's core, in these works, is accessible by way of an imagined warm, open polar sea beyond the icecaps.[44] Familiar works of nineteenth-century hollow earth fiction include Poe's *Narrative of Arthur Gordon Pym* (1837) and various of his short stories, Jules Verne's *Journey to the Center of the Earth* (1864), Edward Bulwer-Lytton's *The Coming Race* (1870), James De Mille's *A Strange Manuscript Found in a Copper Cylinder* (1888), DeWitt Chipman's *Beyond the Verge* (1896), and Edgar Rice Burroughs's *At the Earth's Core* (1914). The majority of these fictions reflect an idea of a polar "verge," first articulated by John Cleves Symmes (1779–1829) to describe the indeterminate space that forms the entrance to the earth's interior. Symmes was a War of 1812 veteran from Ohio who believed the earth was hollow, open at the North and South Poles, and inhabitable inside. He dedicated his life to his theory of concentric spheres, which had some surprising traction amid ridicule, and he advocated his thesis in newspaper missives and on the lecture circuit.[45] Symmes's protégé, Jeremiah N. Reynolds, became a successful advocate for polar exploration and for Charles Wilkes's United

States Exploring Expedition, as well as a literary inspiration to Poe, who is rumored to have cried out Reynolds's name on his deathbed.[46] Credentialed polar explorers might be said to have abandoned, finally, any vague belief in the possibility of a hollow earth (kept alive today in certain internet and occult bookstore corners) in the early twentieth century. The Arctic explorer Vilhjamur Stefansson recalls that the Arctic Club in the early twentieth century had shared a New York neighborhood with William Reed's Hollow Earth Club; when the newly created Explorers Club was looking for rooms in one building, its members tried to drive out the Hollow Earth Club. (They did not succeed.)[47]

Symmes's theories are also known today through their expression in hollow earth fiction, originally, and most provocatively, in *Symzonia* (1820), a parodic fictional narrative that describes an expedition, inspired by Symmes's "sublime theory," that travels through the polar verge to the earth's interior via the South Pole.[48] (The other significant polar event occurring in the year 1820 was the first glimpse of the continent of Antarctica by humans on Russian and British expeditions.) The verge is a spatial concept repeatedly invoked by Symmes to describe the circumpolar regions. The theory that the polar verge could comfortably sustain life was invoked at several moments in the mid-nineteenth-century search for the Franklin expedition. Symmes's son John wrote to Elisha Kent Kane in 1851 in part to hit Kane up for observational evidence the explorer could provide in support of the hollow earth theory, but also to insist that if Franklin "reached the ~~apparent~~ pole he ~~has~~ got tangled in the currents and misconceived the character of the surface of his seas and while sailing back to apparent southern latitudes has been in fact continuing his course ~~over~~ the verge of this crust and in Regions which ~~for~~ the present theories would fail him."[49] In this account, the polar verge is the indeterminate, transitional space between the external and internal worlds—a polar version of the littoral.

In many ways, the verge is an analogue for the indeterminate relationship many humans have to the effects of climate change in the polar regions, and by extension throughout the globe. Voyagers to the inner earth might notice less direct sunlight or a change in vegetation or sea color; the line of demarcation is not clear. "Verge" is a term that can accommodate a variety of meaning: in addition to the familiar sense of *verge* as a boundary, an edging limit, or precinct, the word can also refer to a rod or pole, a wand of authority (*OED*). For the most part, the line between external and internal—verge as boundary or outer limit and verge as pole—is not sharply defined in hollow earth fictions. Symmes's use of the verge keeps both senses in play:

fixed cartographic pole and expansive horizon of potential. We might see an analogue in recent resource claims to North Polar sea zones by Arctic-bordering states.

Hollow earth fictions are fantasies and projections about climatic extremes. A representative example of the hollow earth genre is the novel *A Strange Manuscript Found in a Copper Cylinder* by the Canadian James De Mille, which was serialized in *Harper's Weekly* and published in book form in 1888. The story's frame narrative finds four pleasure cruisers spotting a copper cylinder in the sea which contains leaves of what look like "Egyptian papyrus," or the "common paper of antiquity." A note is affixed to the manuscript in three languages (English, French, and German), which echoes the polar practice of distributing multilingual location forms in bottles or cairns (discussed in chapter 4). The author of the note and manuscript, Adam More, is an Englishman who had been transporting convicts to Tasmania; his name invokes both Thomas More of *Utopia* and Adam Seaborn, the pseudonymous author of *Symzonia*. When separated from his ship in a small boat, he and a companion drift southward until they encounter a warm, volcanic region populated by humans and large prehistoric beasts. Like the Internals of *Symzonia*, the residents of this inner world scorn the acquisition of wealth; many fictions of the polar verge share this critique of capitalism and imperialism. "Here, then, was the South Pole—a world by itself," More writes in his narrative, "not a world of ice and frost, but one of beauty and light, with a climate that was almost tropical in its warmth, and lands that were covered with the rank luxuriance of a teeming vegetable life. I had passed from that outer world to this inner one, and the passage was from death unto life, from agony and despair to sunlight and splendor and joy."[50] The "teeming vegetable life" that More encounters is common to hollow earth fictions; such fecundity was also predicted to exist within the verge by Symmes, whose initial call for a polar expedition in 1818 promised to find "warm and rich land, stocked with thrifty vegetables and animals if not men." ("Thrifty" here indicates, in Symmes's now-rare usage of the word, that the vegetables and animals are flourishing.)[51] In the case of *A Strange Manuscript Found in a Copper Cylinder*, the sojourner to the inner world does not find his way back out before the narrative abruptly ends, as the sailors of the frame story take a break from reading Adam More's account. In other hollow earth fictions, abrupt endings are common, whether because the inner world traveler wakes from a dream or is propelled back to a disbelieving public outside or because a metafictional manuscript is lost. The inconclusive endings suggest the complexity of the range of responses explorers had to returning from the polar extremes to the "world," which might not heed or comprehend their accounts.

In the periodical *South Polar Times* and the book *Aurora Australis*, the polar verge and related concepts find their expression in several pieces of speculative fiction in the guise of nonfiction. A series of linked articles uncover "hieroglyphics" from earlier polar civilizations, for example. "Leaves from an Ancient Papyrus" reveals the contents of "an old document recently uniced in the South frigid zone" (see figure 3.9).[52] This formulation works as a fictional counterpart to the Arctic dead letters I discuss in chapter 4, while also anticipating the twenty-first-century reemergence of nineteenth- and early twentieth-century documents, whisky, zoological sketches, and ships themselves from the polar ice.[53] "Leaves from an Ancient Papyrus," published pseudonymously by Able Seaman Frank Wild in the second volume of the *S.P.T.*, is part of a series that began with "An Old Document" in the first volume. The inaugural piece detailed in "quaint phraseology" the prospect of exploring the "vast country far to the south," the home of "many wonderful birds and beasts, also useful plants and herbs, and vast quantities of gold and precious stones."[54] By 1902 it was evident that Antarctica did not furnish the Northlands with "useful plants and herbs," nor were suppositions about the presence of precious metals borne out, yet the speculative resources of the great southern continent remain in play in Wild's fiction. The "ancient papyrus" that is "uniced" in the southern country reveals that the men of the *Discovery* expedition (the author's own) found "vast dominions" while accomplishing "great work," despite "the dangers and trials and tribulations which they did undergo."[55] In the final installment of the series, "Hieroglyphic Record," we learn that "some more fragments of documents and letters relating to the cruise of the 'Discovery' have been uniced."[56] The narrative portion of the record describes the actual hardships of polar sledging, even as the close of the article hints at the "many wonderful things and curious did they discover, all of which ye may read in the chronicles."[57] Wild's series showcases both the verisimilitude demanded of polar record-keeping as well as the fanciful promise of resources common to fictions of the polar verge. We see, too, how records from the past can emerge from the ice to inform contemporary humans about both temporalities.

An essay on Antarctic history by the *Terra Nova* expedition geologist Thomas Griffith Taylor engages in fantasies of future tourism on the southern continent as part of a disquisition on climate change. "By indirect evidence," Taylor writes of the area near the Ross Ice Shelf, geologists can determine that "Victoria Land has at times been very much warmer than at present and also very much colder. . . . What is to be expected in the future in this region? It may be that increased climatic severity will lead to a recrudescence of the Barrier ice." Yet since it "seems possible still warmer conditions supervene," Taylor continues, Antarctica could eventually play host not just to rugged explorers, experienced with hardship, but to "effete" tourists:

> Forests will cover the slopes of the Western Mountains. In the moraine-fed troughs of the Ferrar and Dry Valleys will dwell a white race, depending partly on the fertile glacial soil, but chiefly on tourists from effete centres of civilisation. . . . The less energetic will proceed in the comfortable steamers of the Antarctic Exploitation Company to the chalets of Beardmore. Here start the summer motor trips to the South Pole. When? Judging the future by the past, about 200,000 A.D.[58]

In a light but cutting detail, Taylor invokes the distant futurity—on the scale of geological time—of the possibility of Antarctic motorcars. The very expedition in which he was engaged, Scott's second polar mission, had attempted to use motorized sledges to travel the Antarctic icescape. They proved to be as useless as the motorcar brought to the South by Shackleton's *Nimrod* expedition in 1907. Taylor's geological and racial forecast for the future polar verge—peopled by a "white race" and lushly fertile—is situated on a historical timeline roughly equidistant from Poe's white supremacist vision of the milky Southern Ocean and the island of Tsalal in *The Narrative of Arthur Gordon Pym*, and conspiracy theories of Nazi submarine bases (or underground cities) in Antarctica that have circulated since World War II. Notably Taylor's "Chapter on Antarctic History" performs the standard moves for hollow earth or polar verge fiction: it imagines a warm, habitable Antarctic zone, populated on its interior of sorts (the inner valleys of the continent) by a "white" race using advanced technology.

A work of speculative fiction in the subsequent issue of the *South Polar Times* takes such questions of race and "civilisation" to their catastrophic extreme. The postapocalyptic climate change story "Fragments of a Manuscript Found by the People of Sirius 8 When They Visited the Earth during the Exploration of the Solar System" is the work of the *Terra Nova*'s meteorologist George Clarke Simpson. The article purports to be an ephemeral found document recovered by extraterrestrial beings long after the end of humans. The first-person narrator, whose story is told in disjointed, elliptical phrases to give verisimilitude to its fragmentary form, feels "impelled to set down the manner of the end" of humanity even though he recognizes that "there will be none to read" the document.[59] The world of the narrator is a decadent one, in which humans focus on "luxury and self-indulgence"; libraries and scientific inquiry have fallen into "oblivion and decay," except for the medical knowledge circulated "mainly with the object of reducing the deathrate" (this story shares with the "Antarctic History" essay a eugenicist interest in "progress"-appropriate birth rates).[60] In this time of dissolution a scientist discovers the Elixir of Life: the "liquid was of crystal clearness, but had the faintest fluorescent glow, which gave it exquisite colours when agitated. . . . . it was the production of great extremes of temperature. . . . . . . electric furnace. . . . . liquid air. . . . . the demand was beyond the supply. No sufficiently large source of energy with the requisite fall of temperature could be found." The necessary "fall of temperature" is found in Antarctica, permitting production of the Elixir of Life. "The ice-bound shores of McMurdo Sound became the centre of the world," we learn. "From it flowed the life-giving fluid which alone sustained the human race. Death was entirely banished, and the race once more became flourishing." At this point Simpson's contribution to the literary subgenre of the found manuscript refocuses its interest from racial supremacy and purity to the consequences of planetary climate change:

> . . . . decrease in the number of blizzards, failure of the Ross Sea to freeze, absence of very low temperatures on the Barrier. . . . . bitterly regretted their failure to keep Meteorological records. . . . . records of the British Antarctic expedition were unearthed from the highest shelves of the lumber rooms of the libraries and were perused with avidity. . . . . the great question of the day was, Does climate change? The greatest authority, the Physiographer of the Expedition 1910–12 was quoted. He took for granted that ice age succeeded tropical age, and tropical age succeeded ice age. . . . . could be no doubt, the temperature was no longer sufficiently low to allow of the production of the Elixir. . . . . I, the writer of this record, am the last of the race, and soon I must follow the companions who have lived with me through the many centuries since the Elixir was discovered. My dying thoughts are of the folly which neglected the teachings of the Scientists of the British Antarctic Expedition 1910–12.[61]

The remarkable conclusion to this story aligns the reader with the alien beings who have recovered the fragmentary evidence that humans had once lived on Earth. To those interplanetary travelers, the tale offers a caution: humans (at least those postdating Scott's 1910 Antarctic voyage) have perished in part because they neither kept good meteorological records nor properly acknowledged climate change. More to the point, they could not survive in an environment that had warmed too much to allow production of the Elixir of Life—whether we choose to read the Elixir as oil, gas, water, or food. Like fossil fuel extraction and development, the Elixir demands transformative amounts of energy. Like water, its purity must be retained. Like food, it is easily tainted. The works of speculative climate fiction in Antarctic newspapers, like hollow earth novels, envision a world in which global warming has reoriented the polar regions. Within the imaginative economies of early twentieth-century polar expeditions, such fictions permit their writers and readers to explore the idea of climate change—and of the relation of the Poles to its processes—without yet facing its geophysical consequences.

The apotheosis of the subgenre of the warm South Polar verge short story within Antarctic publications is "Bathybia," a fantasia written by Mawson and published in *Aurora Australis* during Shackleton's *Nimrod* expedition. (Mawson would go on to his own command of the Australasian Antarctic Expedition, during which his crew produced the newspaper *Adelie Blizzard*.) The story describes a sledging trip to a Far South tropical land teeming with enormous incarnations of known flora and fauna: "All the species represented were but curiously developed forms of types already known to the scientific world."[62] In approaching Bathybia, the narrator first notices a "peculiar appearance in the sky" that seems to indicate "open water," long the fantasy (and increasing present-day reality) of an open polar sea. As "temperatures perceptibly r[i]se," the travelers find themselves "standing on the ruin of a huge volcanoe of unprecedented proportions," the verge of a broad abyss twenty-two thousand feet below sea level, where "temperature average[s] about 70° Fahr." and "crystal" streams abound. Among "dense matted vegetation," the warmth and water produce foot-long spiders, giant ticks, algae containing intoxicating liquids, and enormous phosphorescent fungi, which the men use as umbrella-mushrooms to shield them from the warm rain.[63] The commotion caused by the group's biologist wrestling with a four-foot-long "water bear" coming out of hibernation startles the narrator from what we realize has been his own sleep: it was all a dream. The warm, tropical lands of the polar verge, whether in the fictional worlds of "Seaborn," Poe, Verne, or De Mille, or in Mawson's Bathybia, are realized only in hallucinations. Despite persisting in perpetual darkness, in the shit of a brutal polar winter, the men of the *Nimrod* cannot thrive like the colossal fungi of Bathybia.

FIG 3.11 — Giant mushrooms of Bathybia. Douglas Mawson, "Bathybia," from Shackleton, ed., *Aurora Australis*, n.p. JOHN CARTER BROWN LIBRARY.

We learn several things about Antarctic life, climate, and biology from "Bathybia": for one, that the region is a testing ground for hypertrophic extremes. Take the water bear, whose movements awaken the narrator from the metafictional dream. "Water bear" is another name for the tardigrade, a minute organism that—outside of the fantastic realms of Bathybia—reaches a length of only .04 inches. It is also known as a moss piglet. Mawson's vision of a tardigrade swollen to twelve hundred times its usual dimensions lampoons the outsized importance the men place in their scientific expeditionary work—1200× is a standard magnification on a microscope—even as it emphasizes the otherworldliness of a land that can support monstrous beasts and seemingly unthinkably warm temperatures for the Pole. In magnifying a water bear to facetious lengths, Mawson alludes cheekily to polar bears, charismatic megafauna common to the other Pole. But the water bear has other qualities important to Antarctic existence: the tardigrade, or what we might call charismatic microfauna, can survive extraordinary heat (over 300°F) and cold (less than −300°F), lives for many years without water, subsists in the vacuum of outer space, and is one of the few organisms that has outlasted all five mass extinctions on

Earth to date. The persistence and outsized importance of the water bear of Bathybia take on special interest today, as the earth is on the verge of what scientists identify as the sixth mass extinction and climate extremity threatens human life too.

The News from Poems

The notion that the "outside world" would not believe or heed the meteorological and biological extremities of the South Pole is a common theme in Antarctic volumes. In several instances of polar periodical poetry, the lack of interest taken by temperate-zone readers in the climate news from Antarctica becomes a metafictional reflection on newspapers themselves. A profile of the botanist on the *Discovery*, Reginald Koettlitz, mocks his pedantry and obscurism by presenting his return to Britain as a great joy for journalists, who hang on his every tedious word; an illustration captioned "A rare treat to the journalistic world" shows a crowd of anthropomorphized newspapers vying for his attention (including not just London papers, but also the *S.P.T.*).[64] The joke is that no one back in the metropole will care what Koettlitz has to say. A poem on the difficulty in taking hourly magnetic and climate observations in terrible weather affirms that "magnetic observations while at sea were all the rage." Yet the author, Second Lieutenant Michael Barne, fears that all their work will be unappreciated or shunted aside once it reaches the Magnetic Observatory in London:

> In far off London city there's a place called the M. O.,
> Where we'll send our observations all "pro bono publico,"
> What think you gentle reader with a sympathetic soul,
> Were you to see our observations in a corner pigeon hole?
> Upon them year by year, the dust of ages will collect,
> While we upon our foolishness, in taking them reflect.[65]

Barne's poem is here in conversation with the story "Fragments of a Manuscript Found by the People of Sirius 8," in which the outside world also "neglected the teachings of the Scientists of the British Antarctic Expedition." We see the same concern in a slyly undermining illustration to accompany an otherwise cheerful poem on biological collections. "Bioloveria" is one of at least two Antarctic poems that parodies Isaac Watt's well-known moralistic verse "Against Idleness and Mischief":

How doth the ship Discovery
Let down Agassiz' trawl?
And gather in its meshes wide
All fishes great and small.

. . . .

If all goes well with this stout ship,
While frozen in these Seas;
Collections rich, biological,
Our friends at home will please.[66]

The poem displays a fine sentiment. Yet the illustration positioned at the final line—about pleasing friends at home—shows not an interested person of science but a bald, fleshy, reclining man, fast asleep before a table of specimens "at home," the *Daily Telegraph* (certainly not the news from Antarctica) falling unread from his hand.

Another Watts parody in the *Adelie Blizzard* characterizes the relationship between expeditions and newspaper poetry: "How doth the gay explorer improve the rhyming minute / By editing a newspaper, and printing drivel in it."[67] Watts is not the only source for poetic parody. In chapter 2 I discussed an Arctic take on Poe's "The Raven," and in the fourth volume of the *South Polar Times*, Apsley Cherry-Garrard published "Walt Whitman," a poem in both the style and thematic vein of its titular author. (The *Adelie Blizzard*'s monthly poetry contest would also feature an entry from "Walt Wilkinson," who wrote "with the daring abandonment of Whitman in Iambic Dodecameter.")[68] "Walt Whitman" demonstrates a number of elements found in polar poetry: attention to the weather, a queer playfulness, an emphasis on collective practices, and the use of formal structures associated with national poetic traditions. The poem takes as its subject an improvised form of billiards played by the men in the Antarctic evenings on a converted dining table; the lowest scorer would temporarily wear a medal of shame named after the biblical figure for nautical ill luck, as Cherry-Garrard describes:

Blizz! Blizz! Blizz!
Blizz up, South Wind, along the Ross Sea shore!
Thy whip-stings lash not me, not me;
Behold, am I not snug within?

This is the song of billiards:—
The tight stretched cloth of green, the serried arches,

FIG 3.12 — Detail from "Illustrated Interviews de Reginald Koettliz," *South Polar Times* 2.7 (1903): 47.

The cue—faking the cue, the protests from the players,
The pyramid, the British pluck, the Chinese fluke,
The click of striking balls, the rattle in the ditch,
        the grin of joy,
The minus five, the sorry that it brings;
The interjections of the on-lookingers, the marker, and
        the marker's observations—
Played for, I speakee the true! Champion to Jonah, and
        Jonah to Top Dog!
Oh! Look at his face!—Camerado, the game is o'er.[69]

Attuned to the sharply consonant sounds from within and without its poetic purview, Cherry-Garrard's exclamatory mode registers as a canny reading of Whitman's own sustained attention to conjunctions of work and
leisure, as well as to visions of queer camerados sharing space, song, and
exuberant physicality. And yet here Whitman's expansive, oceanic vision is
reimagined within the battened-down confines of an icebound ship, thousands of miles from the national spaces from which this poetic mode (and
the expeditions themselves) emerge.

In such circumstances, why not toast extremity? As a poem in the
Adélie Mail and Cape Adare Times puts it, "Heres to the Blizzard at plus
seventeen, / Heres to the calm Minus Forty, / The lower degrees that are

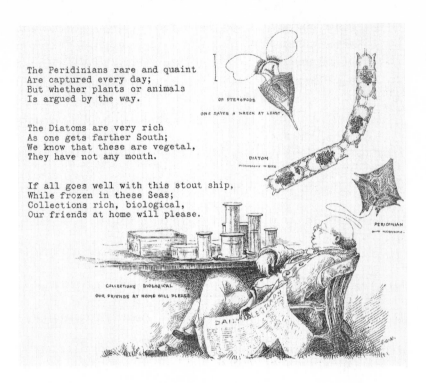

The Peridinians rare and quaint
Are captured every day;
But whether plants or animals
Is argued by the way.

The Diatoms are very rich
As one gets farther South;
We know that these are vegetal,
They have not any mouth.

If all goes well with this stout ship,
While frozen in these Seas;
Collections rich, biological,
Our friends at home will please.

FIG 3.13 — Detail from "Bioloveria," *South Polar Times* 1.3 (1902): 28.

still and serene, / The Blizzard so boisterous and rorty."[70] What Antarctic poems recognize, though, is that despite their authors' distance from "the world," all planetary life is connected. A poem on "Life in the Antarctic; or, The Protoplasmic Cycle" documents the polar food chain, demonstrating that the circularity and codependence of global life functions like "a huge recurring decimal . . . to which no / End is found."[71] On Mawson's 1911–14 expedition, the planetary connection took on a new form: for the first time in Antarctic exploration history, radio contact was established with the outside world via wireless communication. Mawson's crew used a Telefunken 1.5 kilowatt transmitter employing long wave and Morse code telegraphy and relayed messages to Australia through a station they established on Macquarie Island, a bit of land roughly equidistant between New Zealand and Antarctica. Katabatic winds (which commonly exceed 150 miles per hour) at Commonwealth Bay, where Mawson established his continental base, made transmission difficult but not impossible; the commander wrote drily of their attempts to maintain the wireless apparatus in consistently awful weather, "Hurricane conditions were not catered for in

the original aerial system." An article in the first issue of the *Adelie Blizzard*,
"'Wireless'—The Realisation," celebrates the radio technology's success in
establishing communications by remarking how much "money, time, and
life" would have been saved if expeditionary "untoward circumstances" could
have been reported to the outside world. The technology has transformed
the very field itself, Mawson writes: "With the successful application of
wireless to the field of operations, Polar Exploration has taken on a new
phase."[72] The power to call for help is one of many benefits; another is the
expedition's new ability to receive "exact time, and hence, longitude . . .
from civilized lands." Polar research and travel in Antarctica rely on "exact
relative time," and Mawson celebrates the wireless for placing "the inventive
brains of each base at the disposal of all."[73]

Radio technology puts an end to the phase of polar exploration in which
expedition members located themselves out of time, in asynchronous step
with the outer world. The Mawson expedition's employment of the technology, then, forms the chronological endpoint of this book and signals
the end of the heroic age of polar exploration and the beginning of the mechanical age. Polar connection to the outside is not unequivocally a cause
for celebration, however, as Mawson's notebooks reveal. Even as he saluted
the wireless in the *Adelie Blizzard*, he expressed private irritation with "the
chatter which goes on in the aether [the wireless] every evening," which is
"deafening." The Antarctic veteran's searing lament: "We are not free from
'the world' even here."[74] Yet Mawson's newspaper sought to bring the world
to Antarctica in a fashion that had not previously been on display in polar
papers: the *Adelie Blizzard* ran a four-part series of earnest articles on "the
commercialization of Antarctica." These are not the faux real estate ads or
futuristic speculative fiction of Antarctic papers more generally, but instead
discussion of "aspects of economic and scientific interest" that would "form
an invincible retort to those who still say, what's the practical use of these
Antarctic expeditions."[75] The final installment of the series suggests that the
katabatic winds might be harnessed for their energy, but the focus is not all
on renewables; the article also suggests that Antarctica's "geological forma-
tions are most propitious, and mineral discoveries on a commercial scale
are quite likely [to] turn up as further areas of exposed rock are gone over."[76]
The Antarctic Treaty of 1959 dedicated the continent to peace and science,
holding at bay the "commercialization" imagined in the *Adelie Blizzard*. As
the outside world seeped into Antarctic via the Australasian Antarctic Expedition's wireless technology, though, the distinction between inner and
outer polar worlds was collapsing.

What does it mean to be unfree from "the world" in Antarctic writing? As hollow earth and other speculative polar fictions demonstrate, the fantasy of an internal southern realm is interrupted by the external world every time, whether in a return to consciousness, a return to terrestrial reality, or the intrusive chatter of the wireless. The relationship between the outer world and the inner world to which it makes itself known is defined, crucially, by climate extremes, from which the inner world of the Pole ultimately offers no refuge. Climate change today compels humans anew to look to Antarctica and the Arctic in crafting our planetary narratives of survival.

===

FOUR

DEAD LETTER RECKONING

Seeing a cairn near the water's edge, I hurried towards it, and quickly demolished the heap in the expectation of finding some record, but, after an hour's
hard work with pick and shovel, I was horrified to find that it was a grave.
— ALBERT HASTINGS MARKHAM, *The Great Frozen Sea: A Personal*
Narrative of the Voyage of the "Alert" during the Arctic Expedition of
1875–6 (1878)

A rguably the most important document to date in the history of Arctic exploration was found in a cairn at Victory Point on King William Island (Qikiqtaq) in the northern Canadian archipelago in 1859. The
document was a preprinted blank form supplemented with handwritten
updates, one of thousands dispersed throughout the circumpolar North by
British and American ventures throughout the nineteenth century. Arctic
expeditions were expected to leave notice of their whereabouts and operations, depositing them under rock caches, in bottles dropped into the sea,
in copper or tin cylinders, or at other outposts at regular intervals, ideally
in multiple copies. Such multilingual forms (in English, French, Spanish,
Dutch, Danish, and German) left lined blank space at their tops for the
handwritten updates; their bottom halves were imprinted with variations
on the following: "Whoever finds this paper is requested to forward it to
the Secretary of the Admiralty, London, *with a note of the time and place at*
which it was found: or, if more convenient, to deliver it for that purpose to
the British consul at the nearest Port." The U.S. Navy employed an analogous form. This manner of blank form was "usually supplied to discovery
ships for the purpose of being enclosed in bottles and thrown overboard

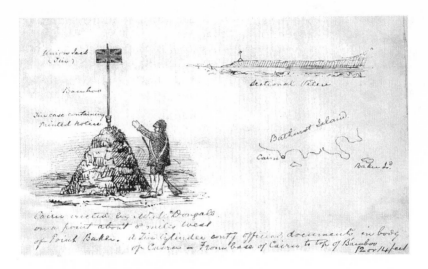

FIG 4.1 — Cairn erected by Mate George F. McDougall, HMS *Resolute*, near Point Baker. The cairn was topped by a bamboo pole hoisting a flag made of tin; under the rocks was a tin cylinder containing official documents. Its height was twelve to fourteen feet. ADM 7/190. NATIONAL ARCHIVES, LONDON.

at sea, in order to ascertain the set of the currents, blanks being left for the date and position."[1] The sending and receiving of messages by humans constitutes a data set of currents and other nonhuman factors. Leaving such records, one officer wrote, "is done every day that the ships are under weigh."[2]

The notice found at Victory Point on King William Island in 1859 was one of the standard multilingual forms. In 1847 it had been written upon briefly and then sealed in a tin cylinder by officers of the large Northwest Passage expedition led by Franklin, which had launched from England in 1845. In 1848, eleven months after the cylinder's first interment, members of the Franklin expedition subsequently returned to the cairn, extracted the notice, and wrote upon it a second time, in script that wended its way around the border of the document, afterward recommitting it to a cairn. There it remained until its discovery twelve years later by the *Fox* expedition, commanded by Francis Leopold M'Clintock (or McClintock), a recovery mission seeking evidence of Franklin's missing voyagers. The 1847 script tells us that Franklin remains in command—"All well"—two years into the voyage. Here is a transcription of the first note:

28 of May 1847 H.M.S.hips Erebus and Terror Wintered in the Ice in Lat. 70°5′ N Long. 98°.23′ W Having wintered in 1846–7 at Beechey Island

in Lat 74°43′28″ N Long 91°39′15″ W After having ascended Wellington Channel to Lat 77° and returned by the West side of Cornwallis Island. Sir John Franklin commanding the Expedition. <u>All well</u> Party consisting of 2 Officers and 6 Men left the ships on Monday 24th May 1847.—Gm. Gore, Lieut., Chas. F. DesVoeux, Mate

Just two weeks after this message had been committed to the cairn, however, Franklin was dead. We learn this from the second inscription, written eleven months after the original. The emphatic "<u>All well</u>" of the previous year takes on a special poignancy in light of the trials hinted at in the 1848 addition, which reads in full:

25th April 1848 HMShips Terror and Erebus were deserted on the 22nd April 5 leagues NNW of this having been beset since 12th Sept 1846. The officers and crews consisting of 105 souls under the command of Captain F. R. M. Crozier landed here—in Lat. 69°37′42″ Long. 98°41′ This paper was found by Lt. Irving under the cairn supposed to have been built by Sir James Ross in 1831—4 miles to the Northward—where it had been deposited by the late Commander Gore in May 1847. Sir James Ross' pillar has not however been found and the paper has been transferred to this position which is that in which Sir J. Ross' pillar was erected—Sir John Franklin died on the 11th of June 1847 and the total loss by deaths in the Expedition has been to this date 9 officers and 15 men.—James Fitzjames Captain HMS Erebus F. R. M. Crozier Captain & Senior Offr And start on tomorrow 26th for Backs Fish River

Franklin and his two ships, *Erebus* and *Terror*, with their crew of 129 men, had been missing for fourteen years when McClintock's *Fox* expedition located the cairn note, stained by rust from the metal container and beginning to deteriorate. At least forty rescue and recovery missions had sought evidence of their whereabouts and mysterious end within those first fifteen years of searching—and they continued through the location of both ships on the Arctic seafloor, the *Erebus* in 2014 and the *Terror* in 2016.[3]

Traces had been found in the early years of the search in the form of Inuit testimony (not always fully credited by white, Western audiences) and in assorted *Erebus* and *Terror* artifacts in abandoned campsites and among Inuit parties. Notably, one Scottish searcher, John Rae, had purchased a number of Franklin materials from the Inuit in 1854; they told him a large party of "kabloonas" (Qabluunak)—white men, around thirty-five to forty of them—had resorted to cannibalism and starved to death in a previous

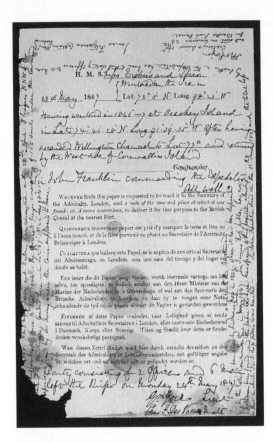

FIG 4.2 — Franklin expedition note found in a cairn by Francis Leopold McClintock, 1859. From McClintock, *The Voyage of the "Fox" in Arctic Seas*, after 282.

winter. (I discuss Rae further in chapter 5.) McClintock's *Fox* expedition itself located many more relics, including, in one small boat that had been hauled from the ship, twine, bristles, wax ends, sailmakers' palms, needle and thread cases, *The Vicar of Wakefield*, several bayonet scabbards cut down into knife sheaths, two rolls of sheet-lead, eleven large spoons, eleven forks, and four teaspoons, many of these last bearing Franklin's crest.[4] Franklin "relics" had been central to the international interest in the expedition's fate for years; indeed Adriana Craciun argues that they were the "most eloquent texts" available to the public.[5] Yet none of these fragments offered an obliging narrative in documentary, written form that explained the outcome of a party the size of the full Franklin expedition. Not until McClintock's cairn discovery was there confirmation that satisfied Anglo-Americans and Europeans that the beset ships had been abandoned to the ice and that Sir John himself was dead, along with twenty-four other expedition members (by circumstances unknown, although causes likely include exposure, starvation, and lead poisoning from poorly soldered tins). The Victory Point cairn note is the only written record that has been found to date that provides any information about the fate of the Franklin expedition.

McClintock was deeply affected by what he read in the cairn message; he reflected in his narrative, "In the short space of twelve months how mournful had become the history of Franklin's expedition; how changed from the cheerful 'All well' of Graham Gore!"[6] For McClintock, the bureaucratic status of the note adds to rather than detracts from its elegiac qualities. "A sad tale was never told in fewer words," he wrote. "There is something deeply touching in their extreme simplicity, and they show in the strongest manner that both the leaders of this retreating party were actuated by the loftiest sense of duty."[7] The duty to which McClintock refers is primarily constituted by the surviving officers' recognition that the expedition was provisioned only through the summer of 1848, and thus they were compelled into the risky act of abandoning the trapped ships. Far less dramatically, but also significantly, the responsibilities of the remaining officers included leaving official records. The forms "are perfect models of official brevity. No log-book could be more provokingly laconic," McClintock observed. "Yet, that *any record at all* should be deposited after the abandonment of the ships, does not seem to have been intended . . . and our gratitude ought to be all the greater when we remember that the ink had to be thawed, and that writing in a tent during an April day in the Arctic regions is by no means an easy task."[8] McClintock fulfilled his own duty: even though he took the original Franklin message back to the Admiralty in England, he created a copy to leave in the cairn and added to it records of his own *Fox* expedition's maneuvers.

We know what message the cairn note conveyed to an Anglo-American public hungry for information in the fall of 1859, almost fifteen years into a series of far-reaching missions of mercy: it provided an elusive cenotaph for the ships and for Franklin himself, even as it left unanswered numerous questions about the expedition's broader fate.[9] But what message was the form *itself* designed to convey, at the original scene of its production and inscriptions? McClintock's analysis of the cairn record oscillates between finding it exceptional (difficult to write, crafted in dire conditions) and mundane (a rote task of "official brevity"). Yet the document found by his party at Victory Point was not an emergency message, specially crafted for potential rescuers or for posterity. Rather it was just another update among hundreds that the expedition would have scattered over three years.

Such updates were often dispersed in multiple copies in order to amplify their chance of detection; indeed not far from the cairn in which this message was discovered, a copy was found, consisting only of the content of the first, 1847 message. Cairn messages, in this sense, bear the charge of the Franklin relics—the cutlery, pins, bits of metal—in their fetishistic promise to reveal the secrets of the vanished men. Yet while cairn messages, like the relics, are bits of mundane ephemera from a life in the Arctic, they are distinctive in one fundamental way: their form is both static (in that they are literally forms, to be filled in) and endlessly narratively adaptable (in the information added to them and in their vague and tenuous locatability). They have an intended circuit, which is to track daily movement; they also have a contingent circuit, determined by polar ecological conditions. The Franklin notice becomes a variation of what I call the Arctic dead letter: the blank form, the procedural information sheet, the status report, the routine paperwork that polar expeditions filed daily in bottles tossed in the sea, in caches built on flinty shores, or in metal casks covered with stones. In the case of the Franklin expedition, a routine notice left in a cairn becomes known as exceptional when it emerges as the only record, partial though it may be, of the fate of 129 men.

I propose that despite the importance it has assumed in the history of polar exploration, the Franklin message in the cairn was in fact routine. In the popular imagination a "message in a bottle" connotes solitude or abandonment, the voice of a singularity desperate to connect against long odds. In the case of Arctic recordkeeping, messages in bottles were generated en masse and as a matter of course; scarcity is a function of their reception, not of their generation. The only thing unusual about the Victory Point Arctic letter, that is to say, is that it actually was received. The cairn message found readers: first in McClintock, then among the broader Anglo-American nineteenth-century world, in polar historians, in me, in you.

I open this chapter by describing the famous cairn message as if its contents were exceptional, but as I've begun to suggest, the Franklin expedition note was just another dispatch among the blanks, forms, notices, and other official documents that circulate in the Arctic region in tenuous and provocative ways, as forms of polar ecomedia that embody oceanic conditions of drift, contingency, dispersal, and annihilation. Nautical ventures in general (naval, exploratory, or commercial voyages other than polar expeditions) produced an enormous volume of writing in the eighteenth and nineteenth centuries, in multiple forms and genres. Recordkeeping, arguably the most common category of sea writing, was as much a mainstay of nautical practice as the exercise of seamanship. In the form of logbooks, weather records, navigational accounts, wind and tide charts, longitude and latitude measurements, course and distance notations, and hydrography, officers and other seamen tracked the progress of their voyages. One aspect of this recordkeeping involved leaving letters, notices, and other forms of mail in whatever circumstances conditions might permit. For standard nautical routes, whether naval or merchant, this meant leaving letters in ports or exchanging them with passing ships. This system was irregular but surprisingly effective. The relative desolation of the polar regions arrested and altered the usual circulation of nautical mail, even as it opened up the possibilities for other forms of oceanic exchange. This chapter studies the unusual and baroque extent of messages sent from Arctic expedition ships, as well as the vagaries and contours of their posting and potential for delivery or receipt.

What I am calling Arctic dead letters comprise the notifications dispatched from ships into the polar regions, in the generally vain hope of future reception. Like letters in postal mail exchange found to be undeliverable and thus labeled "dead," Arctic dead letters lie unclaimed. Like figurative dead letters, Arctic dead letters have passed out of use. Like dead media, they are discarded and possibly obsolete forms of communication. Yet unlike dead-end postal mail—which is eventually consigned to the fire—the circuit remains open for Arctic letters; they retain potential energy. In literary studies our association with dead letters is usually tied to Herman Melville's "Bartleby, the Scrivener: A Story of Wall Street" (1853): after Bartleby's death by starvation in the Tombs, the lawyer-narrator hears a rumor that the scrivener had once worked in the Dead Letter Office. The detail, for many readers, has evoked the alienation of labor under capitalism, especially in light of Bartleby's job, which was to produce duplicates of legal documents (in a manner not unlike the unrelenting duplication of Arctic records at sea). Through abstemiousness, Bartleby prefers to be unproductive: he moves from the Dead Letter Office, to a law office in which he fails to generate document copies, to an actual death that the lawyer-narrator histrionically equates with dead letters. In media studies, Bartleby's dead letters—his rote, unoriginal, and ultimately unproductive copying—can be seen as a form of dead media, one of the processes of reproduction by an alienated human that would soon become reproduction by nonhuman machines.

A different logic for production and reproduction of letters obtains in the polar regions: whereas in "Bartleby" dead letters are a terminus, in the Arctic dead letters are inert components in a circuit that could conceivably blink into conductivity. The messages that have not disintegrated of the thousands cast onto ice or into the seas in the nineteenth century possibly remain in the Arctic in some form, whether in a state of decomposition or in persistent drift or awaiting some potential future reader, perhaps made more accessible in the twenty-first century by climate change. Nautical spaces are inherently resistant to inscription and other forms of demarcation. Recognizing this, polar-voyaging messengers multiply their modes and numbers of address, seeking oceanic registers of circulation both in terms of the wayward proliferation and mass publication scale of their dispatches. Arctic dead letters exemplify the unbounded dimensions of polar ecomedia in their potential for open, ceaseless circulation, and their risk of obliterating dispersal.

Other fundamentally oceanic characteristics of Arctic dead letters are their attenuated temporality and their randomness: any given cairn message or note in a bottle, if found at all, might be picked up decades after its inscription—a scrap of newsprint recovered, say, from Beechey Island by a Franklin search party, labeled by the Admiralty as "piece of brown paper found in washhouse," or an insert from a tin of Superior Chocolate Powder provided to the expedition by Fortnum, Mason & Co.[10] In visiting the expeditionary headquarters of Adolphus Greely's Lady Franklin Bay Expedition decades later, Donald MacMillan found newspaper clippings of various poems whose pathos would be amplified in the Far North: "The Sweet By-and-By," the refrain of which is "We shall meet on that beautiful shore"; Wordsworth's "The World Is Too Much with Us"; and Longfellow's "To Stay at Home Is Best." The men returned home, but their scraps of newsprinted poetry remained at latitude 81°40′ N—at least until 1909, when MacMillan took them up anew.[11]

Neither the interval nor the content of the materials circulating in the oceanic world can be strictly plotted geographically or hydrographically. They can be approximated, though (much like the debris from the 2011 Japanese tsunami that continues to wash ashore periodically on the Pacific coast of North America).[12] Metaphors of mapping likewise falter in representing oceanic diffusion. Unmoored from territorial and temporal fixity, Artic dead letters and other forms of polar ecomedia bear the promise of ceaseless potential yet also stand as bits of the detritus that global-scale human resource extraction has unceasingly left in its wake.

Blank Forms on the Map

Arctic dead letters are a body of records that were produced under the usual conditions of polar recordkeeping, but their primary mode was distribution away from the ship rather than retention aboard it (except in duplicate form—another circuit of Arctic exchange, about which I will say more). Even messages deposited in caches, on more solid surfaces that could be flagged or marked in some way, ran the risk of infrequent encounter. Elisha Kent Kane, for example, the best known of the American Arctic explorers at midcentury, engaged in the standard practices of "build[ing] cairns and leav[ing] notices at every eligible point" during his unsuccessful Grinnell expedition in search of Franklin (1853–55). But appropriate materials were not always at hand, and Kane recalls a time when, "as I had neither paper, pencil, nor pennant, I burnt a K. with powder on the rock, and scratching O.K. with a pointed bullet on my cap-lining, hoisted it as the representative of a flag." One such improvised cairn, "rudely marked," he writes in his narrative, was found by a party sent in aid of Kane's expedition, but "strange to say, [it] was the only direct memorial of my whereabouts communicated from some hundreds of beacons."[13] Other depots were disrupted by polar bears or other Arctic megafauna. McClintock repeatedly encountered supply caches that had been destroyed; in one instance, a previous expedition had left a "small depôt of provisions and three boats" on Cape Hotham across from Beechey Island. "The boats were sound," McClintock found, "but several of their oars, which had been secured upright, were found broken down by bears—those inquisitive animals having a decided antipathy to anything stuck up—stuck-up things in general being, in this country, unnatural."[14] (In blaming this destruction on polar megafauna, McClintock elides the possibility that Westerners on previous search expeditions had ransacked cairns, including Intuit communication cairns, or Inuksuit, looking for messages or supplies.) Oceanic environments work to erode the outcroppings, the "stuck-up," whether through atmospheric attrition or more direct intervention from large organisms. Other Arctic environmental conditions conspired to interfere with cairn messaging. A lieutenant on the Nares expedition, Charles Arbuthnot, labored for some time to locate a message buried near a supply depot. "I regret to say," he reports to his superiors, "that just after I had made one copy of this, and had written a notice of our visit on the back of it, a strong gust of wind took the original record from under a stone where I had placed it, and that although I followed it a long way down the hill, it eventually got amongst the cliffs, and I was unable to recover it."[15] Arbuthnot then had to install the copy in the cairn after making a second copy of the document to bring aboard ship. At every turn Artic conditions demand a multiplication of messages.

The chances that letters in bottles would wash ashore or ride the global oceanic currents to some other reception were vanishingly slim. James Clark Ross (nephew of the Arctic explorer John Ross) worries about this when describing the process of distributing his own versions of the very same standard blank form that was used by the Franklin expedition:

> In the evening a cask was put overboard in lat. 77° s. and long. 187° 24′ E., containing a brief account of our proceedings, and with a request that whoever might find it would forward the paper to the Secretary of the Admiralty. It was my practice to throw a bottle over almost every day containing a paper with our latitude and longitude marked on it, for the purpose of gaining information respecting the joint effects of the prevailing winds and currents in these parts; but amongst ice, and in so turbulent an ocean, I fear but few of them will ever be found to subserve the intended purpose.[16]

The messages, accounts, notices, bulletins, updates, and discarded papers scattered across the ice and waters of the Arctic (or the Southern Ocean, as in Ross's case) are the shipboard press output not created from an imaginative impetus, such as the newspapers, broadsides, and songs I discuss in earlier chapters; such creative publications remained on ship and circulated among expedition members. Instead the blank forms and other informational documents produced or filled out in the circumpolar North were addressed to a conjectural future audience in the Artic itself. The forms note the location of expeditions, the numbers and health of their party, the contents of the supply caches they leave along their routes, the progress of their sledging ventures, and their planned future trajectories. For example, a form sent from the HMS *Lady Franklin* (a Franklin search vessel) via an Inuk or "Esquimaux" carrier that did ultimately reach the Admiralty had been filled in with the following information (other than the date [May 7, 1850] and the latitude and longitude notation): "Beset off Unknown Island since May 4th. H.M.S. Sophia in company. Crews of both ships well. Ice very light. Great appearance of Water to North. Despatches landed at Lively. William Penny, Commander."[17] Cast into oceanic spaces (ice, the pack, open water), these dead letters rarely, however, connected with a reader other than through copies retained aboard ship—and therefore are encountered only far from the scene of their Arctic emplacement, whether by Admiralty secretaries at the conclusion of a voyage or in bound historical records in archives by researchers. Some of the materials that were composed and then deposited within the polar regions, directed to an audience that seldom materialized, remain potentially discoverable—deliverable, in a sense—today, in melting polar regions.[18]

In addition to illuminating the little-known role that Arctic dead letters play in the history of polar literature, this chapter recasts a once commonly held view of the Far North as a "blank." The concept of polar blankness can be seen in the nineteenth-century Arctic sublime of romantic writers, as well as in the imperialist rhetoric of northern European and American expeditions, all of which inaccurately—whether deliberately or not—recast the continuously populated Arctic as barren. My aim is not to heap up evidence of the error of this figuration; there have been many correctives to this view. Instead I consider the notion of Arctic blanks in media and material text terms: What is the role of the printer's blank when employed in polar circulation?[19] A "blank," according to the *OED*, is "a document, 'paper,' or 'form' with spaces left blank to be filled up at the pleasure of the person to whom it is given (e.g., a blank charter), or as the event may determine; a blank form." Neither a printed book nor part of manuscript culture, the blank registers in the history of printing as an element of "job printing," the kind of occasional work for hire done by printers. Job printing could include hand bills, tickets, letterhead, lottery tickets, currency, coupons, and other documents and ephemera. In areas where ready paper was comparatively scarce, job-printed matter could provide manuscript material too, adaptable to the use of the writer. Such was the case for one sailor, who deserted an Arctic whaling ship in 1860 and wrote an account of his experience in a bank passbook printed in the maritime town of Gloucester, Massachusetts. Jobbing accounted for the majority of most printers' work in the nineteenth century but has received comparatively little attention in material text studies. As Lisa Gitelman observes, job printing is often neglected in histories of print culture and the book in favor of "accounts of authors, editors, booksellers, publishers, and readers; cohorts notably missing from the world of blanks. Blanks are printed and used," Gitelman writes pointedly, rather than "authored or read."[20] Scholarly interest in the history of books and the study of cultures of print, in other words, has been primarily focused on readers, writers, and publishers; blanks, by contrast, seem to exist outside of the agency of an author function or the humanism of a reader response. The wide employment of blanks within polar spaces with relatively diffuse human reading populations—as Inuit, Yupik, Iñupiaq, and other circumpolar indigenous populations were not usually targeted as print publics, with a few exceptions—underscores, in some ways, the abstraction of blanks from the intimacy of direct human exchange. If the polar regions themselves were historically figured as blank or barren compared to the verdant temperate zones, then it is possible to think of printed blanks as bearing an analogous relationship to texts with more identifiable authors and readers.

And yet, as James Green and Peter Stallybrass have pointed out, job printing had blank spaces for completion by manuscript hand, as blanks invited direct interaction. Rather than superseding manuscript culture, that is, the various forms of job printing provided an "incitement to writing by hand." Green and Stallybrass observe, "One may or may not read a blank form; but if the form is to fulfill its function, it must be filled in."[21] For Green and Stallybrass, the function of a form like the Franklin cairn message would be notification—ideally, in these terms, to notify the document's readers of the expedition's condition and whereabouts. But the experiential function of forms in the Arctic is not to notify but to leave notes. The designated reader may never appear or may come one year later, or one hundred. The expectation of notification relies on a relative synchronicity between sender and recipient that does not inhere in the frozen oceanic regions. It is happenstance that when McClintock found the Victory Point cairn message eleven years after its second emplacement, the Franklin expedition remained alive enough in the Anglo-American consciousness (if not in its own embodied state) for the discovery or "delivery" of the original message to resonate still, despite the temporal lag between the moment of its release and its receipt.

Virtually all theoretical readers of Arctic documents such as figure 4.3, however, encounter the blanks not in situ but far from the time and space of their inscription and read them necessarily in the form of copies—duplicates created at the scene of their original completion. The copies exist precisely because Arctic blanks are expected to become dead letters. Oceanic spaces are fundamentally characterized by dispersal, extension, and diffusion. In the frozen oceanic spaces of the Arctic, in which monuments and markers can stand for a time, an excess of writing and recordkeeping functions as a mechanism for multiplying possibilities for connection or inscription upon an ice-, land-, and seascape adversarial to permanent markers. Blanks in the Arctic thus function as a response both to the misconceived "blankness" of the regions themselves and to the standard expectations of claims-making by voyages undertaken under the banners of discovery, science, imperialism, or colonialism.[22] Unlike fluid oceanic surfaces, however, the icy polar

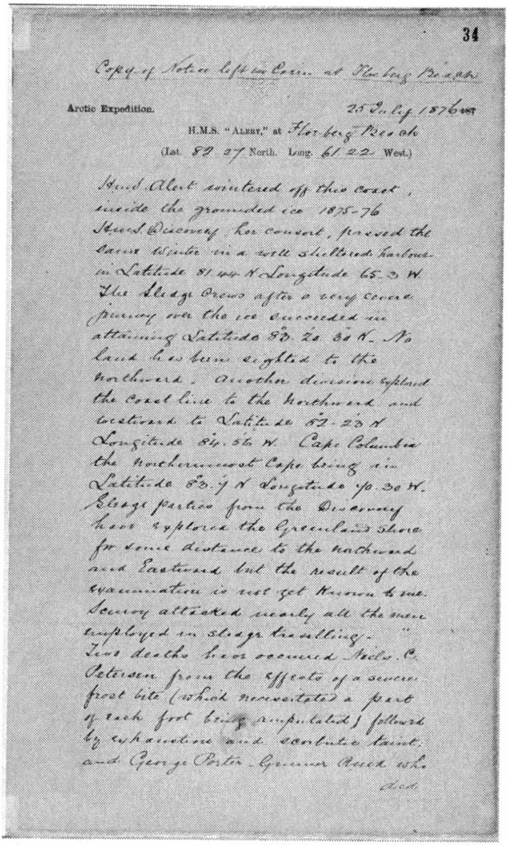
34

Copy of Notice left in Cairn at Floeberg Beach

Arctic Expedition. 25 July 1876

H.M.S. "Alert," at Floeberg Beach

(lat. 82 27 North. Long. 61 22 West.)

H.M.S. Alert wintered off this coast,
inside the grounded ice 1875–76
H.M.S. Discovery her consort, passed the
same Winter in a well sheltered harbour
in Latitude 81.44 N Longitude 65.3 W.
The Sledge Crews after a very severe
journey over the ice succeeded in
attaining Latitude 83. 20. 30 N. No
land has been sighted to the
northward. Another division explored
the Coast line to the Northward and
westward to Latitude 82–23 N
Longitude 84.56 W. Cape Columbia
the northernmost Cape being in
Latitude 83.7 N Longitude 70.30 W.
Sledge parties from the Discovery
have explored the Greenland Shore
for some distance to the northward
and Eastward but the result of the
examination is not yet known to me.
Scurvy attacked nearly all the men
employed in sledge travelling.
Two deaths have occurred Niels C.
Petersen from the effects of a severe
frost bite (which necessitated a part
of each foot being amputated) followed
by exhaustion and scorbutic taint.
and George Porter Gunner R.M.A. who
died

FIG 4.3 — Copy of notice left in cairn at Floeberg Beach by HMS *Alert*, 25 July 1876. May/13/2. © NATIONAL MARITIME MUSEUM, GREENWICH, LONDON.

regions can accept some monuments or markers. But shifting ice, extreme weather, and frozen ground make the forms of inscription customary to voyages of discovery or imperial ventures unreliable. The oceanic forms of knowledge practiced by polar expedition members compel a proliferation of texts, even as the laconic nature of the messages constitutes a proleptic recognition of their likely nonreceipt.

Within the history of material texts, then, we might stress the importance of the *use* made of both Arctic dead letters and other printed blanks as a form of media rather than their "literary" production and consumption. Scholars of book history and print culture have often talked of readerly circulation, of literary economies, but eighteenth- and nineteenth-century job printing is directly the organ and product of economic exchange, generating bills, tax forms, invoices, passbooks, receipts, and other tools of commercial exchange. Arctic circulations also concern economies, but ones whose productivity and return cannot be tracked on linear axes of time and space. If polar exploration is driven by an interest in potential resources, then Artic messages leave open the circuits of potentiality so wide as to render them inactive, foreclosing their prospect of completion through ellipsis. The tenuousness of blank documents in the Arctic brings into relief the epistemological work done by polar expeditions in their attempts to impose models of terrestrial recordkeeping and temporality on oceanic spaces. At the same time, the hyperproliferation of expeditionary documents acknowledges the insufficiencies of that terrestrial and temporal model.

It is not the case that Arctic dead letters never find a recipient, however. In researching this book, I have had access to nineteenth-century polar blanks that exist only, for the most part, as copies made at the scene of their original Arctic creation—copies that were produced as a function of standard shipboard recordkeeping, as well as out of a recognition that the originals would probably never be recovered. I have been able to locate these blanks because they have been preserved in institutional archives by virtue of their association with expeditions deemed historically important, even though the blanks themselves have not been so deemed. I have myself become a recipient of these Arctic letters, in other words. As ecomedia defined by their multitudinous proliferation without regard for spatiality and temporality, some Arctic dead letters do find readers, at some place, in some time. These messages may be printed and collected as ephemera, but they bear the hope of more permanent collection.

A Full Account of the Proceedings

Arctic blanks emerge from a tradition of obsessive accounting of polar expeditionary recordkeeping practices. Twenty-seven years before Franklin's final mission, John Ross embarked upon an Admiralty-sponsored Arctic mission in 1818 to explore Baffin Bay and seek the possibility of a Northwest Passage. In doing so he inaugurated a new, targeted period of British exploration of the northern regions in the nineteenth century. Baffin Bay, off the western coast of Greenland, had been renamed after the early seventeenth-century English captain who had explored the waterway two hundred years earlier, but the ensuing centuries had not been a dynamic period in polar exploration. After the Napoleonic Wars, though, Britain had an excess of naval personnel on active duty, and Second Vice Secretary of the Admiralty John Barrow, who served in that role from 1807 to 1845, found occupation for many of the ships and sailors in nautical and African "discovery" missions. Barrow was a great proponent of Arctic exploration in particular, sponsoring ventures by Ross, Franklin, William Edward Parry, James Clark Ross, and George Back.

Ross's expedition also inaugurated a custom in British polar exploration that placed tight control with the Admiralty of all written materials generated aboard ship. Throughout the long nineteenth century, the Admiralty required that "all persons" on polar expeditions submit any journals, memoranda, logs, and notes, "both of a public and private nature," composed throughout the course of the venture. The full original orders to Ross and his men would be repeated in substance throughout the century:

GENERAL MEMORANDUM

"Pursuant to orders from my Lords Commissioners of the Admiralty, &c. &c. &c.

"You are hereby required and directed to deliver to me, the moment the ship anchors on England, all the charts, logs, journals, and memoranda, both of a public and private nature, which you may have kept during the time you have been on board the ship under my command, which are to be sealed up, and kept at the disposal of their Lordships; and you are to sign an acknowledgment, according to the form annexed, for the satisfaction of their Lordships.

"Given on board the Isabella, this 9th day of November, 1818.

"JOHN ROSS, Captain.

"*To* WM. ROBERTSON, First Lieutenant.
EDW. SABINE, Captain R.A.
JOHN EDWARDS, Surgeon.
A. M. SKENE, Admiralty Midshipman.
J. C. ROSS, Admiralty Midshipman.
J. C. BEVERLY, Assistant-Surgeon,
And all persons on board the Isabella, who may have kept
any of the abovementioned documents.

Form.

"We, the undersigned, do hereby certify, that we have delivered (sealed up) all the logs, journals, and memoranda, we have kept on board the Isabella, between the 1st of May and date hereof, for the purpose of being delivered to the Lords Commissioners of the Admiralty."[23]

In addition to enumerating the officers and men of note aboard ship, the directive covers any other forms of writing done by any of the personnel ("all persons") on the voyage—both officers and men, both public and private writing. The orders to Ross stress the importance of turning shipboard papers over to the Admiralty "the moment the ship anchors on England." A similar sense of urgency is seen in other British naval instructions, such as those given to Parry before his 1819–20 Northwest Passage expedition: "On your arrival in England, you are immediately to repair to this office, in order to lay before us a full account of your proceedings in the whole course of your voyage; taking care, before you leave the ship, to demand from the officers, petty officers, and all other persons on board, the logs and journals they may have kept; together with any drawings or charts they may have made."[24] The tone remained the same later in the century, as can be seen in the orders to George Nares upon the launch of his 1875–76 Arctic expedition: "On your arrival in England, you are forthwith to repair to the Admiralty, to lay before their Lordships a full account of your proceedings; having previously received from the officers and all other persons in the expedition the journals or memoranda they may have kept."[25]

The Admiralty's demand for all written and illustrated accounts of polar proceedings is, in many ways, perfectly consistent with the broader nautical culture of daily (and often hourly) recordkeeping practices. The extremity of the geophysical spaces into which such expeditions ventured, and the infrequency with which subpolar Westerners had visited them, renders the Admiralty's interest in acquiring and processing the results all the more expected. Why, however, would the official orders stress again and again the appropriation of the "private" writings of all persons on board? The answer, in part, lies in the objective to publish the official voyage narratives of polar and other exploring expeditions upon their conclusion, as Craciun argues.[26] The volumes often appeared from the London house of John Murray, known for publishing volumes of travel and exploration; Barrow designated Murray as the Admiralty's official publisher for a time. The Admiralty would have recourse to all public and private shipboard writings in assembling the history, usually under the captain's credited authorship; afterward, as the Nares expedition orders clarified, "such of these journals and documents as may be of an unofficial character will be returned to the writers when no longer required for the public requirements of the expedition."[27] The Admiralty's official narrative was paramount; were the men allowed to keep their private journals, they might rush their accounts into print before the captain had the opportunity to prepare the sanctioned volumes.[28] British voyages of discovery and exploration were somewhat exceptional in their close control of all the manuscript materials generated aboard ship, whether of an official nature or those designated as private; other naval operations did not observe such protocols. When we consider the geophysical spaces of the Arctic regions in their oceanic mutability and abstraction from territorial protocols, however, another reason for Admiralty documentary control emerges. In a hostile environment, the act of tightly regulating and collecting all written materials generated aboard ship serves to provide monuments in the form of writing—by excess of official forms and indiscriminate dispersal of bits of paper—which it cannot erect with any permanence upon the landscape, as nineteenth-century colonial missions did more generally. And since the Arctic dead letters strewn throughout the North were documented so thoroughly, their noncirculation as ecomedia in the polar regions nevertheless quickens into revivification in later readerly circuits.

The Admiralty and analogous regulations, in other words, ensured the survival of Arctic dead letters in the form of copies preserved by accounts-minded crew members, and thus guaranteed their presence in the archive of polar expeditionary history, however miscellaneous these practices. It also provided a fantasy of management in an environment antagonistic to human circulation and control. This was especially the case for messages in bottles, which were generated with daily frequency, although their recovery was exceptionally rare. On his Northwest Passage expedition Parry notes, "A bottle was thrown overboard, containing a printed paper, stating the date and the situation of the ships, with a request, in six European languages, that any person finding it would forward it to the Secretary of the Admiralty, with a notice of the time and place where it was found. One bottle at least was thrown out daily during the voyage, except when the ships were 'beset' in the ice."[29] For John Ross's expedition, "a bottle, or copper cylinder, containing an account of our proceedings, was thrown over-board every day, as soon as the ship's position had been determined."[30] Most, if not all, narratives of polar exploration include similar accounts of daily bottle casting, which I need not multiply here. As a form of Arctic ecomedia, messages in bottles are neither distress calls nor romantic searches for attachment. The machinery of administration—the mundane apparatus of institutional recordkeeping—is filed away in the nonhuman depths of the frozen seas. Messages in bottles embody the contradictions and the promises in trying to account for—and also account *in*—oceanic forms of circulation, both in document and genre.

While many blanks were preprinted before their expeditions launched and were provided in bulk to their officers, many other forms were composed and printed in the polar regions on shipboard presses. These Arctic-generated documents emerged as a particular contingency of the search for the missing Northwest Passage expedition led by Franklin. Most Arctic ships after 1850 brought with them a printing press to aid in the search for the *Erebus* and *Terror*. While the presses were eventually commandeered by the crews in service of shipboard newspapers (as chapters 1 and 2 describe), their original function was to print multiple copies of messages on colored silk or oiled paper that would be transmitted by hydrogen balloon or ship location notices that could be placed in cairns or thrown overboard.[31] To Sherard Osborn, an officer on the HMS *Resolute* search for Franklin, balloon messages were a "novel attempt for distant signalizing, or rather, intercommunication"; the notes contained the location of the searching parties for the benefit of any survivors. "Should these tidings by good fortune have reached their destination," it was hoped that in addition to providing location information, the messages "will have raised up at once fresh hopes and fresh endurance."[32] The *Resolute* expedition also experimented with dispatching messages via carrier pigeon and in collars secured to the necks of Arctic foxes that had been trapped; other stratagems proposed to the Admiralty for signaling the Franklin party included the use of ice hammers, ice blasting, rockets, railway carriages, bladders, stimulating medicines, boots with spikes, kites, gutta percha boats, inflated india rubber balls, aeronauts, velocipedes, and smoke balls.[33] Osborn describes the balloon gambit, a "simple" plan:

> A balloon of oiled silk, capable of raising about a pound weight when inflated, was filled with hydrogen evolved from a strong cask, fitted with a valve, in which, when required for the purpose, a certain quantity of zinc filings and sulphuric acid had been introduced. To the base of the balloon, when inflated, a piece of slow match five feet long was attached, its lower end being lighted. Along this match, at certain intervals, pieces of coloured paper and silk were secured with thread, and on them the information

as to our position and intended lines of search were printed. The balloon, when liberated, sailed rapidly along, rising withal, and as the match burnt the papers were gradually detached, and falling, spread themselves on the snow, where their glaring colours would soon attract notice, should they happily fall near the poor fellows in the "Erebus" and "Terror."[34]

Osborn observes that the greatest distance the balloon messages were documented to have traveled was about fifty miles. (Fewer than ten of the launched notes that were recovered on the ice have made it to present-day archives; the extant messages are copies preserved on the ship.) Nevertheless, he writes, neither the messages' narrow orbit nor "our non-discovery of any papers during our travelling in 1851 can be adduced as a proof against their possible utility and success; and the balloons may still be considered a most useful auxiliary."[35] Robert Randolph Carter, a sailor on a different expedition searching for Franklin, was himself very pleased to find that their own balloon messages had traveled five miles, a tenth of the distance achieved on the *Resolute*. Among the "thousand bits of paper marked with (Date, Ship, position, future intentions, and naming depots of provisions)" that were launched by balloon in bunches of ten, Carter reports that just three of the messages "were found by a party from the Advance about five miles from Beechey Island which were probably some of the first bundle showing that it had worked well thus far."[36] We see here the oceanic optimism maintained by expedition members even in the face of the circumpolar annihilation of their messaging attempts.

In some instances, printed messages were given to local Inuit or Yupik parties for distribution. This strategy was conceived of by Rochfort Maguire, a member of the HMS *Plover* expedition stationed in Point Barrow, Alaska, where active trading routes among Russians and the Yupik and Iñupiat were already established. Maguire wrote in his diary, "I began to turn my attention to the means we might have of extending information along the coast to Eastw [*sic*] through the Natives.... We had a Number of Notices printed today, that I intend asking them here to distribute along the Coast." The scheme does not seem to have worked, however, as Maguire's plan launches in late October: "Unfortunately all their migrations take place in the summer, when they can be of very little use for our purpose."[37] The notices printed for native distribution presumed that Yupik, Iñupiat, or Inuit couriers were not able to read English. In a message "Printed on board H. M. S. Plover, on the 1st of July, 1854," for example, Maguire details the baroque locations of buried caches of food, but remarks of one such cache that

FIG 4.4 — A balloon used by the Franklin search expeditions for distributing messages. AAA 4347. © NATIONAL MARITIME MUSEUM, GREENWICH, LONDON.

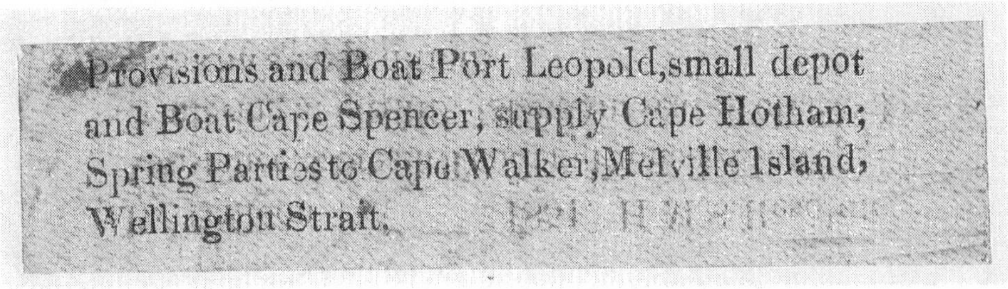

Provisions and Boat Port Leopold, small depot and Boat Cape Spencer, supply Cape Hotham; Spring Parties to Cape Walker, Melville Island, Wellington Strait.

FIG 4.5 — Balloon message on green silk, HMS *Resolute, Assistance*, 1851. The printed text on the other side of the note reads as follows: "By Balloon 1851. H M S Resolute, Assistance, Steam Tenders Pioneer & Intrepid, (wintering at Griffith Island) in search of Sir J Franklin's Expedition." British Library C45.i.ii. © THE BRITISH LIBRARY BOARD.

"it is impossible to say the natives will allow it to remain undisturbed," even as the notice "is printed for distribution among the natives who travel eastward to Barter Point, in the hope that it may fall into the hands of any party of the missing Expedition who may be travelling this way." We learn from the form's conclusion that the supply caches are potentially at risk because the local population is starving: "The natives have been friendly with us but

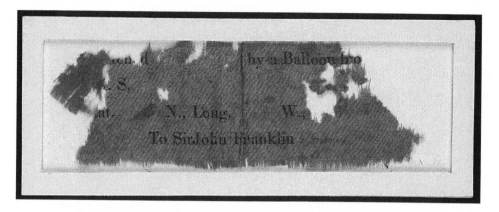

FIG 4.6 — Balloon message, printed in black ink on red silk. AAA3970.2. © NATIONAL MARITIME MUSEUM, GREENWICH, LONDON.

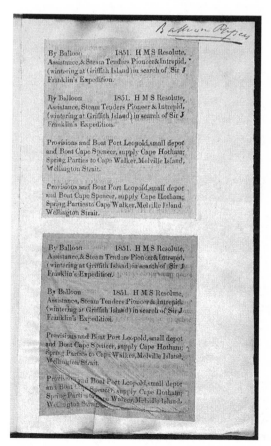

FIG 4.7 — Balloon message on pink and green paper, 1851. The message was printed with the same set of type as figure 4.5 but on different material: oiled pink paper instead of green silk. The printed text on the note reads as follows: "By Balloon 1851. H M S Resolute, Assistance, Steam Tenders Pioneer & Intrepid, (wintering at Griffith Island) in search of Sir J Franklin's Expedition. Provisions and Boat Port Leopold, small depot and Boat Cape Spencer, supply Cape Hotham, Spring Parties to Cape Walker, Melville Island, Wellington Strait." ADM 7/190. NATIONAL ARCHIVES, LONDON.

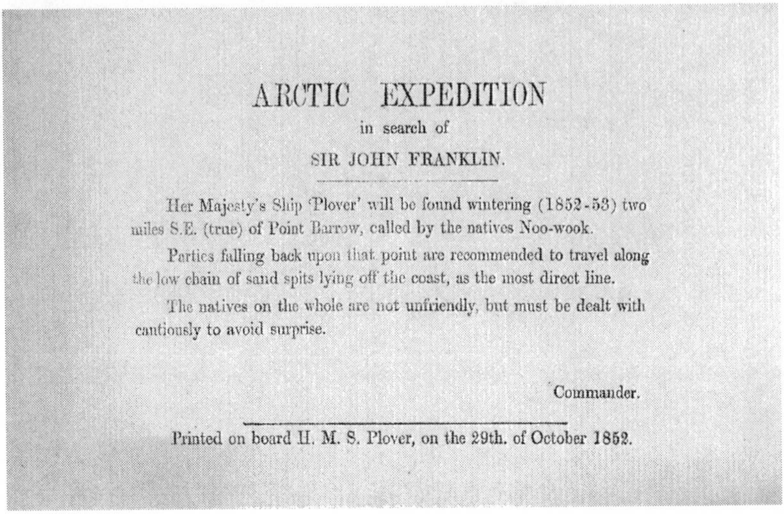

ARCTIC EXPEDITION
in search of
SIR JOHN FRANKLIN.

Her Majesty's Ship 'Plover' will be found wintering (1852-53) two miles S.E. (true) of Point Barrow, called by the natives Noo-wook.

Parties falling back upon that point are recommended to travel along the low chain of sand spits lying off the coast, as the most direct line.

The natives on the whole are not unfriendly, but must be dealt with cautiously to avoid surprise.

Commander.

Printed on board H. M. S. Plover, on the 29th. of October 1852.

FIG 4.8 — HMS *Plover* cairn message, 29 Oct. 1852. Box 4, John Simpson Papers, 1825–1875. DAVID M. RUBENSTEIN RARE BOOK AND MANUSCRIPT LIBRARY, DUKE UNIVERSITY.

ought not to be trusted by strangers, and cannot be relied on for provisions as they frequently suffer from famine themselves."[38] Maguire takes advantage of the "friendliness" and mobility of Arctic indigenous communities while safeguarding his resources, both materially and politically. The paradoxical accessibility and restrictedness of such circuits is painfully underscored by the Inuit recognition that British and American cairns were not communicative media within themselves, but caches of food through which to rummage.

The Oceanic Postbox

I have been describing how messages, notices, and other forms of information circulated in the polar regions in the nineteenth century. These varieties of Arctic ecomedia are not the only body of oceanic letters: these also comprise the letters whose places of emission and destination were aboard ships, to and from captains, sailors, and long-voyaging passengers. Their circuits of delivery and receipt share with the formal post a process of heterogeneous handling, but one stripped of all regularizing processes, patterns, and forms.[39] In this section I address the *intra*oceanic (rather than *trans*oceanic) circuits of nautical letter exchange and mail delivery in the long nineteenth century in order to place into spatial and temporal context the relative "dead"-ness of Arctic blanks. Ships' letters were thrown to the commerce of the sea; indifferently handled, passed along, left behind, or intercepted, correspondence nevertheless often reached its address. The provisional postal exchanges that took place at sea, in ports, in cairns, or at watering spots were surprisingly effective ways of delivering mail. Or so it would seem; in their voyage journals and narratives, sailors describe their postal successes but rarely mention the letters that are lost, adrift, dead.

After writing a letter—in the age of sail as much as today—an individual encloses it in an envelope, places postage upon it, submits it to the handling of the postal service, and trusts that even though multiply handled on various vehicles of transport, the letter will arrive intact, sealed, and ready for the private reception of its intended audience. This process is exceptionally intimate in its presumption of the one-to-one correspondence and shared tactile experience of its sender and its recipient. At the same time, the post is a broadly public form of exchange, predicated upon the hand-to-hand transmission of the agents of delivery, the national postal systems that underwrite it, and the economies of the world of letters on the registers of both the local (the stationers and news agents who provide the materials and tools) as well as the global (Syrian gall ink, for example, and gum from the Sudan, to speak of the materials alone). Even electronic mail replicates historical forms of mail exchange in the digital fragmentation of its modes of transmission, as well as the ambitions it has to privacy despite the medium's demonstrably public exchanges. The letter functions as an itinerant signifier, as Jacques Lacan and Jacques Derrida have memorably argued; while they may diverge on whether "a letter always reaches its destination" (in Lacan's reading) or "always not arrive[s] at its destination" (in Derrida's response), both see the general economy of epistolary exchange as a system of personal and impersonal object relations.[40] In this sense the Victory Point cairn note left by the doomed Franklin expedition can serve simultaneously as just another pedestrian expeditionary update and also as the most important document in Arctic exploration history: its ultimate delivery into the hands of a reader (McClintock; the Anglo-American public; you and me) is conditioned by Franklin's death. Indeed for Derrida in *The Post Card*, death—which demarcates the space between correspondents— may be the inevitable destiny of letters.[41] Failure is the condition of Arctic communication rather than its telos.

Various strategies have been used to circulate mail on an oceanic scale. A visitor today to Floreana Island (formerly Charles Island) in the Galápagos archipelago in the Pacific Ocean can stop at the island's informal post office, at which letters and post cards are left—without postage, by design—to be selectively picked up by visitors who promise to hand-deliver them. It has been in existence for hundreds of years, likely since the 1793 visit to the islands by a British Naval officer, James Colnett, who thought that the islands would be a useful refueling and rest station for whaling fleets working the Pacific. Either Colnett or a slightly later visitor erected an empty whale oil barrel to serve as a postbox, and the spot—which became known as Post-Office Bay—became the center of Pacific Ocean epistolary exchange. U.S. Naval captain David Porter, a major figure in the Pacific during the War of 1812, was one of many visitors to take advantage of the local letter box, by then known as "Hathaway's Post-office." Vessels stopping by the islands for tortoises, wood, or water would leave letters addressed not to individuals, or even specific ships, but to the Pacific community at large. Porter writes of his first stop on Charles (Floreana) Island in 1813:

> Understanding that vessels which stopped there for refreshments, such as turtle and land tortoise, and for wood, were in the practice of depositing letters in a box placed for the purpose near the landing-place, (which is a small beach sheltered by rocks, about the middle of the bay,) I dispatched Lieutenant Downes to ascertain if any vessels had been lately there, and to bring off such letters as might be of use to us, if he should find any. He returned in about three hours, with several papers, taken from a box which he found nailed to a post, over which was a black sign, on which was painted *Hathaway's Post-office*. There were none of them of a late date, but they were satisfactory.[42]

The opportunity for mail exchange was on a par with resource gathering as an impetus to stop on Charles Island, in Porter's description. The contents of the letters, as described by Porter and other sailors, relate the ships' movements, engagements, freight, success, crew health, and future trajectories. Porter quotes from one such letter from a whale ship captain, in part because he is amused by it as a "rare specimen of orthography": "Ship Sukey John Macey 7 1/2 Months out 150 Barrels 75 days from Lima No oil Since Leaving that Port. . . . I leave this port this Day With 250 Turpen 8 Load Wood."[43] On their first stop on Charles Island, Porter's men take with them several of the letters they find in the box; on a return trip, Porter writes in *A Voyage in the South Seas*, they find that another ship has taken away all of the barrel's remaining papers. But when Porter needs to communicate directly—and privately—with his lieutenant on another ship, he buries his

FIG 4.9 — HMS *Lancaster* crew members at post office barrel, Charles Island, 28 Nov. 1917. Las Encantadas, Human and Cartographic History of the Galápagos Islands.

PRIVATE COLLECTION OF JOHN WORAM. USED WITH PERMISSION.

note in a bottle in the sand, as per prearrangement. Should the lieutenant not rendezvous with him on the island, Porter commands, he should "search at the foot of the stake to which the letter-box is attached, where I should bury a bottle containing instructions for him."[44] The presumption is that these postbox letters are public, inasmuch as the small community of whaleships and naval vessels constitutes a public. The Pacific mail-exchange community centered in the Galápagos is a public to a more definitive degree than the circle of Arctic messengers, for whom the inclusion of strangers may be a vain hope.[45]

Porter's experience rhymes with that of other mariners. A number of nineteenth-century seamen describe the Galápagos post office in their narratives; among them is William Nevens, who in his *Forty Years at Sea* writes that the post office "consists of a box made water tight, with a close cover, into which every captain that enters the harbor, puts in an open letter telling his 'where from, where bound, what luck,' and all about. When we came into the harbor there were many letters in the 'post office' and we knew by reading them where all 'the whalers' were bound."[46] Nevens's account is one of many that belie a claim made by the *Beagle*'s captain Robert Fitzroy, that the small settlement that had emerged on Charles Island by the 1830s meant that letters intended for homeward-bound whaleships were now left with the residents rather than in the barrel in Post-Office Bay.[47] Reuben Delano's whaling narrative also affirms the "open" status of this letter point, mentioning the customary epistolary updates: "By a letter which we found in the box, we learned that an English vessel had been there but a few days previous, and had lost two men, one of whom fell dead with a terrapin on his back, from the excessive heat of the sun."[48] The sailors treat the barrel in Post-Office Bay as a convenience and a curiosity, a rare tether in the Pacific to which to affix an epistolary signal. Absent the infrastructure of a port community and the environmental starkness of the polar regions, the largely unsettled Galápagos Islands can support an open post for exchange while still remaining proximate to oceanic forms of relation and circulation. While sailors refer to these missives as "letters," they are, in fact, news, designed to convey information to passing ships.

Melville visited the Galápagos during the time he spent as a sailor; he later wrote about the "enchanted" equatorial isles in "The Encantadas," a series of sketches serialized in *Putnam's Monthly Magazine* in 1854 (and later included in *The Piazza Tales*). Although a working seaman for some years, Melville brings a terrestrial skepticism or pessimism to oceanic forms of mail exchange. In his telling, the Galápagos Islands' post office is catalogued among other signs of "vanishing humanity" detailed in the final sketch of "The Encantadas." It is a "dreary" spot where letters are staked in bottles and rot in the absence of a recipient. "Curious to say," Melville writes,

> that spot which of all others in settled communities is most animated, at the Enchanted Isles presents the most dreary of aspects. And though it may seem very strange to talk of post offices in this barren region, yet post offices are occasionally to be found there. They consist of a stake and a bottle. The letters being not only sealed, but corked. They are generally deposited by captains of Nantucketers for the benefit of passing fishermen, and contain statements as to what luck they had in whaling or tortoise hunting. Frequently, however, long months and months, whole years, glide by and no applicant appears. The stake rots and falls.[49]

Melville highlights the sociability that characterizes land-based post offices, which stands in contrast, in his telling, to the lack of animation to be found on the desert islands. Oceanic letters in Melville's tale are dead, rotting; this is a very different sense of the animation of the spot than can be seen in the writings of his contemporary fellow sailor-authors, for whom the Galápagos mail might not be "of a late date" but is more than "satisfactory."

The oceanic system of mail practiced on the Galápagos serves an arresting function in the story of the historical hermit Patrick Watkins, alias "Oberlus," whose tale Melville adapts from naval captain David Porter's account. (This is only one of many elements of Porter's narrative that Melville borrows in "The Encantadas.") Watkins was an Irish renegade from an English ship, and from his encampment on Charles Island (Melville places him on Hood Island, now Española) he sought to kidnap passing sailors and enslave them. Both Porter and Melville describe how crew members of a ship that had been victimized by Watkins had, in Porter's words, "put a letter in a keg, giving intelligence of the affair, and moored it in the bay" in order to warn other vessels that Watkins was targeting shore parties.[50] In Melville's slight alteration of the line, "they put a letter in a keg, giving the Pacific Ocean intelligence of the affair, and moored the keg in the bay."[51] In fictively moving Watkins off Charles Island, and thus away from Post-Office Bay, Melville removes him from the actual sphere of Pacific epistolary exchange (which he casts as stagnant, in any case). Melville's addition of the whole of the Pacific Ocean to the intended audience for this letter of warning introduces a jape about the open access, as it were, of sea letters, available to those who would put the news to use and share it in turn. For as it happens, Watkins—having deserted his own ship—establishes on the island a Crusoe-esque parody of terrestrial containment, declaring himself sovereign over the island and enslaving men from passing ships, the first of whom is a black sailor. Rather than extending the potential geographical and political mobility offered to him by his oceanic location, Watkins doubles back to land-based models of constraint.

An incident in *Moby-Dick* involving oceanic mail exchange likewise underscores Melville's Derridean emphasis on the morbidity of letters at sea rather than their circulatory potential. In "The Jeroboam's Story," the *Pequod* encounters a plague-beset whaleship whose crew is in thrall to a lunatic sailor who fashions himself a prophet—the archangel Gabriel, in fact. This is the *Jeroboam*'s story: Gabriel had commanded his shipmates not to hunt the white whale, but when the chief mate, Macey, risked doing so, Moby Dick swept him from the boat with a flick of its tail, killing him. In the *Jeroboam*'s aborted gam with the *Pequod*, Gabriel warns Ahab, in turn, to beware the white whale. At this moment, incongruously, Ahab recalls that in his letter bag he has some correspondence for an officer of the *Jeroboam*. "Every whale-ship takes out a goodly number of letters for various ships, whose delivery to the persons to whom they may be addressed, depends upon the mere chance of encountering them in the four oceans," Ishmael narrates.

"Thus, most letters never reach their mark; and many are only received after attaining an age of two or three years or more." The letter that is retrieved from Ahab's letter bag is "sorely tumbled, damp, and covered with a dull, spotted, green mould, in consequence of being kept in a dark locker of the cabin." Its mossiness is a sign of its relative immobility; Ahab's letter bag has not been in circulation but has instead accrued the moisture of oceanic spaces without their fluidity of exchange. Even in the open sea this is a dead letter: "Of such a letter," Melville writes, "Death himself might well have been the post-boy."[52] And such is the case, as it happens. The single letter that Ahab holds for the *Jeroboam* is addressed to the mate Macey, dead by the flukes of the white whale. When Ahab tries to deliver it to the ship despite its absent recipient, the letter attached to a long pole to escape contagion from plague, the cracked archangel Gabriel shriekingly manages to cast the letter back aboard the *Pequod*, telling Ahab that he himself is bound where Macey has gone. The letter for Macey lands back with Ahab: a dead letter for a death-marked monomaniac. Ahab's attempt to circulate the letter, that is, ends with it returned to hand or, literally, to foot, as it falls at his ivory leg—the limb removed from Ahab's own body's circulation. For Melville, letters at sea are always not arriving.

Yet this is not the experience of other mariners, who hunger for absent letters but do not foreclose on the eventuality of their delivery. If we consider Melville's postal pessimism within the context of the countervailing practices and views offered by other sailors, we arrive at a different oceanic order of correspondence. The long establishment of the Galápagos Islands as a nautical watering spot and meeting place—given their relative fixity within the seascape—made them anomalous as a site for seafaring postal exchange. More common would be for ships to exchange letters with other ships or pick up letters in port, in the hope that a given port would have received letters that presumed that that particular ship would indeed have arrived at that particular port. While this method may have been extraordinarily conditional and serendipitous, the majority of sailors spend little to no time lamenting letters that might have been lost or cast astray. Instead they focus on the gratification to be had from their delayed and peripatetic arrival. William Whitecar, aboard a whaler, records the pleasures of receiving news both via letters and in the form of periodicals: "By the ship Alexander, I received letters from home; and although nine months old, they were heartily welcome. . . . Such events are the oases in our desert. Newspapers were also sent to me; and I read them completely through, advertisements and all, with a degree of attention I had never before bestowed on a printed sheet."[53] Walter Colton, aboard a U.S. Navy ship, describes his shipmates' reaction to an unexpected encounter with a homebound whale ship: "All pens were now put in motion to dispatch letters home. Go where you would, fore or aft, nothing was to be heard but the scratch of these pens. . . . How they can carry paper in their clothes-bags is more than I can explain. . . . Each seemed lost in thoughts of the surprise and pleasure which the letters he had thus unexpectedly been able to send back would awaken."[54] Other sailors dealt more strategically with the attenuation and contingency of nautical mail. The captain of J. Ross Browne's whale ship, devoted to his wife and children,

> spent an hour every forenoon reading a package of letters written by his wife to entertain him during his long voyage; and every night he regularly wrote her an account of the proceedings of the day, signed and directed as if for the mail. This arrangement, dictated by affection, brought the devoted couple in mutual communion. While thus separated, the wife had all the letters of the preceding voyage to read, and the husband all those interesting little details of domestic life which had transpired during his previous absence, to make up for the deprivation of being separated from those he loved.[55]

The chronometric slide in the calendar they keep does not sour the correspondence between the captain and his wife, for whom terrestrial time scales are not relevant. Even in the absence of ship-to-ship encounters at which to exchange letters, sailors keep generating material. Aboard the USS *Constitution*, the anonymous author of *Life in a Man-of-War* laments that only twice in twenty-six months had his ship received dispatches; nevertheless, he writes, "month after month, *our* letter bags for the United States were swelled to an enormous magnitude."[56] The sailor's tenuous link to the wider social body he has left behind seems to supersede, temporarily, the promise of oceanic fraternity.

On the Nares Arctic expedition, a relative of one of the officers had contrived to create a Christmas card for each sailor on board, which were then held in reserve until the holiday; in order to simulate postal exchange—"to make it appear as if they had been actually delivered through the post"— the benefactor had affixed "a second-hand postage-stamp" to each envelope, enacting a fantasy that overwrites the dead status of Arctic letters.[57] This fantasy encounters the atemporal status of polar ecomedia too. The nautical posting of letters maintains a pragmatic eventuality in addition to an affective or metaphysical one: because they are not restricted to the private circuit, the mail's "openness" is defined both in terms of time and the multiplicity of participants involved in the transmission of letters. A different fantasy of receipt is at play in the account that Robert Peary gives of a postcard to his wife that he inscribes upon reaching the North Pole, or at least the postcard that he supposedly writes at the moment of his now-discredited claim to have reached the Pole. He is very busy at the North Pole, Peary explains: "I found time, however, to write to Mrs. Peary on a United States postal card which I had found on the ship during the winter." The message:

90 North Latitude, April 7th.

My dear Jo,

I have won out at last. Have been here a day. I start for home and you in an hour. Love to the "kidsies."

"BERT."[58]

Josephine "Jo" Peary (a polar explorer and successful author in her own right) received the North Pole postcard in Sydney, at the other end of the world. The fact of its delivery, for insouciant "Bert," confirms his North Polar claims.

Other Arctic voyagers wrote and occasionally received correspondence, although the deposit points tended to be in the small port towns along Baffin Bay, which was trafficked by whalers and traders. The orders to Edward Belcher from the British Admiralty stipulated that he was "invariably, should any opportunity offer, to leave letters for us at such places as Cape Warrender, Ponds Bay, etc., provided no delay be incurred thereby."[59] Francis Leopold McClintock was so eager to collect any letters waiting for him in Godhavn, Greenland, upon the *Fox* expedition's return trip that they rousted the inhabitants from bed at 3:00 a.m., "demanding our letters, but great indeed was our disappointment at finding only a very few letters and two or three papers, and these for the officers only!"[60] Weather and ice conditions naturally affected mail delivery, and a report from the Nares expedition displays some anxiety about how best to weigh the dispersal or storage of letters against the environmental challenges: "As in the present condition of the straits and at this early season it was impossible to know what our future proceedings would be, or even if we could again visit the cape, and, moreover, the despatches not being in duplicate, I considered it for the best to land now the only loose letters which seemed to comprise some for nearly every member of the expedition, and to reserve the sealed bags until the landing party returned with further information."[61] The temporary post drop proved successful, and the Nares expedition was later able to use the spot to collect correspondence that had been delivered by a separate tender, even though a notice from the "Postmaster-General" aboard ship cautioned that there was "some uncertainty whether the letters will reach their destination."[62] When it was discovered that a search party "had found a mail," the "feelings of all on board were not to be easily-described. . . . After the first exclamations of pleasure and surprise not a word was spoken until the mail-bags were sorted and the lucky ones received their budgets of news."[63] Robert McClure of the Franklin search ship HMS *Investigator* acknowledges, "Communication by post from this region of the globe is rather unprecedented, but nevertheless I hope [a letter] will arrive at its destination safely." His letter had help: McClure wrote to his sister from Mercy Bay in the far northwest of the Canadian Arctic archipelago, and his dispatches ultimately arrived at their destination with the aid of a "skin-clad chief of the tribe fishing at the cape."[64]

The tether between home and the Arctic was more often than not imaginatively constructed in text, however. A mock letter home that appeared as the first contribution of the first number of the *Illustrated Arctic News* finds a crew member writing to his father. He describes with breathless drama the ship's imaginary escapes from destruction in the icepack, near-catastrophes that have made him a "wiser, & I trust, a better man." Thus improved, the sailor recalls "the fact that a small Bill, about £36, is still owing to Looney in Regent Street" for cigars—might his father satisfy the debt?[65] In this comic fantasy of connection, we see Arctic hazards reconfigured as the impetus for moral and economic equity. The joke works only if we recognize that this sailor is, in reality, beyond all accounting.

I close this chapter with a hauntingly evocative dream about Franklin and Arctic communication recorded in the journal of George De Long, an American naval officer and North Polar explorer. De Long commanded the USS *Jeannette* expedition (1879–81), which also ended in tragedy: the ship was crushed by ice, the crew was separated, and twenty of the thirty-three men perished, including De Long, although his body and his papers were later recovered by the survivors. Nearly forty-five years after the Franklin venture, De Long's North Pole expedition had a wider range of technology at hand, and this factors into the dream experienced by a *Jeannette* member:

The doctor relates a curious dream he had last night. He seemed to be accompanying the survivors of Sir John Franklin's last expedition on their journey to the Great Fish River, when suddenly he changed his base to this ship's cabin, and began explaining to Sir John Franklin there present some of our articles of outfit, such as Edison's electric machine, the anemometer, and the telephone. Franklin, after listening to the explanations and viewing the articles, tersely remarked, "Your electric machine is not worth a damn, and your anemometer is just the same." The telephone he seemed to consider a good thing.[66]

When Franklin and his party were heading to the Great Fish River in the late 1840s, both historically and in the dream, they were in their final grim hours. The dream-Franklin rejects the utility of both the anemometer (a machine for gauging wind speed) and the electric lights that a young Edison had offered to the expedition. (Before perfecting the incandescent lightbulb, Edison had toyed with arc lamps; he gave the *Jeannette* a series of arc lamps and the hand-cranked dynamo that De Long found "not worth a damn.")[67] But it is the telephone, a communication device reaching across time and space, that attracts dream-Franklin.[68] Prophetically experienced and recorded before De Long or the ship's doctor could imagine their own deaths on the ice, the dream sifts through possible technologies of ecomedia for illuminating and communicating in the darkness and isolation of the Arctic winter. The doctor's dream nevertheless keeps alive the possibility that a circuit of communication with the dead will yet remain open.

FIVE

INUIT KNOWLEDGE

AND

CHARLES FRANCIS HALL

Teik-ko se-ko? teik-ko se-ko?—Do you see ice? do you see ice?
— CHARLES FRANCIS HALL, *Arctic Researches and*
Life among the Esquimaux: Being the Narrative of an
Expedition in Search of Sir John Franklin, in the Years 1860,
1861, and 1862 (1865)

The search for Sir John Franklin's missing ships that began in 1848 concluded in 2014 and 2016, when the *Erebus* and *Terror* were located on the Canadian Arctic sea floor off King William Island and in Terror Bay, respectively. Identifying the ships has been presented as a triumph of technology, in part: sonar, robot submersibles, subaqueous cameras, and marine archaeology all contributed to the find. It is more properly, however, a confirmation of the accuracy of Inuit reports on the starving, desperate men that have circulated for over 150 years, as some accounts (but far from all) have acknowledged.[1] First Nations sailors were instrumental to the *Terror* find; the ships were eventually found just where the Inuit had repeatedly said they were. From the early searches beginning in the 1840s, various Inuit had told Anglo-American expedition members that they had seen or had heard of abandoned ships, large groups of emaciated men, and mutilated corpses. Arctic whaling captain Thomas Ward of the *Truelove*, conscripted to the search in 1849, turned over to the Admiralty a map

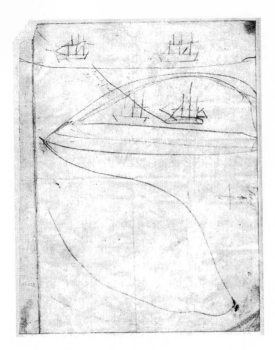

of four iced-in Western ships drawn by an Inuk man; the map attracted little interest or attention. The Inuk translator Adam Beck's 1851 second-hand account of a ship fire and massacre of white men was given no weight by the Admiralty, one member commenting, "Adam Beck's Report is not to be trusted."[2] Scotsman John Rae, most significantly, returned from the North in 1854 with word of Franklin expedition relics in the possession of the Inuit, who had encountered a large party of struggling white men, or "kabloonas" (Qabluunak), who had lost their ship; the Inuit also reported finding bodies a season later. They noted signs of cannibalism among the corpses, Rae wrote in a letter from the Arctic: "From the mutilated state of many of the bodies and the contents of the kettles, it is evident our wretched Countrymen had been driven to the last dread alternative, as a means of sustaining life."[3]

Skeptics of Rae's conclusions feared that Franklin's men had been torn apart by bears or massacred by the Inuit; one of the strongest of these voices was that of Charles Dickens, who characterized Inuit evidence in *Household Words* as "the chatter of a gross handful of uncivilised people."[4] Rae, who learned from indigenous Arctic tactics, presented evidence from Inuit oral history as well as from the remnants of the expedition, but his reports were generally greeted with skepticism, if not hostility or hatred. In making judgments derived from indigenous knowledge that Franklin men may have resorted to cannibalism, Rae might have been seen by the British public as speaking as an Inuit and therefore unreliable as a commentator on British naval practice. Some observers invoked Franklin's harrowing first voyage in 1819 as justification for finding it preposterous that his men would resort to human consumption; although the earlier expedition members had been driven to eating lichen and their shoe leather during a terrible overland crossing to the Coppermine River delta, they allegedly never resorted to cannibalism (even as eleven of the twenty men on the venture died). Franklin became known for this first voyage as "the man who ate his boots." The English commander's own avowed principles were not the only reason Rae received pushback on his reports. A pseudonymous group pamphlet addressed what the authors called the "Great Arctic Mystery":

> It may suit Dr. Rae's purposes to insist upon the tragical termination of cannibalism to the career of the Franklin party, but we well remember the burst of incredulity, mingled with disgust, which was felt by the public when Dr. Rae's unwarranted conclusion from third-hand Esquimaux evidence was published. For it is important to remember that the intelligence reached Dr. Rae in the thrice-diluted form through his Interpreter, who heard it from the Esquimaux, who heard it from other Natives, who said they had been at the spot where the death of forty of the Franklin party is stated to have occurred. These facts show the traditionary nature of the Esquimaux report, and, considered in connection with the conduct of the Natives, who are notoriously addicted to falsehood and deception, naturally lead us to receive the story with very great caution. . . . All the experience of our Arctic Explorers proves that Esquimaux are not to be trusted.[5]

The pamphleteers set out several of the terms that structure this chapter on Inuit knowledge and the newsman-turned-explorer Charles Francis Hall. For one, they characterize indigenous oral communication as "traditionary," which here has a negative valence that would not hold in Hall's own use of the term. "Traditionary" knowledge, by virtue of its orality, must necessarily be passed along by many voices or hands. In referring to Inuit oral history as "traditionary" knowledge, it should be noted, Hall and his contemporaries anticipate a term that has been in use in recent decades among sociologists and other practitioners of what has also been called ethnoecology: TEK, or traditional ecological knowledge, part of a broader body of indigenous wisdom known as TK or IK (traditional knowledge or indigenous knowledge). In her work on glaciers and indigenous epistemology Julie Cruikshank defines TK as "tacit knowledge embodied in life experiences and reproduced in everyday behaviour and speech."[6] For an Anglo-American expeditionary culture that fetishized textual records, Inuit modes of communication were suspect.

In what follows I turn to indigenous circuits of knowledge in the Arctic and the embrace—or rejection—of "traditionary" knowledge by Anglo-American polar expedition members. The Arctic dead letters discussed in chapter 4 adapt Western forms of communication as ecomedia in order to enable the transfer of information in the Far North. Inuit modes of TK, as I explore in this chapter, are variously employed, appropriated, or dismissed by white expedition members. Many members of British and American expeditions were slow or reluctant to adapt to indigenous modes of Arctic survival (such as wearing furs instead of woven cloth). British and American scientific and discovery-minded ventures to the northern polar regions were consistently undertaken as if learning about the Arctic and learning from the Arctic were incommensurate modes of knowledge. I focus on an exception: the American explorer and autodidact Charles Francis Hall (1821–1871), who is usually classified as a colorful footnote to (or doomed eccentric within) the history of Anglo-American polar voyaging. A one-time newspaper editor in Cincinnati with no prior nautical experience, Hall first went to the Arctic as part of a personal quest to find traces of the lost Franklin expedition. Hall became best known to his contemporaries initially, however, for developing a long relationship with an Inuit couple, Ipiirviq (whose name Hall rendered as Ebierbing) and Taqulittuq (or Tookoolito; the couple was known to the whaling crews of Cumberland Sound as "Joe" and "Hannah"). Hall lived with the Inuit for over seven years, in two- and five-year continuous periods—a singular act for a white, Western explorer in the mid-nineteenth century. A provocative tension obtains between Hall's proud amateurism—"If he was enthusiastic in the extreme, there was some method in his enthusiasm," one account puts it—and the broad-based Arctic expertise he adopted from and championed in the Inuit.[7]

Hall's own adventures, sketched briefly here, have had their chroniclers.[8] His first two expeditions in search of Franklin relics were not voyages in the usual Arctic sense, since Hall traveled without his own ship or crew; instead he hitched rides with other vessels (including a whaler out of Connecticut captained by Sidney Buddington or Budington) and prepared for his own residencies among the Inuit. After his initial two years living on

FIG 5.2 — Hall with Taqulittuq and Ipiirviq (or as he spelled their names, Tookoolito and Ebierbing). From Hall, *Arctic Researches and Life among the Esquimaux*, frontispiece.

Baffin Island in the same igloo as Ipiirviq and Taqulittuq, Hall returned to the United States in 1862 along with the Inuit couple and their children. They had already been exposed to the English language and to white Westerners when a whaling captain took them across the Atlantic for a two-year visit to England beginning in 1853, where they were given an audience with Queen Victoria (whose response was to note in her journal that the Inuit couple were "her subjects, very curious, & quite different to any of the southern or African tribes").[9] Hall's treatment of Ipiirviq and Taqulittuq while in America was attentive to their value to his future plans, as the third-person narrative of his second voyage attests: "Hall seems to have been carefully mindful of their welfare. 'Everything,' he wrote to Captain Budington, 'must be done to protect the health of these people; the assistance which I hope to receive from them on my sledge trip is too important for us to relax our exertions to have them comfortable.'"[10] Nevertheless in between his first two Arctic sojourns Hall embarked on a lecture tour and contracted Ipiirviq and Taqulittuq to P. T. Barnum's American Museum as part of his fundraising for his second trip north. Such actions were common in an age of ethnographic and scientific racism, even if Hall reconsidered placing the couple on display shortly thereafter. He wrote to Buddington's wife, "[Barnum] cannot have them again. I do think it would ruin their healths to go through another siege as when they were there. Money would not induce me to run another such risk of their lives."[11] Hall therefore, according to the second narrative, "followed the advice of friends in refusing his consent for their presence at any other lectures than his own."[12] His belated scruples against making Ipiirviq and Taqulittuq into spectacles did not extend to Hall's own public performances of Arctic authenticity, even as he regretted having outsourced the couple for a paying American public.

Although Hall was a relatively agreeable member of the Inuit community in his two northern residencies, he had a more fractious time in the United States and among white sailors. During his second expedition he shot and killed a mutinous member of a whaling crew with whom he had contracted transport. By 1870, however, Hall had established enough polar bona fides that the U.S. Navy entrusted him with command of a state-sponsored North Pole mission, the nation's first. This disastrous final expedition, on the ship *Polaris* (1871–73), ended early for Hall: during the mission's first winter on the ice he was poisoned to death by arsenic at the hands of his own men. Most suspicion rests with the ship's doctor and Hall's rival in expeditionary science, Emil Bessels.[13] The remaining crew of the *Polaris* venture secured an even more sensational place in polar history when nineteen members were separated from the leaking ship and subsequently endured an extraordinary six months on a diminishing ice floe that traveled eighteen hundred miles before their rescue. Among the floe-floating survivors were Taqulittuq and Ipiirviq, the latter of whom (along with another Inuk man, Suersaq or Hans Hendrik) kept the party alive by his skill at seal hunting. All survived the fractured *Polaris* mission except the murdered Hall.

My aim in returning to this sensational history, with a specific focus on Hall's conception and execution of his first voyage, is to consider how knowledge circulated in the oceanic spaces and indigenous knowledge systems of the polar regions, whether through autodidactic, empirical, professional, or intercultural channels. In what follows I discuss how Hall, in his relationship with Ipiirviq and Taqulittuq, mediates not only between U.S. and Inuit histories of Artic expertise but between experiential and speculative modes of knowing as well. The Arctic career of Charles Francis Hall is an example of exchanges of knowledge whose circuits are both routine and extravagant within the Arctic regions and without in the long nineteenth century. While this knowledge took many forms, my interest is the narrative accounts of the circulation of knowledge and historiography between Inuit residents of the Arctic regions and white Westerners such as Hall. As his history demonstrates, a complicated relationship existed between forms of nautical epistemology and indigenous knowledge in the Anglo-American experience of polar exploration. Hall's unusual path to and within the Arctic, guided along the way by Ipiirviq and Taqulittuq, provides a way to think about the place of indigenous knowledge within oceanic models of intellectual circulation. By this I mean that the logic of "discovery," by which travelers import the structures and terms of under-standing of their own cultural and political origin to the space of their ex-ploration, had consistently less success in the polar regions than in other geographical places of imperial, colonial, or economic interest. Hall sought to take the Arctic on its own terms, which has constituted his eccentricity from the circuits of Anglo-American polar histories. And yet it is the fact that Inuit lifeways are empirically verifiable as ways of knowing and sur-viving in the Arctic that underwrites his expeditionary innovations. Hall's speculation was to accede to this fact as an experimental possibility.

North from Cincinnati

Hall was a particularly zealous member of an Arctic-avid public in the late 1850s, a decade of special attention to Franklin's lost ships and to the polar expeditions launched on their behalf. He was born in New Hampshire but spent his adult life in Cincinnati, where he first ran an engraving business and then edited two newspapers between 1858 and 1860, the *Cincinnati Occasional* and the *Daily Press*, for which he wrote much of the noncommer-cial content. His education did not go beyond the eighth grade, which sets him apart from many of the men associated with the leadership of polar ventures; Hall was an autodidact, however, and an obsessive diarist, making detailed notes of the books he read.[14] By the late 1850s those books were mostly about Arctic exploration, a topic he featured in his newspaper col-umns as well as in his private journals.[15] Hall's fixation on accounts of polar expeditions reveals more than his own motivations, of course; his interest reflects both the place of Arctic ventures in the popular Anglo-American imagination, as well as the forms of expression they generated.

The mid- to late 1850s were an active time in polar narrative publication, and in Cincinnati Hall consumed the published voyage narratives that emerged from Anglo-American Arctic travels. In that decade two key pieces of information emerged about Franklin, the first news since his ships' disappearance. For one, Rae's expedition produced not just oral histories of Franklin's distressed men but a large trove of relics from the ships themselves that were purchased from the Inuit. Rae's account did not solve the broader mystery of what happened to both ships and the majority of the crew members, and his news about possible cannibalism was scandalous, but Hall took note of the fact that Rae had made use of Inuit knowledge and lifeways in his search. The second evidentiary announcement came in 1859, when Francis Leopold McClintock's *Fox* expedition found the first written account left by the Franklin expedition: a cached document uncovered on King William Island, as chapter 4 describes.

Hall interpreted these two significant items of news differently than many of his contemporaries. In his view, Rae's report produced hope that members of the Franklin expedition had had not just commerce with the indigenous Arctic residents but also friendly relations that might have extended to the point of rescue, relief, or cohabitation. And while the confirmation of Franklin's own death was affecting, Hall focused not on the confirmed losses but on how many men were still known to have *survived* three years into the doomed expedition—by his conclusions from these fragmentary records, as many as 105 of the original 129. His journals and diaries include numerous extracts from travel narratives whose authors had endured inhospitable regions for extended periods of time, whether polar or otherwise, which Hall apparently found promising antecedents for Franklin's men. In his diary in January 1860, for example, Hall noted that the American sea captain James Riley had survived captivity and sustained deprivation in the North African desert, although his notes exaggerate some aspects of the feat; Hall records Riley as having been enslaved for ten years (it was less than two) and writes that while Riley had "weighed 240 lbs" before his trials, after his redemption he only "weighed 60" (it was 90, still a shocking drop).[16]

Hall followed up his notes on Riley and other travelers with the following draft declaration in his diary in early 1860; it shows his enthusiasm and dedication, which is initially limited only by his theoretical death, then reconsidered as a shorter term of three to four years:

> *Proposal*—I, Chas. F. Hall, of Cin.C. do firmly believe that some of the 105 Companions of Sir John Franklin surviving on the 26th day of

April 1848) [*sic*] are yet living do propose to spend ~~my life~~ the next 3 or 4 years of my life in or in the vicinity of King William Island & that I believe my 1st duty to mankind is to attempt to project an expedition.[17]

One of his preparations for this "duty" made the local papers: one evening in Cincinnati Hall equipped himself with a candle, books, and a bottle of water and pitched a tent near the city's observatory in order to "inure himself to fatigue" and accustom himself to winter exposure. "At eleven o'clock his tent was visited by two Irishmen," the *Daily Press* reported, "armed with a shot-gun" and demanding drink. "We are pretty sure," the paper concluded, that "Mr. Hall considers that he would not have been worse served by the Esquimaux."[18] The newspaper's conflation of the ethnic "Irishmen" with the "Esquimaux" as types both disruptive and comic stages Hall's mission as itself a folly, as his naïve camping experiment in the relatively mild Cincinnati winter might seem to reveal.

Yet Hall's preparations, however amateurish, were not naïve. He filled journals with excerpts from the writings of earlier polar explorers, as well as with inspirational quotations from his reading. ("The greatest discoveries have been made by leaving the beaten path & going into by-paths.")[19] In addition to his research and notes on previous expeditions, he consulted with—and received written endorsements from—the most prominent living Arctic veteran, Israel Isaac Hayes, as well as the benefactor of earlier American Franklin search expeditions, Henry Grinnell, who donated several hundred dollars to his future travels. His wife, whom Hall abandoned along with his children, donated $27 to the expedition. The funding Hall sought more broadly was offered only modestly, however, despite the polite interest his plans; still, he scrupulously acknowledged all contributions, including a single pound of tea offered by one Z. B. Coffin of Cincinnati.[20] In his diary in February 1860 Hall laid out five possible prospects for his Arctic mission: first, he would attempt to secure funding for an actual vessel, at an estimated cost of $2,000; the next two options were similarly oriented. His fourth, penultimate option (which he describes as a "last resort") would be to constitute a joint whaling-exploration venture. Finally, Hall writes—of what would become his actual means of heading north—"see on what terms I can go with [whaling] Capt. Buddington up to Cumberland Inlet."[21] It must be stressed that this was an unusual and possibly unheard of approach to polar exploration in the nineteenth century: no other individual seems to have had the idea of mounting a solo trip relying only on the kindness of strangers, not a fully provisioned expedition, and lived to tell of it. And not just lived to tell: found himself by his third voyage in command of an official U.S. Navy North Pole mission. Hall knew his tactics were uncommon; as he addressed himself in his diary on 17 July 1860, "What do you now propose to do? This case may be an exception to the rule."[22]

He continued to refine his plans throughout the spring and early summer of 1860. Hall came to embrace his status as an unencumbered sojourner in the North, with neither a ship nor an expeditionary team, long before his actually becoming one was classified as an eccentric act: "My object is to acquire personal knowledge of the language & life of the Esquimaux, with a view thereafter to visit the Lands of King William, Boothia & Victoria—to endeavor by my personal investigation to determine more satisfactorily the fate of the 105 Companions of Sir John Franklin, now known to have been living on the 25th day of Apr. 1848."[23] Significantly his employment of the term "Esquimaux," the common one in use at the time among whites and sub-Arctic dwellers, would not be one that Hall would retain. While other Arctic travelers might note that the indigenous population in the eastern Canadian Arctic call themselves Inuit, they generally failed to use that term in their writing beyond ethnographic observation. Hall, on the other hand, adopts "their true designation," the word Inuit, he tells us, "signifying in their language, 'the people,' as distinguishing them from all foreigners." (The singular of Inuit is Inuk.) As Hall clarified on a lecture tour after his first voyage, "The term Esquimaux is not known among these people, it being the name given to them by foreigners, which name signifying eaters of raw fish or meat."[24] Dispensing with the ethnographic distance maintained by other polar explorers, Hall explained to his lecture audiences that his accounts of the Inuit would be coextensive with his account of himself: "As, during my five years of sojourn among these people, I adapted myself in all respects to their habits, customs and manner of living, it follows that in describing these, I am describing my own life during that period."[25] The extent of this immersion and its public reception is suggested in the two titles under which Hall's first-person narrative of his initial expedition appeared in England and the United States in 1865. The English edition was entitled *Life with the Esquimaux*; the American edition that followed shortly thereafter, however, was called *Arctic Researches and Life among the Esquimaux*. The American title has the effect of reinstalling the ethnographic distance that Hall's actual experience came to eliminate, treating his cohabitation with the Inuit as an act of scientific curiosity. The title also seems to separate Hall's living conditions from his research when, as we will see, they were one and the same.

Life among the Inuit

Hall was involved in the publication only of his first narrative, the sole volume that is in his own voice; after his violent death aboard the *Polaris*, the U.S. Navy compiled the accounts of his second and third voyages in the third person from his scores of notebooks.[26] So anxious was Hall to return to the Arctic after his first voyage, he writes in the preface to *Arctic Researches*, that "the last page of the manuscript was written on the morning of my embarkation" on the second voyage (iii); it was datelined "on board bark Monticello, bound for the Arctic Regions" (iv). His exuberant writing style in his private journals and in his first-person narrative is very different from that of most polar voyagers, whose approaches tended to be sober and scientific. Indeed the two third-person narratives compiled posthumously by the U.S. Navy are far more restrained in the material they quote from Hall's notebooks. Published Arctic narratives of the nineteenth century focused not on the personal reactions of expedition members to the region's unfamiliar conditions but on documenting the missions' scientific, exploratory, or hydrographic aims. Many include extensive appendices (or supplementary volumes) of records of observations on the temperature, the magnetic "dip," Arctic fauna, and the solar, lunar, and ocular distortions produced by polar latitudes. The inner lives of the expeditions warrant only a handful of pages in typical polar narratives; this is consistent with the broader nineteenth-century genre of the disinterested travelogue by the scientific-minded observer. Hall, by contrast, based his conclusions not on a preponderance of data but on enthusiasm and a kind of scientific relativity. On spotting an iceberg for the first time, he stages the drama of the encounter: "Then it was we met. Iceberg was silent; I too was silent" (36). He conveyed the relative meaning of Arctic cold for various northern travelers, for example, not by taxonomic charts, but by observations such as the following: "In the Arctic regions one seldom or never hears any remark made with regard to its being cold: this staple topic of conversation is thus entirely lost to the Inuits."[27] And yet Taqulittuq's time in the United States and England gave her a relative sense of what cold could mean; at one point during Hall's second expedition, she "expressed a wish that the lady who told her at the Brooklyn fair in New York that Innuits ought to dress like ladies in the States, could herself take a minute's walk only at this time over the hill near by, when she would be very glad to change her fine hat and hoop-skirts for any one of an Innuit's rough dresses."[28]

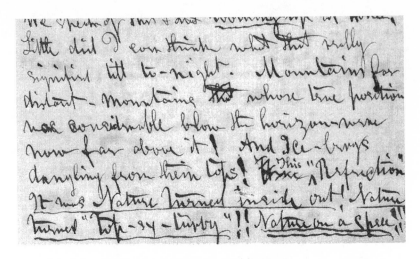

FIG 5.3 — "Nature on a spree," Charles Francis Hall, 013 Journal, Vol. II,
July 1860–November 1860. Charles Francis Hall Collection. NATIONAL MUSEUM OF
AMERICAN HISTORY, ARCHIVES CENTER, WASHINGTON, DC.

Hall approached the polar regions and standard nautical practices with a
version of the gonzo journalism he had practiced while a newspaper editor
in Cincinnati. Upon first observing the maritime visual distortion called
"looming," for example, Hall wrote of it, in a style typical of his narrative:
"This refraction? It was Nature turned inside out! Nature turned topsy-
turvey!! NATURE ON A SPREE!!! Yes, Nature on a spree!" (87). He recognized that this style (the typography and emphases of which he retains in the
published narrative when quoting from his own journals, including the moment just quoted) was a departure from the generic conventions of polar
expedition accounts, writing in the introduction to his *Arctic Researches*,
"This book is to be a work of narrative and adventure, and not one of argument and discussion" (xvii). In the absence of a scientific or navigation
team—usually a given on polar expeditions—Hall had to record all his
own observations with "a knowledge self-acquired." He trusts that "readers
will be able to see, as they move onward with me through my narrative, how
difficult it was—alone, and with no other pair of hands, no other mind, no
other thought, sense, or perception but my own—to record, day by day, the
occurrences that came under my eye" (xvii).

The whaling voyage on which Hall arranged transport was captained by
Sidney Buddington, an experienced Arctic whaler who had brought back to
his Connecticut home an Inuk man he called Kudlago (possibly Kallaarjuk,

writes Kenn Harper).[29] Unlike the representation by white writers of Qala-sirssuaq (who was taken aboard the Franklin search ship *Assistance* in 1850, as chapter 2 details), in Hall's account Kudlago was not an awestruck naïf or "primitive" when introduced to Western forms of technology or knowledge. "He looked upon the works of civilization with interest, but never with wonder," Hall reported. "The first time he saw a locomotive no words escaped his lips, nor did he exhibit any signs but what were consistent with the idea of his having seen the same a thousand times before" (40). When later riding a train, Kudlago observed that the passengers given a broadsheet by an urchin held the circular up to their faces to read it; the Inuk man "held his up before his eyes and *appeared to read*. Though he could not read a word, yet he looked learned" (40). Hall's early exposure to an Inuk man who had been able to play the part of moving between cultures with facility helped shape the Cincinnatian's later engagement with the indigenous populations in the Far North—even though Kudlago himself did not survive the encounter. Hall planned to employ him as his guide and interpreter, but Kudlago died of a respiratory ailment during the voyage from New London to Baffin Island. Even the raw liver and heart of an eider duck, provided to him by concerned whale men, failed to revive him. Hall read "appropriate exhortations from the 'Masonic Manual'" over his sea burial (41), but did not otherwise mystify the Inuk's experience, which struck him with force. (In his journal, in large letters filling a third of the page, Hall wrote, "Death has been among us! 'Cudlango' is dead!!")[30] Kudlago's haunting final words, according to Hall, were "*Teik-ko se-ko? teik-ko se-ko?*—Do you see ice? do you see ice?" (41). Kudlago had hoped to arrive home and be reunited with his family; the absence of ice along the Labrador coast underscored his distance from his Far Northern home.

Hall would come to rely on and learn from other Inuit, several of whom had experience with other U.S. and European expeditions. Here again Hall distinguished himself from most other white explorers, as he looked to forge new social connections rather than recur to a contractual relationship with the handful of experienced go-betweens in Greenland villages. The couple with whom Hall would share much of his Arctic time in intimate quarters, Ipiirviq and Taqulittuq, served him primarily as hunter and translator, respectively. Yet when Hall first meets Taqulittuq, as he records it in his journal, the encounter was shocking not for its ethnographic difference but for its familiarity:

November 2, 1860. About IX this morning, while intently engaged in my little cabin writing, I heard a soft, sweet voice "Good morning, sir!" The tone in which it was spoken, musical, lively, & varied, told me instantly that a lady of refinement was here, greeting me! Was I dreaming? No—I was wide awake—& writing! Was I mistaken? . . . Who should it be but a Lady Esquimaux? . . . Whence came this civilization refinement?[31]

Taqulittuq's "refinement" and her fluency in English (thanks to her trip to England and her encounters with the Arctic whaling crews) was shocking to Hall in their first meeting, even though he had already been told of the Inuk woman by Buddington. In his inclusion of this diary entry—slightly and insignificantly revised—in his published voyage narrative, however, Hall does not position the encounter in its linear, temporal place, which, like most travel and exploration writing, is the form *Arctic Researches* takes. Instead he includes this first meeting as an anecdotal aside much later in the book, hundreds of pages after the reader has already been given extensive evidence of Taqulittuq and her Arctic accomplishments. We see here that Hall is not interested in staging her "civilization" or "refinement" as foremost or sensational in his narrative account. Instead his primary emphasis is on what he learns from her in their conversations and shared acts of polar sustenance during Hall's cohabitation with her and Ipiirviq.

In this and other ways Hall emphasizes the difference in his methods from those of other polar travelers, tactics he developed on his first trip and continued to modify for his second: "I shall not, like previous explorers, set my foot on shore for a few days or weeks, or, like others, journey among men whose language is to me unintelligible. I shall live for two or three years among the Esquimaux, and gain their confidence; and I have the advantage of understanding the language, and of making all my wishes known to them" (iv). Yet the tone of the published narrative, which makes an argument for how "patiently [he] acquired the language and familiarized [him]self with the habits of the Esquimaux" (iii), has a calmness of reflection that his journal entries made on the spot do not evince. In his initial Arctic residence Hall was early exposed to the raw meat diet of the Inuit, which has vital antiscorbutic qualities but was deemed repulsive by most whites (who, in consequence, suffered greatly from scurvy). Hall wrote in his diary on 10 November 1860:

I therefore et abundantly of frozen whale! Let those who will think evil of it—one thing is certain, neither my conscience or—Stomach condemned the deed! The fact is, to effect the purpose I have at heart—to carry out such what I have motivation to perform—to visit King Williams Land & lands adjacent—to continue & complete the History of

Sir John Franklin & his manned Expedition, <u>I must learn to live as Esquimaux do!</u> To carry out this Mission, <u>I shall</u> "eat to live," discarding altogether the common idea—at least for three years—of "living to eat"![32]

The force of revelation was strong with Hall, and he took up Inuit ways with the zeal of the convert. This interest was reciprocated; on Baffin Island, where they had taken up residence, Ipiirviq and Taqulittuq treated Hall as kin, as he describes after witnessing a healing ceremony: "This people, knowing that I did not make fun of them or taunt them for believing as they do, had confidence in me.... It is against their customs to have any but the family present, but hitherto I have always had access to their meetings."[33]

His embrace of indigenous means of survival was what most characterized him to his contemporaries as eccentric. The editors of his posthumous second expedition narrative, for example, find it odd that Hall would choose an igloo over a ship for his winter residence: "Strange as it might seem to any one but Hall... he still lived in his snow hut, in daily sight and sound of the [whaling] ships, which were now comfortably housed for the winter.... He would not depart from his rough Arctic diet."[34] This strangeness (or what we can call Hall's polar method) may simply have been *ex-centric*, emerging from a sphere beyond the social and political centers of Western culture, for Hall's interest in Inuit culture and practices formed the basis for his significant education about survival in the polar regions, which distinguished him from other, more celebrated but less successful explorers (the Briton Robert Falcon Scott in the South first and foremost). While British and American polar expeditions would hire Inuit hunters or guides, they routinely resisted adaptation to indigenous means for Arctic survival—slow to learn the use of sled dogs, for example, and relying on the hugely debilitating practice of "man-hauling" sledges. (Other than Hall, exceptions include the Scotsman John Rae, the American Frederick Schwatka, and the Canadian Vilhjamur Stefansson.) The outfitting lists drawn up by white captains detail stores of flannel shirts, knitted frocks, worsted stockings, cloth boots, Welsh wigs (wool caps), and comforters, in one example from Horatio Austin; still, that particular Briton recognized that a "sealskin jumper" would be "much preferable" to a wool jacket, "being longer, less bulky and cumbrous, much lighter and impervious to wind, snow, or wet. I would suggest that dressed sealskin be purchased from the Esquimaux for this purpose, and made up on board."[35] Hall's peculiarity within the history of Anglo-American polar exploration lay in his embrace of native lifeways. Yet his more significant departure from Western tradition can be found in his no less strong embrace of Inuit scientific, historical, and hydrographic observation.

"Traditionary" History

Hall privileged Inuit hydrographic knowledge—what we would today call TEK, or traditional ecological knowledge—over long-standing Anglo-American charts and beliefs. One of the first revisions he made to Arctic hydrography on the basis of Inuit experience concerned the question of the form taken by the body of water on Baffin Island known to Westerners as Frobisher Strait, after the explorer who had sailed sixty miles up it in 1576. Nearly three hundred years later, Hall recorded the error of this judgment: "'Frobisher Strait,' so called, does not exist, according to my firm belief! I have had from intelligent Esquimaux travellers" that it is a bay.[36] Hall included in his published narrative several maps and other forms of Inuit ecomedia, including one of Frobisher Bay "drawn by Koopernkung while we were at Cape True, 1862" (583). Experiential observation was the order of Hall's Arctic residency. "On one occasion, when I was speaking with Tookoolito concerning her people," Hall recorded, "she said, 'Innuits all think this earth once covered with water.' I asked her why she thought so. She answered, 'Did you never see little stones, like clams and such things as live in the sea, away up on the mountains?'" (572). Inuit experiential knowledge translates to geological and paleontological interpretive conclusions on an oceanic scale.

Recall that Hall had come north seeking information on Franklin and his crew, whom he believed might have survived if they had, themselves, embraced Inuit subsistence practices. In his second expedition Hall did, in fact, uncover more Franklin relics as well as an Inuit narrative of contact with the expedition; when meeting with natives in Pelly Bay,

> *Kok-lee-arng-nŭn*, their head man, showed two spoons which had been give to him by *Ag-loo-ka* (Crozier), one of them having the initials F.R.M.C. stamped upon it. His wife, *Koo-narng*, had a silver watchcase. This opened up the way for immediate inquiries. Through Too-Koo-li-too who as usual soon proved a good interpreter, it was learned that these Innuits had been at one time on board of the ships of *Too-loo-ark*, (the great *Esh-e-mut-ta*, Sir John Franklin), and had their *tupiks*

[sealskin summer tents] on the ice alongside of him during the spring and summer. They spoke of one ship not far from Ook-kee-bee-jee-lua (Pelly Bay), and two to the westward of Neit-tee-lik, near Ook-goo-lik. *Kok-lee-arng-nǔn* was "a big boy when very many men from the ships hunted *took-too* [tuktu, or caribou]. They had guns, and knives with long handles, and some of their party hunted the *took-too* on the ice; killing so many that they made a line across the whole bay of Ook-goo-lik." The Pelly Bay men described the *Esh-e-mut-ta* as an old man with broad shoulders, thick and heavier set than Hall, with gray hair, full face, and bald head. He was always wearing something over his eyes (spectacles, as Too-koo-li-too interpreted it), was quite lame, and appeared sick when they last saw him. He was very kind to the Innuits;—always wanting them to eat something.[37]

The description is a good likeness of the portly, sexagenarian Franklin. Among the native communities on Baffin Island Hall found a compelling story of several survivors within the repository of indigenous historical memory. What he learned from his companions was that "strangers" had come among them, strangers described as white men. Hall distinguishes what he calls the Inuits' "traditionary" oral history from "written" history and finds that this information, as well as other Inuit memories of "strangers," rhymed with written records of expeditions going back hundreds of years. While Hall did not travel far from Frobisher Bay, he did learn something crucial about Martin Frobisher's expedition to Baffin Island in 1576, which the Inuit talked about as if it had just happened. At one point in *Arctic Researches* Hall asks a community elderwoman about the reports he is hearing of lost vessels (which he originally thought referred to Franklin). The elder tells him that the community recalled multiple ships: "First two, then two or three, then many—very many vessels." In his dawning realization that this account does not refer to Franklin's voyage of two ships but to an earlier and larger expedition, he consults a history of Arctic discovery he had brought with him:

> Turning to the account of Frobisher's voyages, I read what had been given to the world by means of writing and printing, and compared it with what was now communicated to me by means of oral tradition. *Written* history tells me that Frobisher made three voyages to the arctic regions as follows:

First voyage in 1576, with *two* vessels.

Second voyage in 1577, three vessels.

Third voyage in 1578, fifteen vessels.

Traditionary history informs me that a great many, many years ago the vessels of white men visited the bay (Frobisher's) three successive years:

First, in *two* vessels.

Second, in *three* vessels.

Third, in many vessels. (279)

Hall makes a pointed distinction between the knowledge that circulates in the world by means of "writing and printing" and the knowledge gained by oral or "traditionary" history, or TK. Western explorers too often dismissed oral histories of encounters in the polar regions throughout the nineteenth century, even as they drew from Inuit geographical knowledge. Anglo-Americans also consistently misunderstood and even destroyed the informational cairns called Inuksuit that are used by the Inuit and other northern people to navigate the land- and waterscape ("Inuksuk" [sing.] means "that which acts in the capacity of a human").[38]

Hall continues his account by recognizing the value of Frobisher's own embrace of Inuit hospitality and knowledge, which enabled his crew's survival of at least one Arctic winter ashore:

But this is not all that traditionary history gave me on that day. *Written* history states that Frobisher lost *five* of his men on his first voyage when conveying a native on shore. *Oral* history told me that five white men were captured by Innuit people at the time of the appearance of the ships a great many years ago; that these men wintered on shore (whether one, two, three, or more winters, could not say); that they lived among the Innuits; that they afterward built an oomien (large boat), and put a mast into her, and had sails; that early in the season, before much water appeared, they endeavored to depart; that, in the effort, some froze their hands; but that finally they succeeded in getting into open water, and away they went, which was the last seen or heard of them. This boat, as near as I could make out at the time, was built on the island that Frobisher and his company landed upon, viz., *Niountelik.* (279–80)

Upon the conclusion of the woman's testimony, Hall wondered "if such facts concerning an expedition which had been made nearly three hundred years ago can be preserved by the natives, and evidence of those facts obtained, what may not be gleaned of Sir John Franklin's Expedition of *only sixteen years ago*?" (280). He feels "great astonishment" at the Inuit "powers of memory, and the remarkable way in which this strange people of the icy North, who have no written language, can correctly preserve history from one generation to another" (281). Such modes of knowing were outlandish to Hall's Anglo-American contemporaries; in a testimonial used to publicize his lecture tour in between his first two expeditions, for example, a Yale professor emphasized the difference between written and experiential knowledge: "Mr. Hall possesses much knowledge not found in books—the fruits of his own experience."[39] In a region that had been seen as outside of history (as indigenous or "primitive" peoples often have been) in the particularity of its inhospitableness to colonial settlement or territorial claims, such knowledge creates a world whose circuits oscillate beyond Western evidentiary understanding, much less time and space. This world is oceanic both materially and conceptually, in the sense that its forms of circulation are independent of (or indifferent to) political or doctrinal boundaries.

These collaborations were long-standing. Neither the elder who conveys information about the centuries-earlier Frobisher voyage nor Ipiirviq and Taqulittuq were the first Inuit to assist Western expeditions. William Edward Parry and John Ross had relied on native knowledge during their 1820s British expeditions. And not just the knowledge: in several notable cases Inuit collaborators provided the hydrography and illustrations of their encounters as well. The information they provided, however, was treated mostly as a curiosity by the British Admiralty and Anglo-American geographers and hydrographers. Taqulittuq's abilities in this regard were compared by the U.S. Navy editors who posthumously compiled the narrative of Hall's second voyage to those of the Inuk woman who had assisted Parry decades earlier: "Too-koo-li-too showed an unexpected knowledge of the geography of her country, reminding Arctic students of the native woman *Iligliuk*, and of her chart drawn for Parry."[40] But even as Iligliuk and Taqulittuq served as translators both of language and of geography, their native knowledge did not translate outside of the North on its own terms; that is, it registered as a curious aside rather than as constitutive to Arctic life. In a similar vein, the carved, wooden, three-dimensional coastal maps used by Greenlandic Inuit when kayaking were valued for their aesthetics rather than their utility when compared to written charts.

FIG 5.4 — Part of Greenland Coast (and Islands), Kunit fra Umivik (Inuit, Greenland), 1884. Wood. GREENLAND NATIONAL MUSEUM AND ARCHIVES, NUUK.

Polar Orientations

The example of Hall brings into relief the terms of the ongoing popular fascination with the Arctic and Antarctica, regions that historically have been considered nonnational spaces but that have nevertheless also been the ongoing object of nationally sponsored scientific and exploratory missions. The knowledge produced and circulated by and around such expeditions, in turn, has found purchase in both national and nonnational units of inquiry. What does the example of the "amateur" Charles Francis Hall tell us about the possibilities and limits of "native" knowledge of the poles compared to knowledge generated by national or professionally scientific Western missions? In the afterlife of Hall's expeditions his gleanings from "traditionary" history were rejected in favor of a narrative of contact that for centuries preferred the seeming blankness of the ice to an articulate indigeneity. It was Hall's very estrangement from Anglo-American, Western modes of scientific exploration that enabled his inhabitation of TK or TEK and other native forms of epistemology and survival. I have traced the circuits of indigenous knowledge retold, rejected, and reimagined in the period after Hall's Arctic residence as a way to consider the potentialities of the polar ecomedia and TEK for our moment of climate extremity today, in which present-day Inuit experience of climate change is not a quirk or curiosity for later confirmation by Western science, but the reverse. Hall's history resides not within national traditions of exploration of historiography but within indigenous and oceanic histories of the dispersal and collection of knowledge.

A final example of Hall's divergence from expected modes of polar travel and exploration underscores the value and broader applicability of both his own epistemological practices and polar and oceanic modes of knowledge production. Even within a tradition of voluminous polar expeditionary narrative production, Hall is exceptional. In his years in the Arctic he filled over 250 extant journals (a handful of which are seen in figure 5.5), and we know from the narratives of former shipmates that many more were lost or destroyed (whether by Hall himself or by the officers on the *Polaris* voyage on which he was murdered).[41] His excess of writing, in all its forms, can be seen as a way to inscribe something upon a landscape that is hostile to permanent records. Shifting ice, extreme weather, and frozen ground make unreliable the forms of inscription customary to voyages of discovery or imperial ventures. On the other hand, the cold and aridity helped preserve bodies and other organic remnants for decades or centuries longer than a temperate climate would—as it preserved Hall's own body, intact enough to test for arsenic poisoning a century after he died. Most polar expeditions left written records in cairns, in multiple iterations so as to maximize the possibility of their being found. Since his first two Arctic trips were not tethered to any expeditionary crew or patron, Hall did not himself practice constant cairning but instead made monuments of his own excess of writing.

Hall was attentive to the technological production of texts, of information, of the demands of polar ecomedia. In addition to the many scores of notebooks he kept while winterbound, he engaged in other meticulous acts of literary practice, including making typographical corrections to a copy of Nathaniel Bowditch's famous *Practical Navigator*, which he passed along to the volume's publisher upon his return to the United States.[42] He worked on solutions to the problem of frozen ink in temperatures that reached 70

FIG 5.5 — Thirty-eight small notebooks with notes of sledge journey to Ig-loo-lik and back, Feb. to June 1868. Charles Francis Hall Collection, Collection 702, Box 11, Folder 100. NATIONAL MUSEUM OF AMERICAN HISTORY, ARCHIVES CENTER, WASHINGTON, DC.

degrees below zero; the ink was stored in "a deposit of icy ink-blocks outside of the *igloo*; slices from these were chipped off, crushed and thawed inside." He developed an ingenious system of writing upon heated metal plates:

> I have before me a lamp with two wicks kept constantly burning. The brass sheets are 10 inches each by 5; and while one is heated the other, which has been made hot, is under the leaf on which I write, warming it; this, in turn, keeps my fingers warm and the ink from freezing in the pen, and dries the writing. Changing the plates after writing on each half a dozen lines, I am able to make up my journals, the thermometer at my side showing 42° below the freezing point. It is a plan of my own.[43]

"It is a plan of my own": such might be the alternative title to the story of Charles Francis Hall. But as I have been arguing, the plans that Hall made and enacted were always emergent from collectivities of knowledge, initially from the published narratives of previous Arctic voyagers and ultimately from shared Inuit knowledge. This latter indigenous knowledge, too, was as much a part of a technological production of experiential knowing as the histories of Anglo-American exploration. Hall's life with the Esquimaux functioned as a mechanism for generating narratives, however ephemeral, that are parallel to the epistemological tasks of science. Hall's fractiousness—his survival and then nonsurvival—are ultimately subordinate to his seemingly indiscriminate but actually exceptionally discerning ability to collate ecomedia and "traditionary" knowledge from circuits on an oceanic scale.

CONCLUSION

MATTERS OF LIFE

AND

DEATH

Over the eons of time the sea has grown ever more bitter with
the salt of the continents.

— RACHEL CARSON, *The Sea around Us* (1951)

In September 2018 I was scheduled to join an Arctic expedition sailing
through the Northwest Passage. The warm open polar sea of nineteenth-
century speculation has become a reality: once unattainable, the Passage
has been transformed by anthropogenic climate change into ice-free open
water in many recent summers. Northwest Passage Project expedition
members included STEM students, scientists, and a documentary film
crew; I signed on to be the ship's "Arctic humanities scholar" during the
venture's second leg as we explored the effects of climate change on the Far
North and the Northwest Passage with the support of the National Science
Foundation and a collection of university and museum partners. In preparation for the Arctic expedition, I recorded a webinar on ice in the Western
imagination and closely followed the science team's extensive preliminary
work surveying contemporary student and public knowledge on climate
change and the Arctic regions.

On the morning of the second day of the expedition, the ship—the
Finnish-built *Akademik Ioffe*, an ice-strengthened cruise ship sailing under
a Russian flag and crew—ran aground in the Canadian Arctic archipelago.

After a tense day, all passengers and staff on the listing, compromised vessel were safely rescued, cruising cancelled for the season.[1] While the cause of the ship's accident has not been determined as of this writing, less than 10 percent of the North American Arctic is sufficiently charted, even after half a millennium of exploratory voyages to the region by Europeans and North Americans. There is more than one way for a ship to run aground; this was to be the Northwest Passage Project's second attempt at Arctic transit, in fact. The voyage was first scheduled to occur in summer 2017, but two months before it launched the contracted tall ship unexpectedly pulled out of the project, and the expedition was postponed a year.[2] As my disappointment in not heading north in 2017 or 2018 began to ease (I live in hope for 2019!), it struck me that the grounded Arctic expedition was another polar cautionary tale: here we were spending years marshalling resources, recruiting patrons, and laying the scientific and scholarly groundwork, but were thwarted—like centuries of explorers before us—by the capriciousness of polar conditions.

Accounting for the persistent insufficiencies of Western methods has historically been one way to gauge the climatic and geographical extremity of the Arctic. Consider the lament made by an open polar sea exponent and Arctic explorer, George De Long: "I frequently think that instead of recording the idle words that express our progress from day to day I might better keep these pages unwritten, leaving a blank properly to represent the utter blank of this Arctic expedition."[3] De Long's U.S. Arctic expedition aboard the *Jeannette* was cataclysmic; the ship was trapped by ice, adrift for two years before being crushed and sunk. De Long was among the twenty men who died of a crew of thirty-two; his journal was preserved by the survivors. The emblematic "blank of [his] Arctic expedition"—swallowed by ice, ruinous—masks the "unfathomable force" of the terraqueous world that seethes beneath the representational text. Like the whiteness of Ahab's "pasteboard mask" in Melville's *Moby-Dick* or the "shrouded human figure" with skin "of the perfect whiteness of snow" that rises from the warm polar South to engulf the travelers at the end of Poe's *Narrative of Arthur Gordon Pym*, De Long's blank indicates the inadequacy of standard literary forms of textual media to speak for oceanic and polar extremes.[4]

In the twentieth century the logic of exploration has been associated with the rationale given by George Mallory for his attempts to ascend Mount Everest: "Because it's there." Mallory never returned from his 1924 venture to the summit; his broken body, complete with snow goggles and camera, was identified on the mountain's ice face in 1999. It is tempting to see Mallory's corporeal reemergence after more than seventy-five years as a kind of Himalayan dead letter, giving mountaineers and historians new data for the "there" to which the Englishman was seeking access. (And since bodies on Everest cannot effectively be removed, the mountain has become an above-ground frozen graveyard for the hundreds who have died in summit attempts in the past century.) The logic of "Because it's there" registers differently, if it applies at all, in polar terms, however; the "there" is not fixed. The South Pole flag is restaked every year to account for the ice sheet movement that renders the polar marker's previous Antarctic location obsolete. The North Pole is not on land and thus cannot be flagged at sea level. On 2 August 2007, however, a Russian submarine reached 14,000 feet below sea level at the North Pole and planted a titanium flag on the Arctic seafloor. The flag remains at an invisible remove from the world, seen only through the undersea video taken by expedition members.[5] None of these points are stable other than by the abstraction of longitude and latitude lines; even the magnetic North and South Poles are located several degrees away from the geophysical poles. The vague, shifting locations underscore the ephemeral nature of the polar "there." Everest too, the great Chomolungma, is on the move: plate tectonics ensure that Everest is adding—or subtracting—height by a few millimeters a year, and shifting horizontally. Nineteenth-century polar imaginaries of blank spaces, holes in the terrestrial verge, or an open polar sea are a kind of polar magical thinking: they are fantasies of circulation that run into trouble because the points of the axis of the spherical globe are ever in retreat.

Throughout *The News at the Ends of the Earth* I have discussed ephemeral modes of polar ecomedia created by Arctic and Antarctic expedition members as they sought to represent, in textual form, the space and time of climate extremity. Yet as I have argued, representation alone is often not what constitutes the data of polar ecomedia. Elements of polar ecomedia are rather the shifts, gaps, interrupted circuits, and representative failures that are themselves recorded (whether gathered or memorialized) as a collection of data. In a moment when human and nonhuman life feels increasingly ephemeral within the broader scope of planetary climate crisis—even as human actions have propelled these extreme conditions—polar and oceanic perspectives offer representational keys with which we might begin to find conceptual language instrumentalizable to life (and endurance) in the Anthropocene.

One template for Anthropocenic accounts is the work of Rachel Carson, that exemplary theorist of oceanic spaces. In *The Sea around Us*

(1951), Carson is interested in deep time from the perspective of the sea. In a textual instantiation of geology that anticipates Dana Luciano's work on rocks as Anthropocenic media, she proposes that "the story of how the young planet Earth acquired an ocean . . . is founded on the testimony of the earth's most ancient rocks."[6] In a similar vein, the sedimentary layer of the sea floor, which in Carson's quietly moving image accretes as if the longest imaginable snowfall, likewise bears witness, this time in verse: "The sediments are a sort of epic poem of the earth. When we are wise enough, perhaps we can read in them all of past history. For all is written here. In the nature of the materials that compose them and in the arrangement of their successive layers the sediments reflect all that has happened in the waters above them and on the surrounding lands" (76).[7] Carson reads both the rocks themselves (which present "a sort of epic poem") and the shifting seas, ice floes, and human and nonhuman matter that surround them. Not a metaphor, "the book of the sediments" (76) provides its own thin leaves to the skilled interpreter, much as ice core samples do for glaciologists and paleoclimatologists tracking global warming trends, or atmospheric evidence recorded in the earth's stratigraphic record does for geologists determining epochs of geological time.

Deep time also provides a way for Carson to comment upon contemporary trends in global warming and sea level increases. Consider the cool observational pleasure that she takes in documenting warming temperatures and rising seas before the mid-twentieth century, when *The Sea around Us* was published. This tone is characteristic of her luminous yet spare prose; a systems thinker, interested in cycles, Carson notes the function of the oceans as a "global thermostat" and finds that "the evidence that the top of the world is growing warmer is to be found on every hand" (182). What is more, she writes, "we live in an age of rising seas" (97). This "is an interesting and even an exciting thing because it is rare that, in the short span of human life, we can actually observe and measure the progress of one of the great earth rhythms. What is happening is nothing new" (97). What is arresting about rereading this argument today, when rising seas are projected to whelm major world coastal cities within the next hundred years, is in part its seeming prescience. Will soon "the surf . . . break against the foothills of the Appalachians," Carson wonders. With a shrug, she says simply, "No one can say" (98). What is equally startling to realize about her rising seas meditation, however, is that the logic of rhythmic return ("nothing new," another cycle of planetary time) is also the rejoinder made by climate change deniers (nothing new, natural variability) to the alarms about global warming raised by the very environmental activists and climate scientists to whose movement, and to whose research, Carson has been foundational.

Carson's cycles recur in the writing of contemporary environmental humanists. Oceanic forms of thought lend themselves to spiralizing notions of time—time understood "not as laminar flow, but as spiral of unforeseen propinquity," as Jeffrey Jerome Cohen stipulates. "Water does not periodize like stone or landlocked texts," Cohen writes. "Its archive eddies, whirls, conveys dangerously, transforms the submerged into the rich and strange."[8] The Anthropocene demands that we reject linear progression, must look for new models of accounting. In both Carson's and Cohen's imagination, inspiration for these new models is found in the medium of water. Water is not an indiscriminately fluid medium, however, as the hydrography of the polar regions underscores. For even in their power, the seas are responsive to the lands that interrupt them. Sea water is salty, for instance, because of terrestrial mineral diffusion and circulation. As Carson explains, "From the moment the rain began to fall, the lands began to be worn away and carried to the sea. It is an endless, inexorable process that has never stopped—the dissolving of the rocks, the leaching out of their contained minerals, the carrying of the rock fragments and dissolved minerals to the ocean." It is difficult, reading *The Sea around Us* in the twenty-first century, not to attach new meaning to Carson's words: that the leached minerals stand in for oil and gas resource extraction in the Arctic Ocean, or that the fragments carried to the sea substitute for plastiglomerates or other hybrid bits of organic and inorganic waste, as Stacy Alaimo warns.[9] These very minerals have brought salt to the sea, "and over the eons of time," Carson writes hauntingly, "the sea has grown ever more bitter with the salt of the continents" (7). The very practices of resource extraction that have helped demarcate the Anthropocene have accelerated the processes by which the salt tang of the seas has become instead something too warm, too polluted, too bitter to contemplate. The seas, human and nonhuman life itself, may be spiraling out of our grasp; do we still we recognize our earth, and the sea around us, as our home? For how much longer will humans exist to call it such? Estranged from the cyclical renewal of an earth that in Carson's time was in less overtly cataclysmic climate crisis, we now find that we cannot count on an idealized terrestrial home, an engulfing Mother Earth. This does not make our planet an utterly alien one, however; we need to form new relationships to and with it, new forms of stewardship and perspective.

I have sought to tell survival stories in *The News at the Ends of the Earth*, even when prospects might seem dim. Historical polar voyagers struggled to survive; expedition members battled to subsist, to preserve their records. The polar ecomedia they circulated was largely ephemeral; some examples endure, many do not. The question for humans in the Anthropocene is whether we too can write a survival story while in extremity. Perhaps some of the practices of polar expedition members—their triumphs and mistakes, yes, but also their ecomedia production and reproduction processes—can provide a model and some hope. These are matters of life and death.

NOTES

Preface

1 Grolier Club, press release, October 2005, author's collection.
2 Stam and Stam, *Books on Ice*. I refer to items 2.5, 2.6, 10.10, 6.7, 7.7, 6.14.
3 *Facsimile of the Illustrated Arctic News*. Five numbers were published: 31 Oct., 30 Nov., 31 Dec. 1850, 31 Jan. and 14 Mar. 1851.
4 *Illustrated Arctic News* 3 (31 Dec. 1850): 31.

Introduction

Epigraphs: George Simpson, "Fragment of a Manuscript Found by the People of Sirius, when they visited the Earth during their exploration of the Solar System," *South Polar Times* 3.2 (1911): 78; Gilman, *Letters Written Home* (2 Jan. 1858).

1 R. E. Priestley, "The Psychology of Exploration," 1, in Priestley Collection, Polar Papers, MS 1097/23.
2 De Long, *The Voyage of the* Jeannette, 2:456.
3 See the "private family circle" invoked in the *Port Foulke Weekly News* of the *United States* Arctic expedition, or "*our own little circle*" as defined within the *North Georgia Gazette, and Winter Chronicle* of William Edward Parry's first Arctic voyage (emphasis in original). *Port Foulke Weekly News* 1 (11 Nov. 1860), 1, New-York Historical Society; *New Georgia Gazette, and Winter Chronicle*, North Georgia Gazette Collection, GB/015/GB, MS 438/12, Scott Polar Research Institute, University of Cambridge.
4 Versions of this question have been raised by a number of scholars. See, for example, Chakrabarty, "The Climate of History"; Latour, "Agency at the Time of the Anthropocene"; Dimock, "*Gilgamesh*'s Planetary Turn"; LeMenager, "The Humanities after the Anthropocene"; Ghosh, *The Great Derangement*; Baucom and Omelsky, "Knowledge in the Age of Climate Change"; Alaimo, "Sustainable This, Sustainable That"; and Nixon, *Slow Violence and the Environmentalism of the Poor*.

5 Gitelman, *Always Already New*, 7. She clarifies that in this sense "structures include both technological forms and their associated protocols, and . . . communication is a cultural practice, a ritualized collocation of different people on the same mental map, sharing or engaged with popular ontologies of representation."

6 David H. Stam and Deirdre C. Stam, Grolier Club press release, Oct. 2005, author's collection.

7 "A 5°C Arctic in a 2°C World."

8 Department of Northern Affairs and National Resources, "Explorers' Records Found in the Canadian Arctic Archipelago in 1960," 28 Mar. 1961, MG24 H47, File 4, Library and Archives Canada/Bibliothèque et Archives Canada.

9 Department of Northern Affairs and National Resources, "Explorers' Records Found in the Canadian Arctic Archipelago in 1960," appendices A–I, MG24 H47, vol. 1, File 5, Library and Archives Canada/Bibliothèque et Archives Canada.

10 Kane, *Arctic Explorations*, 1:228.

11 Leane and Miles, "The Poles as Planetary Places," 271. As New Materialists such as Stacy Alaimo have observed, the environmental is not external to the human.

12 Gould, *Time's Arrow, Time's Cycle*, 3, is adapting a trope of embodiment similar to that used by John McPhee.

13 I elaborate on these ideas in my essay "Speaking Substances: Ice."

14 Estrin, "Photographing Climate Change Refugees." Indeed, at Ice³, a conference on Arctic art, literature, and science hosted by the Columbia University Society of Fellows, presenters noted with some chagrin that a substantial majority of us included the same now iconic image of a polar bear cub on a dissolving berg mentioned by Estrin. (I was among the guilty.)

15 Bradfield, "Polar Explorer Robert Falcon Scott (1912)," in *Approaching Ice*, 60.

16 "Police News," *Adélie Mail and Cape Adare Times* 1911–12, n.p. [1910–13 Scott] MS 1506, EN, Scott Polar Research Institute, University of Cambridge. When Levick and Priestly were not documenting penguin shenanigans, they were writing comic poems about the odor of the gas lamp.

17 Russell et al., "Dr. George Murray Levick."

18 The photographic negatives were taken by a member of the ill-fated Ross Sea Party, the supply wing of Shackleton's 1914–17 Imperial Trans-Antarctic Expedition; they were located in Scott's Cape Evans hut in 2013 by members of the New Zealand Antarctic Heritage Trust. "Ross Sea Party Photos," Antarctic Heritage Trust, https://www.nzaht.org/pages/ross-sea-party-photos.

19 See "Shackleton's Whisky," Antarctic Heritage Trust, https://www.nzaht.org/pages/shackletons-whisky. I have secured one of the pricey reproductions and have saved it to toast this book's publication.

20 "Levick's Notebook," Antarctic Heritage Trust, https://www.nzaht.org/pages/levicks-notebook.

21 Commenter "Sage-on-the-Hudson," on Rhodi Lee, "100-Year-Old Notebook Found Encased in Antarctic Ice Is Part of Robert Scott's Expedition Team," *Tech Times*, 25 Oct. 2014, http://www.techtimes.com/articles/18712/20141025/100

-year-old-notebook-found-encased-in-antarctic-ice-is-part-of-robert-scotts
-expedition-team.htm#disqus_thread.

22 Scott's hut, Cape Evans, Google Street View, https://www.google.com/streetview
/#antarctica/scotts-hut-cape-evans-on-ross-island. Shackleton's hut on Cape Royds
is also available: https://www.google.com/streetview/#antarctica/shackletons-hut
-cape-royds-on-ross-island.

23 Cohen, "The Emancipation of Boyhood." Emphases in original.

24 Hayes, *The Open Polar Sea*, 177, 178–79.

25 T. W. Edgeworth David, "The Ascent of Mount Erebus," in Shackleton, *Aurora Australis*, n.p.

26 "Menu," British Arctic Expedition 1875–1876, MS 1479, D (Playbills, poems etc., 48 leaves), Scott Polar Research Institute, University of Cambridge.

27 C. W. Emmerson, "The Arctic Twins," British Arctic Expedition 1875–1876, MS 1479, Scott Polar Research Institute, University of Cambridge.

28 "King Henry V. (not by Shakespeare)," *South Polar Times* Contributions (unpublished), MS 1505/5, Scott Polar Research Institute, University of Cambridge.

29 The project is entitled ISRU [In Situ Resource Utilization] Based Robotic Construction Technologies for Lunar and Martian Infrastructure. "Nasa Research," USC School of Architecture, https://arch.usc.edu/topics/nasa-research.

30 LeMenager, "Climate Change and the Struggle for Genre," 221–22.

31 Thoreau, *Walden*, 397.

32 LeMenager, "Climate Change and the Struggle for Genre," 221–22.

33 In a long passage in the conclusion to *Walden*, Thoreau refers to the polar voyages of Martin Frobisher, Charles Wilkes, Sir John Franklin, Elisha Kent Kane, and Henry Grinnell, as well as to the hollow earth theory of John Cleves Symmes. His claim is that "it is easier to sail many thousand miles through cold and storm and cannibals, in a government ship, with five hundred men and boys to assist one, than it is to explore the private sea, the Atlantic and Pacific Ocean of one's being alone" (577–78).

34 A conversation with Lisa Swanstrom helped me develop these ideas, and I am grateful to her for her insights on ecomedia.

35 An ecomedia studies interest group is a relatively recent addition to the Association for the Study of Literature and Environment, for example, and is engaged in the study of "non-print media as it applies to environmental discourse and action." ASLE 2011 Ecomedia Seminar, http://asle-seminar.ecomediastudies.org/?page_id=10. For especially strong examples of recent ecomedia studies work see Starosielski, *The Undersea Network*; Smith, *Eco-Sonic Media*; Peters, *The Marvelous Clouds*; see as well the media archaeology work of Parikka, *A Geology of Media* and *What Is Media Archaeology?*; Zielinski, *Deep Time of the Media*; the Dead Media Project of writer Bruce Sterling at http://www.deadmedia.org/.

36 Parikka, *What Is Media Archaeology?*, 2–3.

37 Gitelman, *Always Already New*, 4–5.

38 Smith, *Eco-Sonic Media*, 5.

39 Parikka, *What Is Media Archaeology?*, 5.

40 Zielinski, *Deep Time of the Media*, 33.

41 Peters, *The Marvelous Clouds*, 2, 1.

42 Boes and Marshall, "Writing the Anthropocene," 64.

43 In arguing that polar ecomedia might help humans mediate the acceleration and effects of climate change, I have in mind Sean Cubitt's definition of mediation as "the effervescent commonality of human, technical, and natural processes." Cubitt clarifies, "Mediations are not communications (though all communications are mediated). Mediating does not require messages, nor even senders and receivers.... Mediation names the material processes connecting human and nonhuman events" (*Finite Media*, 3–4).

44 In specifying that I am speaking *from* a discipline rather than *to* a field I am invoking the call issued by Stephanie Foote and Stephanie LeMenager in their opening manifesto to the journal *Resilience* ("Editors' Column," 2).

45 Chakrabarty, "The Climate of History," 215.

46 Nixon, *Slow Violence and the Environmentalism of the Poor*, 3, 2.

47 Menely and Taylor, introduction to *Anthropocene Reading*, 3, 5.

48 Baucom and Omelsky, "Knowledge in the Age of Climate Change," 2.

49 LeMenager, "Climate Change and the Struggle for Genre," 222, 220.

50 LeMenager, "The Environmental Humanities and Public Writing," 13.

51 Foote and LeMenager, "Editors' Column," 8.

52 His provocative call to arms creates what some reviewers have found to be an unsustainable distinction between what Ghosh in *The Great Derangement* calls "serious fiction" and the many writers of speculative fiction and other forms of genre writing that have engaged with climate change. Such writing has been called cli-fi, or climate fiction.

53 Foote, "The Stuff of Fiction"; Morton, *Hyperobjects*.

54 For a trenchant critique of the discourse of sustainability and its appropriation by corporate and neoliberal forces, see in particular Alaimo, "Sustainable This, Sustainable That": "We may well ask how it is that environmentalism as a social movement became so smoothly co-opted and institutionalized as sustainability" (559).

55 I have written further about oceanic studies in Blum, "The Prospect of Oceanic Studies" and "Introduction: Oceanic Studies." See also the Theories and Methodologies cluster on Oceanic Studies in *PMLA* 125.3 (2010): 657–736.

56 Steinberg, "Of Other Seas," 165.

57 Steinberg, "Of Other Seas," 157.

58 Starosielski, *The Undersea Network*, 6.

59 Warner, "Critique in the Anthropocene."

60 Starosielski, *The Undersea Network*, 5.

61 Peters, *The Marvelous Clouds*, 38.

62 Starosielski, *The Undersea Network*, 17.

63 See in particular Paul J. Crutzen's influential formulation of the term "Anthropocene" in "Geology of Mankind," 23, as well as his revised work in, for example,

Steffen et al., "Anthropocene." The concept has been especially attractive to humanists; as Boes and Marshall note in their introduction to a special issue, "Writing the Anthropocene," in the *Minnesota Review*, "The ability of the Anthropocene to lodge itself firmly within various cultural forms—from popular media to film, fiction, and television—has far outpaced its scientific accounting" (60). An earlier date for the onset of the Anthropocene, the year 1610, has been proposed by Simon A. Lewis and Mark A. Maslin, "Defining the Anthropocene," which reflects the genocidal impact of European colonization of the Americas. See Dana Luciano's meditation on this "Orbis hypothesis" in "The Inhuman Anthropocene." In 2016 the Working Group on the "Anthropocene" of the Subcommission on Quaternary Stratigraphy proposed to the International Commission on Stratigraphy that the Anthropocene be recognized as a formal geological epoch, succeeding the Holocene. While the subcommission initially acknowledged that "the beginning of the 'Anthropocene' is most generally considered to be at *c*. 1800 CE, around the beginning of the Industrial Revolution in Europe (Crutzen's original suggestion); other potential candidates for time boundaries have been suggested, at both earlier dates (within or even before the Holocene) or later (e.g. at the start of the nuclear age)," subsequent deliberation has fixed the "golden spike" of the Anthropocene at 1950, the nuclear age. Jan Zalasiewicz et al., "Working Group on the 'Anthropocene.'"

64 Harper, "Franklin Discovery Strengthens Canada's Arctic Sovereignty."

65 Rignot et al., "Widespread, Rapid Grounding Line Retreat of Pine Island, Thwaites, Smith, and Kohler Glaciers." An article in *Nature Geoscience* in March 2015 made similar claims for an immense glacier in East Antarctica: Greenbaum et al., "Ocean Access to a Cavity beneath Totten Glacier in East Antarctica." See also Gillis, "Miles of Ice Collapsing into the Sea."

66 Moskvitch, "Mysterious Siberian Crater Attributed to Methane."

67 Boes and Marshall, "Writing the Anthropocene," 62. See also the recent work of Latour, particularly "Agency in the Time of the Anthropocene"; Colebrook, *Death of the PostHuman*; and Timothy Morton's recent work, particularly *Hyperobjects*, as well as work by Chakrabarty, Foote, LeMenager, Alaimo, Dimock, and Nixon.

68 Luciano, "The Inhuman Anthropocene."

69 Alaimo, "Sustainable This, Sustainable That," 562.

70 Warner, *Publics and Counterpublics*, 66.

71 Anderson, *Imagined Communities*.

1. Extreme Printing

Epigraphs: Samuel Taylor Coleridge, "Captain Parry" (1825), in *The Collected Works*, 1037; advertisement in *Queen's Illuminated Magazine*, 1852, material printed on HMS *Assistance*, MS 1481/1, 1852–54, Scott Polar Research Institute Archives, University of Cambridge.

1 Nordenskjöld and Andersson, *Antarctica*, 290.

2 *Printing the "Arctic Eagle,"* Fiala-Ziegler Expedition, private collection, used with permission. My research has uncovered no other photographs of printing in action, although the illustrations in chapter 3 show the unattended press and type case used to print the book *Aurora Australis* during Shackleton's *Nimrod* expedition in Antarctica (1909). The act of printing is not otherwise sketched or illustrated, to the best of my searching.

3 The man on the top bunk is John Vedoe, assistant quartermaster, and the bearded sailor on the lower left bunk is Pierre Le Royer, dog caretaker, according to a note on the back of a copy of the photograph. The reclining man on the right is not identified. Anton M. Vedoe Papers, 1895–1963, MSS 233, Box 2, Folder 12, Stefansson Collection, Dartmouth College.

4 For more information on Golding presses, see "Golding Printing Presses," *Handset Press*, accessed 10 July 2016, http://www.handsetpress.org/golding/.

5 Fiala, "Christmas Near the North Pole," 25.

6 Of these newspapers, I have located copies of all except the *Ice-Blink*, *Gleaner*, *Minavalins*, and *Ostgrönländische Zeitung*. There is no trace of the *Ice-Blink* in any of the many archives that hold material related to Elisha Kent Kane and the Second Grinnell Expedition, and librarians and Kane historians have no knowledge of its location. The *Gleaner* and *Minavilins* were both suppressed before their expeditions returned home, and no copies seem to have survived. The *Ostgrönländische Zeitung* is mentioned in the journal of Carl Koldewey, a German polar explorer, who indicates that at least two manuscript editions were produced. The newspaper cannot be located today, and according to my correspondence with Reinhard Krause of the Alfred Wegener Institute for Polar and Marine Research in Germany, "a lot of papers of the expedition (owned by the geographical society in Bremen) were destroyed in a firestorm during WW 2 in the office of Herbert Abel at the Überseemuseum Bremen." Email correspondence with Reinhard A. Krause, 2 December, 2010.

7 "A Catalogue of the Library Established on Board H.M.S. Assistance, Captain Sir Edward Belcher, C.B., Commanding the Arctic Squadron in Search of Sir John Franklin and His Companions: Printed & Published on Board H.M.S. Assistance, Wellington Channel, Arctic regions, H. Briant, Printer, 1853," Arctic Pamphlets, 1852–54, courtesy Royal Geographical Society (with the Institute of British Geographers).

8 On the publisher John Murray's role in facilitating these publications in Britain, see Craciun, *Writing Arctic Disaster*; Keighren et al., *Travels into Print*; Cavell, *Tracing the Connected Narrative*.

9 For more on sailors' literacy and literary culture, see Blum, *The View from the Masthead*.

10 *Facsimile of the Illustrated Arctic News* 2 (30 Nov. 1850): 18.

11 Greely, *Three Years of Arctic Service*, 1:162. In another example, the school established on the *Fox*, a Franklin search, was led by the ship's doctor (a common stand-in schoolmaster on polar voyages); according to Commander McClintock,

the doctor "intends to make [the pupils] acquainted with the trade-winds and atmosphere. This subject affords an opportunity of explaining the uses of our thermometer, barometer, ozonometer, and electrometer, which they see us take much interest in. It is delightful to find a spirit of inquiry amongst them." McClintock, *The Voyage of the "Fox" in Arctic Seas*, 61.

12 For more on British naval theatricals, see Isbell, "Illustrated Reviews of Naval Theatricals"; Isbell, "P(l)aying Off Old Ironsides and the Old Wagon"; Isbell, "When Ditchers and Jack Tars Collide"; Pearson, "'No Joke in Petticoats'"; O'Neill, "Theatre in the North"; Davis, "British Bravery, or Tars Triumphant."

13 *North Georgia Gazette, and Winter Chronicle*, in Parry, *Journal of a Voyage*.

14 Edward Sabine, "Advertisement" [appendix], *North Georgia Gazette, and Winter Chronicle*, iii.

15 Stam and Stam, "Bending Time."

16 Rudy, "Floating Worlds." See also Rudy's book *Imagined Homelands*, and Blum and Rudy, "First Person Nautical."

17 "Notice," *R.M.S. City of Paris Gazette, Printed on Board* 12 (3 Nov. 1891).

18 "Prospectus," *Austral Chronicle. A Bi-Weekly Journal* 1.1 (1886).

19 *Cunard Cruise News* 1 (26 Aug. 1933): 2.

20 Tocqueville, *Democracy in America*, 602–3.

21 Cooper, *Sensus Communis*, 1.

22 Anderson, *Imagined Communities*, 33.

23 Anderson, *Imagined Communities*, 34, 36.

24 Scholars of print culture such as Trish Loughran and Meredith McGill have described how paying closer attention to the operations of transnational and local spheres of circulation dismantles some elements of Anderson's model and shores up others. Anderson presumes the simultaneity of newspaper reading among far-flung individuals, for example, although Loughran has argued persuasively that in the early United States such presumptions are not historically accurate. Rather than a networked national print culture, Loughran describes localized, fragmented communities of print that are more akin to what we see aboard polar ships. She writes, "If the newspaper denies, in its casual columnar form, the scatteredness of the spaces from which it collects its information, it nevertheless bears ... the telltale traces of that scatteredness" (*The Republic in Print*, 11).

25 Warner, *Publics and Counterpublics*, 12.

26 Anderson, *Imagined Communities*, 35.

27 Shields, *Civil Tongues and Polite Letters in British America*.

28 *Umbria Express, and Atlantic Times* 14 (1 Oct. 1887): 4; E. Alsheimer, "Creeds," *All Aboard: The Journal of R.M.S. "Transylvania"* 14.4 (1931): 14.

29 *Bound Home or The Gold-Hunters' Manual* (2 Mar. 1852).

30 Quoted in Lewis, *Sea Routes to the Gold Fields*, 92.

31 See Blum, *The View from the Masthead*.

32 Elaine Hoag documents several examples of wartime shipboard printing during the Revolutionary and Napoleonic Wars in "Caxtons of the North," 81–82.

33 Morillo, "Venesolanos que habeis seguido a Bolivar."

34 See Berkey, "Splendid Little Papers from the 'Splendid Little War'"; Berkey, "Traces of the Confederacy." In World War I, the men of the British destroyer HMS *Blenheim* printed a paper called the *Tenedos Times* while stationed off the Aegean isle by that name; "the pressure of stirring events" cut short its publication in 1914. "Preface," *Tenedos Times: A Monthly Journal of the Mediterranean Destroyer Flotilla during the Early Part of the War*, [5].

35 Harris, *Personal Impressions*, 13.

36 Accountant General's Record Book, 1852, l. 467, 9 Feb. 1852, ADM 47/21, National Archives, London.

37 "Organ and printing press landed at Woolwich from the late Polar expedition to be repaired," Admiralty correspondence index for 1852, cut 68-5a, 25 Feb. [1852], ADM 12/558, National Archives, London.

38 Hoag, "Caxtons of the North," 85–88.

39 *Arctic Miscellanies*, xiii.

40 Maguire, *The Journal of Rochfort Maguire*, 106–7.

41 Rochfort Maguire's *Journal* mentions the illustrations in his explanation of the origin of the name of the paper *Weekly Guy*: "A weekly publication is likely to be undertaken by Doctor Simpson, but as it received its name and an accompanying set of illustrations, from a kind friend to all arctic adventurers at the Admiralty, its time has not yet come" (*The Journal of Rochfort Maguire*, 106–7). Hoag reports that these were Cruikshank images ("Shipboard Printing on the Franklin Search Expeditions," 28).

42 "The Rise and Progress of Arctic Printing," in *Arctic Miscellanies*, 246–47.

43 "The Rise and Progress of Arctic Printing," in *Arctic Miscellanies*, 247–48. Clements Markham confirms, "wood blocks were cut of the Royal arms and other adornments" by the sailors for the playbills, printed on silk (*The Lands of Silence*, 255).

44 *Queen's Illuminated Magazine*, 24 [40].

45 "A Catalogue of the Library Established on Board H.M.S. Assistance." I discuss the presence of Melville's two novels in "Melville in the Arctic," *Leviathan* 20.1 (March 2018): 74–84.

46 Belcher, *The Last of the Arctic Voyages*, 1:19.

47 Accountant General's Record Book, 1852, l. 1179, 5 Apr. 1852, ADM 47/21, National Archives, London.

48 Seitz, Polar Diaries, 1901–5, 12 June 1903, MSS 244.

49 "Arctic Eagle Printed in Barren Polar Land," *Brooklyn Daily Eagle* (10 Sept. 1905): 3.

50 An example of some "Fialisms," parenthetical comments in the original:

> (After being told that a large mass of dog feces was in the water bbl.)—"Let it go! It is too blamed much trouble to have it cleaned!"
>
> (After fainting)—"Why, this is strange! Just before coming away, I won over four strong men, one after the other, at fencing."
>
> "And at the banquet the General said that the only main in Troop 'C' whom he would be afraid to meet in personal combat, was Anthony Fiala."

"I will fight any man, upon the return of the Exped., with any weapon, from a saber to a cannon."

"I'll fight you all! I'll fight you all!—But not on this Exped."

(Speaking of the "Glory Hole")—"Oh, my! How comfortable you are here! Why, you've the finest quarters in the ship!"

(To each individual member of the field party)—"You are the only man who will receive $50 per mo. All the others have signed for $25."

"Oh, my! Isn't the atmospheric scenery glorious!"

"I am the only male member of the 'Ladies Aid Society.'"

"Fialisms," in Shorkley Papers, I-4, Stef MSS 207. For a lively, detailed account of this expedition, see Capelotti's *The Greatest Show in the Arctic*; Capelotti finds Shorkley to be an "uninformed malcontent" (406).

51 *Port Foulke Weekly News* 1 (11 Nov. 1860): 1–2.
52 Koldewey, *The German Arctic Expedition*, 377–78.
53 *Arctic Miscellanies*, xiii–xviii.
54 The following is a transcription of the advertisement:

> The ARCTIC Printing Office
>
> Messrs. Giffard & Symons beg to inform the Public that they have obtained—at an immense cost & with infinite trouble—possession of the extensive premises lately occupied by Mr Clements Markham situated in Trap Lane within half a minutes walk of the foremost Quarter Deck Ladder, and easily accessible to all parts of the City.
>
> They have fitted up their new establishment—*regardless of expense*—with all the *latest inventions* and *newest machinery* to enable them to carry on the Noble Art of Printing in a Style & with a Rapidity hitherto quite unattainable.
>
> They therefore expect from the Public that support & assistance which it always gives to the *truly deserving.*
>
> Charges moderate. No credit given. All work required to be executed to be paid for in advance.
>
> N.B. Everything undertaken promptly and correctly executed.
>
> H.M.S. Alert.
> July. 28. th.
> 1875.

("The Arctic Printing Office," May, Sir William Henry, Admiral of the Fleet, 1849–1930, May/13/2, National Maritime Museum, Greenwich, London)

55 Markham, *The Great Frozen Sea*, 189–90.
56 "The Arctic Printing Office."
57 In Warner's terms, "A public is always in excess of its known social basis. It must be more than a list of one's friends. It must include strangers" (*Publics and Counterpublics*, 74).

58 *Port Foulke Weekly News* 1 (11 Nov. 1860): 1.

59 Elizabeth Leane gives a great taste of the twentieth-century Antarctic papers in "The Polar Press." Stephanie Pfirman, an Arctic environmental scientist at Barnard College and Columbia University, told me, "On our Arctic expeditions today we always have a newsletter, and it's always kept private. What goes [on] in the Arctic stays in the Arctic." Conversation with the author, 16 Apr. 2016.

60 Pierre Berton's *Arctic Grail*, for example, devotes a half-sentence to Arctic newspapers in nearly seven hundred pages of its narrative of Northwest Passage and North Pole quests. Douglas Wamsley's comprehensively researched biography *Polar Hayes* mentions the *Port Foulke Weekly News* in four sentences out of 571 pages, and the paper does not make the volume's index. Francis Spufford's well-known *I May Be Some Time* invokes the *South Polar Times* of Robert Falcon Scott a handful of times. Fergus Fleming's popular history of early nineteenth-century British exploration, *Barrow's Boys*, devotes a few sentences to Parry's *North Georgia Gazette* (judging it "downright appalling" for the quality of its puns) but does not otherwise mention shipboard printing or periodicals. Adriana Craciun's book on the relationship between Arctic exploration and British print culture, *Writing Arctic Disaster*, devotes two paragraphs to printing in the region. *The Coldest Crucible*, Michael Robinson's history of American Arctic exploration, doesn't refer to expeditionary winter pastimes at all. Benjamin Reiss notes a similar curiosity in the relative disregard of an asylum newspaper, the *Opal*, in medical commentary by the asylum's officials (*Theaters of Madness*, 34).

61 See in particular Hoag, "Caxtons of the North," and "Shipboard Printing on the Franklin Search Expeditions"; Stam and Stam, "Bending Time"; Stam, "The Lord's Librarians"; Leane, *The Adelie Blizzard* and *Antarctica in Fiction*.

62 Hoag, "Caxtons of the North," 82.

63 In a model of digitally mediated scholarly exchange, the Arctic scholars Russell Potter and Elaine Hoag take up a conversation in the comments on Wilkins's blog post, in which Potter proposes a possible source for the balloon message: a Virginian who served as an officer on an American Franklin search ship in 1850, some of whose family members' papers appear in the Virginia Historical Society collections. Katerine Wilkins, "Message from a Balloon: How Did It Come to the VHS?," *Virginia Historical Society's Blog*, 4 Mar. 2013, https://vahistorical.wordpress.com/2013/03/04/message-from-a-balloon-how-did-it-come-to-the-vhs/.

64 I have also taken advantage of digitized records, when available, as such resources are relatively scarce for this type of material. Most North American and British archives have not digitized their manuscript and ephemeral printed polar holdings as of this writing, with the exception of Franklin search artifacts, which the UK's National Maritime Museum has made available in its digital collections. My resources for archival travels have not yet enabled me to travel to Australia or New Zealand, the launching points for many Antarctic missions, both of which have rich Antarctic holdings; antipodean libraries have digitized a number of Antarctic holdings, however.

65 I am grateful to Michael Winship for this suggestion. Hoag, however, notes that the Admiralty provided expeditionary ships with paper in a variety of colors; see her excellent bibliographic account in "Caxtons of the North," 93–94.

66 I am grateful to Fritz Swanson of the University of Michigan's Wolverine Press for showing me examples of hand-carved wood type and advising me how to identify print made from such type.

67 For especially sharp discussion on archival incompleteness and its ideological and research implications, see Gardner, *Black Print Unbound*. The librarians with whom I have worked throughout this project have been unfailingly superb and helpful. When polar materials have been uncatalogued or hard to locate, this has been due to changing research and cataloguing interests over time, library resource scarcity, or my own deficiencies, not those of any archivists or librarians with whom I have consulted.

68 Harris, *Personal Impressions*, 11.

69 *The Boys and Girls Favorite* 1 (1874): 2.

70 "Our Printers," *West Philadelphia Hospital Register* 1.2 (1863): 7. Each contributor to the paper received five free copies; one copy was allotted to every five patients, and extras cost two cents for soldiers and three cents for nonsoldiers. A year's subscription was one dollar, and four hundred copies of each number were printed for Reading Room use. "The Library and Reading Room," *West Philadelphia Hospital Register* 1.1 (1863): 2.

71 "The Library and Reading Room," *West Philadelphia Hospital Register* 1.1 (1863): 2. The library at the hospital grew rapidly by charitable donation. As this same article documents, its holdings were diverse: "The Library at the present time consists of about 625 bound volumes, and about 900 Magazines and other unbound literature. We make our appeal to the benevolent public, in every part of the country, to send us Books in any language. It should be remembered, that we have Soldiers of different nations in our armies. They too, are found in our Hospital." By the fifth number of the *West Philadelphia Hospital Register* there were 1,142 bound volumes and 1,300 unbound claimed for the library.

72 *West Philadelphia Hospital Register* 1.2 (1863): 6.

73 Reiss, *Theaters of Madness*, 28.

74 Foucault, "Of Other Spaces."

75 Cohen, "The Emancipation of Boyhood." Emphases in original.

76 *Shells and Seaweed* had a healthy pool of exchanges established by just its second number, as it documented in an article entitled "The Amateur's Department":

Twenty-one papers, besides all the city papers, are regularly received.

Telephone,	Premier,
Amateur Scientist,	American Sphinx,
Langill's Leisure,	Our Compliments,
Boys' Favorite,	Lake Breezes,
Amateur Emblem,	Radiator,

Boys' Folio,	Boys' Doings,
New Century,	Northern Breezes,
Times of '84,	Wise and Otherwise,
Progressive Youth,	Asteroid,
Fact and Fancy,	Huffman Amateur,
Nugget,	all have our thanks.

("The Amateur's Department," *Shells and Seaweed* 2 [May 1884]: 2)

77 *Shells and Seaweed* 1 (Apr. 1884): 3.

78 *Letters Written during the Late Voyage of Discovery in the Western Arctic Sea*, 59.

79 Craciun, *Writing Arctic Disaster*, 6.

80 See Cavell, *Tracing the Connected Narrative*; Potter, *Arctic Spectacles*.

81 *Arctic Miscellanies*, xiii–xviii.

82 On sailor literacy and cultures of reading, see Blum, *The View from the Masthead*.

83 Markham, *The Great Frozen Sea*, 191.

84 Markham, *The Great Frozen Sea*, 169.

85 *Arctic Miscellanies*, 204–5.

86 Osborn, *Stray Leaves from an Arctic Journal*, 153–54.

87 *Arctic Miscellanies*, xiii–xviii.

88 Markham, *Life of Admiral Sir Leopold McClintock*, 113.

89 Documents Relating to Arctic Expeditions, 343, ADM 7/195, National Archives, London.

90 "Education Sheet, [for/from] Giffard and Symons, MS 1815/28, Ephemera Collection, British Arctic Expedition of 1875–76, Scott Polar Research Institute Archives, University of Cambridge.

91 Kane, *Arctic Explorations*, 1:145. Neither I nor the other polar researchers and archivists with whom I have consulted have located a copy of the *Ice-Blink*.

92 Maguire, *The Journal of Rochfort Maguire*, 122.

93 Fiala, "Christmas Near the North Pole," 25.

94 *Arctic Eagle* 1.1 (1903): 2.

95 Preface to *Facsimile of the Illustrated Arctic News*.

96 "Preface," *Arctic Miscellanies*, xxiii.

97 "Preface," *Arctic Miscellanies*, xxiv.

98 *Arctic Moon* 1.1 (1881): 1.

99 Preface to *Facsimile of the Illustrated Arctic News*.

100 The "Native Dance" was conciliatory; its object was "to restore that amicable feeling with which [our neighbors of Noo-wook] have until lately regarded us . . . and, avoiding any just cause of offence, to inspire them with confidence in our friendly disposition towards them; so that, having no injuries to avenge, they may be induced to treat with kindness any of our countrymen belonging to Sir John Franklin's party, or to the Ships in search of him, who may fall into their hands in a defenceless state." Box 4, Miscellaneous Printed Material Nov. 1844–20 Jan. 1875, undated, Simpson Papers.

101 Maguire, *The Journal of Rochfort Maguire*, 112.

102 Advertisement, *Queen's Illuminated Magazine*, Material printed on HMS *Assistance*, MS 1481/1, 1852–54, Scott Polar Research Institute Archives, University of Cambridge.

103 Kane, *Arctic Explorations*, 2:14.

104 Nares, *Narrative of a Voyage to the Polar Sea*, 1:191.

105 *Arctic Expedition, 1875–6*, 73. Writing of that same expedition, Albert Markham recalled:

> The sun . . . took its final departure on the 11th of October. From this date darkness gradually settled upon us, reaching its greatest intensity on the 21st of December. The type of a leading article in the *Times* newspaper was taken by us as a test of the darkness. This was last read in the open air at mid-day on the 6th of November, and then only by a few with a great deal of difficulty. Many unsuccessful attempts were made on subsequent days. (*The Great Frozen Sea*, 203)

106 Moss, *Shores of the Polar Sea*, 45.

107 Nansen, *Farthest North*, 1:382.

108 Blake, *Arctic Experiences*, 257–58. Emphasis in original.

109 Nansen, *Farthest North*, 2:395.

110 *Arctic Miscellanies*, xviii.

111 Belcher, *The Last of the Arctic Voyages*, 1:188. Extreme weather could be an issue for passenger liners engaged in shipboard newspapers. The *Makura Journal* of the Canadian Australasian Line, en route to Sydney from Vancouver, offered an apology to readers of its fourth number for the paper's appearance: "It was with difficulty that it was printed at all, for the equatorial heat made the rollers of the press like jelly." The *Makura Journal* was edited and published by two passengers and was offered "free as the air of the Pacific Ocean." "With Apologies to The Boston Journal. En Route Vancouver to Sydney," 1.4 (1909): 1.

112 *Facsimile of the Illustrated Arctic News* 1 (31 Oct. 1850): 4.

113 *The Blizzard* 1 (May 1902): 2. MS 859, Scott Polar Research Institute Archives, University of Cambridge.

114 *Arctic Miscellanies*, 204–5.

115 Greely, *Three Years of Arctic Service*, 1:180.

116 *Weekly Guy* 7 (17 Dec. 1852): 26–27.

117 "Editorial," *Port Foulke Weekly News* 1.3 (1860): 1. Hayes invokes the Biblical story from the Book of Daniel, in which mysterious writing appears on the wall of the Babylonian king Belshazzar's palace. Daniel interprets "MENE, MENE, TEKEL UPHARSIN" as a warning that the king's dynasty will fall.

118 Photographs scrapbook, Anton M. Vedoe Papers, 1895–1963, MSS 233, Box 3, Stefansson Collection, Dartmouth College.

119 Peary, *The North Pole*, 180.

120 Markham, *The Great Frozen Sea*, 208–9.

121 Stam, "The Lord's Librarians."

122 Peary, *The North Pole*, 179–80.

123 Nansen, *Farthest North*, 1:382.

124 For more on Arctic shipboard theatricals, see note 12.

125 The manuscript copy of the *North Georgia Gazette, and Winter Chronicle* (which was entitled *New Georgia Gazette, and Winter Chronicle* before the expedition learned that a northern land had already been named New Georgia), held in the Scott Polar Research Institute, includes the script of *The North West Passage or Voyage Finished*, which was not included in the version of the *North Georgia Gazette* that was printed upon the expedition's return to London in 1821. *New Georgia Gazette, and Winter Chronicle*, MS 438/12, Scott Polar Research Institute Archives, University of Cambridge.

126 Here is a fuller plot summary of the *Pantomime of Zero*:

> This talented and original piece was composed expressly for this theatre (Royal Arctic); and abounds in wit and humour. Turning all the dangers and inconveniences to which we are exposed in these inhospitable climates into evil spirits that are leagued against us, it supposes them continually watching every opportunity to surprise an unfortunate travelling party, till at length their power is destroyed by the appearance of the more puissant good spirits, Sun and Daylight. Then the metamorphosis takes place: the good spirits become Harlequin and Columbine, and frosty old Zero, who has all along been the leader of the evil spirits, is changed into First Clown; a bear, which had been for some time prowling about, was then fired at, and falling to pieces, discovers Pantaloon and Second Clown. Then commences the pantomime of fun and frolic, which was carried on with great spirit by the two Clowns and Pantaloon, while they were at intervals relieved by the graceful and elegant *pas de deux* of Harlequin and Columbine. Several songs, alluding to the Expedition, its purposes and position were also introduced. (*Arctic Miscellanies*, 204–5)

127 Markham, *The Great Frozen Sea*, 244.

128 British Arctic Expedition of 1875–76, MS 1479, Scott Polar Research Institute Archives, University of Cambridge.

129 Ship's surgeon Alexander Fisher notes of a performance of *The North West Passage: or, the Voyage Finished* that the temperature "was as low as 19° during the whole time; but the pleasure they derived from seeing a scene exhibiting their own character in so favourable a point of view, completely overcame any inconvenience they may have suffered from the state of the weather" (*A Journal of a Voyage of Discovery*, 165–66).

130 *Arctic Miscellanies*, 204–5.

131 *Port Foulke Weekly News* 1.1 (1860): 4–5.

132 Hayes, *The Open Polar Sea*, 184.

133 A descendent of the expedition's sailing master, Samuel Jarvis McCormick, has generously provided me with transcripts of his ancestor's diary, *An Abstract of a Journal in the Arctic Ocean during the Years of 1860 and 61 by F L Harris, U.S. Navy*, as well as the diaries of Steward Francis L. Harris and Seaman Harvey Scott Heywood, also of the *United States*. McCormick's journal reveals his distrust of Dodge's competency, and Harris's journal in particular documents over and over Dodge's extreme intoxication (and the abuse of alcohol in general aboard ship). Here are some selections from Harris's diary: "The 2nd mate Dodge had been in the navy as an ordinary seaman and could boast of how many floggings he had for smuggling liquor and getting drunk, which he fully demonstrated by getting beastly drunk every opportunity, even stealing the liquor to carry out his purposes, as he was not possessed with any manly courage"; "Dodge was so badly intoxicated that he did not remember of having his supper"; "Dodge steals liquor and gets beastly intoxicated"; "Dodge feels that he has been neglected and swears revenge because he is not allowed free access to the liquor"; "Dodge gets gloriously drunk"; "All winds up in a drunken frollics. Dodge is number one on that list"; "At 2 am. Mr Dodge yells out at the top of his voice that he can not get rum enough to make him drunk"; "Dodge being to drunk [sic] to sleep attempts to pick a quarrel with some of the men." I am indebted to Thomas Walker for sharing these journals with me.

134 *Port Foulke Weekly News* 1.3 (1860): 8–9.

135 See Blum, *The View from the Masthead*; Cohen, *The Novel and the Sea*.

2. Arctic News

Epigraphs: Pynchon, *Mason and Dixon*, 123; Henry Dodge, "Literature," *Port Foulke Weekly News* 1.3 (1860): 9, New-York Historical Society.

1 Anderson, *Imagined Communities*, 35.

2 Cavell, *Tracing the Connected Narrative*; Craciun, *Writing Arctic Disaster*; Keighren et al., *Travels into Print*. See also Potter, *Arctic Spectacles*.

3 The original manuscript version was entitled *New Georgia Gazette, and Winter Chronicle*, after the land that Parry named "New Georgia." Upon the expedition's return, however, Parry discovered that there already was a New Georgia, so the name of the land and of the gazette was changed in future iterations to "North Georgia." Henceforth all references to the paper were to the *North Georgia Gazette, and Winter Chronicle*.

A note on sources: The *North Georgia Gazette* was printed as an appendix to Parry's journal of the voyage. When I quote from the printed version, I refer to the pagination in Parry's journal as well as the periodical's number. Elsewhere in this chapter I cite the manuscript version of the *New Georgia Gazette*, which contains material that is not printed in the North Georgia version in Parry's journal; when I refer to the manuscript version, I cite the newspaper's number, as there is no pagination in the manuscript version.

4 Parry, *Journal of a Voyage for the Discovery of a North-West Passage*, 99.

5 *North Georgia Gazette*, vi.

6 A manuscript copy of the *New Georgia Gazette, and Winter Chronicle*, MS 438/12, held at the Scott Polar Research Institute at the University of Cambridge identifies the anonymous contributors to the newspaper.

7 These categories were not necessarily trifling. The genre of the riddle, as David Shields has written, presumes an audience "something more than witless"; as such, riddles "could be considered the citizenship exam for membership in the republic of letters" (*Civil Tongues and Polite Letters in British America*, 162).

8 The few reviewers who commented on the *North Georgia Gazette* accepted this cue, noting that standard critical energies would be inappropriate. One review explained, "Though the volume before us has a claim beyond that of most, if not of all others, that we have ever perused, to be excepted from the severities, and even the justice of criticism; we may be permitted equally to admire and eulogize those compositions, which sprang into existence amidst the regions of eternal frost." The only complaint of most reviewers was the high half-guinea price for the volume. Review of *North Georgia Gazette, and Winter Chronicle, European Magazine, and London Review* 79 (June 1821): 541.

9 A manuscript edition of the newspaper that Parry later gave to his sister is preserved at the Scott Polar Research Institute. Parry's copy was written in ink but has been corrected with penciled annotations (including a number of grammatical or minor stylistic emendations), presumably in his hand. The most visible editorial marks indicate the excision of a good number of letters, articles, and other pieces for the newspaper. In some examples individual paragraphs are crossed out; in most, the penciled hand strikes through whole contributions. In several instances the word "omit" has been written at the head of an entry. In all cases but one the omissions proposed in the manuscript paper were indeed left out of the printed version. *New Georgia Gazette, and Winter Chronicle*, MS 438/12, Scott Polar Research Institute Archives, University of Cambridge.

10 This degree of rank-based exclusivity would be significantly smaller in the polar publications in the decades to come.

11 "A Journal of a Voyage of Discovery to the Arctic Regions, in his Majesty's Ship Hecla and Griper, in the years 1819 and 1820," *Gentleman's Magazine* (May 1821): 99.

12 Fisher, *A Journal of a Voyage of Discovery*, 152.

13 "Literary Notices," *Examiner* 14 (3 June 1821): 348. Cavell and Craciun note that competitive journalistic and publishing pressures affected the reviews of Parry's narrative and of the *Chronicle* printing.

14 The play, *The Revolutionary Philannthropist* [*sic*], or *The Hecatomb of Haïti*, was composed aboard the prison ship by a French prisoner of war. Theatre bill for H.M. Prison ship "Crown," 1807, Newspapers and Playbills, THP/1, National Maritime Museum, Greenwich, London.

15 *Flight of the Plover* 1 (1 Mar. 1848): 1.

16 Hoag, "Caxtons of the North," 85–87. Hoag notes how scant and lacking in detail Admiralty records are in identifying precisely what models of presses were sent to the Arctic aboard the various search expeditions; mentions of "a small press" are the most specific the surviving records can be. None of the presses that traveled to the Arctic survives or has been identified to date; they may have been requisitioned for other uses. On the cairn messages left by the *Plover*, with their occasional address to the Inuit, see chapter 4.

17 The finding aid for the manuscript newspaper in Duke University's special collections describes this manuscript version as "the handwritten proofs of *The Flight of the Plover or North Pole Charivari*, the newsletter that Simpson printed while aboard the *Plover*," which would make it the first printed Arctic newspaper. I suspect that this finding aid is in error, however, as there are no other printed materials extant from this particular expedition, although much printed matter, including the printed newspaper *Weekly Guy*, has been collected from the *Plover*'s subsequent voyage in 1852 (which I imagine is the source of the finding aid's confusion). Guide to the John Simpson Papers.

18 *Flight of the Plover* 1 (1 Mar. 1848): 1.

19 Albert Hastings Markham notes that as of the month of June the Nares Expedition's press had been long dismantled for the season: "The return of the sledge travelers was celebrated, on the 29th of June, by the best dinner we could afford to put on the table. As our printing-press had long been dismantled, a written menu was given to myself and Aldrich as the leaders of the two extended sledge parties" (*The Great Frozen Sea*, 377).

20 *Flight of the Plover* 1 (1 Mar. 1848): 1–2.

21 Markham, *The Great Frozen Sea*, 326; Greely, *Three Years of Arctic Service*, 2:201–2; "A Catalogue of the Library Established on Board H.M.S. *Assistance*, Captain Sir Edward Belcher, C.B., Commanding the Arctic Squadron in Search of Sir John Franklin and His Companions: Printed & Published on Board H.M.S. *Assistance*, Wellington Channel, Arctic regions, H. Briant, Printer, 1853," Arctic Pamphlets, 1852–54, courtesy Royal Geographical Society (with IBG), handwritten ships' newspaper (on blue paper) for HMS *Assistance*, "Aurora Borealis," Baffin Bay, June 1850, HRR/4/10, National Maritime Museum, Greenwich, London.

22 According to the OED, the British expression "to take the piss," or to deride, does not come into use until the mid-twentieth century, but "piss on," or to show scorn, is in use beginning in the seventeenth century.

23 *Flight of the Plover* 1 (1 Mar. 1848): 1.

24 *Facsimile of the Illustrated Arctic News* 1 (31 Oct. 1850): 1.

25 Regarding indigenous communication networks, Claudio Aporta, Michael Bravo, and Fraser Taylor have created an extraordinary digital atlas of Inuit Arctic trails: *Pan Inuit Trails*, http://paninuittrails.org/.

26 *Facsimile of the Illustrated Arctic News* 1 (31 Oct. 1850): 5.

27 Markham, *The Great Frozen Sea*, 5.

28 *Arctic Expedition, 1875–6,* 464.

29 Markham, *The Great Frozen Sea,* 188–89.

30 Nansen, *Farthest North,* 1:277–80. A manuscript edition of the *Framsjaa* in the original Norwegian is located in the National Library of Norway.

31 *Queen's Illuminated Magazine* 1.1 (28 Oct. 1852): 2–3. Note: the bound copy in the British Library has inconsistent and often contradictory page numbering; in subsequent citations, I give both numbers where available.

32 Markham, *The Great Frozen Sea,* 188–89.

33 Craciun devotes attention to the collectivity of London-published official Arctic voyage accounts in *Writing Arctic Disaster,* chapter 2.

34 *Midnight Sun* 1.1 (1901): 2.

35 "Arctic Eagle Printed in Barren Polar Land," *Brooklyn Daily Eagle* (10 Sept. 1905): 3.

36 Rudy, "Floating Worlds." See also Rudy's book *Imagined Homelands.*

37 "Songs of the North," *Facsimile of the Illustrated Arctic News* 1 (31 Oct. 1850): 3.

38 "The Epilogue, at the Close of the Season, at the Royal Arctic Theatre," MS 1482/1–3;D Playbills, 1851 [Printed in HMS *Assistance*], Scott Polar Research Institute Archives, University of Cambridge.

39 "Prologue, Spoken at the Re-Opening of the Arctic Theatre, on Thursday, 18th November, 1875," Printed Programmes of Theatrical Entertainment, Museum Register 995, Scott Polar Research Institute Archives, University of Cambridge.

40 British Arctic Expedition of 1875–76.

41 Markham notebook, GB 15 British Arctic Expedition of 1875–76, MS 396/1; BJ, Scott Polar Research Institute Archives, University of Cambridge.

42 "Stray Shots," *Facsimile of the Illustrated Arctic News* 1 (31 Oct. 1850): 7.

43 See Rudy, "Floating Worlds" and *Imagined Homelands.*

44 "The Ravings," *Arctic Eagle* 1.3 (1903): 4.

45 *Weekly Guy* 3 (19 Nov. 1852): 10–12.

46 Hirsch, *A Poet's Glossary,* 514.

47 Kenn Harper, a historian of the Canadian Arctic and of the Inuit, recommends the spelling "Qalasersuaq" in keeping with modern Greenlandic orthography. Email correspondence with Kenn Harper, 10 July 2018.

48 Murray, *Kalli, the Esquimaux Christian,* 15.

49 "Arctic Highlanders" was the descriptor given to the Inughuit or Greenlandic Inuit by the British Arctic explorer John Ross in 1818.

50 "From Erasmus York, of the Arctic Highlands, to the Editor of the Aurora Borealis," *Arctic Miscellanies* 5 (Dec. 1850): 91–92.

51 *Queen's Illuminated Magazine,* MS 2 [28].

52 *Facsimile of the Illustrated Arctic News,* 8.

53 "To the Editor of the Aurora Borealis," *Arctic Miscellanies* 4 (Nov. 1850): 51.

54 "To the Editor of the Aurora Borealis," *Arctic Miscellanies* 3 (Oct. 1850): 24.

55 *Facsimile of the Illustrated Arctic News,* 10.

56 *Midnight Sun* 1.1 (1901): 1.

57 *Facsimile of the Illustrated Arctic News,* 10.

58 "The State of the Country," *Port Foulke Weekly News* 1.1 (1860): 3–4. The second
mate Dodge writes:

> Our domestic policy remains undisturbed. The provinces, and cities of our
> dominions are some of them in a flourishing conditions. Of others we have
> unhappily less encouraging information. The neighboring colony Etah
> has become ours by right of conquest, but upon taking possession of the
> capital, we found, to our mortification, that it was inhabited only by an old
> woman and boy,—both dead. They were immediately secured. . . .
>
> We are living in harmony with the Bears. We are not disturbed by the
> Bulls (Wall St or otherwise.) A war has been successfully waged against the
> Reindeer, but they have beat a retreat, and an armistice alike honorable to
> both parties, has been declared. The foxes continue to despise our traps, on
> which account war will be declared. (3–4)

59 *Arctic Moon* 1.1 (1881): 3–4, Adolphus Greely Papers, 1876–1973, Stefansson Collection, Dartmouth College.

60 *Facsimile of the Illustrated Arctic News*, 9.

61 *Queen's Illuminated Magazine*, MS 25.

62 *Arctic Eagle* 1.3 (1903): 1.

63 *Queen's Illuminated Magazine*, MS 8.

64 *Arctic Eagle* 1.3 (1903): 5.

65 See chapter 1, note 133 on Dodge's habitual intoxication. He was a skilled writer
for the *Port Foulke Weekly News* in any event.

66 "Wanted Immediately," *Arctic Miscellanies* 5 (Dec. 1850): 129.

67 "Nuts for the Arctic Public," *Arctic Miscellanies* 5 (Dec. 1850): 131.

68 "Thursday Pops" (10 Feb. 1876), Printed Programmes of Theatrical Entertainment, Museum Register 995, Scott Polar Research Institute Archives, University
of Cambridge.

69 Markham, *The Life of Sir Clements R. Markham*, 122.

70 Belcher, *The Last of the Arctic Voyages*, 1:187.

71 *Our Lost Explorers*, 284; *The Arctic Moon*, Adolphus Greely Papers, II-20.1.

72 Royal Terror Theatre, 6 Aug. 1902, "Dishcover Minstrel Troupe" Programme, Stefansson Collection, Dartmouth College. For more on blackface minstrel performances in the polar regions, see Tomasz Filip Mossakowski, "'The Sailors Dearly
Love To Make Up': Cross-Dressing and Blackface during Polar Exploration"
(PhD diss., Kings College London, 2015).

73 *Arctic Eagle* 1.3 (1903): 2.

74 Ross, *A Voyage of Discovery*, 236–37.

75 *North Georgia Gazette* MS 438/12.

76 Entry, 11 Sept. 1861, in Heywood, *The Arctic Diary*. I am indebted to Thomas
Walker for sharing these journals with me and for giving me permission to quote
from them.

77 Peary had two children by Allakasingwah or Alaqasinnguaq: Samik or Saamik
and Kale or Kaale. Matthew Henson's son Anaukkaq eventually met his relatives

at a reunion of American and Inuit Hensons in the United States shortly before he died in 1987 at the age of 80. The efforts of Allan Counter, who studied black explorers, helped bring Henson's achievements into wider attention. Email correspondence with Kenn Harper, 10 July 2018; see also Counter, *North Pole Promise*.

78 The primary target of Coleridge's poem, which was published in *News of Literature and Fashion* in 1825, is the publisher John Murray; a subsequent stanza describes bookmaking as the point of polar expeditions: "Captain Parry! Captain Parry! / Thy vocation stops not here: / Thou must dine with Mr. Murray / And a quarto must appear" ("Captain Parry," in *The Collected Works*, 1035–38). See also Cavell, "Making Books for Mr Murray," 61.

79 Arctic Exploration Letterbook, Elisha Kent Kane Papers, American Philosophical Society, Philadelphia.

80 *Queen's Illuminated Magazine*, MS 11 [15–16].

81 Markham, *The Arctic Navy List*, iv–v.

82 Markham, *The Arctic Navy List*, 4.

83 Roland Huntford's description of Markham's homosexuality has received the angriest response to date, which may be related to his sharp criticism of Markham's preference for man-hauling over the use of sled dogs, which Huntford judged outdated and disastrous. Huntford, *Scott and Amundsen*. Others have resorted to the long-standing historiographical canard of "no evidence"; see, for example, David Crane's book on Robert Falcon Scott, in which he concedes that Markham was attracted to men but concludes improbably that there is "not a shred of evidence" that he acted on his desires (*Scott of the Antarctic*, 62).

84 Henry P. Hartt to George Shorkley, 22 Mar. 1905, Box 1, Folder 8, Papers of George Shorkley, Stefansson Collection, Dartmouth College. P. J. Capelotti documents a chronic anal fissure from which Hartt suffered and suggests that its causes "ranged from the restricted diet, the more or less constant drinking, or from the homosexual activity Hartt would later hint at in his correspondence" (*The Greatest Show in the Arctic*, 422).

85 Quoted in Leane, *Antarctica in Fiction*, 99.

86 C. W. Emmerson, "The Arctic Twins," British Arctic Expedition of 1875–76, MS 1479.

87 Bradfield, "Against Solitude," in *Approaching Ice*.

88 [Herbert Ponting], "The Sleeping Bag," *South Polar Times* 3.1 (1911): 43.

89 Sex between men at sea can be a form of situational homosexuality, or the practice of homosexual acts when there is no opportunity for heterosexual practice, such as is found in the military, in boarding schools, and in prisons. As a naval saying summarizes homosexuality at sea, "It's only queer when you're tied to the pier."

90 *Facsimile of the Illustrated Arctic News*, preface.

91 *Queen's Illuminated Magazine*, MS n.p.

92 *Queen's Illuminated Magazine*, MS 40.

93 "Nuts for the Arctic Public," *Arctic Miscellanies* 5 (Dec. 1850): 131.

94 *Weekly Guy* 6 (14 Jan. 1852): 42.

95 This is the full transcription provided by Nansen:

> Up and down on a night so cold,
> Kvirre virre vip, bom, bom,
> Walk harpooner and kennelman bold,
> Kvirre virre vip, bom, bom,
> Our kennelman swings, I need hardly tell,
> Kvirre virre vip, bom, bom,
> The long, long lash you know so well,
> Kvirre virre vip, bom, bom,
> Our harpooner, he is a man of light,
> Kvirre virre vip, bom, bom,
> A burning lantern he grasps tight,
> Kvirre virre vip, bom, bom,
> They as they walk the time beguile,
> Kvirre virre vip, bom, bom,
> With tales of bears and all their wile,
> Kvirre virre vip, bom, bom,
>
> "Now suddenly a bear they see,
> Kvirre virre vip, bom, bom,
> Before whom all the dogs do flee,
> Kvirre virre vip, bom, bom,
> Kennelman, like a deer, runs fast,
> Kvirre virre vip, bom, bom,
> Harpooner slow comes in the last,
> Kvirre virre vip, bom, bom,
> and so on. (*Farthest North*, 304–6)

96 Anton M. Vedoe Papers, 1895–1963, MSS 233, Box 2, Folder 11, Stefansson Collection, Dartmouth College. The smelly shipmate was Eddie Coffin; the crew member with a "spongy and thin" pecker was likely the first mate, Edward Haven, who hailed from Lynn, Massachusetts.

97 Markham, *The Life of Sir Clements R. Markham*, 120–21. According to the OED, "manavilins" is nautical slang for odds and ends and usually refers to leftover scraps of food.

98 Hoag, "Caxtons of the North," 111n69.

99 Markham, *The Life of Sir Clements R. Markham*, 122.

100 *Arctic Miscellanies* 3 (Oct. 1850): 23.

101 Koldewey, *The German Arctic Expedition of 1869–70*, 391.

102 *Facsimile of the Illustrated Arctic News*, 21.

103 Maguire, *The Journal of Rochfort Maguire*, 305.

104 *Arctic Moon* 1.1 (1881): 4.

105 *Weekly Guy* 6 (17 Dec. 1852): 28.

106 *Weekly Guy* 10 (7 Jan. 1853): 40.

107 *Discovery News* (27 Nov. 1875): 1.

108 *Discovery News* (6 Dec. 1875): 1.

109 Henry Dodge, "The Grumbler," *Port Foulke Weekly News* 1.7 (1860).

110 Dodge, "The Grumbler," *Port Foulke Weekly News* 1.7 (1860); Dodge, "The Grumbler," *Port Foulke Weekly News* 1.6 (1860).

111 Dodge, "The Grumbler," *Port Foulke Weekly News* 1.6 (1860).

112 *Port Foulke Weekly News* 1.1 (11 Nov. 1860).

113 Hayes, *The Open Polar Sea*, 179–80.

3. Antarctic Imprints

Epigraph: [Edward Frederick Bage], "To the Editor," *Adelie Blizzard* 1.3 (1913): 90.

1 Murray and Marston, *Antarctic Days*, 15.

2 A comprehensive bibliography is kept at the website Antarctic Circle, coordinated by Robert B. Stephenson: http://www.antarctic-circle.org/aurora.details.htm.

3 While many scholars today observe a strict distinction between the North and South Polar regions, for important geological, political, and sociological reasons, some of the most prominent Western explorers of the long nineteenth century ventured to both ends of the earth (John Clark Ross, George Nares, Jean-Baptiste Charcot, Roald Amundsen, plus Edmund Hillary).

4 [Louis Bernacci], "When One Goes Forth a Voyaging, He Has a Tale to Tell—," *South Polar Times* 2.6 (1903): 21. "Poodle-faker" is British military slang for a young officer who devotes excessive attention to the social world of young ladies.

5 [Reginald Koettlitz], "Polar Plant Life," *South Polar Times* 1.1 (1902): 13–15.

6 "100 Year Old Fruitcake Found," Antarctic Heritage Trust, https://www.nzaht .org/pages/100-year-old-fruit-cake-found-in-antarcticas-oldest-building#.

7 Leane and Pharaoh, "Introduction," *Adelie Blizzard*, xii.

8 Superb bibliographic information on the book is available here: "*Aurora Australis* Production Details," Antarctic Circle, http://www.antarctic-circle.org/aurora .production.htm.

9 Murray and Marston, *Antarctic Days*, 106.

10 Shackleton, *The Heart of the Antarctic*, 131–32.

11 "Details on Copies of the *Aurora Australis*," Antarctic Circle, http://www .antarctic-circle.org/aurora.details.htm. The copies I have examined that contain stencils (not all I have seen do)—the "butter," "oatmeal," "pates," "fruit," and "stewed kidneys" editions—are held in the following institutions, respectively: Scott Polar Research Institute, University of Cambridge; Stefansson Collection, Dartmouth College; Columbia University; Huntington Library; John Carter Brown Library, Brown University.

12 "To Let," *Adélie Mail and Cape Adare Times* (1911–12): n.p.

13 "Mining Properties for Sale," *Adelie Blizzard* 1.4 (1913): 168.

14 Title page, *Adelie Blizzard* 1.1 (1913).

15 Gillis and Chang, "Scientists Warn of Rising Oceans from Polar Melt." More recently climate scientists have updated their models to stipulate an even faster melting scenario than originally predicted. A summary of these findings appears in Gillis, "Climate Model Predicts West Antarctic Ice Sheet Could Melt Rapidly."

16 Peggy Nelson, "About Me," https://eshackleton.com/about-me/.

17 Comparing the tactics of Nordic to British expeditions has been a common theme in histories of Antarctic exploration, most notably in the 1912–13 "race to the pole" undertaken by the Norwegian Roald Amundsen and the Briton Robert Falcon Scott. Amundsen was the first to reach the Pole; Scott and his companions died. Amundsen skied to the South Pole, using sled dogs as both transportation and food; Scott and his team "man-hauled" their sledges, laden with rocks for scientific collection, and froze to death twelve miles from a supply depot. For the most Scott-critical account, see Huntford, *The Last Place on Earth*. For defenses of Scott's tactics, see Fiennes, *Captain Scott*; Solomon, *The Coldest March*.

18 The quotations in this paragraph are taken from Ernest Shackleton, http://twitter.com/EShackleton, on the following dates: 1 March 2014, 11:00 a.m.; 14 May 2014, 1:00 p.m., 2:00 p.m., and 3:00 p.m.; 6 June 2011, 7:17 a.m.; 14 May 2014, 9:30 a.m., 10:00 a.m., and 12:00 p.m.

19 Hamilton, *America's Sketchbook*, 27.

20 Aston, *Alone in Antarctica*, 183–84.

21 Shackleton, *South*, 211. The Shackleton phantom man is thought to be the source of the following moment in T. S. Eliot's "The Waste Land":

Who is the third who walks always beside you?
When I count, there are only you and I together
But when I look ahead up the white road
There is always another one walking beside you
Gliding wrapt in a brown mantle, hooded
I do not know whether a man or a woman
But who is that on the other side of you? (68)

22 Scott, *Scott's Last Expedition*, 1:136.

23 Scott, *Scott's Last Expedition*, 2:408.

24 Jacobson, "Desiring Natures."

25 They are interested in books of travel, magazines, and nautical writing; other than Marryat and Dickens, he reports, novels are not much in favor. Scott, *The Voyage of the "Discovery,"* 297.

26 [Apsley Cherry-Garrard], "Editorial," *South Polar Times* 3.1 (1911): 1.

27 Prospectus, *South Polar Times*, MS 366/16/34, ER.

28 Prospectus, *South Polar Times*.

29 Scott, *The Voyage of the "Discovery,"* 311.

30 Scott, *The Voyage of the "Discovery,"* 362.

31 Armitage, *Two Years in the Antarctic*, 88.

32 Scott, "Preface," v–vi.

33 [Ernest Shackleton], "The South Polar Times," *South Polar Times* 1.1 (1902): 1.

34 The large Antarctic volcanoes Erebus and Terror were named after his ships by James Clark Ross in 1841 during his expedition to the southern continent; Ross sailed on the very ships *Erebus* and *Terror* that a decade later would be abandoned to the ice by Sir John Franklin's men in 1847 and recovered on the Arctic seafloor in 2014 and 2016.

35 [*South Polar Times*], Draft Editorial by Ernest Shackleton, 23 April 1902, MS 1537/2/51/17, Scott Polar Research Institute Archives, University of Cambridge. The strikethroughs are Shackleton's.

36 [*South Polar Times*], Draft Editorial by Ernest Shackleton.

37 Scott, "Preface," *South Polar Times*, vi. Emphasis added.

38 Sea Leopard [Arthur Lester Quartley], "South Pole Volunteers, *South Polar Times* 2.6 (1903): 14. The Arctic commander George Nares, it should be noted, had also missed the "outer world," the land of "home" and "friends" (Nares, *Narrative of a Voyage*, 2:175).

39 [Ernest Shackleton], Editorial, *South Polar Times* 1.2 (1902): 2.

40 Nordenskjöld and Andersson, *Antarctica or Two Years amongst the Ice of the South Pole*, 186.

41 "The Evolution of Women," *Adelie Blizzard* 1.1 (1913): 20.

42 Lisa Mastro and Jim Mastro, "Life in Antarctica," *Antarctica Online*, http://www .antarcticaonline.com/culture/culture.htm.

43 "Editorial: Marooned," *Adelie Blizzard* 1.1 (1913): 1.

44 M. P. Shiel's *The Purple Cloud* (1901) also has affinities with the genre. The notion of a hollow earth is one of the constitutive tenets of Mormonism; Joseph Smith believed that the Lost Israelites were located in a balmy land at the North Pole, beyond the reach of ice. In addition to Smith's writings, there are nineteenth-century Mormon hollow earth writings by LDS Elders, such as *The Inner World* (1886) by Frederick Culmer. Some late nineteenth-century explorers claimed the native inhabitants they encountered in northern Canada spoke Hebrew. For lively if uneven histories of hollow earth theories and fictions, see Standish, *Hollow Earth*, and Fitting, *Subterranean Worlds*. See also my "John Cleves Symmes and the Planetary Reach of Polar Exploration."

45 The circular in which Symmes first detailed his ideas appeared in U.S. newspapers in April 1818 and was addressed "TO ALL THE WORLD!" Symmes's language in his first brief manifesto relies more on the rhetoric of personal conviction than that of scientific theory or even scientific speculation. "I declare the earth is hollow," Symmes writes in the circular. "I pledge my life in support of this truth, and am ready to explore the hollow, if the world will support and aid me in the undertaking." The planned exploration should involve "one hundred brave companions, well equipped, [who will] start from Siberia in the fall season, with Reindeer and slays, on the ice of the frozen sea. . . . I engage we find warm and rich land, stocked with thrifty vegetables and animals if not men." Symmes, "Light Gives Light."

46 For a review of theories on this deathbed utterance, see Peeples, *The Afterlife of Edgar Allan Poe*.

47 Vilhjamur Stefansson, "The Hollow Earth," 17 March 1954, Unpublished Articles by Stefansson, Box 68, Folder 24, Stefansson Collection, Dartmouth College.

48 [Seaborn], *Symzonia*, vi.

49 John C. Symmes, Letter to Elisha Kent Kane, 20 Oct. 1857, Elisha Kent Kane Papers, Series I, MSS.B.K132, Box 10, American Philosophical Society, Philadelphia.

50 De Mille, *A Strange Manuscript Found in a Copper Cylinder*, 9, 56.

51 Symmes, "Light Gives Light."

52 [Frank Wild], "Leaves from an Ancient Papyrus," *South Polar Times* 2.7 (1903): 32.

53 See, for example, the case of George Murray Levick's photographic notebook in the introduction.

54 [Frank Wild], "An Old Document," *South Polar Times* 1.4 (1902): 13.

55 [Wild], "Leaves from an Ancient Papyrus," 32.

56 [Frank Wild], "Hieroglyphic Record," *South Polar Times* 2.8 (1903): 28.

57 [Wild], "Hieroglyphic Record," 30. Wild would also produce "An Ancient Manuscript" in the book *Aurora Australis*, writing there under the pen name Wand Erer; that contribution was an epic tale of Shackleton's fundraising for the *Nimrod* voyage, written in the King James style.

58 [Thomas Griffith Taylor], "A Chapter on Antarctic History," *South Polar Times* 3.1 (1911): 8, 14–15.

59 [George Clarke Simpson], "Fragments of a Manuscript Found by the People of Sirius 8 When They Visited the Earth during the Exploration of the Solar System," *South Polar Times* 3.2 (1911): 75. Here is the full story (ellipses in original):

> I know not why I write for there will be none to read; but the history of the human race since the dawn of civilisation has been written, and I feel impelled to set down the manner of the end. With this intent . . . . The great intellectual activity which had its dawn in the Victorian age was followed by a reaction resulting in a desire for nothing but luxury and self-indulgence . . . .
> . . . . human race had become almost uniform and there were no barbarian tribes to overrun and destroy the effeminate . . . . . . the pains of motherhood and the responsibilities of parentage . . . . only by the most stringent laws could the birthrate be kept even approximately equal to the deathrate, although the latter, by largely increased medical knowledge, was greatly reduced from what it had been previously. The personal habits . . . .
> . . . . . . large towns and solitary country resorts. Only in a few places were the sciences and arts cultivated, and the great libraries containing the results of the fervid striving after knowledge, which had been characteristic of the previous ages, were deserted and given over to oblivion and decay. The Science of medicine was the only one which continued to be pursued with vigour, and this was mainly with the object of reducing the deathrate. The love of truth for its own sake had departed. . . . .
> . . . . thousand students. Its large medical laboratory was a scene of the greatest excitement. After years of study and experiment, Professor Archibald B. Clarence discovered the Elixir of Life. He was a proud man

and the highest honours in the land were showered upon him . . . .
liquid was of crystal clearness, but had the faintest fluorescent glow, which
gave it exquisite colours when agitated . . . . it was the production
of great extremes of temperature . . . . electric furnace . . . . . . liquid air
. . . . . . the demand was beyond the supply. No sufficiently large source of
energy with the requisite fall of temperature could be found . . . .
remained the privilege of the few and these the ruling classes.

     . . . . volcanoes. The energy was sufficient, but the fall of tem-
perature was just short of that required . . . . bookworm, loved to
retire to his study with the geographical books of the twentieth century .
. . . . "The Voyage of the Discovery" . . . . "The Heart of the
Antarctic" . . . . . . "The Conquest of the South Pole" . . . . Erebus"
. . . .

    The ice-bound shores of McMurdo Sound became the centre of
the world. From it flowed the life-giving fluid which alone sustained the
human race. Death was entirely banished, and the race once more became
flourishing. The laws which had maintained the birthrate were no longer
of vital importance and were gradually allowed to lapse so that within a few
countries the birthrate again equalled the deathrate and both were nil! . . . . .
. . . . decrease in the number of blizzards, failure of the Ross
Sea to freeze, absence of very low temperatures on the Barrier . . . .
. . . . . bitterly regretted their failure to keep Meteorological records . . . .
. . . . . records of the British Antarctic expedition were unearthed from the
highest shelves of the lumber rooms of the libraries and were perused with
avidity . . . . the great question of the day was, Does climate change?
The greatest authority, the Physiographer of the Expedition 1910–12 was
quoted. He took for granted that ice age succeeded tropical age, and tropi-
cal age succeeded ice age . . . . could be no doubt,
the temperature was no longer sufficiently low to allow of the production
of the Elixir . . . . I, the writer of this record, am the last of the race,
and soon I must follow the companions who have lived with me through
the many centuries since the Elixir was discovered. My dying thoughts are
of the folly which neglected the teachings of the Scientists of the British
Antarctic Expedition 1910–12. (75–78)

60 [Simpson], "Fragments of a Manuscript Found by the People of Sirius 8," 76.

61 [Simpson], "Fragments of a Manuscript Found by the People of Sirius 8," 76–78.
Ellipses in original.

62 Another work of short fiction in the *S.P.T.* also imagines a southern continent of
outsized creatures: "The Last of the Terrorcas" is a fantasy about a dragon-like
killer whale fighting an immense flying insect. [Griffith Taylor], "The Last of the
Terrorcas," *South Polar Times IV*, 1912, MS 505/4, EN, Scott Polar Research Institute, University of Cambridge.

63 [Douglas Mawson], "Bathybia," *Aurora Australis*, n.p.

64 "Illustrated Interviews de Reginald Koettliz," *South Polar Times* 2.7 (1903): 46–48.

65 [Michael Barne], "Observations," *South Polar Times* 1.1 (1902): 22.

66 "Bioloveria," *South Polar Times* 1.3 (1902): 27–28.

67 [Bage], "To the Editor," 90.

68 "Calendar Rhymes," *Adelie Blizzard* 1.3 (1913): 125.

69 [Apsley Cherry-Garrard], "Walt Whitman," *South Polar Times IV*, 1912, MS 505/4, EN, Scott Polar Research Institute, University of Cambridge. I discuss this poem further in "First Person Nautical," coauthored with Rudy.

70 "A Lament," *Adélie Mail and Cape Adare Times* 1911–12 MS 1506, EN.

71 "Life in the Antarctic; or, The Protoplasmic Cycle," *South Polar Times* 3.1 (1911): 4.

72 [Douglas Mawson], "'Wireless'—the Realisation," *Adelie Blizzard* 1.1 (1913): 16.

73 [Mawson], "'Wireless'—the Realisation," 16.

74 Mawson, Notebook 5, 1–6 April 1913, *Mawson's Antarctic Diaries*, 187.

75 "Editorial: The Merry Month of May," *Adelie Blizzard* 1.2 (1913): 29.

76 "The Commercial Resources of Antarctica IV: General," *Adelie Blizzard* 1.5 (1913): 213.

4. Dead Letter Reckoning

Epigraph: Markham, *The Great Frozen Sea*, 251.

1 McClintock, *The Voyage of the "Fox" in Arctic Seas*, 283–84. Emphasis in original.

2 The writer continues:

> The principal object of this custom is, that, by comparing the times and places of the throwing out and the picking up of the bottles, if found at sea, or immediately after they are driven ashore, a calculation may be made of the direction and the motion of the currents of the water by which the bottles have been conveyed along. A bottle of this kind, I am informed, was found on the north-west coast of Ireland, which had been thrown overboard in the former voyage to Baffin's Bay. It had been ten months in the sea, and must have been carried by the currents upwards of a thousand miles in that time. The chance of conveying, by the same means, to all concerned, intelligence of the state of a ship, is, of itself, sufficient to engage those on board to its adoption. (*Letters Written during the Late Voyage of Discovery*, Saturday 22d, 6)

3 Parks Canada discovered the *Erebus* on a Canadian state-sponsored mission; her sister ship *Terror* was found by a private search team.

4 The full list of items found in the boat follows:

> Five or six small books were found, all of them scriptural or devotional works, except the 'Vicar of Wakefield.' One little book, 'Christian Melodies,' bore an inscription upon the titlepage from the donor to G.G. (Graham Gore?) A small Bible contained numerous marginal notes, and whole

passages underlined. Besides these books, the covers of a New Testament and Prayerbook were found.

Amongst an amazing quantity of clothing there were seven or eight pairs of boots of various kinds—cloth winter boots, sea boots, heavy ankle boots, and strong shoes. I noted that there were silk handkerchiefs—black, white, and figured—towels, soap, sponge, toothbrush, and hair-combs; macintosh gun-cover, marked outside with paint A 12, and lined with black cloth. Besides these articles we found twine, nails, saws, files, bristles, wax-ends, sail-makers' palms, powder, bullets, shot, cartridges, wads, leather cartridge-case, knives—clasp and dinner ones—needle and thread cases, slow-match, several bayonet-scabbards cut down into knife-sheaths, two rolls of sheet-lead, and, in short, a quantity of articles of one description and another truly astonishing in variety, and such as, for the most part, modern sledge-travellers in these regions would consider a mere accumulation of dead weight, but slightly useful, and very likely to break down the strength of the sledge-crews. . . .

In the after-part of the boat we discovered eleven large spoons, eleven forks, and four teaspoons, all of silver; of these twenty-six pieces of plate, eight bore Sir John Franklin's crest, the remainder had the crests of initials of nine different officers, with the exception of a single fork which was not marked; of these nine officers, five belonged to the 'Erebus,' Gore, Le Vesconte, Fairholme, Couch, and Goodsir. Three others belonged to the 'Terror,'—Crozier, (a teaspoon only), Hornby, and Thomas. I do not know to whom the three articles with an owl engraved on them belonged, nor who was the owner of the unmarked fork, but of the owners of those we can identify, the majority belonged to the 'Erebus.' (McClintock, *Voyage of the "Fox" in Arctic Seas*, 295–97)

5 Craciun, *Writing Arctic Disaster*, 37.

6 McClintock, *Voyage of the "Fox" in Arctic Seas*, 287.

7 McClintock, *Voyage of the "Fox" in Arctic Seas*, 288.

8 McClintock, *Voyage of the "Fox" in Arctic Seas*, 303–4. Emphasis in original.

9 The news was heavily covered on both sides of the Atlantic; *Harper's Weekly*, for example, published a photoengraving of a facsimile of the cairn message on its cover on 29 October 1859, rather than leading with news of John Brown's raid on Harpers Ferry (Potter, *Arctic Spectacles*, 153). My focus in this chapter, however, is not on the history of the broad search for the Franklin expedition, nor on the industry in theories about its disappearance, both of which have held sustaining interest for over 170 years, with scores of volumes written on their progressions.

10 ADM 7/190, National Archives, London. In a recent interview, ship captain Sean Bercaw, who has been launching messages in bottles ever since a childhood spent sailing around the world with his family, emphasized as well the open timeline for such ecomedia: "The cool thing about it, is it's not simply black and white: succeed or fail. Even if no one finds [the bottle] now, there is always that possibility.

That hope always exists that some one may find it a hundred years later." Brogan, "Messages in a Bottle Chart a Lifelong Romance with the Sea."

11 Miscellaneous clippings found at Greely Headquarters, Fort Conger, 10 June 1909, M118.7: Notes, Clippings, Ephemera, and Realia, 1884–1985, n.d., Box 6, Folder 26, Donald Baxter MacMillan Collection, George J. Mitchell Department of Special Collections and Archives, Bowdoin College Library.

12 See also Steinberg's smart reading of the drift of a container of Nike sneakers after it fell from a container ship in *The Social Construction of the Ocean*, 1–4.

13 Kane, *Arctic Explorations*, 58. He left his mark throughout the region, in name and, suggestively, in specie: "I built a large cairn here, and placed within it a copper penny, on which was scratched the letter K; but, like many other such deposits, it never met the eyes for which it was intended" (207). On Kane's Arctic inscriptions, see Craciun, *Writing Arctic Disaster*.

14 McClintock, *Voyage of the "Fox" in Arctic Seas*, 176.

15 *Arctic Expedition, 1875–6*, 476.

16 Ross, *Voyage of Discovery and Research in the Southern and Antarctic Regions*, 233.

17 ADM 7/190, National Archives, London.

18 Antarctica was also the scene of the distribution of documentary forms, to a less extensive degree, but the fact of its continental mass—its more stable land and ice, its nonarchipelagic state—keeps my focus in this chapter on the Arctic messages. Just one example from the South, then: in James Clark Ross's Antarctic venture in the early 1840s on the *Erebus* and *Terror*, the very ships targeted by Franklin searchers, he noted the messages left by previous expeditions:

> Two painted boards, erected upon poles in a conspicuous spot, attracted our attention, and an officer was immediately sent to examine them. They proved to be records of the visits of the French expedition under D'Urville, and of one of the vessels of the American exploring expedition [commanded by Charles Wilkes]. The first, a white board with black letters, as follows:—"Les corvettes Françoises L'Astrolabe et la Zélée, parties de Hobart Town le 25 Février, 1840, mouillées ici le 11 Mars, et réparties le 20 du dit pour la New Zéland. Du 19 Janvier au 1 Février, 1840, découverte de la Terre Adélie et determination du pole magnétique Austral!"
>
> The second, a black board with white letters, stated,—"U.S. brig Porpoise, 73 days out from Sydney, New Holland, on her return from an exploring cruize along the antarctic circle, all well; arrived the 7th, and sailed again on the 10th March, for the ZBay of Islands, New Zealand."
>
> A paper was also found inclosed in a bottle, which had been so imperfectly corked that some water had got into and so obliterated some parts of the writing, that we had difficulty in deciphering it. Its purport was, that the Porpoise had touched here for water, and that during their cruize they had coasted along the Icy Barrier, and had touched here for water. (Ross, *Voyage of Discovery and Research in the Southern and Antarctic Regions*, 133–34)

19 In this sense I speak to conversations about blanks ongoing by others in material textual studies, most notably Lisa Gitelman and James Green and Peter Stallybrass.

20 Gitelman, *Paper Knowledge*, 25.

21 Green and Stallybrass, *Benjamin Franklin*, 89.

22 On the perceived blankness of Arctic spaces in the British imperial imagination, see in particular Carroll, *An Empire of Air and Water*; Hill, *White Horizon*.

23 Ross, *A Voyage of Discovery*, 236–37.

24 Parry, *Journal of a Voyage for the Discovery of a North-West Passage*, xxviii.

25 Nares, *Narrative of a Voyage to the Polar Sea*, xviii. Here is a further example, from a Franklin search expedition's orders: "The various logs and private journals, with drawings, plans, etc., are to be sent to this office on the return of the Expedition" (Belcher, *The Last of the Arctic Voyages*, 5).

26 In Craciun's account, *Writing Arctic Disaster*, the Admiralty injunction was designed to ensure that the first narratives of the voyages appearing in print would have the official imprint of the Admiralty.

27 Nares, *Narrative of a Voyage to the Polar Sea*, xviii.

28 Precisely such a crisis of polar expedition printing within the metropole happened after the return of Parry's first expedition, when ship surgeon Alexander Fisher's journal was published so quickly that the Admiralty investigated to see if he had withheld copies of his private papers. As a review of his journal stated, he was "unjustly suspected of having kept a duplicate of his Journal, in order to forestall Capt. Parry's promised work" (*A Journal of a Voyage of Discovery to the Arctic Regions*, 442–43). Within the tradition of British polar missions, it was acceptable for other members of an expedition to publish narratives of their experiences eventually, but such accounts were expected to appear subsequent to the volume or volumes first appearing with the implied or explicit imprimatur of the Admiralty. "The Public are probably aware," one publisher wrote in a preface to a volume of letters written during an Arctic expedition, "that, agreeably to a regulation of the Admiralty, all Journals of Voyages of Discovery, kept by Officers or others, are required to be temporarily surrendered for the use of that Board: hence it has happened, that we have been unable until now to submit to our Readers full details" of the most recent voyage (*Letters Written during the Late Voyage of Discovery*, iii). See chapter 2 for further discussion of Parry's oversight of post-voyage publications; Craciun discusses this in "Writing the Disaster: Franklin and Frankenstein," particularly footnote 62, as well as in *Writing Arctic Disaster*.

29 Parry, *A Journal of a Voyage for the Discovery of a North-West Passage*, 3.

30 Ross, *A Voyage of Discovery*, 211.

31 One such message cast in a bottle reads as follows:

> Thrown overboard from H. M. Ship North Star, lying at single anchor in Erebus and Terror Bay, Beechy Island, on the 25. of September 1852. Wind at the time light from North; a N.E. gale having just subsided. Ship not yet housed in; Ice not have made, although there is much soft sludge in the

bay, which is driven about constantly by wind and tide. Union Bay closed up with ice. Temperature of the air when this was thrown overboard 25.5. Sea 29. All well.

Should any one pick this up; please forward it to the following address.—
On H.M. Service.

————————

To the Secretary of the Admiralty

LONDON

Stating, in what Latitude & Longitude it was picked up; with the date, condition of the cask &c; in fact any particulars respecting the document.

P.S. Two bottles with a similar notice were thrown overboard at the same time.

Printed at Beechy Island.

Copy of HMS *North Star* message in a bottle thrown overboard, 25 Sept. 1852, ADM 7/195, National Archives, London

32 *Arctic Miscellanies*, 246.

33 Examples digested from proposals collected by the British Admiralty, ADM 7/608, National Archives, London.

34 Osborn, *Stray Leaves from an Arctic Journal*, 172–73.

35 Osborn, *Stray Leaves from an Arctic Journal*, 173.

36 Carter, *Searching for the Franklin Expedition*, 66–67.

37 Maguire, *The Journal of Rochfort Maguire*, 114.

38 Bequeathed by Colonel John Barrow, F.R.S., formerly Keeper of the Records of the Admiralty, Vol. IX (III. ff. 409): 1. "Captain [Richard] Collinson, C.B., H.M. Discovery Ship 'Enterprize,' 1850"; 15 Jan. 1850–5 June, 1875: 58, Add MS 35308, British Library.

39 I am not concerned in this discussion with the nineteenth-century transatlantic mail system by which one could send a letter from the United States to France, say, paying postage in both country of origin and destination as well as a separate "sea postage" to the carrier; these letters both originated from and were addressed to terrestrial recipients and used the ocean only as a medium for transport.

40 Lacan, "The Purloined Letter," 205; Derrida, *The Post Card*, 444.

41 In *The Post Card*, Derrida sees no difference between the "Division of Dead letters" and what he would call the "division of living letters"; all remain in suspension (124).

42 Porter, *A Voyage in the South Seas*, 35

43 Porter, *A Voyage in the South Seas*, 35–36.

44 Porter, *A Voyage in the South Seas*, 50.

45 Warner, *Publics and Counterpublics*, 74.

46 Nevens, *Forty Years at Sea*, 225.

47 Fitz-Roy, *Narrative of the Surveying Voyages*, 490.

48　*Wanderings and Adventures of Reuben Delano*, 44–45.

49　Melville, "The Encantadas," 172.

50　Porter, *A Voyage in the South Seas*, 39.

51　Melville, "The Encantadas," 168.

52　Melville, *Moby-Dick*, 317.

53　Whitecar, *Four Years in a Whaleship*, 127.

54　Colton, *Deck and Port*, 69–70.

55　Browne, *Etchings of a Whaling Cruise*, 478.

56　*Life in a Man-of-War*, 230.

57　Markham, *The Great Frozen Sea*, 221.

58　Peary, *The North Pole*, 300.

59　Belcher, *The Last of the Arctic Voyages*, 5.

60　McClintock, *Voyage of the "Fox" in Arctic Seas*, 342–43.

61　*Arctic Expedition, 1875–6*, 471.

62　The order for the dispatch of mail to the Nares expedition was printed as a broadside:

> POLAR EXPEDITION
> DESPATCH OF MAILS FOR
>
> MAILS for the Polar Ships "Alert" and "Discovery" will be made up for conveyance from Portsmouth on or about the 25th May by the Steam Yacht "Pandora," Captain Allen Young having kindly consented to convey letters for the officers and crews of the Polar Ships, to be deposited at the depots.
>
> All letters should be sent through the Post Office prepaid the inland rate of postage, and addressed "Arctic Yacht Pandora, Portsmouth."
>
> It should be understood that these letters will be deposited at the depots on the chance of Captain Nares being able to communicate with the entrance of Smith's Sound by means of a small sledge party in the autumn of the present year, and that there is, therefore, some uncertainty whether the letters will reach their destination.
>
> It is requested that the friends of the officers and men of the Polar Expedition will make their letters as few and light as possible.
>
> No letters containing articles of value should be sent.
>
> No newspapers should be sent, as the Admiralty will send a sufficient supply.
>
> By Command of the Postmaster-General

15th May 1876: Message with information about the dispatch of mails for the Polar Ships "Alert" and "Discovery," 1 leaf, printed. Ephemera Collection, British Arctic Expedition of 1875–76, MS 1815/30, Scott Polar Research Institute, University of Cambridge.

63　Nares, *Narrative of a Voyage to the Polar Sea*, 175.

64 Robert McClure to his sister, 10 Apr. 1853, The Arctic Dispatches, Arctic Pamphlets 2 1852–53, Royal Geographical Society.

65 *Facsimile of the Illustrated Arctic News* 1 (31 Oct. 1850): 1.

66 De Long, *The Voyage of the* Jeannette, 162–63.

67 On Edison's contributions to the *Jeannette* expedition, see Sides, *In the Kingdom of Ice*.

68 The telephone dream resonates with a late twentieth-century moment of environmental extremity and death: the disastrous 1996 climbing season on Mount Everest, in which a blizzard took eight lives in one day. Rob Hall, an experienced New Zealand mountaineer and guide, was trapped and died on the mountain; while he was unable to be reached for rescue, he did have the technology to communicate with Base Camp, which was able to patch his radio via satellite phone through to his wife in New Zealand in order to say a farewell (Krakauer, *Into Thin Air*).

5. Inuit Knowledge and Charles Francis Hall

Epigraph: Hall, *Arctic Researches and Life among the Esquimaux*, 41.

1 Excellent exceptions include Woodman, *Unravelling the Franklin Mystery*; Eber, *Encounters on the Passage*; Potter, *Finding Franklin*; and the work of Louie Kamookak, an Inuit historian who lived in Gjoa Haven.

2 Deposition of Adam Beck, 3 Mar. 1852, 202, ADM7/192, National Archives, London.

3 John Rae to Archibald Barclay, 1 Sept. 1854, in Rae, *John Rae's Arctic Correspondence*, 342.

4 Dickens, "The Lost Arctic Voyagers," 392.

5 Φίλοι Συμβουλευόμενοι [Friendly Consultants], *The Great Arctic Mystery*, 9.

6 Cruikshank cautions scholars, however, not to view TK as "static, timeless, and hermetically sealed" (*Do Glaciers Listen?*, 9–10).

7 Hall, *Narrative of the Second Arctic Expedition*, 33.

8 The foremost historian of Hall's adventures is Chauncey Loomis, whose biography *Weird and Tragic Shores* offers a richly detailed account of his life and of his death. Bruce Henderson's account of the *Polaris* expedition, *Fatal North*, also covers Hall extensively.

9 Journal of Her Majesty, Queen Victoria, 3 Feb. 1854, Royal Archives, Windsor Castle. Perhaps a sense of similar receptions by white people over the course of his life is behind a plea with which Ipiirviq closes a letter written much later: "Pleas call haff wite man no Esquimaux Joe." Cited in Russell Potter, "A Letter from Ebierbing," *Visions of the North*, blog, https://visionsnorth.blogspot.com/2017/12/a-letter-from-ebierbing.html.

10 Hall, *Narrative of the Second Arctic Expedition*, 23–24.

11 Quoted in Loomis, *Weird and Tragic Shores*, 153.

12 Hall, *Narrative of the Second Arctic Expedition*, 23–24.

13 Loomis's exhumation of Hall's body in 1968 confirmed his death by arsenic poisoning.

14 The Smithsonian's Charles Francis Hall Collection covers only the years 1860–71, and yet consists of over 250 notebooks, in addition to hundreds of other letters, notes, scientific observations, and memoranda.

15 His biographer Loomis speculates that the death in 1857 of the best-known American Arctic explorer, Elisha Kent Kane, catalyzed his interest. Kane's body traveled on an extensive funeral train throughout the country (second only to Abraham Lincoln's), arriving in Hall's Cincinnati in March 1857. Loomis, *Weird and Tragic Shores*, 39–41.

16 Collection 702, Box 1, Folder 1, Diary, with Notes opening 1 Jan. 1860, Hall Collection.

17 Box 1, Folder 1, Diary, with Notes opening 1 Jan. 1860, Hall Collection.

18 Box 11, Folder 109, Newspaper clipping, n.d., Hall Collection.

19 Box 1, Folder 2, Journal, with preparations for the first expedition, Hall Collection.

20 Hall, *Arctic Researches*, 587. All future references to this edition will be cited parenthetically.

21 Box 1, Folder 1, Diary, 21 Feb. 1860, Hall Collection.

22 Box 1, Folder 1, Diary, 17 July 1860, Hall Collection.

23 Box 1, Folder 4, Journal for months preceding the first expedition, Hall Collection.

24 Box 4, Folder 46, Notes for lectures on the 1st expedition, 1863–64, Hall Collection. The etymological definition for "Eskimo" used by Hall was in long-standing use through the late twentieth century but has been challenged by Ives Goddard of the Smithsonian, who finds the term instead coming from an Algonkian language, Montagnais, and meaning "she who nets snowshoes." Goddard, *Handbook of North American Indians*, Vol. 5, 6.

25 Box 4, Folder 46, Notes for lectures on the 1st expedition, 1863–64, Hall Collection.

26 The preface to the second narrative explains that the U.S. Navy had intended initially to produce a narrative only of the third, dramatic *Polaris* expedition but found they had a volume of material on the second voyage at hand: "Under the act of Congress approved June 23, 1874, the Navy Department purchased from his family, for the sum of $15,000, the manuscripts of his several explorations, some of which were made use of by the late Admiral Davis in preparing for the Department the widely-appreciated 'Narrative of the North Polar Expedition [in the *Polaris*].' The larger number of the manuscripts, however, have been found to belong to the Second Expedition, and form the basis of the Narrative now prepared by the orders of the Department." Hall, *Narrative of the Second Arctic Expedition*, xi–xii.

27 Box 4, Folder 46, Notes for lectures on the 1st expedition, 1863–64, Hall Collection.

28 Hall, *Narrative of the Second Arctic Expedition*, 207.

29 Harper, "Burial at Sea."

30 Charles Francis Hall, 012 Journal, Vol. I, January 1860–July 1860, Hall Collection.

31 Box 1, Folder 14, Journal, Vol. III, August 1860–November 1860, Hall Collection.

32 Box 1, Folder 14, Journal, Vol. III, August 1860–November 1860, Hall Collection.

33 Hall, *Life with the Esquimaux*, 57.

34 Hall, *Narrative of the Second Arctic Expedition*, 289–90.

35 Horatio Austin, "Scheme of equipment for 2nd Arctic Expedition drawn up [?] 1850 to _____ drawn up for the Arctic on the return of the Expedition in 1851," MCL 35 *Printed Papers*, National Maritime Museum, Greenwich.

36 Box 1, Folder 14, Journal, Volume III, August 1860–November 1860, 13 Sept. 1860, Hall Collection.

37 Hall, *Narrative of the Second Arctic Expedition*, 255–56.

38 Hallendy, *Tukiliit*, 60.

39 Quoted in Loomis, *Weird and Tragic Shores*, 155.

40 Hall, *Narrative of the Second Arctic Expedition*, 25.

41 In one example of destroyed journals, the narrative of a survivor of the *Polaris* trials reveals that an "expressive article was found" at a campsite of some of the separated crew, "namely, a log-book, out of which was torn all reference to the death of Captain Hall" (Blake, *Arctic Experiences*, 354).

42 "On his return he had presented to Mr. J. Ingersoll Bowditch the corrections of a number of typographical and other errors in 'The Navigator,' which were adopted in the subsequent editions, in regard to which corrections he had replied to an inquiry from Mr. G. W. Blunt by saying that 'he had made them while working through Bowditch during a winter in the igloos'" (Hall, *Narrative of the Second Arctic Expedition*, 32).

43 Hall, *Narrative of the Second Arctic Expedition*, 148.

Conclusion

Epigraph: Carson, *The Sea around Us*, 7.

1 The grounding happened at the beginning of the expedition's first leg; I was scheduled to join its second leg. Ed Struzik, a Canadian writer aboard the *Akademik Ioffe* for the project's first leg, wrote a deeply sobering account of the ordeal and its implications; see Struzkik, "In the Melting Arctic, a Harrowing Account from a Stranded Ship."

2 In sharing the story of the 2017 postponement with a friend who is a scholar-sailor I learned that she and other experienced mariners had been concerned about the design and safety of the ship on which we had originally been set to sail. "You dodged a bullet," she said, and assured me that the other vessel options for the postponed expedition were sound. The twice-delayed expedition is as of this writing scheduling a fall 2019 journey. Northwest Passage Project, https://northwestpassageproject.org/.

3 De Long, *The Voyage of the* Jeannette, 2:456.

4 Melville, *Moby-Dick*, 164; Poe, *The Narrative of Arthur Gordon Pym*, 1179. The "shrou[d]" seen on the huge figure at the end of *Pym* in its "whiteness" also evokes the only burial garment or covering the sailor can expect: the sewed-up shroud of his white canvas hammock.

5 In the footage the claw of a robotic arm embeds the flag in the seabed. The video still that illustrated many media reports of the claim-staking shows a rounded camera lens, bounded by black, that composes the scene to afford a view of the North Pole as if a sphere seen from space. "It's like putting a flag on the moon," a Russian official proclaimed. The comparison is pointed: the submersible that planted the flag was named *Mir 1*, just as Russia's now-decommissioned space station was named Mir, after the Russian word meaning "peace" or "world" (Parfitt, "Russia Plants Flag on North Pole Seabed"). I discuss the Russian flag planting at greater length in Blum, "John Cleves Symmes and the Planetary Reach of Polar Exploration." Elizabeth DeLoughrey has found the polar and oceanic regions to be figuratively consistent with "extraterrestrial" spaces" ("Satellite Planetarity and the Ends of the Earth," 260).

6 Carson, *The Sea around Us*, 3. Subsequent references will be noted parenthetically in the text.

7 In a similar vein, Stacy Alaimo writes, "The synchronic depth and breadth of the oceans present a kind of incomprehensible immensity that parallels the diachronic scale of anthropogenic effects. . . . To begin to glimpse the seas, one must descend, not transcend, be immersed in highly mediated environments that suggest the entanglements of knowledge, science, economics, and power" (*Exposed*, 161).

8 Jeffrey Jerome Cohen, "Anarky," in Menely and Taylor, *Anthropocene Reading*, 27, 34.

9 "A more potent marine transcorporeality would submerge the human within global networks of consumption, waste, and pollution, capturing the strange agencies of the ordinary stuff of our lives" (Alaimo, *Exposed*, 113).

BIBLIOGRAPHY

Primary Sources

Accountant General's Record Book. 1852. National Archives, London.

Adélie Mail and Cape Adare Times. Scott Polar Research Institute Archives, University of Cambridge.

Admiralty Correspondence Index for 1852. National Archives, London.

Admiralty Records. National Archives, London.

Albanov, Valernian. *In the Land of White Death.* New York: Modern Libraries, 2000.

All Aboard: The Journal of R.M.S. "Transylvania." Kemble Maritime Ephemera Collection. Huntington Library, San Marino, California.

Amundsen, Roald. *The North West Passage.* London: Archibald Constable, 1908.

Amundsen, Roald. *The South Pole: An Account of the Norwegian Antarctic Expedition in the Fram, 1910–1912.* New York: Cooper Square Press, 2000.

The Antarctic Book, Winter Quarters, 1907–1909. London: William Heinemann, 1909.

The Antarctic Petrel. Alexander Turnbull Library, Wellington, New Zealand.

The Arctic Eagle. Harrie H. Newcomb Papers. George J. Mitchell Department of Special Collections and Archives, Bowdoin College Library.

Arctic Expedition, 1875–6: Journals and Proceedings of the Arctic Expedition, 1875–6, under the Command of Sir George S. Nares. London: Her Majesty's Stationery Office, Harrison and Sons, 1875–77.

Arctic Exploration Letterbook (Private). Volume 10. Elisha Kent Kane Papers. American Philosophical Society, Philadelphia.

Arctic Miscellanies: A Souvenir of the Late Polar Search by the Officers and Seamen of the Expedition. London: Colburn, 1852.

The Arctic Moon. Adolphus Greely Papers, 1876–1973. Stefansson Collection, Dartmouth College.

Arctic Pamphlets, 1852–54. Royal Geographical Society, London.

Armitage, Albert. *Two Years in the Antarctic: Being a Narrative of the British National Antarctic Expedition.* London: Edward Arnold, 1905.

Aston, Felicity. *Alone in Antarctica: The First Woman to Ski Solo across the Southern Ice*. Berkeley, CA: Counterpoint, 2014.

Aston, Felicity. *Call of the White: Taking the World to the South Pole*. Chichester, UK: Summersdale Press, 2011.

Aurora Borealis. National Maritime Museum, Greenwich, London.

Austin, Horatio. Collection. Scott Polar Research Institute Archives, University of Cambridge.

Austral Chronicle. A Bi-Weekly Journal. Kemble Maritime Ephemera Collection. Huntington Library, San Marino, California.

Back, George. *Arctic Artist: The Journal and Paintings of George Back, Midshipman with Franklin, 1819–1822*. Montreal: McGill-Queen's University Press, 1994.

Barrow, John. *Voyages of Discovery and Research within the Arctic Regions, from the Years 1818 to the Present Time*. London: John Murray, 1846.

Beechey, Frederick William. *Narrative of a Voyage to the Pacific and Beering's Strait*. London: H. Colburn and R. Bentley, 1831.

Beechey, Frederick William. *A Voyage of Discovery towards the North Pole, Performed in His Majesty's Ships* Dorothea *and* Trent, *under the Command of Captain David Buchan, R.N.; 1818; to which is added, a summary of all the early attempts to reach the Pacific by way of the Pole*. London: Richard Bentley, 1843.

Belcher, Edward. *The Last of the Arctic Voyages: Being a Narrative of the Expedition in* H.M.S. Assistance, *Under the command of Captain Sir Edward Belcher, C.B., in search of Sir John Franklin, during the years 1852–53–54*. London: L. Reeve, 1855.

Blake, E. Vale, ed. *Arctic Experiences: Containing Capt. George E. Tyson's Wonderful Drift on the Ice-Floe, a History of the Polaris Expedition, the Cruise of the Tigress, and Rescue of the Polaris Survivors. To Which Is Added a General Arctic Chronology*. New York: Harper and Brothers, 1874.

The Blizzard. Scott Polar Research Institute Archives, University of Cambridge.

Bound Home or The Gold-Hunters' Manual: A Newspaper Published on Board the Pacific Mail S.S. Co.'s Steamship "Northerner," Capt. Henry Randall, on Her Trip from San Francisco to Panama. Kemble Maritime Ephemera Collection. Huntington Library, San Marino, California.

The Boys and Girls Favorite. Huntington Library, San Marino, California.

British Arctic Expedition of 1875–76 Collection. Scott Polar Research Institute Archives, University of Cambridge.

Browne, J. Ross. *Etchings of a Whaling Cruise, with Notes of a Sojourn on the Island of Zanzibar, to Which Is Appended a Brief History of the Whale Fishery, Its Past and Present Condition*. New York: Harper and Brothers, 1846.

Bull-Dog Gazette. Kemble Maritime Ephemera Collection. Huntington Library, San Marino, California.

Byrd, Richard E. *Alone*. New York: Ace Books, 1938.

Carter, Robert Randolph. *Searching for the Franklin Expedition: The Arctic Journals of Robert Randolph Carter*. Edited by Harold B. Gill Jr. and Joanne Young. Annapolis, MD: Naval Institute Press, 1998.

Catapult of the U.S.S. Maryland. Kemble Maritime Ephemera Collection. Huntington Library, San Marino, California.

Cherry-Garrard, Apsley. *The Worst Journey in the World.* 1922. New York: Carroll and Graf, 1989.

Colton, Walter. *Deck and Port; or, Incidents of a Cruise in the United States Frigate Congress to California.* New York: A. S. Barnes, 1850.

Cook, Frederick A. *My Attainment of the Pole.* New York: Cooper Square Press, 2001.

Cunard Cruise News. Kemble Maritime Ephemera Collection. Huntington Library, San Marino, California.

Davis, J. E. [John Edward]. *A Letter from the Antarctic.* London: William Clowes and Sons, 1901.

de Bray, Emile Frédéric. *A Frenchman in Search of Franklin: De Bray's Arctic Journal, 1852–1854.* Toronto: University of Toronto Press, 1993.

De Long, George W. *The Voyage of the Jeannette: The Ship and Ice Journals of George W. De Long, Lieutenant-Commander U.S.N. and Commander of the Polar Expedition of 1879–1881.* Edited by Emma De Long. Boston: Houghton, Mifflin, 1883.

De Mille, James. *A Strange Manuscript Found in a Copper Cylinder.* New York: Harper and Brothers, 1888.

Dickens, Charles. "The Lost Arctic Voyagers." *Household Words* 246 (9 Dec. 1854): 392.

Discovery News. Nares Expedition. Private collection. Used with permission.

Documents Relating to Arctic Expeditions. National Archives, London.

Ephemera Collection. British Arctic Expedition of 1875–76. Scott Polar Research Institute Archives, University of Cambridge.

Facsimile of the Illustrated Arctic News, Published on Board H.M.S. Resolute, Captn Horatio T. Austin, C.B. in Search of the Expedition under Sir John Franklin. London: Ackermann, 1852.

Fiala, Anthony. "Christmas Near the North Pole." *New York Times,* 23 Dec. 1906, 25.

Fiala, Anthony. *Fighting the Polar Ice.* London: Hodder and Stoughton, 1907.

Fisher, Alexander. *A Journal of a Voyage of Discovery to the Arctic Regions: In His Majesty's Ships Hecla and Griper, in the Years 1819 and 1820.* London: Longman, Hurst, Rees, Orme, and Brown, 1821.

Fitz-Roy, Robert. *Narrative of the Surveying Voyages of His Majesty's Ships Adventure and Beagle, between the Years 1826 and 1836.* London: Henry Colburn, 1839.

Flight of the PLOVER. John Simpson Papers. David M. Rubenstein Rare Book and Manuscript Library, Duke University.

Franklin, John. *Narrative of a Journey to the Shores of the Polar Sea, in the Years 1819–20–21–22.* London: John Murray, 1824.

Gilder, William H. *Schwatka's Search: Sledging in the Arctic in Quest of the Franklin Records.* New York: Charles Scribner's Sons, 1881.

Gilman, William Henry. *Letters Written Home.* Exeter, NH, 1911.

Greely, Adolphus W. *A Handbook of Polar Discoveries.* Boston: Little and Brown,
1907.

Greely, Adolphus W. *Three Years of Arctic Service: An Account of the Lady Franklin
Bay Expedition of 1881–84 and the Attainment of the Farthest North.* New York:
Charles Scribner's Sons, 1886.

Guide to the John Simpson Papers, 1825–75. David M. Rubenstein Rare Book and
Manuscript Library, Duke University.

Hall, Charles Francis. *Arctic Researches and Life among the Esquimaux: Being the Narrative of an Expedition in Search of Sir John Franklin, in the Years 1860, 1861, and
1862.* New York: Harper and Brothers, 1865.

Hall, Charles Francis. Collection. National Museum of American History, Archives
Center, Washington, DC.

Hall, Charles Francis. *Life with the Esquimaux: The Narrative of Captain Charles
Francis Hall of the Whaling Barque "George Henry" from the 29th May, 1860, to
the 13th September, 1862; with the Results of a Long Intercourse with the Innuits
and Full Description of Their Mode of Life, the Discovery of Actual Relics of the
Expedition of Martin Frobisher of Three Centuries Ago, and Deductions in Favor of
Yet Discovering Some of the Survivors of Sir John Franklin's Expedition.* London:
Sampson Low, Son, and Marston, 1864.

Hall, Charles Francis. *Narrative of the Second Arctic Expedition Made by Charles F.
Hall: His voyage to Repulse Bay, Sledge Journeys to the Straits of Fury and Hecla
and to King William's Land and Residence among the Eskimos during the Years
1864–69.* Washington, DC: Government Printing Office, 1879.

Harris, Francis L. *An Abstract of a Journal in the Arctic Ocean during the Years of 1860
and 61 by F L Harris, U.S. Navy.* Private collection. Used with permission.

Hayes, Isaac Israel. *An Arctic Boat Journey in the Autumn of 1854.* Boston: Ticknor and
Fields, 1867.

Hayes, Isaac Israel. *The Open Polar Sea: A Narrative of a Voyage of Discovery towards the
North Pole, in the Schooner "United States."* New York: Hurd and Houghton, 1867.

Henson, Matthew. *A Negro Explorer at the North Pole.* New York: Cooper Square
Press, 2001.

Heywood, Harvey Scott. *The Arctic Diary of Harvey Scott Heywood, Volunteer Seaman on the Hayes expedition to the Arctic, 1860–61.* Private collection. Used with
permission.

Kane, Elisha Kent. *Arctic Explorations: The Second Grinnell Expedition in Search of Sir
John Franklin, 1853, '54, '55.* Philadelphia: Childs and Peterson, 1856.

Koldewey, Carl. *The German Arctic Expedition of 1869–70, and Narrative of the Wreck
of the "Hansa" in the Ice.* Translated by L. Mercier and edited by H. W. Bates.
London: Sampson Low, Marston, Low, and Searle, 1874.

Leane, Elizabeth, ed. *The Adelie Blizzard: Mawson's Forgotten Newspaper.* Adelaide:
Friends of the State Library of South Australia, 2010.

*Letters Written during the Late Voyage of Discovery in the Western Arctic Sea, by an Of-
ficer of the Expedition.* London: Printed for Sir Richard Phillips, 1821.

Life in a Man-of-War, or Scenes in "Old Ironsides" during Her Cruise in the Pacific. Philadelphia: Lydia R. Bailey, 1841.

Lyon, G. F. *The Private Journal of Captain G. F. Lyon, of H.M.S.* Hecla, *during the recent voyage of discovery under Captain Parry.* London: John Murray, 1824.

MacMillan, Donald Baxter. Collection. George J. Mitchell Department of Special Collections and Archives, Bowdoin College Library.

Maguire, Rochfort. *The Journal of Rochfort Maguire 1852–1854: Two Years at Point Barrow, Alaska, aboard H.M.S.* Plover *in the Search for Sir John Franklin.* Edited by John Bockstoce. London: Hakluyt Society, 1988.

Makura Journal, With Apologies to The Boston Journal. En Route Vancouver to Sydney. Kemble Maritime Ephemera Collection. Huntington Library, San Marino, California.

Markham, Albert Hastings. *The Great Frozen Sea: A Personal Narrative of the Voyage of the "Alert" during the Arctic Expedition of 1875–6.* London: Daldy, Isbister, 1878.

Markham, Albert Hastings. *A Polar Reconnaissance: Being the Voyage of the "Isbjörn" to Novaya Zemlya in 1879.* London: C. Kegan Paul, 1881.

Markham, Albert Hastings. *A Whaling Cruise to Baffin's Bay and the Gulf of Boothia. And an Account of the Rescue of the Crew of the "Polaris."* London: Samson Low, Marston, Low, and Searle, 1874.

Markham, Clements R. *The Arctic Navy List, or a century of Arctic and Antarctic officers, together with a list of officers of the 1875 expedition, and their services, 1773–1873.* London: Griffin, 1875.

Markham, Clements R. *The Lands of Silence: A History of Arctic and Antarctic Exploration.* 1921. Cambridge, UK: Cambridge University Press, 2015.

Markham, Clements R. *Life of Admiral Sir Leopold McClintock.* 1909. Cambridge, UK: Cambridge University Press, 2014.

Markham, Clements R. *The Life of Sir Clements R. Markham.* London: John Murray, 1917.

Material printed on HMS *Assistance,* 1852–54. Scott Polar Research Institute Archives, University of Cambridge.

Mawson, Douglas. *Mawson's Antarctic Diaries.* Edited by Fred Jacka and Eleanor Jacka. Crows News, New South Wales: Allen and Unwin, 1988.

May, William Henry. Collection. Scott Polar Research Institute Archives, University of Cambridge.

McClintock [M'Clintock], Francis Leopold. *The Voyage of the "Fox" in Arctic Seas: A Narrative of the Discovery of the Fate of Sir John Franklin and his Companions.* London: John Murray, 1859.

McClure, Robert. *The Arctic Dispatches: Containing an Account of the Discovery of the North-West Passage.* London: J. D. Potter, 1853.

Melville, George W. *In the Lena Delta: A Narrative of the Search for Lieut.- Commander De Long and his Companions Followed by an Account of the Greely Relief Expedition and A Proposed Method of Reaching the North Pole.* Boston: Houghton, Mifflin, 1885.

Midnight Sun. Ernest deKoven Leffingwell Papers, 1900–1961. Stefansson Collection, Dartmouth College.

Morillo, Pablo. "Venesolanos que habeis seguido a Bolivar" Frigata *Diana* Imprenta del Exèrcito expedicionario: 1 Jan. 1815: 1. John Carter Brown Library, Brown University.

Moss, Edward L. *Shores of the Polar Sea: A Narrative of the Arctic Expedition of 1875–6.* London: M. Ward, 1878.

Murdoch, W. G. Burn. *From Edinburgh to the Antarctic: An Artist's Notes and Sketches during the Dundee Antarctic Expedition of 1892–93.* London: Longmans, Green, 1894.

Murray, James, and George Marston. *Antarctic Days: Sketches of the Homely Side of Polar Life by Two of Shackleton's Men.* London: Andrew Melrose, 1913.

Murray, Thomas Boyles. *Kalli, the Esquimaux Christian: A Memoir.* London: Society for Promoting Christian Knowledge, 1856.

Nansen, Fridtjof. *Farthest North.* Westminster, UK: Archibald Constable, 1897.

Nares, George S. *Narrative of a Voyage to the Polar Sea during 1875–6 in H.M. Ships "Alert" and "Discovery."* London: Sampson, Low, Marston, Searle, 1878.

Nevens, William. *Forty Years at Sea: Or a Narrative of the Adventures of William Nevens.* Portland, ME: Thurston, Fenley, 1846.

New Georgia Gazette, and Winter Chronicle. North Georgia Gazette Collection. Scott Polar Research Institute Archives, University of Cambridge.

Nordenskjöld, N. Otto G., and Johan Gunnar Andersson. *Antarctica or Two Years amongst the Ice of the South Pole.* London: Hurst and Blackett, 1905.

North Georgia Gazette, and Winter Chronicle. In William Edward Parry, *Journal of a Voyage for the Discovery of a North-West Passage from the Atlantic to the Pacific: Performed in the Years, 1819–20, in His Majesty's Ships* Hecla *and* Griper *under the Orders of William Edward Parry.* Philadelphia: Abraham Small, 1821.

Northern Regions; or, Uncle Richard's relation of Captain Parry's voyages for the discovery of a north-west passage, and Franklin's and Cochrane's overland journeys to other parts of the world. New York: O. A. Roorbach, 1827.

Observer of the U.S. Aircraft Carrier Lexington. Kemble Maritime Ephemera Collection. Huntington Library, San Marino, California.

Ommanney, Erasmus. Collection. Scott Polar Research Institute Archives, University of Cambridge.

Osborn, Sherard. *Stray Leaves from an Arctic Journal, or, Eighteen Months in the Polar Regions: In Search of Sir John Franklin's Expedition, in the Years 1850–51.* London: Longman, Brown, Green, and Longmans, 1852.

Our Lost Explorers: the Narrative of the Jeannette Arctic Expedition as Related by the Survivors, and in the Records and Last Journals of Lieutenant De Long, edited by Raymond Lee Newcomb. Hartford, CT: American Publishing Co., 1883.

Parry, Edward. *Memoirs of Rear-Admiral Sir W. Edward Parry, Kt, F.R.S.* New York: Protestant Episcopal Society for the Promotion of Evangelical Knowledge, 1857.

Parry, William Edward. *Journal of a Second Voyage for the Discovery of a North-West Passage from the Atlantic to the Pacific; Performed in the Years, 1821–22–23, in His Majesty's Ships* Fury *and* Hecla *under the Orders of William Edward Parry.* London: John Murray, 1824.

Parry, William Edward. *Journal of a Voyage for the Discovery of a North-West Passage from the Atlantic to the Pacific; Performed in the Years, 1819–20, in His Majesty's Ships* Hecla *and* Griper *under the Orders of William Edward Parry.* Philadelphia: Abraham Small, 1821.

Parry, William Edward. *Narrative of an Attempt to Reach the North Pole, in Boats Fitted for the Purpose and Attached to His Majesty's Ship* Hecla. London: John Murray, 1828.

Peary, Robert. *The North Pole: Its Discovery in 1909 Under the Auspices of the Peary Arctic Club.* New York: Frederick A. Stokes, 1910.

Playbills, 1851 [printed in HMS *Assistance*]. Scott Polar Research Institute Archives, University of Cambridge.

Ponting, Herbert G. *The Great White South.* London: Duckworth, 1930.

Port Foulke Weekly News. New-York Historical Society.

Porter, David. *A Voyage in the South Seas, in the Years 1812, 1813, and 1814 with Particular details of the Gallipagos and Washington Islands.* London: Phillips, 1823.

Priestley, Raymond. Collection, Polar Papers. Scott Polar Research Institute Archives, University of Cambridge.

Printed Programmes of Theatrical Entertainment. British Arctic Expedition of 1875–76. Scott Polar Research Institute Archives, University of Cambridge.

Pynchon, Thomas. *Mason and Dixon.* New York: Picador, 2004.

Queen's Illuminated Magazine and North Cornwall Gazette. Published in Winter quarters, Arctic Regions. British Library, London.

Rae, John. *John Rae's Arctic Correspondence 1844–1855.* Victoria, Canada: TouchWood Editions, 2014.

Richardson, John. *Arctic Searching Expedition: A Journal of a Boat-Voyage through Rupert's Land and the Arctic Sea, in search of the discovery ships under command of Sir John Franklin.* London: Longman, Brown, Green, and Longmans, 1851.

R.M.S. *City of Paris Gazette, Printed on Board.* Inman and International Steamship Company. Kemble Maritime Ephemera Collection. Huntington Library, San Marino, California.

Ross, James Clark. *Voyage of Discovery and Research in the Southern and Antarctic Regions, during the Years 1839–43.* London: John Murray, 1847.

Ross, John. *A Voyage of Discovery, Made under the Orders of the Admiralty, in His Majesty's Ships* Isabella *and* Alexander, *for the Purpose of Exploring Baffin's Bay, and Inquiring into the Probability of a North-West Passage.* London: J. Murray, 1819.

Ross, John. *Narrative of a second voyage in search of a North-west passage, and of a residence in the Arctic regions, during the years 1829, 1830, 1831, 1832, 1833 by Sir John Ross.* Philadelphia: E. L. Carey and A. Hart, 1835.

Sabine, Edward. *Remarks on the account of the late voyage of discovery to Baffin's Bay published by Captain J. Ross, R.N.* London: Printed by R. and A. Taylor for John Booth, 1819.

Schwatka, Frederick. *The Children of the Cold.* New York: Cassell, 1895.

Scott, Robert Falcon. "Preface." In *South Polar Times I: April to August 1902*, v–viii. London: Smith, Elder, 1907

Scott, Robert Falcon. *Scott's Last Expedition.* New York: Dodd, Mead, 1913.

Scott, Robert Falcon. *Tragedy and Triumph: The Journals of Captain R. F. Scott's Last Polar Expedition.* London: Prospero Press, 2000.

Scott, Robert Falcon. *The Voyage of the "Discovery."* London: Smith, Elder, 1905.

[Seaborn, Adam]. *Symzonia: A Voyage of Discovery.* New York: J. Seymour, 1820.

Seitz, Charles L. Polar Diaries. Stefansson Collection, Dartmouth College.

Shackleton, Ernest, ed. *Aurora Australis.* Antarctica: Printed at the Sign of "The Penguin" by Joyce and Wild, 1908.

Shackleton, Ernest. *The Heart of the Antarctic: Being the Story of the British Antarctic Expedition 1907–1909.* Philadelphia: Lippincott, 1914.

Shackleton, Ernest. *South.* New York: Macmillan, 1920.

Shells and Seaweed. Huntington Library, San Marino, California.

Shorkley, George. Papers. Stefansson Collection, Dartmouth College.

Simpson, John. Papers. David M. Rubenstein Rare Book and Manuscript Library, Duke University.

South Polar Times. Scott Polar Research Institute Archives, University of Cambridge.

South Polar Times Contributions (unpublished). Scott Polar Research Institute Archives, University of Cambridge.

Stefansson, Vilhjamur. Papers. Rauner Library, Dartmouth College.

Stefansson Collection on Polar Exploration. Rauner Library, Dartmouth College.

Symmes, John Cleves. "Light Gives Light, to Light Discover—'Ad Infinitum.'" St. Louis, MO: April 10, 1818.

Tenedos Times: A Monthly Journal of the Mediterranean Destroyer Flotilla during the Early Part of the War. Originally Printed on Board H.M.S. "Blenheim." London: George Allen & Unwin, 1917.

Thoreau, Henry David. *Walden.* In *A Week on the Concord and Merrimack Rivers, Walden; or, Life in the Woods, The Maine Woods, Cape Cod.* New York: Library of America, 1985.

Umbria Express, and Atlantic Times. Kemble Maritime Ephemera Collection. Huntington Library, San Marino, California.

Vedoe, Anton M. Papers. Stefansson Collection, Dartmouth College.

Wanderings and Adventures of Reuben Delano, Being a Narrative of Twelve Years Life in a Whale Ship! Worcester, MA: Thomas Drew Jr., 1846.

Weekly Guy. John Simpson Papers, David M. Rubenstein Rare Book and Manuscript Library, Duke University.

West Philadelphia Hospital Register. Library Company of Philadelphia.

Whitecar, William B. Jr. *Four Years in a Whaleship: Embracing Cruises in the Pacific, Atlantic, Indian, and Antarctic Oceans, in the years 1855, '6, '7, '8, '9*. Philadelphia: J. B. Lippincott, 1860.

Worsley, F. A. *Endurance*. New York: Norton, 2000.

Φιλοι Συμβουλευομενοι [Friendly Consultants]. *The Great Arctic Mystery*. London: Chapman and Hall, 1856.

Secondary Sources

"A 5°c Arctic in a 2°c World: Challenges and Recommendations for Immediate Action." Briefing Paper for Arctic Science Ministerial, 28 Sept. 2016. Columbia Climate Center, Columbia University.

Alaimo, Stacy. *Bodily Natures: Science, Environment, and the Material Self*. Bloomington: Indiana University Press, 2010.

Alaimo, Stacy. *Exposed: Environmental Politics and Pleasures in Posthuman Times*. Minneapolis: University of Minnesota Press, 2016.

Alaimo, Stacy. "Sustainable This, Sustainable That: New Materialisms, Posthumanism, and Unknown Futures." *PMLA* 127.3 (2012): 558–64.

Allewaert, Monique. *Ariel's Ecology: Plantations, Personhood, and Colonialism in the American Tropics*. Minneapolis: University of Minnesota Press, 2013.

Alexander, Caroline. *The* Endurance: *Shackleton's Legendary Antarctic Expedition*. New York: Knopf, 1998.

Anderson, Benedict. *Imagined Communities: Reflections on the Origin and Spread of Nationalism*. London: Verso, 1991.

Anthony, Jason C. *Hoosh: Roast Penguin, Scurvy Day, and Other Stories of Antarctic Cuisine*. Lincoln: University of Nebraska Press, 2012.

Antarctic Circle. Edited by Robert B. Stephenson. http://www.antarctic-circle.org/.

Aporta, Claudio, Michael Bravo, and Fraser Taylor. *Pan Inuit Trails*. Accessed 1 Dec. 2016. http://paninuittrails.org/.

Baucom, Ian, and Matthew Omelsky. "Knowledge in the Age of Climate Change." *South Atlantic Quarterly* 116.1 (2017): 1–18.

Beattie, Owen, and John Geiger. *Frozen in Time: Unlocking the Secrets of the Doomed 1845 Arctic Expedition*. New York: Plume, 1990.

Benjamin, Walter. "The Storyteller: Reflections on the Work of Nikolai Leskov." In *Illuminations: Essays and Reflections*. 1968. New York: Harcourt Brace Jovanovich, 2007.

Bennett, Jane. *Vibrant Matter: A Political Ecology of Things*. Durham: Duke University Press, 2010.

Berkey, James. "Splendid Little Papers from the 'Splendid Little War': Mapping Empire in the Soldier Newspapers of the Spanish-American War." *Journal of Modern Periodical Studies* 3.2 (2012): 158–74.

Berkey, James. "Traces of the Confederacy: Soldier Newspapers and Wartime Printing in the Occupied South." In *Literary Cultures of the Civil War*, edited by Timothy Sweet. Athens: University of Georgia Press, 2016.

Berton, Pierre. *Arctic Grail: The Quest for the Northwest Passage and the North Pole, 1818–1909*. 1988. New York: Lyons Press, 2000.

Bloom, Lisa. *Gender on Ice: American Ideologies of Polar Expeditions*. Minneapolis: University of Minnesota Press, 1993.

Blum, Hester. "Introduction: Oceanic Studies." *Atlantic Studies* 10.2 (2013): 151–55.

Blum, Hester. "John Cleves Symmes and the Planetary Reach of Polar Exploration." *American Literature* 84.2 (2012): 243–71.

Blum, Hester. "Melville in the Arctic." *Leviathan* 20.1 (2018): 74–84.

Blum, Hester. "The Prospect of Oceanic Studies." *PMLA* 125.3 (2010): 770–79.

Blum, Hester. "Speaking Substances." *Los Angeles Review of Books*, 21 Mar. 2016. https://lareviewofbooks.org/article/speaking-substances-ice/.

Blum, Hester. *The View from the Masthead: Maritime Imagination and Antebellum American Sea Narratives*. Chapel Hill: University of North Carolina Press, 2008.

Blum, Hester, and Jason R. Rudy. "First Person Nautical: Poetry and Play at Sea." *J19: Journal of Nineteenth-Century Americanists* 1.1 (2013): 189–94.

Boes, Tobias, and Kate Marshall. "Writing the Anthropocene: An Introduction." *Minnesota Review* 83, new series (2014): 60–72.

Bradfield, Elizabeth. *Approaching Ice: Poems*. New York: Persea Books, 2010.

Brogan, Jan. "Messages in a Bottle Chart a Lifelong Romance with the Sea." *Boston Globe*, 12 Feb. 2013.

Buell, Lawrence. *The Future of Environmental Criticism: Environmental Crisis and Literary Imagination*. London: Wiley-Blackwell, 2005.

Capelotti, P. J. *The Greatest Show in the Arctic: The American Exploration of Franz Josef Land, 1898–1905*. Norman: University of Oklahoma Press, 2016.

Carroll, Siobhan. *An Empire of Air and Water: Uncolonizable Space in the British Imagination, 1750–1850*. Philadelphia: University of Pennsylvania Press, 2015.

Carson, Rachel. *The Sea around Us*. 1951. New York: Oxford University Press, 1991.

Carter, Robert Randolph. *Searching for the Franklin Expedition: The Arctic Journal of Robert Randolph Carter*. Edited by Harold B. Gill Jr. and Joanne Young. Annapolis, MD: Naval Institute Press, 1998.

Cavell, Janice. "Making Books for Mr Murray: The Case of Edward Parry's Third Arctic Narrative." *The Library* 14.1 (2013): 45–69.

Cavell, Janice. *Tracing the Connected Narrative: Arctic Exploration in British Print Culture, 1818–1860*. Toronto: University of Toronto Press, 2008.

Chakrabarty, Dipesh. "The Climate of History: Four Theses." *Critical Inquiry* 35 (Winter 2009): 197–222.

Cohen, Jeffrey Jerome. *Stone: An Ecology of the Inhuman*. Minneapolis: University of Minnesota Press, 2015.

Cohen, Lara Langer. "The Emancipation of Boyhood: Postbellum Teenage Subculture and the Amateur Press." *Common-Place* 14.1 (2013). Accessed 10

Feb. 2014. http://www.common-place-archives.org/vol-14/no-01/cohen/#
.W19pothKjMI.

Cohen, Margaret. *The Novel and the Sea*. Princeton: Princeton University Press, 2010.

Cohoon, Lorinda B. *Serialized Citizenships: Periodicals, Books, and American Boys,
1840–1911*. Lanham, MD: Scarecrow Press, 2006.

Colebrook, Claire. *Death of the PostHuman: Essays on Extinction*. Ann Arbor: University of Michigan Library, Open Humanities Press, 2014.

Coleridge, Samuel Taylor. *The Collected Works of Samuel Taylor Coleridge 16: Poetical
Works*. Edited by J. C. C. Mays. Princeton: Princeton University Press, 2001.

Cooper, Anthony Ashely. *Sensus Communis: An Essay on the Freedom of Wit and
Humour*. London, 1709.

Counter, S. Allen. *North Pole Promise: Black, White, and Inuit Friends*. Petersborough, NH: Bauhan, 2017.

Craciun, Adriana. *Writing Arctic Disaster: Authorship and Exploration*. Cambridge,
UK: Cambridge University Press, 2016.

Craciun, Adriana. "Writing the Disaster: Franklin and Frankenstein." *Nineteenth-
Century Literature* 65.4 (2011): 433–80.

Crane, David. *Scott of the Antarctic: A Life of Courage and Tragedy*. New York: Knopf,
2006.

Cruikshank, Julie. *Do Glaciers Listen? Local Knowledge, Colonial Encounters, and
Social Imagination*. Vancouver: University of British Columbia Press, 2005.

Crutzen, Paul J. "Geology of Mankind." *Nature* 415 (3 Jan. 2002): 23.

Cubitt, Sean. *Finite Media: Environmental Implications of Digital Technologies*. Durham: Duke University Press, 2017.

David, Robert G. *The Arctic in the British Imagination, 1818–1914*. Manchester, UK:
Manchester University Press, 2000.

Davis, Jim. "British Bravery, or Tars Triumphant: Images of the British Navy in Nautical Melodrama." *New Theatre Quarterly* 4.14 (1988): 122–43.

DeLoughrey, Elizabeth M. *Routes and Roots: Navigating Caribbean and Pacific Island
Literatures*. Honolulu: University of Hawai'i Press, 2007.

DeLoughery, Elizabeth M. "Satellite Planetarity and the Ends of the Earth." *Public
Culture* 26.2 (2014): 257–80.

Derrida, Jacques. *The Post Card: From Socrates to Freud and Beyond*. Translated by
Alan Bass. Chicago: University of Chicago Press, 1987.

Dimock, Wai Chee. "*Gilgamesh*'s Planetary Turn." In *The Planetary Turn: Art, Dialogue, and Geoaesthetics in the 21st-Century*, edited by Amy J. Elias and Christian
Moraru. Evanston, IL: Northwestern University Press, 2015.

Dimock, Wai Chee. *Through Other Continents: American Literature across Deep
Time*. Princeton: Princeton University Press, 2006.

Dimock, Wai Chee, and Lawrence Buell, eds. *Shades of the Planet: American Literature as World Literature*. Princeton: Princeton University Press, 2007.

Eber, Dorothy Harley. *Encounters on the Passage: Inuit Meet the Explorers*. Toronto:
University of Toronto Press, 2008.

Eber, Dorothy. *When the Whalers Were Up North: Inuit Memories from the Eastern Arctic*. Montreal: McGill-Queen's University Press, 1989.

Eliot, T. S. "The Waste Land." In *The Annotated Waste Land with Contemporary Prose*. New Haven: Yale University Press, 2006.

Estrin, James. "Photographing Climate Change Refugees, by Drone and on Foot." *New York Times,* 28 Dec. 2016. http://lens.blogs.nytimes.com/2016/12/28 /photographing-climate-change-refugees-drone-foot-josh-haner/.

Fiennes, Ranulph. *Captain Scott*. London: Hodder and Stoughton, 2004.

Fitting, Peter. *Subterranean Worlds: A Critical Anthology*. Middletown, CT: Wesleyan University Press, 2004.

Fleming, Fergus. *Barrow's Boys*. London: Granta Books, 1998.

Foote, Stephanie. "The Stuff of Fiction: The Rise of the Environmental Novel." Presentation at Penn State University, 5 Dec. 2016.

Foote, Stephanie, and Stephanie LeMenager. "Editors' Column." *Resilience: A Journal of the Environmental Humanities* 1.1 (2014): 1–9.

Foucault, Michel. "Of Other Spaces." Translated by Jay Miskowiec. *Diacritics* (Spring 1986): 22–27.

Fuller, Matthew. *Media Ecologies: Materialist Energies in Art and Techoculture*. Cambridge, MA: MIT Press, 2005.

Gardner, Eric. *Black Print Unbound: The* Christian Recorder, *African American Literature, and Periodical Culture*. New York: Oxford, 2015.

Ghosh, Amitav. *The Great Derangement: Climate Change and the Unthinkable*. Chicago: University of Chicago Press, 2016.

Giddings, J. Louis. *Ancient Men of the Arctic*. New York: Knopf, 1967.

Gillis, Justin. "Climate Model Predicts West Antarctic Ice Sheet Could Melt Rapidly." *New York Times*, 30 Mar. 2016. http://www.nytimes.com/2016/03/31/science /global-warming-antarctica-ice-sheet-sea-level-rise.html.

Gillis, Justin. "Miles of Ice Collapsing into the Sea: Antarctic Dispatches." *New York Times,* 18 May 2017. https://www.nytimes.com/interactive/2017/05/18/climate /antarctica-ice-melt-climate-change.html.

Gillis, Justin, and Kenneth Chang. "Scientists Warn of Rising Oceans from Polar Melt." *New York Times,* 12 May 2014. http://www.nytimes.com/2014/05 /13/science/earth/collapse-of-parts-of-west-antarctica-ice-sheet-has-begun -scientists-say.html.

Gitelman, Lisa. *Always Already New: Media, History, and the Data of Culture*. Cambridge, MA: MIT Press, 2006.

Gitelman, Lisa. *Paper Knowledge: Toward a Media History of Documents*. Durham: Duke University Press, 2014.

Glasberg, Elena. *Antarctica as Cultural Critique: The Gendered Politics of Scientific Exploration and Climate Change*. New York: Palgrave-Macmillan, 2012.

Goddard, Ives. *Handbook of North American Indians: Arctic*. Volume 5. Washington, DC: Smithsonian Institution, 1984.

Gould, Stephen Jay. *Time's Arrow, Time's Cycle: Myth and Metaphor in the Discovery of Geological Time*. Cambridge, MA: Harvard University Press, 1987.

Green, James, and Peter Stallybrass. *Benjamin Franklin: Writer and Printer.* New Castle, DE: Oak Knoll Press, Library Company of Philadelphia, British Library, 2006.

Greenbaum, J. S., D. D. Blankenship, D. A. Young, T. G. Richter, J. L. Roberts, A. R. A. Aitken, B. Legresy, D. M. Schroeder, R. C. Warner, T. D. van Ommen, and M. J. Siegert. "Ocean Access to a Cavity beneath Totten Glacier in East Antarctica." *Nature Geoscience* 8 (16 Mar. 2015): 294–98.

Hallendy, Norman. *Inuksuit: Silent Messengers of the Arctic.* Toronto: Douglas and McIntyre, 2001.

Hallendy, Norman. *Tukiliit: An Introduction to Inuksuit and Other Stone Figures of the North.* Vancouver: Douglas and McIntyre and University of Alaska Press, 2009.

Hamilton, Alice Jane. *Finding John Rae.* Vancouver: Ronsdale Press, 2017.

Hamilton, Kristie. *America's Sketchbook: The Cultural Life of a Nineteenth-Century Literary Genre.* Athens: Ohio University Press, 1989.

Harper, Kenn. "Burial at Sea: The Death of Kudlago." *Nunatsiaq News* (ᓄᓇᑦᓯᐊᕐ ᐱᕐᑳᑦᑐᐊᕐᑦ) 30 June 2006. http://nunatsiaq.com/stories/article/taissumani _july_1_1860_burial_at_sea_the_death_of_kudlago/.

Harper, Kenn. *Give Me My Father's Body: The Life of Minik, the New York Eskimo.* New York: Washington Square Press, [1986] 2001.

Harper, Stephen J. "Franklin Discovery Strengthens Canada's Arctic Sovereignty." *Globe and Mail,* 12 Sept. 2014.

Harris, Elizabeth M. *Personal Impressions: The Small Printing Press in Nineteenth-Century America.* Boston: David R. Godine, 2004.

Hatfield, Philip J. *Lines in the Ice: Exploring the Roof of the World.* Montreal: McGill-Queen's University Press, 2017.

Heise, Ursula. *Sense of Place and Sense of Planet: The Environmental Imagination of the Global.* Oxford: Oxford University Press, 2008.

Henderson, Bruce. *Fatal North: Adventure and Survival Aboard USS* Polaris, *the First U.S. Expedition to the North Pole.* New York: New American Library, 2001.

Hill, Jen. *White Horizon: The Arctic in the Nineteenth-Century British Imagination.* New York: SUNY Press, 2007.

Hirsch, Edward. *A Poet's Glossary.* New York: Houghton Mifflin Harcourt, 2014.

Hoag, Elaine. "Caxtons of the North: Mid-Nineteenth-Century Arctic Shipboard Printing." *Book History* 4 (2001): 81–114.

Hoag, Elaine. "Shipboard Printing on the Franklin Search Expeditions: A Bibliographic Study of the *Plover* Press." *Papers of the Bibliographic Society of Canada* 31.8 (2000): 7–71.

Huntford, Roland. *The Last Place on Earth: Scott and Amundsen's Race to the South Pole.* New York: Modern Library, 1999.

Huntford, Roland. *Scott and Amundsen.* London: Hodder, 1979.

Hutchinson, Gillian. *Sir John Franklin's* Erebus *and* Terror *Expedition: Lost and Found.* London: Adlard Coles Nautical Press, 2017.

Ingersoll, Karin Amimoto. *Waves of Knowing: A Seascape Epistemology.* Durham: Duke University Press, 2016.

Isbell, Mary. "Illustrated Reviews of Naval Theatricals." *Nineteenth Century Theatre and Film* 38.2 (2013): 67–74.

Isbell, Mary. "P(l)aying Off Old Ironsides and the Old Wagon: Melville's Depiction of Shipboard Theatricals in *White Jacket*." *Leviathan* 15.1 (2013): 6–30.

Isbell, Mary. "When Ditchers and Jack Tars Collide: Benefit Theatricals at the Calcutta Lyric Theatre in the Wake of the Indian Mutiny." *Victorian Literature and Culture* 42 (2014): 407–23.

Jacobson, Kristin. "Desiring Natures: The American Adrenaline Narrative." *Genre* 35.2 (2002): 355–82.

Keighren, Innes M., Charles W. J. Withers, and Bill Bell. *Travels into Print: Exploration, Writing, and Publishing with John Murray, 1773–1859*. Chicago: University of Chicago Press, 2015.

Kirkpatrick, Robert J. *From the Penny Dreadful to the Ha'penny Dreadfuller: A Bibliographic History of the Boys' Periodical in Great Britain, 1762–1950*. London: British Library and Oak Knoll Press, 2013.

Krakauer, Jon. *Into Thin Air*. New York: Villard, 1997.

Lacan, Jacques. "*The Purloined Letter*." In *The Seminar of Jacques Lacan, Book II: The Ego in Freud's Theory and in the Technique of Psychoanalysis 1954–1955*, edited by Jacques-Alain Miller and translated by Sylvana Tomaselli. New York: Norton, 1988.

Larkin, Brian. *Signal and Noise: Media, Infrastructure, and Urban Culture in Nigeria*. Durham: Duke University Press, 2008.

Latour, Bruno. "Agency at the Time of the Anthropocene." *New Literary History* 45.1 (2014): 1–18.

Leane, Elizabeth. *Antarctica in Fiction: Imaginative Narratives of the Far South*. Cambridge, UK: Cambridge University Press, 2012.

Leane, Elizabeth, and Mark Pharaoh. "Introduction." In *The Adelie Blizzard: Mawson's Forgotten Newspaper*, edited by Elizabeth Leane. Adelaide: Friends of the State Library of South Australia, 2010.

Leane, Elizabeth. "The Polar Press: A Century of Australian Antarctic 'Newspapers.'" *Australian Antarctic Magazine* 22 (2012). www.antarctica.gov.au/magazine/2011 -2015/issue-22-2012/polar-press/the-polar-press-a-century-of-australian-antarctic -newspapers.

Leane, Elizabeth, and Graeme Miles. "The Poles as Planetary Places." *Polar Journal* 7.2 (2017): 270–86.

LeMenager, Stephanie. "Climate Change and the Struggle for Genre." In *Anthropocene Reading: Literary History in Geologic Times*, edited by Tobias Menely and Jesse Oak Taylor. University Park: Pennsylvania State University Press, 2017.

LeMenager, Stephanie. "The Environmental Humanities and Public Writing: An Interview with Rob Nixon." *Resilience: A Journal of the Environmental Humanities* 1.2 (2014).

LeMenager, Stephanie. "The Humanities after the Anthropocene." In *The Routledge Companion to the Environmental Humanities*, edited by Ursula K. Heise, Jon Christensen, and Michelle Niemann. New York: Routledge, 2017.

LeMenager, Stephanie. *Living Oil: Petroleum Culture in the American City*. Oxford: Oxford University Press, 2014.

Lewis, Oscar. *Sea Routes to the Gold Fields: The Migration by Water to California in 1849–1852*. New York: Knopf, 1949.

Lewis, Simon A., and Mark A. Maslin. "Defining the Anthropocene." *Nature* 519 (12 Mar. 2015): 171–80.

Loomis, Chauncey. *Weird and Tragic Shores: The Story of Charles Francis Hall, Explorer*. New York: Knopf, 1971.

Lopez, Barry. *Arctic Dreams*. New York: Scribner's, 1986.

Loughran, Trish. *The Republic in Print: Print Culture in the Age of U.S. Nation Building, 1770–1870*. New York: Columbia University Press, 2007.

Luciano, Dana. "The Inhuman Anthropocene." *Avidly: A Channel of the Los Angeles Review of Books*, 22 Mar. 2015. http://avidly.lareviewofbooks.org/2015/03/22/the-inhuman-anthropocene/.

Mastro, Lisa, and Jim Mastro. "Life in Antarctica." *Antarctica Online*. Accessed 15 Sept. 2017. http://www.antarcticaonline.com/culture/culture.htm.

McGhee, Robert. *The Last Imaginary Place: A Human History of the Arctic World*. Oxford: Oxford University Press, 2005.

Melville, Herman. "The Encantadas." In *The Piazza Tales and Other Prose Pieces, 1839–1860*. Evanston, IL: Northwestern University Press and Newberry Library, 1987.

Melville, Herman. *Moby-Dick: or, The Whale*. Evanston, IL: Northwestern University Press and Newberry Library, 1988.

Menely, Tobias, and Jesse Oak Taylor, eds. *Anthropocene Reading: Literary History in Geologic Times*. University Park: Pennsylvania State University Press, 2017.

Metayer, Maurice. *I, Nuligak*. New York: Pocket Books, 1966.

Miller, Paul D. *The Book of Ice*. New York: Mark Batty, 2011.

Morton, Timothy. *Ecology without Nature: Rethinking Environmental Aesthetics*. Cambridge, MA: Harvard University Press, 2009.

Morton, Timothy. *Hyperobjects: Philosophy and Ecology after the End of the World*. Minneapolis: University of Minnesota Press, 2013.

Moskvitch, Katia. "Mysterious Siberian Crater Attributed to Methane." *Nature*, 13 July 2014. http://www.nature.com/news/mysterious-siberian-crater-attributed-to-methane-1.15649.

Mossakowski, Tomasz Filip. "'The Sailors Dearly Love to Make Up': Cross-Dressing and Blackface during Polar Exploration." PhD diss., Kings College London, 2015.

Mott, Frank Luther. *American Journalism: A History, 1690–1960*. New York: Macmillan, 1962.

National Research Council. *The Arctic in the Anthropocene: Emerging Research Questions*. Washington, DC: National Academies Press, 2014.

Nelson, Peggy. *Shackleton*. Accessed 10 Dec. 2014. https://eshackleton.com/.

Nixon, Rob. *Slow Violence and the Environmentalism of the Poor*. Cambridge, MA: Harvard University Press, 2011.

Nord, David Paul. *Communities of Journalism: A History of American Newspapers and Their Readers*. Urbana: University of Illinois Press, 2001.

O'Neill, Patrick B. "Theatre in the North: Staging Practices of the British Navy in the Canadian Arctic." *Dalhousie Review* 74.3 (1994): 356–86.

Parrish, Susan Scott. *The Flood Year 1927: A Cultural History*. Princeton: Princeton University Press, 2016.

Parfitt, Tom. "Russia Plants Flag on North Pole Seabed." *The Guardian*, 2 Aug. 2007. www.guardian.co.uk/world/2007/aug/02/russia.arctic.

Parikka, Jussi. *A Geology of Media*. Minneapolis: University of Minnesota Press, 2015.

Parikka, Jussi. *What Is Media Archaeology?* Cambridge, UK: Polity Press, 2012.

Pearson, Mike. "'No Joke in Petticoats': British Polar Expeditions and Their Theatrical Presentations." *Drama Review* 48.1 (2004): 44–59.

Peeples, Scott. *The Afterlife of Edgar Allan Poe*. Rochester, NY: Camden House, 2004.

Peters, John Durham. *The Marvelous Clouds: Toward a Philosophy of Elemental Media*. Chicago: University of Chicago Press, 2015.

Phillips, Dana. *The Truth of Ecology: Nature, Culture, and Literature in America*. Oxford: Oxford University Press, 2003.

Poe, Edgar Allan. *The Narrative of Arthur Gordon Pym*. In *Poetry and Tales*. New York: Library of America, 1984.

Potter, Russell A. *Arctic Spectacles: The Frozen North in Visual Culture, 1818–1875*. Seattle: University of Washington Press, 2007.

Potter, Russell A. *Finding Franklin: The Untold Story of a 165-Year Search*. Montreal: McGill-Queen's University Press, 2016.

Potter, Simon James. *Newspapers and Empire in Ireland and Britain: Reporting the British Empire, c. 1857–1921*. Dublin: Four Courts Press, 2004.

Pratt, Lloyd. *Archives of American Time: Literature and Modernity in the Nineteenth Century*. Philadelphia: University of Pennsylvania Press, 2010.

Rawlins, Dennis. *Peary at the North Pole: Fact or Fiction?* New York: R. B. Luce, 1973.

Reidy, Michael S. *Tides of History: Ocean Science and Her Majesty's Navy*. Chicago: University of Chicago Press, 2008.

Reiss, Benjamin. *Theaters of Madness: Insane Asylums and Nineteenth-Century American Culture*. Chicago: University of Chicago Press, 2008.

Rignot, E., J. Mouginot, M. Morlighem, H. Seroussi, and B. Scheucl. "Widespread, Rapid Grounding Line Retreat of Pine Island, Thwaites, Smith, and Kohler Glaciers, West Antarctica, from 1992 to 2011." *Geophysical Research Letters* 41 (27 May 2014): 3502–9.

Robinson, Michael. *The Coldest Crucible: Arctic Exploration and American Culture*. Chicago: University of Chicago Press, 2006.

"Ross Sea Party Photos." Antarctic Heritage Trust. Accessed 4 Aug. 2017. https://www.nzaht.org/pages/ross-sea-party-photos.

Rubery, Matthew. *The Novelty of Newspapers: Victorian Fiction after the Invention of the News*. Oxford: Oxford University Press, 2009.

Rudy, Jason R. "Floating Worlds: Émigré Poetry and British Culture." *ELH* 81 (2014): 325–50.

Rudy, Jason R. *Imagined Homelands: British Poetry in the Colonies.* Baltimore: Johns Hopkins University Press, 2017.

Russell, Douglas G. D., William J. L. Sladen, and David G. Ainley. "Dr. George Murray Levick (1876–1956): Unpublished Notes on the Sexual Habits of the Adélie Penguin." *Polar Record* 48.247 (2012): 387–93.

Shields, David S. *Civil Tongues and Polite Letters in British America.* Chapel Hill: University of North Carolina Press, 1997.

Sides, Hampton. *In the Kingdom of Ice: The Grand and Terrible Voyage of the USS Jeanette.* New York: Doubleday, 2014.

Smith, Jacob. *Eco-Sonic Media.* Oakland: University of California Press, 2015.

Solomon, Susan. *The Coldest March: Scott's Fatal Antarctic Expedition.* New Haven: Yale University Press, 2001.

Spufford, Francis. *I May Be Some Time: Ice and the English Imagination.* New York: St. Martin's Press, 1997.

Stam, David H. "The Lord's Librarians: The American Seamen's Friend Society and Their Loan Libraries, 1837–1967. An Historical Excursion with Some Unanswered Questions." *Coriolis* 3.1 (2012): 45–59.

Stam, David H., and Deirdre C. Stam. "Bending Time: The Function of Periodicals in Nineteenth-Century Polar Naval Expeditions." *Victorian Periodicals Review* 41.4 (2008): 301–22.

Stam, David H., and Deirdre C. Stam. *Books on Ice: British and American Literature of Polar Exploration.* New York: Grolier Club, 2005.

Standish, David. *Hollow Earth: The Long and Curious History of Imagining Strange Lands, Fantastical Creatures, Advanced Civilizations, and Marvelous Machines below the Earth's Surface.* Cambridge, MA: Da Capo Books, 2006.

Starosielski, Nicole. *The Undersea Network.* Durham: Duke University Press, 2015.

Steffen, Will, Jacques Grinevald, Paul Crutzen, and John McNeill. "Anthropocene: Conceptual and Historical Perspectives." *Philosophical Transactions of the Royal Society* 369 (2011): 842–67.

Steinberg, Philip E. "Of Other Seas: Metaphors and Materialities in Maritime Regions." *Atlantic Studies* 10.2 (2013): 165.

Steinberg, Philip E. *The Social Construction of the Ocean.* Cambridge, UK: Cambridge University Press, 2001.

Sterling, Bruce. Dead Media Project. Accessed 3 June 2016. http://www.deadmedia.org/.

Struzkik, Ed. "In the Melting Arctic, a Harrowing Account from a Stranded Ship." 29 Aug. 2018. *Yale Environment 360.* https://e360.yale.edu/features/in-the-melting-arctic-harrowing-account-from-a-stranded-ship.

Swanstrom, Lisa. *Animal, Vegetable, Digital: Experiments in New Media Aesthetics and Environmental Poetics.* Tuscaloosa: University of Alabama Press, 2016.

Tocqueville, Alexis de. *Democracy in America.* Translated by Arthur Goldhammer. New York: Library of America, 2004.

Wamsley, Douglas. *Polar Hayes: The Life and Contributions of Isaac Israel Hayes,* M.D. Philadelphia: American Philosophical Society, 2009.

Warner, Michael. "Critique in the Anthropocene." Paper presented at Situation Critical! Critique, Theory, and Early American Studies, McNeil Center for Early American Studies, Philadelphia, 2 Apr. 2016.

Warner, Michael. *Publics and Counterpublics.* New York: Zone Books, 2002.

Williams, Kevin. *Read All about It! A History of the British Newspaper.* London: Routledge, 2010.

Wilson, Eric G. *The Spiritual History of Ice.* London: Palgrave, 2001.

Woodman, David C. *Strangers among Us.* Montreal: McGill-Queen's University Press, 1995.

Woodman, David C. *Unravelling the Franklin Mystery: Inuit Testimony.* Montreal: McGill-Queen's University Press, 1991.

Zalasiewicz, Jan, et al. "Working Group on the 'Anthropocene.'" Subcommission on Quaternary Stratigraphy. Accessed 15 May 2017. http://quaternary.stratigraphy .org/workinggroups/anthropocene/.

Zielinski, Siegfried. *Deep Time of the Media.* Cambridge, MA: MIT Press, 2008.

INDEX

dead media, 29, 183

deep time, xix, 10, 31, 36, 42, 167, 234

Delano, Reuben, 202

De Long, George, 2, 4, 123, 207–8, 232

De Mille, James, 37, 163, 165

Derrida, Jacques, 199, 203

diaries: as genre of polar writing, 37, 86, 215, 252n133

Dickens, Charles, 103–4, 210

Discovery (ship), xv, 15, 40, 76, 84, 141, 150, 156–59, 166, 171–72. *See also* Nares, George; Scott, Robert Falcon

Discovery News, 15, 40, 132

Dodge, Henry, 88–90, 122, 133, 251n133, 255n58

dogs, 24, 95, 11, 115, 124, 129–30, 135–36, 138, 151–52, 223, 259n17

drama. *See* theater

drunkenness, 53, 88–89, 118, 122, 251n133, 256n84

Drygalski, Erich von, 4, 141

Ebierbing. *See* Ipiirviq

ecocriticism, 29, 38

ecomedia: polar, 5–6, 11–14, 28–35, 38–39, 41–42, 44–45, 56, 70, 78, 82, 83, 93, 95, 99, 132, 137, 148, 149–50, 153, 182, 184, 190, 193–94, 198, 205, 208, 212, 224, 229, 230, 233, 236

Edison, Thomas Alva, xv, 208

Egyptology, 165–66

Eliot, T. S., 259n21

Endurance (ship), 6, 141, 142, 147–48, 150, 152–54. *See also* Shackleton, Ernest

environmental humanities, 31–32, 36, 38–39, 42

ephemera, xv, xix, 2–3, 5–9, 14, 28–31, 34, 38–40, 44, 45, 51–53, 55–56, 68–69, 74, 82, 83, 150, 167, 182, 187, 190, 230, 233, 226

Erebus (ship), xvi, xviii, 47, 49, 102, 178–79, 194, 209, 260n34, 263n4, 265n18. *See also* Franklin, John; Ross, John Clark

Eskimo or Esquimaux. *See* Inuit

Everest (Chomolungma), 155, 232–33, 269n68

Expedition Topics, 141

Explorers Club, 164

Fiala, Anthony, 4, 15, 45, 59, 62–63, 110, 112, 142, 244n50. *See also* Fiala-Ziegler Expedition

Fiala-Ziegler Expedition, 45–46, 56, 59, 77, 85, 112–13, 126, 130. *See also* Fiala, Anthony

fiction: about polar regions, 37–38, 140, 163–165, 260n44; written by expedition members, 166–71, 96, 176, 262n62. *See also* novels

Fisher, Alexander, 100–01, 250n129, 266n28

Fitzroy, Robert, 201

Fleming, Fergus, 246n60

Flight of the Plover, or the North Pole Charivari, 15, 47, 102–5, 113, 253n17

Foote, Stephanie, 32, 240n44

forms: blank, 30, 41, 165, 177–79, 181–94, 238n5, 265n18

fossil fuels. *See* resource extraction

Fox (ship), 178–81, 206, 216, 242n11. *See also* McClintock, Francis Leopold

Fram (ship), 15, 49, 81, 83, 85, 107–8, 129. *See also* Nansen, Fridtjof

Framsjaa, 15, 49, 83, 107, 129

Frankenstein (Shelley), 9, 37

Franklin, John, xvi, 4, 47, 49, 102, 148, 164, 191, 207–8; searches for, 6, 8, 35, 40, 44, 56–57, 68–69, 71, 73, 75, 77, 83, 102, 108, 110–11, 115, 117–18, 130, 132, 178–85, 194–99, 209–212, 215–18, 221, 223, 224–25, 263n4, 264n9

Franz Josef Land, 77

Frobisher Bay, 224–27

Frobisher, Martin, 3, 225–27

Frost Fairs, Thames, 55, 59

Galápagos Islands, 199–204

genre: of polar writing, xviii, 3, 5–6, 28, 30, 32, 44, 52, 68, 74, 93, 115, 137, 153, 165, 194, 240n52 geological time. *See* deep time

Ghosh, Amitav, 32, 240n52

Giffard, George, 65, 76, 245n54

Gitelman, Lisa, 6, 30, 187, 238n5

Glacier Tongue, 141

glaciers, 9, 11, 154, 212

Gleaner, 15, 47, 130–31

global warming. *See* climate change

Gore, Graham, 179, 181

Gould, Stephen Jay, 10

Greely, Adolphus, 4, 15, 49–50, 78, 84, 123

Green, James, 188

Greenland, 3, 8, 9, 116, 124, 135, 221, 227

Greenwich Mean Time, 70, 78, 92

Griper (ship), 15, 50, 86. *See also* Parry, William Edward

Grolier Club, xv–xvii

gryphons, 133–35

Hall, Charles Francis, 4, 6, 41, 82, 83, 211–31, 271n41

Hamilton, Kristie, 153

Hamlet, 87, 88, 123

Hannah. *See* Taqulittuq

Hansa (ship), 15, 64, 65. *See also* Koldewey, Carl

Harper, Kenn, 221, 255n77

Harper's Weekly, 81–82, 165, 264n9

Harris, Elizabeth, 55, 71

Harris, Francis L., 251n133

Hartt, Henry P., 126, 256n84

Hayes, Isaac Israel, 4, 15, 18–19, 63–64, 65, 71–72, 84, 88, 133–36, 217

Hecla (ship), 15, 50, 86. *See also* Parry, William Edward

Hendrik, Hans (Suersaq), 214

Henson, Matthew, 4, 123, 124, 255n77

Heywood, Harvey Scott, 124, 134

hierarchies: nautical, 64–65, 99–101

Hirsch, Edward, 116

Hoag, Elaine, 56, 57, 68, 102, 131, 253n16

hollow earth: theories of, 6, 36, 37, 163–67, 176, 260n44

homoeroticism: among expedition members, 123–30, 172–73, 256n83–84, 256n89

Hooper, William Hulme, 103–5

Hoppner, Henry Parkyns, 98

Hudson, Henry, 3

Huntford, Roland, 256n83, 259n17

Hurley, Frank, 141–42, 147–48

Ice-Blink, 47, 72, 77, 242n6

Iligliuk, 124, 227

Illustrated Arctic News, xvi–xvii, 15, 35, 38, 40, 47, 49, 54, 64, 65, 77–78, 79, 105, 107, 110, 11, 120, 129, 130, 132, 207

imperialism. *See* colonialism

indigenous knowledge (IK), 5, 41, 106, 117, 211–230

infrastructure, 28, 33–34

ink, 45, 83–84, 141, 142, 144, 181, 229–30

Inuit, 4, 5, 6, 9, 37, 39, 41, 43, 79, 82, 85, 105, 106, 109, 111, 115–17, 124, 127, 135, 151, 179, 186, 187, 195, 198, 209–30; as guides and translators, xv, 116, 117, 210, 221, 227

Inuksuit, 6, 37, 185, 226

Inuktitut, 113, 116, 117

Iñupiat, 5, 105, 109, 116, 187, 195

Investigator (ship), 86, 207. *See also* Mc-Clure, Robert

Ipiirviq, 41, 212–215, 221–23, 227, 269n9

Jacobson, Kristin, 155

Jeannette (ship), 2, 87, 123, 207–8, 232. *See also* De Long, George

Jewett, Sarah Orne, 37

job printing, 71, 187–89

Joe. *See* Ipiirviq

journalism: amateur, 18, 70–73, 142, 247n76

Joyce, Ernest, 142

kabloonas (Qabluunak), 179, 210

Kalli or Kallihirua. *See* Qalasirssuaq

Kalli, the Christian Esquimaux, 116–17

Kane, Elisha Kent, 4, 9, 37, 71, 72, 77, 80, 124, 164, 185, 265n13, 270n15

privacy: and polar writing, 5, 52–53, 66–67, 94–95, 99, 101, 120, 123–23, 128, 191–93, 246n59, 266n28

Proteus (ship), 15. *See also* Greely, Adolphus

public sphere: of polar writing, 38, 50, 52, 53, 66–67, 77–79, 95, 98, 101

Pullen, William, 88

Punch, 104, 112

Qalasirssuaq, 116–18, 221

Queen's Illuminated Magazine, 15, 47, 59, 64, 75, 79, 108, 117, 121–22, 124, 129, 148, 245n57

raciness, 122, 129. *See also* censorship

racism, 10, 53, 117, 123, 167–68, 214

Rae, John, 4, 179, 210–11, 216, 223

reading: by expedition members, 18, 49–50, 80–82; 89–90, 95–96, 100, 108, 117, 160, 187–90, 217, 221. *See also* fiction; literacy; novels; poetry

Reiss, Benjamin, 72, 246n60

relics: of Franklin expedition, xvi, 180, 182, 210, 212, 216, 224

Resolute (ship), xvi, 15, 69, 77, 83, 86, 87, 105, 107, 111, 118, 120, 122, 130, 131, 194, 195. *See also* Austin, Horatio; Belcher, Edward

resource extraction, xviii, 7–8, 14, 30, 35–39, 105, 135, 149, 163, 165, 184, 235

Reynolds, Jeremiah N., 163–64

Riley, James, 216

Rilliet, Charles, 126

Rime of the Ancient Mariner, The (Coleridge), 37

Robinson, Michael, 246n60

Ross, James Clark, 4, 179, 186, 190, 191, 260n34, 265n18

Ross, John, xv, 4, 75, 190, 191, 227

Royal Arctic Theatre, 58, 88, 122, 126, 250n126

Rudy, Jason R., 51, 112

Russia, 35, 36, 77, 195, 233, 272n5

Sabine, Edward, 94–100, 191

Sacheuse, John, xv

Sami, 5, 105, 109, 151, 152

Satterlee Hospital, 71

schools: shipboard, 49–50, 73–75, 157, 242n11

Schwatka, Frederick, 223

Scott, Robert Falcon, xv, 4, 6, 11, 12, 13, 15, 40, 84, 123, 138, 141, 147, 151, 155, 157–59, 161, 167, 259n17

Scott, Walter, 49

sea clocks, 69, 78, 91–92

seals, 82, 111, 120, 127, 152, 214

Second Grinnell Expedition, 37, 71, 72, 77, 80, 185. *See also* Kane, Elisha Kent

Seitz, Charles, 59

sexual relations. *See* homoeroticism

Shackleton, Ernest, xv, 4, 6, 12–13, 15, 40, 138, 139, 141, 142, 147–48, 150–62, 167, 169, 259n21, 261n57

Shaftesbury, Earl of (Anthony Ashley Cooper), 52

Shields, David, 53, 252n7

Shorkley, George, 63, 126, 244n50

Siberia, 36, 163

silk: as printing medium, 57–58, 69, 76, 83, 151, 194–95

Simpson, George Clarke, 167–69

Simpson, John, 69, 102–3, 105, 253n17, 261n59

sledging, 2, 4, 11, 83, 102, 111, 115, 131, 147, 150, 166, 169, 213, 223, 253n19, 259n17

sleeping bags, 25, 127–28

Smith, Jacob, 30

social media: polar newspapers as, 24–25, 43, 105, 120, 149. *See also* Twitter

songs: sung by expedition members, 47, 65, 74, 76, 95, 110, 111, 115–16, 123

South Polar Times, 6, 15, 40, 84, 128, 138, 140, 141–42, 149, 156–62, 166, 167, 172, 261n59, 262n62

South Pole, 1, 2, 11, 12, 139–40, 147, 152, 162, 163–67, 171, 233, 259n17

Spofford, Harriet Prescott, 37

Spufford, Francis, 246n60

Stallybrass, Peter, 188, 266n19

Stam, David H., xv, 7, 50, 68, 85

Stam, Deirdre C., xv, 7, 50, 68

Starosielski, Nicole, 34

Stefansson, Vilhjamur, 164, 223

Steinberg, Philip E., 33, 265n12

Stephenson, Robert B., 146

Stewart, Spencer, 45–46

Strange Manuscript Found in a Copper Cylinder (De Mille), 37, 140, 163, 165

sublime: polar, 37–38, 68, 83, 187

Suersaq (Hans Hendrik), 214

Sverdrup, Otto, 4

Swedish Antarctic Expedition, 44, 168. *See also* Nordenskjöld, Otto

Symmes, John Cleves, 163–65, 260n44–45

Symons, Robert, 65, 76, 245n54

Symzonia ([Seaborn]), 37, 164–65

Taqulittuq, 41, 212–15, 219, 221–23, 227

tardigrades, 170

Taylor, Jesse Oak, 31

Taylor, Thomas Griffith, 166–67, 262n62

temporality: of polar regions, xix, 3, 7, 10, 13, 28, 30, 38–39, 41, 44, 46, 51, 55, 68, 73, 78, 81, 91–93, 110, 131, 154, 160–61, 184, 190

Terra Nova (ship), 12, 13, 15, 141, 157, 166, 167. *See also* Scott, Robert Falcon

Terror (ship), xvi, xviii, 47, 49, 102, 178–79, 194, 209, 260n34, 263n4, 265n18. *See also* Franklin, John; Ross, John Clark

theater: on polar ships, xvi, 47, 49, 50, 58, 66, 68–69, 84, 86–88, 92, 95, 101, 111, 122, 126, 127, 132, 140, 250n126

"The Encantadas" (Melville), 202–3

"The Raven" (Poe), 112, 133, 172

Thoreau, Henry David, 28–29, 238n33

Tocqueville, Alexis de, 52–53

Tookoolito. *See* Taqulittuq

traditional ecological knowledge (TEK), 5, 41, 106, 117, 211–230

Trudens, John, 126

Twitter, 150–54

Typee (Melville), 59, 104

typewriters: in polar regions, 142, 156

Tyson, George E., 81–82

United States (ship), 15, 18, 63, 65, 72, 88, 89, 90, 122, 124, 133–36, 251n133. *See also* Hayes, Isaac Israel

United States Exploring Expedition, 164

Universal Yankee Nation, 136–37

Vedoe, Anton, 85, 130, 257n96

Venesta, 144–46

verge: polar, 148, 163–69

Vicar of Wakefield, The (Goldsmith), xvi, 148, 180, 263n4

Victoria, Queen, 213

Vulture, 130

Wamsley, Douglas, 246n60

Ward, Thomas, 209

Warner, Michael, 34, 38, 53, 245n57

Watkins, Patrick (Oberlus), 203

Watt, Isaac, 171–72

Weekly Guy, 15, 40, 47, 64, 77, 79, 84, 115–16, 129, 132, 244n41, 253n17

West Philadelphia Hospital Register, 71–72, 247n70–71

whaling: Arctic, 8, 116, 140, 209, 212–13, 214, 217, 220, 222, 234; Pacific, 200–06

whisky: Shackleton's, 12–13

Whitecar, William, 204

Whitman, Walt, 172–73

Wild, Frank, 142, 166

Wilkes, Charles, 4, 102, 163, 265n18

Wilson, Edward, 156

wireless technology, 33, 55, 174–76

Worsley, Frank, 154

Wyatt, Benjamin, 76, 132

York, Erasmus. *See* Qalasirssuaq

Yupik, 5, 102, 105, 109, 115–16, 151, 187, 195

Zakaeus, Hans. *See* Sacheuse

Zielinski, Siegfried, 30